# New Directions in American Politics

T0399551

*New Directions in American Politics* introduces students not just to how the American political system works but to how political science works. La Raja brings together top scholars to write original essays across the standard curriculum of American government and politics, capturing emerging research in the discipline in a way that is accessible for undergraduates. Each chapter combines substantive knowledge with the kind of skill building and analytical inquiry that is being touted in higher education everywhere. Contributors to *New Directions* highlight why the questions they seek to answer are critical for understanding American politics and situate them in the broader context of controversies in research.

The teaching of American politics follows a well-worn path. Textbooks for introductory courses hew to a traditional set of chapters that describe the Founding, American institutions, the ways citizens participate in politics, and sometimes public policy. The material rarely engages students in the kind of questions that animate scholarship on politics. One hurdle for instructors is finding material that reflects quality scholarship—and thus teaches students about why, not just what—and yet is accessible for undergraduates. Articles in scholarly journals are typically unsuited for undergraduate courses, particularly introductory courses. What is needed is a book that conveys exciting trends in scholarship across vital topics in American politics and illustrates analytical thinking. *New Directions in American Politics* is that book and will be an ideal companion to standard textbooks that focus mostly on nuts and bolts of politics.

- Contributions from a top-notch cast of active scholars and a very highly regarded editor
- A focus on analytical thinking that addresses questions of causality
- Full coverage of the American politics curriculum
- Short interviews with each contributor on a companion Web site to help the research come alive and prompt critical thinking questions for students
- Work that draws on the highest-quality research in political science but is written specifically for first-year undergraduate students.

**Raymond J. La Raja** is associate professor in the department of political science at the University of Massachusetts, Amherst. He is the author of *Small Change: Money, Political Parties and Campaign Finance Reform* and numerous articles on campaign finance and political parties. La Raja is founder and co-editor of *The Forum: A Journal of Applied Research in Contemporary Politics*.

# New Directions in American Politics

The Routledge series *New Directions in American Politics* is composed of contributed volumes covering key areas of study in the field of American politics and government. Each title provides a state-of-the-art overview of current trends in its respective subfield, with an eye toward cutting edge research accessible to advanced undergraduate and beginning graduate students. While the volumes touch on the main topics of relevant study, they are not meant to cover the "nuts and bolts" of the subject. Rather, they engage readers in the most recent scholarship, real-world controversies, and theoretical debates with the aim of getting students excited about the same issues that animate scholars.

Titles in the Series:

# New Directions in
# American Politics

## Edited by Raymond J. La Raja

Routledge
Taylor & Francis Group

NEW YORK AND LONDON

Please visit the companion website for this book at
www.routledge.com/cw/laraja

First published 2013
by Routledge
711 Third Avenue, New York, NY 10017

Simultaneously published in the UK
by Routledge
2 Park Square, Milton Park, Abingdon, Oxon OX14 4RN

*Routledge is an imprint of the Taylor & Francis Group, an informa business*

© 2013 Taylor & Francis

The right of the editor to be identified as the author of the editorial
material, and of the authors for their individual chapters, has been
asserted in accordance with sections 77 and 78 of the Copyright,
Designs and Patents Act 1988.

*Library of Congress Cataloging in Publication Data*
New directions in American politics / edited by Raymond J. La Raja.
   p. cm. – (New directions in American politics)
   1. United States – Politics and government.
   I. La Raja, Raymond J., 1965–
   JK276.N48 2012
   320.973–dc23                                    2012029543

ISBN: 978-0-415-53554-0 (hbk)
ISBN: 978-0-415-53557-1 (pbk)
ISBN: 978-0-203-11240-3 (ebk)

Typeset in Minion
by HWA Text and Data Management, London

To my parents,
Adriana and Raymond,
who inspired me with their of love of books and learning

# Contents

## OVERVIEW
## New Directions in
## American Politics                                                  1

## PART I
## Governing Institutions                                            17

   *Federalism is not merely a theoretical debate about state versus
   federal power—it sets the stage for vibrant conflict over major policies
   in America, including abortion, healthcare, and immigration. This
   chapter analyzes how American political institutions endure and
   transform through history in ways that reveal contemporary political
   undercurrents.*

*There is widespread agreement that the United States is headed for a train wreck of massive proportions if its leaders do not move beyond partisan gridlock and address the problem of the national debt. Palazzolo shows that structural constraints, such as polarization and electoral incentives, do not necessarily prevent leaders from acting to solve the nation's problems. This case study analysis challenges theories that rely too heavily on single-factor explanations of policy outcomes.*

*Paradoxically, wars appear to have a positive effect on domestic politics. Yet, we often fail to see the connection because scholars tend to separate foreign and domestic policy in their analyses. Saldin explains how wars have helped extend rights to previously marginalized groups in America by altering expectations about citizenship. This chapter demonstrates how major events have the capacity to stimulate political change, including the recent wars in Iraq and Afghanistan.*

# Figures

# Tables

# Contributors

**Kevin Arceneaux** is associate professor of political science and an Institute for Public Affairs Faculty affiliate at Temple University. He specializes in the study of mass political behavior, focusing on how people arrive at political judgments. His ongoing research uses experimental methods in both field and laboratory settings to study how political rhetoric and mass communication influence political attitudes and behavior. Professor Arceneaux's work has appeared in a number of scholarly journals, including the *American Journal of Political Science*, *The Journal of Politics*, *Quarterly Journal of Political Science*, *Political Behavior*, *Political Analysis*, and *Political Psychology*.

**Jack Citrin** is Heller Professor of political science and director of the Institute of Governmental Studies at the University of California, Berkeley. His research centers on political trust, national identity, immigration, and multiculturalism in the United States and Europe. Among his publications are *Tax Revolt: Something for Nothing in California*; *California and the American Tax Revolt*; *How Race, Ethnicity, and Immigration are Changing the California Electorate*; and, with David Sears the forthcoming *American Identity and the Politics of Multiculturalism*. Among his recent articles and book chapters dealing with immigration and national identity are "Testing Huntington: Is Hispanic Immigration a threat to American Identity?" (2007); "Saved by the Stars and Stripes, Protest Imagery and Immigration Attitudes" (2010); "Alternative Measures of National Identity: Implications for the Ethnic-Civic Distinction (2012); and "Do Patriotism and Multiculturalism Collide? Competing Perspectives from Canada and the United States?" (2012).

**Cornell W. Clayton** is director of the Thomas S. Foley Institute of Public Policy and Public Service and the C.O. Johnson Distinguished Professor of political science at Washington State University. His research focuses on judicial politics and American political institutions. He has published numerous articles and books, including: *Supreme Court Decision-Making: New Institutionalist Approaches* and *The Supreme Court in American Politics:*

*New Institutionalist Interpreations* (both co-edited with Howard Gillman); *The Politics of Justice: The Attorney General and the Making of Legal Policy*; and *Government Lawyers: The Federal Legal Bureaucracy and Presidential Politics*. He and J. Mitchell Pickerill are currently working on a book about the Supreme Court and regime politics.

**Jennifer R. Garcia** is a PhD student in the department of political science at the University of California, Irvine. Her research interests focus on the representation of Latinos and Blacks in the U.S. Congress, race, public opinion, and political participation. Garcia has published co-authored works in these areas. She is affiliated with the Center for the Study of Democracy at UC Irvine.

**Matt Grossmann** is assistant professor of political science at Michigan State University and director of the Michigan Policy Network. He is the author of *The Not-So-Special Interests: Interest Groups, Public Representation, and American Governance* (Stanford University Press). His research also appears in the *Journal of Politics, American Politics Research*, and twelve other journals. His next book, *Artists of the Possible: Governing Networks and American Policy Change Since 1945* is under contract. He is also co-author of *Campaigns & Elections: Rules, Reality, Strategy, and Choice*.

**Martin Johnson** is associate professor of political science and operates the Media & Communication Research Laboratory at University of California, Riverside. His research investigates political communication, public opinion, and public policy with a particular interest in U.S. subnational politics. His research has been published in the *American Journal of Political Science, British Journal of Political Science, Journal of Politics, Political Research Quarterly*, and *Social Science Quarterly*, among other journals. Professor Johnson's research has been supported by the John Randolph and Dora Haynes Foundation and the National Science Foundation.

**Raymond J. La Raja** is associate professor of political science at the University of Massachusetts, Amherst, and editor of *The Forum*, an electronic journal of applied research in contemporary American politics. His research on American political parties, interest groups, campaign finance, and electoral reform has appeared in the *Journal of Politics, Legislative Studies Quarterly*, and other noted journals and edited volumes. He is the author of *Small Change: Money, Political Parties and Campaign Finance Reform*, which explains how political finance laws shaped parties and elections through American history. He serves on the Academic Advisory Board of the Campaign Finance Institute in Washington, DC.

**Keena Lipsitz** is an associate professor of political science at Queens College, City University of New York. Her main field is American political behavior with a focus on how political campaigns affect voters, but she has broader interests in democratic theory, public opinion, election law, and media effects as well. She is the author of *Competitive Elections and the American Voter* (2011) and *Campaigns and Elections: Rules, Reality, Strategy, Choice* (with John Sides, Daron Shaw, and Matt Grossman, 2012). Her research has appeared in a variety of journals, including *Political Behavior* and *Journal of Political Philosophy*. She received her PhD from the University of California, Berkeley in 2004.

**Seth Masket** is associate professor and chair of the political science department at the University of Denver. He is the author of *No Middle Ground: How Informal Party Organizations Control Nominations and Polarize Legislatures* (2009). He writes and teaches on the subjects of party organizations, state legislatures, political networks, and campaigns and elections. Masket received his PhD from UCLA in 2004.

**Joanne M. Miller** is an associate professor of political science and adjunct associate professor of psychology and journalism and mass communication at the University of Minnesota. She received her PhD in social psychology in 2000 from the Ohio State University. Her research addresses the ways in which the media affect political attitudes and the motivations underlying a wide array of political behaviors (voting, protesting, volunteering, contributing money, becoming a party delegate, and the like). Her work has been supported by grants from the National Science Foundation and has appeared in journals such as the *American Journal of Political Science*, *Public Opinion Quarterly*, and *Political Psychology*.

**Daniel J. Palazzolo**, PhD, is a professor of political science at the University of Richmond, where he teaches courses on American government, campaigns and elections, legislative process, and public policy. He is author of two books, including *Done Deal? The Politics of the 1997 Budget Agreement*, and author or co-author of more than twenty articles or book chapters. He is also co-editor, with James W. Ceaser of the University of Virginia, of *Election Reform: Politics and Policy*. His current research, with Randall Strahan of Emory University, seeks to explain the formation of coalitions in Congress that involve bipartisan cooperation in an era of polarized parties.

**Paul J. Quirk**, a dual citizen of the United States and Canada, is Phil Lind Chair in U.S. politics and representation at the University of British Columbia. He received his PhD at Harvard University, was a research associate at the Brookings Institution, and held faculty positions at several American universities—most recently, the University of Illinois at Urbana-Champaign—before moving to Canada in 2004. He has published widely in several areas of American politics: administrative politics, public policy, the presidency, Congress, and public opinion. He is author or co-author of *Industry Influence* *in Federal Regulatory Agencies* (1981); The *Politics of Deregulation* (1985); and *Deliberative Choices: Debating Public Policy in Congress* (2006) and co-editor of *The Legislative Branch* (2005). His work on public opinion includes articles and essays on "The Rising Hegemony of Mass Opinion," "Reconsidering the Rational Public," "Misinformation and the Currency of Citizenship," and "The Conceptual Foundations of Citizen Competence." His awards include the Louis Brownlow Book Award of the National Academy of Public Administration and the Aaron Wildavsky Enduring Achievement Award of the Public Policy Section of the American Political Science Association.

**David Brian Robertson** is curators' teaching professor of political science at the University of Missouri-St. Louis. His most recent book is *Federalism and the Making of America* (2011). He also is the political analyst for KSDK Television (NBC).

**Andrew Rudalevige** is Thomas Brackett Reed Professor of government at Bowdoin College. He has held teaching and visiting posts at Dickinson College, Harvard University, the University of East Anglia, and Sciences Po (Lyon). Rudalevige has written extensively on presidential power, inter-branch relations, presidential management of the bureaucracy (especially via the Office of Management and Budget), and public policy. His books include *Managing the President's Program*; *The New Imperial Presidency: Renewing Presidential Power after Watergate*; and the edited volumes *The George W. Bush Legacy* and *The Obama Presidency: Appraisals and Prospects*. In a former life, Rudalevige was a city councilor and state senate staffer in his native Massachusetts.

**Robert P. Saldin** is an associate professor of political science at the University of Montana. He writes and teaches about American government, political development, and public policy. His first book, *War, the American State, and Politics since 1898*, was published in 2011, and his articles have appeared in outlets such as *The Journal of Politics*, the *Journal of Policy History*, *Political Research Quarterly*, and *The Forum*. Previously, Saldin was a Robert Wood Johnson Scholar at Harvard University, the Patrick Henry Scholar at Johns Hopkins University, a Fellow at the Miller Center of Public Affairs, and a visiting scholar at the University of California, Berkeley's Institute of Governmental Studies. He received his PhD from the University of Virginia in 2008.

**JoBeth Surface Shafran** is a graduate student at the University of Texas, where she studies American politics and public policy. She is a graduate research fellow with the Policy Agendas Project.

**Katherine Tate** is professor of political science at the University of California, Irvine. She is also affiliated with UC Irvine's African American Studies

Program and the Center for the Study of Democracy. She is the author of several books, including *Concordance: Black Lawmaking in the U.S. Congress from Carter to Obama* (2013). Her PhD in political science is from the University of Michigan.

**Sean M. Theriault** is an associate professor at the University of Texas. He is the author of *The Power of the People, Party Polarization in Congress* and *The Gingrich Senators*. His research, ranging from presidential rhetoric to congressional retirement and the Louisiana Purchase to the Pendleton Act, has been published in a number of different journals. Professor Theriault has earned numerous teaching awards and is a member of the Academy of Distinguished Teachers.

**Matthew Wright** is an assistant professor in the department of government at American University. He received his PhD from the University of California, Berkeley, in 2010. In his research, he has explored numerous topics relevant to American politics and comparative politics more generally. These include: the causes and implications of political identity; immigration, assimilation, and citizenship policies; the politics of ethnic diversity; national identity and patriotism; religion and politics; political culture; social capital, civic engagement, and trust; and U.S. voting behavior. He has published work in a number of peer-reviewed journals, including *Comparative Political Studies, American Politics Research, Political Research Quarterly, Psychological Science, Canadian Journal of Political Science, Political Psychology,* and *Perspectives on Politics.*

# Preface

This book aims to invigorate learning about American politics by engaging students in cutting-edge questions in political science research. Though introductory textbooks provide solid information about American government, they gloss over the most interesting questions about the study of politics. Students in introductory courses rarely have the opportunity to learn how experts think about the subject. And students are typically not encouraged to ask whether an assertion about politics is true or how one would go about discovering its veracity. By integrating basic knowledge about politics with lessons in the practice of research, this book should help deepen students' understanding of American politics, sharpen their analytical skills, and prepare them better for responsibilities of citizenship.

The original essays in this volume cover most of the topics in an introductory American politics course. However, scholars drill down on some of the most intriguing questions in their respective fields. Each chapter highlights a critical research agenda, explaining why it advances knowledge about American politics. Scholars provide a concise overview of accumulated knowledge about a research puzzle and then explain how they address it. Along the way, students learn about the kind of choices scholars make in framing a question, designing research, and evaluating evidence. In this way, the book combines substantive knowledge about American politics with the kind of analytical inquiry and skill building that is touted at top universities and colleges across the country.

Used alongside a traditional textbook on American politics, this volume will enliven class discussions by raising major questions that animate scholarship. And it does so without the professional jargon that makes standard professional journal articles difficult to use in undergraduate classrooms. As a practical guide, each chapter begins with headnotes that summarize findings and highlight key concepts or design elements of the research. Many findings are counter-intuitive and should inspire students to rethink standard narratives about American politics. The hope is that the research illustrated in these pages sparks full-throated conversations in classes and dorm rooms: Wars increase minority representation? Hard-hitting campaign ads can be good for democracy?

The contributing scholars are outstanding researchers and teachers. They shared a vision for this book and responded amiably to requests for revisions, advice, and additional assignments, despite their busy lives and the small compensation for their efforts. I am grateful to have such wonderful colleagues.

This volume exists because Michael Kerns, the acquisitions editor at Routledge Press, had a vision for bringing current research into the classroom through a series of books on different topics in American politics. It was challenging to produce a volume for an introductory course, given the scope of topics and the fact that these courses typically enroll students whose knowledge of politics ranges widely. However, through my experience in teaching introductory American politics, I recognized the value of the project. I had been trying, without much luck, to find examples of political science research that were fresh and insightful while also accessible to undergraduates. I am grateful to Michael for bringing his ideas, encouragement, and editorial talents to this venture. I also want to thank the editorial assistant, Darcy Bullock, and production editor Sioned Jones for bringing the book to fruition with their expert guidance. A special thanks goes to the scholars who reviewed the proposal and chapters: David Wells, Mark Joslyn, Alan Abramowitz, Michael Wagner, Kristin Kanthak, Gregory Koger, John Barnes, Mark Eisner, Janet Box-Steffensmeier, and additional anonymous reviewers. They offered invaluable suggestions to improve this book, and their enthusiasm for the project increased my pleasure in working on it.

*Amherst, Massachusetts*
*January 2013*

# Overview

## New Directions in American Politics

# Introduction

*Raymond J. La Raja*

Several years ago, comedian Jon Stewart organized a "Rally to Restore Fear and/ or Sanity" on the Washington Mall. In his speech to roughly 200,000 fans, he excoriated the press, or what he called "the country's 24-hour political pundit perpetual panic conflictuator." Stewart's point was that partisan news shows on Fox News and MSNBC were pushing the nation into two tribes because these programs emphasized the conflict between Democrats and Republicans and proffered extremist opinions that most Americans did not share. Many prominent citizens shared his view, including veteran journalists such as the esteemed Ted Koppel, formerly of ABC News.

Stewart is surely right that these news programs lack the objective style that was common among broadcast networks more than a decade ago. And yet he and others may overstate the power of Fox News to shape public opinion. We know this because political scientists study closely how the media influence politics. In this volume, two scholars, Kevin Arceneaux and Martin Johnson, develop an innovative experiment to show how people behave when they watch TV. It appears that the vast majority of citizens use their television remote controls to skip news programs in favor of alternative entertainment shows. The fact that so few people *choose* to watch these partisan programs suggests that they may not harm or divide viewers as much as people believe. Arceneaux and Johnson explain that the partisan press is hardly a new phenomenon in American history and point to previous research debunking the notion that the media "brainwash" citizens. The chapter shows in a clear, jargon-free style how experts *think* about answering questions related to politics. Jon Stewart says Fox News is harmful, but how do we *really know*? If we take at face value that partisan news shows really push people into warring tribes, efforts to attenuate aspects of polarization might be misguided if this assertion is wrong. Instead, if we want to remedy the deleterious effects of polarization, a genuine understanding of underlying causes might help advance effective solutions rather than attacking Fox News or MSNBC.[1]

This is the work of political science. It involves framing important questions, developing theories about politics, and evaluating the evidence systematically. The task is not always easy. Politics is messy and complicated, with players and events always in motion. Political scientists cannot typically control the environment to isolate "cause and effect" the way physicists or chemists do through experiments. They take what the real world gives them and devise innovative ways of building knowledge through historical documents, interviews, statistical data and even, at times, experimentation. Political science research also borrows ideas abundantly from related fields such as psychology, economics, anthropology, and sociology. With a range of tools, scholars of American politics seek to understand questions that get at the heart of democratic governance: Who governs and how? How do political institutions engage and respond to citizens? What factors shape public policies? By addressing these questions, scholars hope to advance knowledge that enriches our understanding about American democracy and enhances the public welfare.

## Why This Book?

There has hardly been a more critical time to learn deeply about how the nation's politics "works." The country faces daunting challenges as it emerges from the most damaging financial crisis in eight decades. At the same time, leaders must figure out how to curtail ballooning national debts that threaten long-term prosperity and social stability. Regarding national security, the government must continue to protect against terrorist threats at home and abroad without curbing fundamental liberties. Americans look to Washington for some answers but ruefully observe partisan bickering and policy gridlock. A Gallup poll in June 2012 shows that just 17 percent of Americans approve of the job that Congress is doing.[2] To be sure, American politicians have not typically been the favorites of the American people, but there is a pervasive sense that politics is not working as it should.

This book offers no easy answers about the challenges facing American democracy. Instead, it asks readers to take the plunge into a deeper understanding of politics. Though traditional textbooks typically describe the political process for novices, this book goes further. It compels readers to think *analytically* about the changes and continuities in American political institutions and citizenship. It does this by introducing vexing *puzzles* that intrigue scholars who have dedicated careers to increasing knowledge about politics. Why, for example, do citizens bother to vote at all when their vote is unlikely to make a difference in an election? What exactly makes interest groups powerful, and how powerful are they? What can presidents actually do unilaterally with their executive power, and why don't they do more of it to get things done? These questions, and others that are addressed in this volume, reveal the scope of new scholarship on American politics.

The purpose of this book, then, is to engage readers in exciting research and demonstrate how to think systematically about politics. The core idea is to bring state-of-the-art developments in research to the classroom and beyond. Scholars in this edition were selected precisely because they are both top researchers and noted teachers who write well for non-expert audiences. Uniquely, the book covers the *breadth* of topics one finds in introductory texts but provides the analytical *depth* to learn how experts ponder research questions. Seeing how scholars examine questions brings to life knowledge in an introductory course and gives students a model for how to evaluate critically the material in textbooks and news media. Ultimately, the habits formed through this kind of teaching of politics should help make students more capable of contributing to civic life and improving the democratic process.

This book emerged from my teaching experience in which I was increasingly concerned about leaving my students in introductory classes with a shallow understanding of American government and politics. I typically require students to read about politics in the newspapers before class. I was struck by how easily students accepted "the facts" conveyed by commentators on television or in newspapers. They agreed uncritically, for example, with a journalist's pronouncement that the president is falling in the polls because he can't "connect with voters." The problem with such accounts is that they are often devoid of structural context or broader perspective. It would be helpful to know, for instance, that research shows presidents tend to struggle with voters when the economy is doing poorly, whereas those fortunate to preside over a strong economy are considered great communicators. In other words, the state of the economy matters a great deal on public perceptions of the president.

It would also be helpful to understand that journalists face professional imperatives that encourage them to overemphasize the influence of discrete events and candidate behaviors on election outcomes. Endowing the days' stories with special meaning and providing "horse-race" coverage is what sells newspapers. My comments are not so much a criticism of journalism as an acknowledgment that consumers of the news often lack the wherewithal to critically evaluate political information filtered to us by news organizations.

The problem with my teaching was that I did not provide a learning environment in which students wondered aloud about how political outcomes came to be. In short, I did not ask them to think analytically very much. Instead, they tended to memorize a lot of information or read about "real-world" politics without pausing to consider: *How do we know this?* On a number of occasions, however, I recognized that students really enjoyed when I talked about research. They particularly loved findings that demonstrated something counter-intuitive or revealed misconceptions about a problem. During these moments, learning about politics became less a matter of absorbing information from PowerPoint slides than a process of discovery. In a moment of self-awareness, I realized that *my* excitement in discussing research increased *their* excitement about learning.

These experiences caused me to believe that there is an important place for exposing students to research in an introductory political science course.

Traditional textbooks often provide excellent roadmaps to learn about politics, but they necessarily focus on rather dry "nuts-and-bolts" information. The very best textbooks offer opportunities for students to examine data in a graph or table but do not ask students to reflect on a research question in the field and grapple with how to answer it. And yet we know from studies of learning that achieving mastery of a subject means moving beyond basic recall of facts and mechanically applied solutions to a list of problems. True mastery means acquiring the concepts and tools of inquiry that can be applied to new questions. By modeling higher-level thinking skills, students are stirred toward deeper reflection about politics (or any other subject). Ultimately, this kind of analytical thinking helps students understand the material better and retain what they have learned in textbooks and lectures. More importantly, they engage in the kind of reasoned inquiry that should help them participate as thoughtful citizens beyond the classroom.

The opportunity to probe scholarly developments rarely happens in an introductory-level course. Even at top universities, students do not get to observe the kind of cutting-edge research that opens up new ways of understanding the political world. One hurdle for instructors is finding material that reflects quality scholarship and yet is accessible for undergraduates. Articles in scholarly journals are typically unsuited for undergraduate courses, particularly introductory courses. And where undergraduate readers exist for scholarly work, they are typically confined to a single topic for upper-division courses on Congress or public opinion. Many readers simply summarize the research findings but do not illustrate how the scholar makes decisions about how to study a problem and why they choose a particular kind of analysis. Some good introductory readers organize "classics" in the field but focus on the arguments rather than making the research process visible. This volume, however, tries to convey the immediacy of generating new research on contemporary questions by presenting examples of how experts approach politics analytically.

Two trends in higher education appear to support this approach. For better or worse, American colleges and universities have entered the era of public "accountability" as the public grows anxious about the cost of higher education and postgraduate employment prospects. Students, parents, and the government are demanding to know what kind of knowledge and skills they are getting for their money. Many campuses have responded by emphasizing the acquisition of analytical skills rather than absorption of basic material. To some degree, this trend is reflected in recent textbooks, which now incorporate boxed "call-outs" to encourage students to analyze basic evidence. This volume goes further because, by exposing students to the practice of research (e.g., selecting, clarifying, integrating), it helps them build strong competencies that can be applied in a variety of contexts.

The other driver of change is technology. In the coming decade, many courses will become "blended" experiences that include face-to-face class discussions in combination with coursework conducted online. Fostered by new technologies, instructors will have opportunities to deepen classroom discussions by providing knowledge in online formats and devoting class time to higher-level inquiry and problem solving. To support this blended environment, *New Directions in American Politics* provides online materials, such as interview videos with scholars and testbank questions to assess comprehension (discussed further). One vision for this book is to encourage instructors to exploit technology by changing the character of an introductory course. Personally, I would like to see more of the "basics" about American politics offered online (e.g., via electronic textbooks and other materials) while allocating a large portion of class time to informed dialogue about contemporary political questions and how to answer them.

## What Is Included in This Book

The scope of this book is broad, containing many of the same topics found in traditional texts on American politics. To accommodate non-experts, the chapters contain overviews of the existing literature on a research topic, without overburdening the student with too much information. The central element in each chapter is a research puzzle, which is placed in the broader context of knowledge about a particular subject. In other words, the authors give a sense of the standard approaches to understanding a topic, and then they explain how their approach, which often differs from these standard accounts, lends new insights about a question. Typically, the findings challenge conventional wisdom or appear counterintuitive at first blush.

A key aspect of the book is the way scholars explain how they go about addressing the puzzle. Some of this explanation requires learning concepts and frameworks for organizing knowledge. However, the writing is clear and devoid of jargon found in many professional journals. For the most part, no additional knowledge is needed to understand a chapter beyond what is provided in a textbook. Many findings are presented with basic graphics and tables, which do not require advanced analytical training. The authors typically conclude by indicating how their approach might help address pressing questions about contemporary American politics. Indeed, almost all the chapters raise normative concerns implied by the research findings, (e.g., should the president be more or less constrained in exercising power?). They also try to engage the students on the direction of future research and remaining unanswered questions.

To provide one example, the chapter on the presidency by Andrew Rudalevige poses the broad question, "What can presidents do, and how can presidents do it?" It begins by acknowledging the genuine concerns about executive power raised by Framers during the Constitutional Convention, and examines how power has been used recently by presidents to pass laws or pursue war. Equally important, it discusses how *difficult* it has been to study presidential power, and why scholars have focused so much on personal characteristics to explain the exercise of power. Then it offers an approach that focuses more on "institutional" understanding of presidential power, which means looking at the processes and patterns of decision-making rather than individual "quirks". It does all of this while focusing on the puzzle of how presidents pursue legislative goals. Throughout, Rudalevige leads the reader through a series of key choices about how to analyze different aspects of presidential decision making, drawing on his own work to make key points about the research process. In the end, he arrives at an important conclusion that the kind of strategies that help presidents manage the executive branch may hurt them in trying to gain influence in the legislative branch. The conclusion has significant implications for understanding the constraints that all presidents face in a separated system and raises larger questions about how much power presidents have and how much we *want* them to have.

In this way, the chapter on the presidency, like other chapters in the volume, combine many ideas to enlarge the reader's perspective about American politics. Not only does it provide rich substantive content that draws students into an ongoing intellectual dialogue about American political institutions but it lays bare an analytical process for contributing to this dialogue in an intelligent way. In short, it helps students think analytically about contemporary American politics.

There are several common themes across the chapters. One strong substantive theme is partisan polarization and how this dynamic affects American political institutions and the behavior of citizens. So, for example, chapters on the Supreme Court, Congress, parties, interest groups, immigration, and national debt give considerable attention to how the growing partisan divide creates new challenges in governing, while also providing additional insights into the malleability of institutions. Rather than viewing polarization pessimistically, the research in this volume suggests that good governance remains plausible. Strong differences between the parties do not necessarily lead to stalemate or unusually sub-par policies.

The other notable element in this volume is methodological. Scholars devote considerable attention to the challenge of identifying *causal relationships*—that is, one thing or set of things causing something else rather than just being connected. In describing their research, they are careful to explain whether and how the way they conducted the research (the research design) helps demonstrate whether one set of factors can explain a particular outcome. As important, many do an excellent job explaining the limits of their research design and suggest plausible future research to improve our understanding of causality in politics. After all, as social scientists, we want to know not just what is happening in politics but why. Through this volume, you will find that the authors are decidedly pluralist in their willingness to use a variety of approaches to address questions. Many chapters combine multiple methods to address a puzzle, including historical analysis (an approach often referred to as American political development), quantitative, qualitative, and experimental analyses. Readers will hopefully see that different questions often require different methods and sometimes combinations of them. There are many useful methods of conducting research in studying politics.

## Chapter Summaries

The book is divided into three parts. The first part, *Governing Institutions,* covers the constitutionally created institutions of federalism, Congress, the presidency, and courts. The second part, *Influencing Politics,* examines how groups in society and individual citizens engage in politics through political parties, interest groups, the media, public opinion, political campaigns, and diverse forms of political participation. Finally, the third part, *Politics and Policy,* looks at salient public issues that the political system grapples with, including immigration, race, the national debt, and wars.

Starting with the first part about governing institutions, two sub-themes emerge. First, these chapters challenge a common premise of political science scholarship that predicts institutional outcomes based on the sum of individual behaviors. Much research on Congress, for example, simply arrays all Members of the House along an ideological continuum and then focuses on the median Member—the elected representative who is exactly in the middle—to predict the policy that gets passed by this chamber. In this volume, however, the scholars suggest that institutions are both more consequential and allow for greater nuance across policies and depending on the political environment. For instance, in a typical year, balancing the budget is extremely difficult: the median member of Congress may prefer to keep taxes low without cutting spending. However, then public opinion shifts toward a desire to balance the budget in the aftermath of a financial crisis. Members readjust to the new context and may adopt new rules in Congress that encourage members, both liberal and conservative, to compromise on a plan to balance the budget.

Another sub-theme is that these chapters reveal how intertwined American governing institutions are and, more specifically, how they affect each other through time: the Supreme Court by electoral politics of the era, presidents by partisan coalitions in Congress, and federalism by the tug-and-pull of politics in all three branches in Washington.

In the first chapter, for example, David Robertson shows how federalism is a virtual battleground over policies Americans care deeply about. The nation engages in an ongoing dispute about the degree to which issues such as abortion, health care, or immigration are the purview of states or the federal government. Robertson shows how groups strategically use appeals to federalism to favor their preferred policy, rather than an ideologically pure defense of national or state power. Through this push-and-pull dynamic, the nation draws on past practices but also shapes new meanings for federalism. This chapter is a prime example of using historical analysis to demonstrate continuity and change in American political institutions.

The subsequent chapter on Congress, by Sean Theriault and JoBeth Surface Shafran, challenges a prevailing orthodoxy in studying how Congress makes decisions. As the most powerful representative body in the world, the U.S. Congress claims the considerable attention of scholars. In discussing the policies shaped by Congress, Theriault and Shafran praise the significant research on Congress that employs "formal models" and quantitative analysis of roll call votes, but they argue that this view obscures too much, even as it claims to explain most outcomes in Congress. One might observe that they are criticizing the "lumpers" of political science who assume that differences in the policymaking process are not as important as overarching similarities. Theriault and Shafran, in contrast, appear to be "splitters" who think differences matter a great deal in explaining the form and substance of policy debates in Congress. They see nuance in how problems get on Congress's agenda, how coalitions are put together, and when politics are polarized or bipartisan. Their view offers a glimpse into how and why politicians do not always vote in lockstep with the party or with their ideological preferences. The research urges scholars to employ case studies in combination with conventional quantitative analysis to understand how the process works on major policy questions before Congress.

Turning to the presidency, Andrew Rudalevige takes on the timeless question about power. How much power do presidents really have, especially with respect to Congress? Important for the purposes of this book, Rudalevige provides a roadmap for understanding how political scientists think about power and how they study it. In his analysis, he explains the special challenges of research when there are "only" forty-four presidencies to study. His innovative analysis of presidential decision making shows when presidents choose to keep decisions close to them in the White House and when they allow executive agencies to take the lead, with important implications for each strategy. As critical, the findings illustrate the formidable constraints on the president, even when he tries to do things unilaterally such as using executive orders.

In the chapter on the judiciary, Cornell Clayton returns to the theme of power and how judges make decisions. The Supreme Court has played an increasingly influential role in policy decisions, ranging from abortion (*Roe v Wade*), presidential elections (*Bush v Gore*), money in politics (*Citizens United v Federal Elections Commission*) and health care (Affordable Care Act). These decisions are controversial, and many have claimed that the Court is merely political with their actions reflecting the kind of partisan politics observed in the other branches. Indeed, a considerable body of research evaluates judges as if they were merely legislators with fixed ideological preferences, but Clayton argues that the courts are unique. Though judging is a political process, the judges do, in fact, strive for norms of objectivity in deciding cases. Clayton broadens the lens by demonstrating how the courts are shaped by the wider politics of an era—what he calls "regime politics"—but this does not mean that they completely fail at the task of being judges in the traditional and impartial sense. They bring their experiences to the bench, which include the same political forces shaping the other branches, but they are steeped in professional norms of law schools and legal vocation. Clayton's research is another good example of using historical analysis to provide a broader and integrated view of political institutions in the United States.

Part II, *Influencing Politics*, includes several chapters that elaborate on the dynamics of partisan polarization in American politics. It begins with Seth Masket's seemingly simple question: "What is a political party?" The era of the strong party "boss" seems long gone, and yet partisans appear to get things done even without someone's giving directions from the top. Employing a relatively new method called social network analysis allows Masket to demonstrate that the party is more than the formal party organization. It includes interest groups, officeholders, and activists who coordinate activities to achieve partisan goals. Studying relationships among political actors provides a rich portrait of the variety of influences that shape decisions to nominate party candidates, raise money, or pass legislation.

On the topic of interest groups, Matt Grossman examines Americans' perennial fears of special interests' dominating Washington and undermining the common good. Grossman uses a variety of innovative methods, ranging from old-fashioned archival research to meta-analysis of historical books and statistical study of legislative outcomes. He shows which groups *appear* powerful but then goes on to show that even these groups have little to show for their efforts. His research raises excellent questions about the difficulties of demonstrating whether political contributions and lobbying affect policy outcomes.

The news media comprise another political actor many Americans love to hate. They are especially concerned about the power of the media to distort how citizens view politics. As we saw at the start of this Introduction, close observers point to the highly shrill and partisan media epitomized by Fox News and MSNBC, which appear to be pulling Americans further apart by exaggerating differences between the parties and villainizing the opposition. Kevin Arceneaux and Martin Johnson devise a creative experiment with college students to observe how citizens actually behave when they watch TV. Their findings suggest that fears of media power are overblown, chiefly because most Americans choose to ignore these highly partisan shows (and the small audience that remains is like preaching to the choir). Their research raises perhaps a larger concern about whether Americans are getting *any* political news in this era of hyper-choice. The research does an outstanding job explaining research design issues of *internal* validity (identifying the causal relationships) and *external* validity (generalizing findings to the broader population).

Another source of information for citizens potentially comes from political campaigns. However, many Americans appear turned off by the negative advertising, believing that there is nothing worth listening to in these mudslinging battles. Keena Lipsitz takes a closer look at these advertisements, observing whether they support essential democratic values that would help voters make choices. Her study assembles a unique dataset of TV ads and matches it to specific House races, showing how even slight increases in political competition elevate the substance of campaign information, even as they also increase the amount of negative advertising. Americans may claim to dislike campaign ads, but they appear to be a valuable part of democratic process of learning about issues and candidates. Lipsitz's work raises questions about what can be done to ensure that more campaigns provide good information to voters.

Looking at public opinion, Paul Quirk takes on the controversial question in the scholarly literature about whether partisan polarization is being pushed by elites or reflects the changing behavior of mass citizens. Quirk does a critical analysis of the literature and arrives at the conclusion that Americans themselves bear a large share of the responsibility for polarization, but it appears to be the rather narrow and ideological constituencies on the right and left who are pushing this dynamic. Quirk introduces the concept of "polarized populism" to describe the way in which politicians respond to ideologically extreme citizens at the expense of traditional elite deliberation and the fabled "median voter." His analysis points to the need for future research to understand underlying sources of polarization and the possibility of ameliorating the situation through electoral reforms.

The final chapter in this part examines the longstanding and fundamental question about why some people participate in politics more than others. Previous research emphasizes that those who have more "resources," such as education and income, tend to participate at higher rates. However, Joanne Miller argues these explanations do not account for some underlying patterns of behavior and why some people prefer different forms of participation. She turns to social-psychological theories to explain the intensity and scope of participation showing that *motivation* matters. Her work probes the sources of theses motivations and how they powerfully shape political engagement. This chapter is another excellent example of using mixed methods, particularly experiments in the field and laboratory to untangle causal relationships.

Part III, *Politics and Public Policy* addresses controversial policy matters from political angles. The common element in these chapters is their use of rich historical analysis of institutions, in combination with data on public opinion to understand how Americans grapple with major policy issues such as immigration, race relations, debt crises, and war. Regarding the immigration issue: In the past few decades, the United States has experienced one of the most massive waves of immigration in its history. Despite the nation's mythology about being a land of immigrants, Jack Citrin and Matthew Wright show that Americans are highly ambivalent about current immigration policies. The authors combine public opinion data with a richly drawn historical perspective to recurring American concerns about the loss of national culture and identity, even as they remain open to the principle of immigration as a positive force in American life. In juxtaposing elite perspectives on immigration with mass opinion, the chapter raises important questions about the politics of immigration policy that American leaders have yet to address.

Turning to issues of race and ethnicity, Jenny Garcia and Katherine Tate describe how the nation has come a long way since the days of denying citizenship to blacks, Latinos, and Asians but show that formidable obstacles remain. Despite the historic election of a black president, the nation is not colorblind in choosing its leaders. They point to recent research that reveals persistent disparities in the representation of minorities and public opinion data showing the racialized views of whites toward minority groups and leaders. As formal barriers to political participation recede, race and ethnicity remain markers of difference for non-white Americans in less transparent ways. The authors address the power of institutions to shape behavior of leaders in Washington and how political dynamics may change as nonwhites become a greater share of the American electorate.

Dan Palazzolo takes a look at the spiraling debt crisis in the United States and asks whether political leaders will be able to organize viable solutions to address the problem. As in Theriault and Shafran's work on Congress, Palazzolo challenges the conventional wisdom that the political parties are too far apart to achieve policy resolution. Drawing on historical case analysis, he employs a "process tracing" approach that highlights situations in which crises, shifts in public opinion, and even small changes in institutional procedures can lead to outcomes that never would have been predicted by conventional regression models. His chapter reveals the capacity of the American political system, with the right-minded leaders, to respond to crises despite structural constraints.

In the final chapter, Robert Saldin provides a new lens for understanding policy change in the United States. He looks specifically at the effect of war on domestic policy. Casting aside artificial distinctions between foreign and domestic, he shows just how intertwined they are. Paradoxically, foreign wars can be good on the home front. Specifically, they have a positive impact on extending the rights and privileges of citizenship to previously marginalized groups. His analysis shows how pragmatic and moral concerns motivated the nation's leaders to end forms of discrimination and expand rights of blacks, women, and gays. His larger argument reveals how war reshapes political institutions and attitudes in American society in ways that may affect a range of domestic issues.

## How to Use This Book

As stated previously, this volume aims primarily to introduce good research in American politics as a way of demonstrating to students the value of analytical and systematic inquiry. The hope is that by supplementing the traditional approach of conveying basic facts with discussions about political science research, students will be more engaged in learning about American politics. At the same time, these discussions should elevate the quality of thinking by students. The chapters are designed to encourage readers to consider how logic, creativity, and evidence help address important and controversial questions about politics.

This book is not designed to convey a lot of elementary knowledge about American government. To be sure, coverage is broad, and many chapters provide excellent histories of political institutions. However, the material "drills down" on a research question by summarizing seminal work on the topic and offering a new way of studying it. Students will see how scholars frame questions, how they attempt to build on previous knowledge, and how they apply theories and concepts to address a question. In this way, the volume presents an expert's approach to understanding politics without assuming expertise on the part of students. In short, it makes the research process both transparent and accessible.

Given the unique nature of this book, it would be best to use it in introductory courses as a supplement to other materials that provide elementary facts about American politics, either through lectures, textbooks, or online resources. With basic knowledge about American politics, students can readily sink their teeth into the questions that are probed in this volume. No special instruction in research design or methods is necessary. The volume, however, would be useful for undergraduates taking courses in "scope and methods" in political science or even graduate students participating in a broad field seminar about American politics.

As accessible as the readings are, students will need a roadmap before they begin. This is new territory for many and research narratives are not the same as textbook narratives. For this reason, I highly recommend that students focus on the following essential questions as they read each chapter:

1. What is the puzzle or problem the chapter tries to address?
2. How will addressing this puzzle help increase knowledge about this topic?
3. How does the scholar try to answer the question?

Several features are included in the book to help guide students. First, each chapter begins with a *short summary* to introduce the topic, highlight the findings, and point out interesting features of the research that novices might otherwise overlook.

The second helpful tool includes online videos of *interviews with a scholar*. These five-minute segments connect readers to a flesh-and-blood professor talking about his or her work. Students hear how scholars conceived the project, how they made decisions about the research and grappled with particular challenges, and what they view as the central insight. The videos offer a multi-method approach to learning the material for students with different learning styles. At the same time, multimedia bring alive the research by seeing scholars talk to viewers directly about why their work is meaningful.

To aid with comprehension and assessment, the publisher is providing to instructors a testbank for help in creating exams based on the book. For each chapter, there is a set of multiple choice questions, short answers, and an essay question. Of course, the questions in the testbank can also be used with "clickers" in the classroom or uploaded to a learning management system to be used as quizzes.

To make the most of this book, however, this is no substitute for robust *class discussion*. I would begin by focusing on the main question. Be sure students know what question the scholars want to address and why it is important. Next, ask students how scholars have tried to address the question previously. They should be able to explain the standard approaches to understanding a question (as described in the accessible literature review in each chapter). Then discuss the approach used in the chapter and whether it is different. Does the approach seem reasonable for addressing the question?

Though each chapter addresses different topics, all of them provide rich fodder for discussing aspects of research design. It is often easiest to begin with the basic concepts and measures. For example, what do students think of how Lipsitz measured "diversity" of campaign ads in Chapter 9? Many chapters also speak to the concept of "power" and how we might know when it is exercised and in what manner (see, for example, Chapter 2 on the presidency or Chapter 6 on interest groups). Other chapters speak directly to the concept of representation. In Chapter 11, for example, Citrin and Wright make clear that elites and lawmakers think differently about immigration. In a democracy, should the voters' preferences prevail over the preferences of elites, even if voters lack good information about the issue and prefer policies that might inflict harm on the economy and civil liberties?

Almost all the chapters speak directly to the issue of causality, providing many opportunities to ask students how to distinguish between correlated and causally-related events. In Chapter 6, for example, Grossman explains why a politician's vote may not necessarily be induced by a political contribution. These discussions of causality become especially helpful in chapters that include experiments (e.g., Chapter 7 on media and Chapter 10 on political participation). Fortunately, students will observe a variety of research approaches in which they can gain some elementary competencies, including American political development, experimental methods, and basic quantitative analysis.

In summary, here is a possible list of broad questions for class discussion:

1. What are the standard approaches to addressing this question?
2. How does the approach in this chapter differ, if at all?
3. Does this approach provide new insights that challenge conventional wisdom?
4. Where is the research headed and what are some unanswered questions?
5. What does this research tell us about contemporary American politics?

By using this book and asking these questions, I hope that introductory courses on American politics will nurture the kind of disciplined thinking that will prepare students for a life of questioning, problem solving, and informed citizenship.

## Notes

1  It is entirely possible, of course, that Fox News or MSNBC are pushing citizens into warring tribes although not *directly*. As the two scholars point out, one possibility is that these programs influence opinion leaders who watch them and that *these* people then influence others around them.
2  http://www.gallup.com/poll/155144/Congress-Approval-June.aspx

# Part I

# Governing Institutions

# Chapter 1

# American Federalism as a Political Weapon

*David Brian Robertson*

Federalism is not merely a theoretical debate about state versus federal power. According to David Robertson, federalism sets the stage for vibrant conflict over major policies in America, including abortion, health care, and immigration. In Robertson's analysis, federalism is a "battleground" over the future direction of the nation. Values and interests clash in a recurrent dynamic, pitting one level of government against the other. Robertson emphasizes an historical approach to understanding institutional change and continuity, commonly referred to as American political development (or APD). He demonstrates that Americans continually give new shape to the practice of federalism through ongoing contestation over the degree of control between levels of government. At the same time, federalism exhibits a "path-dependent" nature, meaning that practices from the past influence future directions. Viewed historically, one observes how political leaders strategically use arguments over federalism to advance preferred policy goals depending on the political context (e.g., when Republicans control Washington, liberals emphasize state power to pursue agendas concerning the minimum wage or gay marriage). The strategic deployment of federalism has only grown during this era of intense partisan polarization. This chapter is an excellent example of analyzing how American political institutions endure and transform through history in ways that reveal contemporary political undercurrents.

Ken Cuccinelli, the Virginia Attorney General who filed a lawsuit challenging the Affordable Health Care Act of 2010, sparked a roar of approval from conservative Tea Party supporters when he told them, "If we lose that case, state sovereignty has been whittled to nothing and federalism is dead."[1] Twenty other state attorneys general mounted a legal challenge to the health care law, charging that it infringed on state prerogatives.[2] Meanwhile, leaders in Arizona who disagreed with the Obama administration's immigration policy enacted a controversial state law that required police checks of immigration documents and added many state criminal charges for undocumented immigrants. Alabama, Georgia, Indiana, South Carolina, and Utah followed the Arizona example in 2011.[3] Political opponents use federalism as a political weapon in debates over many other important issues, including labor, economic policy, abortion, gay marriage, election law, and climate change.

Why is federalism—the division of government authority between the national government and regional governments—at the heart of so many conflicts in this era of political polarization? Does federalism really matter? Does it have a real impact on politics and policy results? Some American scholars argue that the actual impact of federalism has greatly diminished. However, newer scholarship shows that federalism is still a powerful political tool for partisans, presidents, judges, and state officials. Though today's American political leaders have adapted federalism to new conflicts, they are using federalism as a weapon, as leaders always have used it: an advantageous political institution that helps them win political battles or to defeat opponents. Federalism's role in political conflict has gained renewed urgency because so many of today's active policies have been layered on top of the federal system and depend on state cooperation for their success. A history of the development of American federalism shows that national activism has multiplied federal-state conflicts even as these conflicts became more specialized and less visible.

This chapter examines the resurgence of federalism as an important and visible weapon used in American politics. Using the perspective of APD, an approach that analyzes the way government and politics have evolved over time, the chapter identifies federalism as a durable institution that plays a constantly evolving political role. It describes how federalism became a wider, more fragmented, and often less visible tool in political conflicts. It assesses the political inheritance from several periods of the development of federalism: the nineteenth century, the Progressive Era, the New Deal, and the 1960s and 1970s. Finally, the chapter analyzes the way conservatives and liberals have used federalism to win political victories since the 1980s.

## Does Federalism Make a Difference? Conventional Scholarship

The oldest tradition of federalism scholarship explores the philosophical meaning of federalism, scrutinizing different theories about the value of federalism as an institutional arrangement. Montesquieu, James Madison, Alexis de Tocqueville, and John C. Calhoun wrote landmark arguments for the value of federalism for liberty and a well-governed republic. More recently, scholars have explored both original and contemporary justifications of American federalism.[4]

Law professors Malcolm Feeley and Edward L. Rubin discount these philosophical defenses of federalism as romantic arguments that are not grounded in current reality. They claim that federalism does not actually make a difference in American politics today, that it may not be "of any use," and that it may not even exist in the United States because national rules, laws, and regulations have greatly reduced the independent impact of state policy.[5]

Many of the books and articles on federalism since the 1960s have left the impression that Feeley and Rubin's skepticism is warranted. A number of textbook authors emphasize the way the intergovernmental system of national, state, and local governments implements American public policy.[6] Generally, these works describe the changing patterns of national grants and regulation, the degree of discretion that state and local governments exercise over federal grants-in-aid, cooperation or conflict among these governments, and management issues.[7] These studies often list the stages of the development of federalism over time, beginning with "dual federalism" in the nineteenth century, when the federal and state governments exercised power over distinct and separate spheres of public policy. Dual federalism, often compared to a "layer cake" with separate federal and state responsibilities, gradually evolved into "cooperative federalism" during the twentieth century, as federal responsibilities increased. Cooperative federalism is a kind of "marble cake" in which federal and state responsibilities swirl together, so that policy responsibility is mixed together and interdependent.[8] Federal, state, and local government relationships often are labeled "intergovernmental relations" today.[9] The term *intergovernmental relations* tends to focus on administrative challenges of this system, while downplaying the substantive political differences that federalism makes.

Even some scholars who disagree with Feeley and Rubin have conceded that federalism makes much less of a difference today than it did in the past. Political scientist Martha Derthick wrote that federalism "as a constitutional principle was sharply devalued" by the 1960s, and though not dead, federalism had "undeniably atrophied over time." In Derthick's view, states governed geographical areas that differed from one another, and federalism represented the state governments' cultural, economic, and political diversity. The nationalization of politics and policy has undermined the importance of states as distinct geographical regions. Politics is no longer organized by state and region but rather by class, race, gender, and other categories of groups that transcend state boundaries. "Historically," concluded Derthick, "the place-based community, often defined as a unit of government, had played a preeminent part in American politics and governance." However, today, states matter much less because geography matters much less.[10]

## Does Federalism Make a Difference? New Directions

New approaches to federalism, however, emphasized that federalism still makes a difference in American politics and policy. Political scientists who take a "rational choice" approach have applied economic analysis to federalism; they dissect the way incentives shape the behavior of state and federal government actors, and describe the conditions under which federal systems can sustain themselves.[11] Rational choice and other political scientists have produced hundreds of studies of the way states develop innovative solutions to public problems, and scholars, interested in states as laboratories that diffuse policy experiments, have analyzed the way political and policy innovations spread across states in the American federal system.[12] Historians have demonstrated the energetic role of government at the state level throughout the development of the United States.[13] Some of the most exciting current research on other nations examines the political role of federalism abroad.[14]

Scholars in the field of APD bring a fresh perspective to contemporary partisan conflict over federalism because they show how it consistently is used as a powerful political weapon. APD scholars improve our understanding of past and current political events by analyzing the origins, continuity, and changes in long-lasting institutions such as federalism.[15] For example, Robert Lieberman showed that American policy makers used federalism to put off difficult choices about race, a delay whose consequences have rippled through American history to the present.[16] Suzanne Mettler demonstrated how New Deal policymakers used federalism to construct a more generous welfare state for white men than for women and blacks, decisions that affect American social policy today.[17] Kimberley Johnson showed how federal government activism a century ago employed the states to achieve national action, a template that continues in the major federal domestic initiatives of the twenty-first century.[18] The rest of this chapter applies an APD approach to American federalism, demonstrating that federalism has and continues to make a huge difference in American politics and government.

### Federalism as a Political Weapon

Federalism still serves as a potent weapon in the polarized American politics of the 2000s, as health care and immigration policy demonstrate. The American Recovery and Reinvestment Act of 2009 (ARRA), the economic stimulus bill that the administration championed from the start of the Obama presidency, passed Congress by largely partisan votes, and several conservative Republican state governors fought it as an intrusion on the states.[19] Republican Governor Rick Perry of Texas used "states' rights" as the cornerstone of his wide-ranging criticism of a century of "progressive" policies, most especially those of the Obama administration.[20] Conservative research institutions urged Americans to embrace federalism and cut national power in domestic affairs.[21] In the contest for the 2012 Republican presidential nomination, "the quest to sharply shrink government that all the Republican candidates embrace, driven by the fervor of the Tea Party, has brought a sweeping anti-federal government stance to the fore on education, as in many other areas."[22] This use of federalism as a political weapon is not new.

History shows that American federalism regularly has been used to win political conflicts, just as it is being used now. It is true that federalism and states' rights no longer serve as the unifying battle cry that bonded the states that tried to leave the union in the 1860s or the states that resisted civil rights in the 1950s. The conflicts over federalism have fractured into many narrower issues even as the battlefield of federalism expanded into thousands of controversies over jobs, health care, race, education, environmental protection, immigration, abortion, gay marriage, energy, roads, taxes, and many more. As an issue, federalism seems submerged because these conflicts are less momentous than the Civil War, because federal leadership is accepted in principle and presumed in practice and because the media often overlook the political significance of the administrative complexity and technical details where the politics of federalism often thrive. When a person fully understands the huge responsibilities of the states and the wide scope of these many conflicts, federalism's importance is much easier to appreciate.

### Why States Matter

Political opponents use federalism as a weapon because the states have enormous authority, because they use that authority in different ways, and because they produce different results. State governments employ more civilians than the federal government. State and local government spending was roughly the same as federal spending before the long recession drove up federal expenditures and cut state revenue.[23] State governments regulate almost one-fifth of the American economy; states oversee the insurance industry, charter corporations, license occupations, and protect public health and safety.[24] American corporations do not have to exist legally in the state where they are headquartered. Many choose to incorporate in Delaware, which maintains laws that are very favorable to business. Many of the largest firms in the world, such as Wal-Mart, McDonald's, Coca-Cola, and the Walt Disney Company, legally exist as Delaware corporations. Delaware's favorable corporate laws, in turn, help produce more favorable corporate laws across the nation, because they put competitive pressures on other states to provide laws that are attractive to business.[25]

Just as important, states shape the political ambitions and careers of nearly all the nation's important political leaders. After the presidency, the most visible and prestigious American political offices are contested at the state level: U.S. Senator, state governor and, in seven states, seats in the U.S. House of Representatives. Ambitious governors, state attorneys general, and other officials have very strong incentives to enhance their prestige by pursuing policies that differ from, and often clash with, policies enacted in Washington, DC.

These state officials manage deeply contentious issues such as education, criminal justice, assistance to the needy, and activities ranging from marriage and divorce to gambling. American states enrolled about fifty million students in state-regulated public elementary and secondary education systems in the late 2000s, and another eighteen million in public higher education.[26] Most American criminal trials are held in state courts. Most of the million and a half prisoners in the United States are held in state or local prisons, and states have carried out all but three of the 1,277 executions in the United States since 1976.[27] State policy innovations influence other states and often national policy.[28] States are even an important part of national defense. Between 2001 and 2007, a quarter of a million state National Guard troops served in wars in Iraq and Afghanistan.[29]

### Why Federalism Is Used as a Political Weapon

Federalism is an attractive weapon in politics because when important choices are left to the states, the states produce results different from the national government's. First, different states desire different results from one anotherr. Political preferences and attitudes differ widely across the states. Conservative beliefs (such as limited government and traditional social values) tend to dominate in many Southern and Rocky Mountain states, and these beliefs support policies ranging from low taxes to capital punishment, abortion limitations, and bans on gay marriage. States on the Pacific coast, the mid-Atlantic and in New England have more liberal political beliefs, tend to support more active government, and are more tolerant of abortion rights and gay marriage. The Gallup polling organization found great variation across the states when it asked whether residents considered themselves conservative, moderate, or liberal. Nationally, 40 percent identified themselves as "conservative" in 2011, whereas 36 percent considered themselves "moderate" and 21 percent liberal. However, fully 53 percent of people in Mississippi identified themselves as conservative. In Massachusetts, 30 percent identified themselves as liberal, and only 29 percent identified themselves as conservative. Figure 1.1 maps the range of political beliefs across the states, with the darkest-shaded states indicating more conservative states than average and the lightest-shaded states more liberal than average.

These relatively stable patterns correspond to voting behavior. For example, the most conservative states on the map all voted for the Republican presidential candidate in the elections of 2000, 2004, and 2008 (with only one exception, Indiana, in 2008). Alaska is more libertarian than liberal and routinely votes for Republican presidential candidates. All the rest of the most liberal states in the figure voted for the Democratic presidential candidate in these three elections (except for New Hampshire in 2000).[30] Not surprisingly, state officials elected in conservative states, such as Texas governor Perry, are among the most prominent and vocal state officials who used federalism to challenge the Obama administration.

Second, states would do things differently than the Federal government even if their preferences were the same, because the states have a different, more

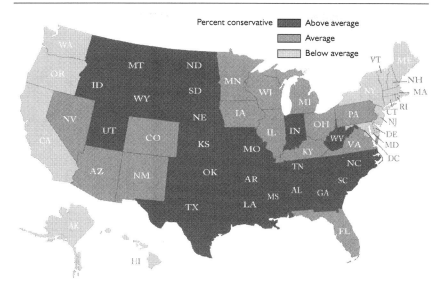

*Figure 1.1* Percentage of Americans who identify themselves as conservative, by state, 2011[31]

Note: Based on Gallup Daily Tracking polls, January 1 through December 31, 2011. The sample size is 218,537 adults; the margin of error is ±4 points (±3 in most states).

limited set of policy tools than the federal government's. None of the states have as many policy tools as the federal government. The U.S. Constitution allocated specified powers to the national government, such as printing currency and regulating trade with other nations and among the states. The states kept the remaining powers, including the power to govern everyday American life. Unlike a national government, states cannot print money or impose tariffs on goods imported into the state. Virtually all now require balanced budgets. With powers over trade, currency, and debt, national governments often shield companies and workers from economic competition originating in other nations.

Because the states lack a national government's economic tools, they are exposed to intense and immediate competition from enterprises in other states. State policymakers always feel very strong pressures to promote short-term economic growth, and they support business and strong resistance to policies that inhibit business profits or freedom.[32] States, then, generally have produced social welfare policies and business regulations more slowly than the national government and implement business regulations that are weaker and more geographically varied. Yet, because states have so much authority to deal with everyday life, most of the important political battles of American history were conducted at the state and local level before they were brought to the national government.

Third, because the states do things differently from each other and from the federal government, decentralizing policy allows a political interest to win a victory in *some* states if the interest cannot win a victory at the national level or in *all* the states. Each state's history, economy, and culture differ from the rest, so that each state is building on a different political foundation. Federalism is about inequality, as political scientist Aaron Wildavsky wrote: "It is inequality of result, not merely in income (some states choosing high tax, high services, others the opposite) but also in lifestyle, that distinguishes federalism as a living system from federalism as a front for a unitary power."[33]

It, therefore, makes a great difference whether the federal or the state governments control public policy. Because it makes a difference, the struggle over federalism has been constant and pervasive in APD. The real goal behind battles over state versus national power is to get government to do something or prevent government from doing something. If states control a policy, they are likely to produce more limited and uneven results than centralized policy, but a few may implement experiments that begin to lay the foundation for federal government action. In the twenty-first century, opponents of the Obama health care plan used federalism to undermine it. However, proponents of stricter rules on carbon emissions had much more success in some states than in the federal government.

## How American Federalism Evolves

Durable government institutions such as federalism are intended to change slowly, but they do change over time. Those who seek to advance their interests often find creative ways to adjust to institutions such as federalism and to invent new ways to use them. At any one time, political parties, interest groups, and reform movements have had to learn how to use federalism to achieve their principal goals. Federalism helps explain why political parties and interest groups grew to be so decentralized in the United States. These political organizations focused on the state governments, which controlled most of the power over domestic policy when they emerged and took root.

Federalism's impact on American politics has been gradual. It has shaped new institutions and public policies that modified the path of political development. This process of slow institutional evolution is termed *path dependence*, a tendency for an established way of doing things to become self-reinforcing and to shape future events.[34] Put another way, the path forward for new policy is heavily dependent on the path that past policy has taken. An APD scholar trying to understand the politics of American race relations today, for example, would analyze the path of racial policy development, from slavery in the Constitution, through the interstate disagreements about federalism and slavery that led to the Civil War, the period of state laws that segregated the races in the first half of the twentieth century, the laws designed to overcome these state policies in the 1960s, to the continuing national and state conflicts over affirmative action, racial profiling, and economic inequality today.[35] In this way, an institution such as federalism gradually shapes the development of public policy and the way people battle to control the way government uses its power.

Efforts to use federalism—and to adjust to it—have caused it to change over time, recasting the politics of federalism by broadening its policy scope and submerging its visibility. Federalism induced national policymakers to employ four tools to establish nation-wide policies without violating state prerogatives. These tools all have changed the politics of federalism.

First, *constitutional amendments* established specific new national rules or federal powers. Amendments in the Civil War era aimed to protect the civil and political rights of African Americans. The Sixteenth Amendment (1913) authorized the national government to levy income taxes. The Eighteenth Amendment (1919) aimed to ban alcohol. Second, *partial national rules*, established in federal legislation or federal court rulings, placed national restrictions on the states' powers or prescribe state actions. Since the 1930s, the federal government has banned state racial segregation laws, mandated states to provide access for disabled people, and required state antipollution actions, among many others. Third, through a process of *layering*, the federal government has induced the states to assume new responsibilities in return for some federal benefit such as land or a cash grant. Layering usually involves the process of adding new federal grants to the state and local governments or new requirements to existing grants in an effort to move the states in a common policy direction. These federal efforts build new tasks on top of long-established state duties, stimulating a national policy effort by enlisting all the states to implement a national goal. For example, the Morrill Act (1862) boosted higher education by granting federal land to each of the states on the condition that each provide college-level training in science, engineering, and agriculture. With so little federal authority to regulate, efforts to create national policies relied heavily on this kind of layering. Once layering was an established solution to the problem of national action, it also was used in later federal regulatory policies (such as air and water pollution) even after the Supreme Court broadened federal regulatory authority. Fourth, *bypassing* occurs when federal authorities establish new, separate local institutions to achieve specific policy goals. Federal grants to community-based nonprofit organizations in the 1960s aimed to connect federal policy makers directly to poor communities, bypassing the states. Partial national rules, layering, and bypassing constrain state discretion but also reinforce the states' residual discretion.

These tools have profoundly shaped the *sequence* of the American government growth since the late nineteenth century.[36] Most important, layering through federal grants is a tool more deeply established and expedient than partial national rules. The federal government enjoyed broad authority to manage public land and to collect revenue long *before* the two great surges in government activism in the Progressive Era (about 1890 to 1920) and in the New Deal from 1933 to 1945). Through federal grants to the states, the national government in both periods expanded its role in managing roads, education, and social welfare, among others. By the late 1930s, federal grants-in-aid to the states were a widely used and deeply embedded part of American government. Because the Supreme Court conceded that the federal government could police domestic economic affairs only *after* the growth of government activism through grants was well underway, the strategy of partial national rules did not begin to expand greatly until the next period of government activism, in the 1960s and 1970s.

American politics today has inherited many features from each stage of this evolutionary sequence. Remnants of each of four different periods in the evolution of federalism—dual federalism, the Progressive Era, the New Deal, and the liberal 1960s and 1970s—affect American politics today.

### The Inheritance of Dual Federalism

The 1800s left three unique institutional legacies for subsequent APD. Advocates of national political change in the twentieth century had to adjust to the robust institutional strength of state-based governance in the nineteenth-century United States.

First, dual federalism entrenched state policy authority and, therefore, made state-level public offices very desirable. Nineteenth century American politics often focused on state and local governments because these governments controlled the authority to address economic growth; race and gender; social welfare; elections; and other politically explosive issues. Political parties primarily competed to win state and local elections so they could control the state and local offices. Party members who won key offices learned to dole out appointments to party loyalists, who then worked to help their party retain these public offices. Party control of offices became the bond that kept political parties strong at the state and local level.[37] European nations after 1900 developed disciplined national political parties with coherent platforms, while American national parties remained rooted in the state and local politics of the nineteenth century. In the twentieth century, American parties remained relatively undisciplined collections of state and local organizations, loose coalitions in which state factions supported different policies because they represented varied regional and state interests.[38]

Second, a century of largely unimpeded self-rule allowed the states to construct diverse institutions and policies, tailored to particular state interests, making political cooperation across states very difficult. In first half of the nineteenth century, some states phased out slavery, while others strengthened it. After slavery was banned in the 1860s, Southern states passed so-called Jim Crow laws to keep African Americans politically and economically subordinate;

these states enforced racial segregation until the 1960s. State policies supported the different crops and businesses within each state, sometimes creating rivalries with other states. States rich in coal, precious metals, or other natural resources implemented laws to foster their mining industries. States with growing industrial cities, such as Massachusetts, initiated new regulations to control the effects of industrialization. These state regulations sometimes induced businesses (such as textile producers) to invest in other, more rural states with less regulation. Decentralized policy was tailored to local politics, ensuring that any effort to nationalize policy would meet some opposition from states invested in the status quo.

Third, federalism became and remains a potent rhetorical weapon used to frame major political issues. The ambiguity of the dividing line between state and federal power, along with reverence for the Constitution, created an open invitation for political opponents to frame a political conflict as a Constitutional issue over state versus national power instead of a disagreement over policy substance. Opponents of policy change often use the principle of federalism to obstruct, slow, and fragment initiatives they oppose and to protect states' authority to deal with the issue in a way they find more satisfactory. This use of federalism has been utilized frequently, but not exclusively, to block racial and cultural policy changes. Proponents of national policy change—whether Republicans or Democrats—often argue for federal government supremacy and power to make the policy. Thus, by framing the contested issue in terms of federalism, American politics has been complicated by a double battleground. The first battleground involves whether the government *should* take action at all. The second battleground involves *which level* of government should have the authority to take action. Federalism is used today—as it has been used for more than two centuries—to frame a conflict for political advantage.

### The Inheritance from Progressive-Era Federalism

The state authority entrenched in the nineteenth century posed a huge challenge for the ambitious reformers of the Progressive Era. Determined to adjust government to the needs of a dynamic industrial nation, these reformers sought government action to address emerging nationwide needs, including more professionalized administration, better factory and mining conditions, more highway construction, education for a manufacturing economy, and a democracy free of political corruption. To do so, they constructed policy that attempted to transcend state boundaries. They put in place new policy institutions, including uniform state laws, federal government grants to the states, and specialized policy communities.

In the 1890s, progressives began to lobby states to enact identical "model," or "uniform," laws to create commercial, child labor, and factory regulations that would be the identical laws everywhere in the United States. For example, reformers lobbied for state "mother's aid" programs that could provide for a stipend to fatherless families. Such efforts had some success; thirty-nine of the states had enacted mother's aid programs by the end of the 1910s, and these laws laid a foundation for the development of American welfare policy.[39] However, uniform law campaigns inevitably fell short of establishing the same law in states with diverse cultures, economies, and politics. The uniform law strategy took enormous sustained effort. Powerful state and local interests often defeated the strategy in precisely those states where stronger rules were most needed. Despite these limitations, the uniform laws strategy is still used today.[40]

The well-established national power to spend money presented an easier path to national policy in the federal system. Reformers urged new federal grant-in-aid programs to induce each state to establish a specific kind of program if it matched federal assistance with state funds. Reformers liked grants because they offered even impoverished states a financial incentive to initiate a policy. The states and their Congressional representatives liked the grants because they provided tangible benefits and allowed states to make important choices about the program. New grants-in-aid layered new policy initiatives on the existing federal system. The Federal Road Act of 1916 provided five million dollars in federal aid to each state for constructing rural roads and creating a state highway department.[41] The Smith-Hughes Vocational Education Act of 1917 provided grants for teachers' salaries and training.[42] The Smith–Lever Act of 1914 gave the states grants to institute cooperative extension services, managed by the state land-grant colleges and the U.S. Department of Agriculture.[43] These early grant-in-aid successes provided a ready template for extending national activism subsequently.

Reformers simultaneously built networks of professional policy experts and interest groups that supported uniform laws and federal grants.[44] For example, highway grants helped forge functional alliances of state and national road improvement groups, highway-building groups, and farm groups.[45] Farm extension agents constructed local "farm bureaus," which then organized at the state and national level and became the powerful farm lobbying groups.[46] Such networks became very influential in state and national policy making.[47]

Reformers also sought to make state politics more democratic and professional. Most of the states forced the political parties to employ primary elections to open up the nomination process.[48] Nearly half the states gave voters the power to bypass legislatures by passing laws through ballot measures.[49] New public agencies sought to prod national action on issues in their jurisdiction and to professionalize government.

## The Inheritance from New Deal Federalism

President Franklin Roosevelt's "New Deal" transformed American federalism in the 1930s, elevating the national government to a senior partner and broadening its role to new policy areas. During the New Deal, federal spending tripled and began to exceed state and local spending.[50]

New federal grants-in-aid programs multiplied, and grants spending grew sixteen-fold from 1932 to 1940. These grants-in-aid helped pull together the loosely confederated New Deal Democratic Party, a coalition that included urban liberals in the North and conservatives in the South. Delegating authority to the states allowed state and local Democrats to adopt national activism to a wide variety of circumstances.[51] Grants would require the states to meet national standards where the parts of the Democratic coalition agreed (such as more money for construction projects and relief) while at the same time permitting the states to control policy where Democrats disagreed with one another (as on racial segregation).

Federal regulatory authority also expanded late in the New Deal. The Supreme Court accepted a very broad interpretation of federal power to regulate the economy. This broader interpretation of the Constitution's commerce clause generally has been upheld since the 1930s, allowing the federal government to expand regulation. However, the new grant-in-aid programs, established in part because of previously accepted limits on federal power, already had been institutionalized.[52] Even in regulation, the New Deal pragmatically accommodated state power, leaving considerable state authority intact. Instead of fully nationalizing the regulation of such important areas as public utilities and oil, federal policy often left state regulatory authorities intact and required cooperation with federal regulatory commissions.[53]

State and local governments also strengthened during the New Deal and thereafter because the New Deal enlisted the states as partners in national activism.[54] Though the states accepted more federal policy leadership, their own governing capacity expanded. Court decisions allowed state governments and the federal government to expand their policy efforts.[55] Despite the growth of national government spending, the size of the state and local workforce continued to exceed the size of the federal workforce.[56] Federal activism often worked by proxy, with the states bearing the responsibility for implementing federal programs. This established pattern expanded further in the decades after World War II.

### The Inheritance of 1960s and 1970s Federalism

Political liberals in the 1960s built upon the New Deal system of intergovernmental activism. These reformers channeled more money to state and local governments, layered many new rules onto grants, and tried to establish new organizations to bypass existing policy networks.

During the presidency of Lyndon Johnson (1963–1969), Congress enacted 210 new grant programs, and federal grants expenditures doubled from 1964 and 1968.[57] These new grants addressed new problems, including systemic

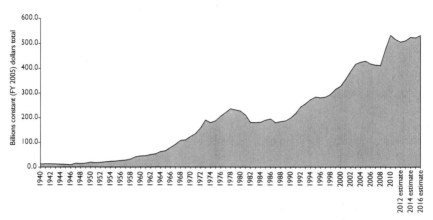

*Figure 1.2* Federal grant-in-aid spending, 1940–2015, in billions of constant (2005) dollars[58]

poverty and racial exclusion. They expanded federal influence into most of the important areas that state and local governments had monopolized since 1789, such as education and crime control. Income support, education, and training; Medicaid health funding for the needy; and other programs received substantial federal money. By 1978, one in every six dollars of federal spending was directed to grants-in-aid and, after dropping temporarily in the 1980s, the percentage of federal spending directed to grants is still about the same today, and the amount spent on grants generally has grown larger over time (Figure 1.2). Federal grants for health care alone now constitute nearly half of all federal grants spending, a fact that has fueled support for federal health care reform.

To leverage national results, these grants imposed more rules on grant recipients. The federal government had imposed only four requirements for federal grants in 1960. By 1978, there were more than 1,000 such federal requirements.[59] The 1964 Civil Rights Act, for example, prohibited discrimination in any program receiving federal grants. Environmental laws required the states to develop and meet antipollution standards.

These federal requirements greatly expanded the number of potential disagreements between the states and the national government. At the same time, many of these conflicts were narrowly focused on specific administrative choices and received only local, limited, and short-term publicity. Thus, while fights over federalism had multiplied in an important sense, these fights were submerged and were less visible than the great conflicts over federalism in the nineteenth century.

Many of the federal grants in the 1960s bypassed the state governments, channeling money instead to cities, counties, businesses, and non-for-profit groups. Liberal activists believed that direct funding for these actors would get around the obstruction, backwardness, and parochialism that characterized many state governments. Democrats were attracted to bypassing because it could shift more funds toward their urban constituency.[60] These grants further expanded the intergovernmental system and strengthened the networks that supported grant activism. At the same time, conflicts among the recipients increased. Richard Nixon's New Federalism aimed to reduce federal control over grants and redirect some funding to state and suburban governments, which were more Republican than the cities. By 1980, then, the stage was set for a more partisan approach to grants and to federalism more generally.

## Conservatives and Federalism in Polarizing America

Federalism has played a part in nearly every major domestic policy conflict in the last three decades. Republicans and Democrats, conservatives and liberals, have all found federalism a very useful strategic battleground for waging political warfare, as the United States has become more politically polarized.

When Ronald Reagan became president in 1981, conservative support had been growing for cutting the federal government's domestic policy role and elevating the role of the states. As president, Reagan championed federalism, arguing that the federal government "takes too much taxes from the people, too much authority from the States, too much liberty with the Constitution."[61] Reagan's signature budget initiative, the Omnibus Budget Reconciliation Act of 1981, removed 140 grants programs, cut federal grants spending, and gave state governments more power to determine how to spend federal grants. Grants spending shrank during the Reagan administration (see Figure 1.2).

Conservative presidents have used federalism very selectively, however. They have decentralized power when they believed it was likely to produce conservative results, whereas they expanded national rules and limited state authority where state control could undermine more important substantive priorities, such as freeing business from government regulation. For example, the Reagan administration sought national rules to reduce the states' power to regulate transportation, communications, and banking. During Reagan's presidency alone, the federal government preempted state authority in dozens of civil rights, commercial, financial, and health and safety programs.

In several ways, the federal government regulated states more tightly at the end of Reagan's term than at the start.[62] After Reagan left office, Republicans continued to use federalism selectively to achieve substantive goals. Sometimes these conservatives preempted the states, and sometimes they added more federal regulations for states to obey. The Republican-sponsored Telecommunications Act of 1996, the Financial Services Modernization Act of 1999, the Public Company Accounting Reform and Investor Protection Act of 2002, and the Energy Policy Act of 2005 all limited the states' authority to regulate business.

George W. Bush's No Child Left Behind Act layered additional federal rules on elementary and secondary education.[63]

Conservatives strengthened federalism more consistently through appointments to the courts and the control of many state governments. Guided by Reagan's appointments, such as Chief Justice William Rehnquist (1986–2005), the U.S. Supreme Court ruled that several federal laws were invalid because they encroached on state authority.[64] In the words of one journalist covering the Court, "These days, federalism means war."[65]

A number of states with conservative governors, legislatures and voters used state governments as conservative policy laboratories. They implemented stricter criminal sentences, stringent rules for welfare, restrictions on abortion, and bans on affirmative action and gay marriage. For example, many states made access to abortions more difficult by tightly restricting abortion clinics and requiring waiting periods for an abortion. By 2012, state abortion limits were increasing, and states were experimenting with new tactics to discourage abortion, such as requiring an ultrasound of the fetus.[66] Conservative state defiance of the Obama administration is an intensification of long-simmering partisan trends in the states.

## Liberals and Federalism in Polarizing America

Paradoxically, the conservative decentralization of national power helped energize liberals to use the states to achieve their goals.[67] Liberals, like conservatives, have advanced their agendas at the state level during Republican presidencies.[68] In the 1990s, state attorneys general sued the tobacco companies for the damages that smoking inflicted on citizens' health and engineered a $200 billion legal settlement.[69] A number of state attorneys general aggressively fought for financial reforms and for consumer and environmental protection.[70] In the early 2000s, state policies tried to limit carbon emissions, raise the legal minimum wage, expand anti-discrimination laws, and make it possible for undocumented residents to pay in-state tuition at public colleges.[71] The state of Massachusetts developed a health care plan that served as a model for the Patient Protection and Affordable Care Act of 2010. Though conservative states banned gay marriage, six states by 2012 allowed gay couples to marry, and another nine recognized spousal rights for same-sex couples.[72] States also built durable regional agreements to address problems that transcend their individual boundaries, such as water quality, homeland security, and access to prescription drugs.[73]

Like Democratic presidents before them, Bill Clinton and Barack Obama actively enlisted states and employed new intergovernmental tools to achieve their national policy goals. While Clinton supported new mandates on the states early in his term, he also supported more authority for the states.[74] Grant-in-aid spending increased 70 percent during Clinton's presidency. Clinton championed the Children's Health Insurance Program (SCHIP, now CHIP), a new grant program to enable states to provide health insurance for children in families without health insurance and who did not qualify for Medicaid[75]

President Obama also depended on the states to help advance his agenda. The Obama administration's stimulus bill provided tens of billions of dollars to the financially hard-pressed states to weather the recession. States played an important role in Obama's health care reforms, beginning with an expansion of the CHIP during Obama's first weeks in office.[76] The Patient Protection and Affordable Care Act of 2010 expanded federal-state Medicaid coverage to persons with incomes up to 133 percent of the poverty level, and it obliged states to implement insurance exchanges to provide access to health insurance.

The Clinton and Obama administrations have developed a new kind of "executive" federalism to achieve their goals by easing federal rules and allowing states to experiment with liberal policy.[77] This new executive federalism depends heavily on waivers. A waiver is permission from the executive branch for a state to experiment with new health, welfare or other services, serve new clients, or control costs. These waivers are produced by bargaining between federal and state executive branch officials. The Clinton administration actively used waivers to boost presidential power and bypass Congress. For example, Clinton used waivers to expand health care coverage after the defeat of his national health care proposal.[78] President Obama also used "executive" federalism vigorously, granting ten states waivers for implementing the No Child Left Behind Act and granting more than 1,200 waivers for the administration's health care reform.[79]

## Conclusion

Modern American politics was constructed upon the foundation of federalism. The durable and dynamic federal system remains important to contemporary American political parties, interest groups, politicians, and citizens. Federalism always has new strategic possibilities for those who seek government action because state governments are strong, innovative, and influential political units. Throughout American history, new efforts, from alcohol prohibition to environmental protection, emerged in the states before the federal government made them national policy.

It is not surprising that the use of federalism in American politics today is still "pragmatic and politically driven," as it always has been.[80] From the start of the American republic, partisan, ideological, or institutional opponents have used federalism as an expedient weapon in political conflicts. Federalism is a powerful weapon because states produce results different from those of the national government.

A new generation of Americans is inheriting layers of political and policy innovation in the federal system. They face enduring questions in the new context of the evolving politics of our time. How will political opponents invent new ways to use federalism to frame issues, or implement policies, in ways that advance their political interests? How will Republicans and Democrats balance federalism and national power to bring about political victories in the near and medium future? How will victories by Republicans or Democrats, conservatives or liberals alter the path of American political development?

Federalism is resurgent because political polarization has induced political opponents to use every available institution to their advantage in the bitter partisan conflicts of the early twenty-first century. Just as President Obama used the states as indispensable tools for implementing his signature health policy initiative, his opponents used federalism as an indispensable tool to defeat it. The political development of federalism has not eliminated its strategic utility, but it has broadened, fragmented, and often submerged it.

Federalism, then, is a "common carrier," like a railroad, that carries a diverse cargo of political interests. Although conservatives seem to invoke federalism much more than liberals today, American political development shows that liberals have depended heavily on federalism for social change and that conservatives often preferred federal power over the states to achieve their goals. Few political actors, whether liberal or conservative, will defend federalism if it interferes with substantive results they seek.

However, if federalism has few disinterested defenders, it clearly serves as a foundation of democracy in America, because it nurtures political opposition to those in power. A free political opposition is essential for a vigorous democracy. In an effective federal system, when one of the political parties is out of power in Washington, its members can still use policy levers at the state level to advance an opposition agenda and build an opposition base. In this way, federalism ensures a lively debate on important political issues. In the early twenty-first century, when Republicans controlled the national government during the Bush administration, Democratic state officials used their government powers to press for an alternative policy agenda. When Democrats controlled national power during the early Obama administration, state Republican officials turned the tables and built opposition using state policy instruments. The political polarization of the early twenty-first century, in short, has restored some of the vitality and visibility of American federalism.

## Notes

1  Bill Bartel, "Cuccinelli Shines Among GOP Stars at Tea Party Rally." *The Virginian-Pilot*, October 10, 2010. http://hamptonroads.com/2010/10/tea-party-activists-treat-cuccinelli-rock-star (accessed November 24, 2010).
2  National Conference of State Legislatures, "State Legislation and Actions Challenging Certain Health Reforms, 2011." http://www.ncsl.org/?tabid=18906 (accessed January 8, 2012).
3  National Conference of State Legislatures, "Arizona's Immigration Enforcement Laws." July 28, 2011. http://www.ncsl.org/?tabid=20263 (accessed December 20, 2011); "Immigration-Related Laws and Resolutions in the States (Jan. 1–Dec. 7, 2011)"

http://www.ncsl.org/default.aspx?TabId=23960 (accessed December 26, 2011). See also See Lina Newton and Brian E. Adams, "State Immigration Policies: Innovation, Cooperation or Conflict?" *Publius* 39:3 (Summer 2009): 408–431.

4 Daniel J. Elazar, *Exploring Federalism* (Tuscaloosa, AL: University of Alabama Press, 1987); Samuel H. Beer, *To Make a Nation: The Rediscovery of American Federalism* (Cambridge, MA: Belknap Press, 1993); Dimitrios Karmis and Wayne Norman, eds., *Theories of Federalism: A Reader* (Basingstoke, England and New York: Palgrave Macmillan, 2005); Alison LaCroix, *The Ideological Origins of American Federalism* (Cambridge, MA: Harvard University Press, 2010).

5 Malcolm Feeley and Edward L. Rubin, *Federalism: Political Identity and Tragic Compromise* (Ann Arbor, MI: University of Michigan Press, 2008), 5.

6 Carol S. Weissert, "Beyond Marble Cakes and Picket Fences: What U.S. Federalism Scholars Can Learn from Comparative Work," *Journal of Politics* 73:4 (October 2011), 965–979, esp. 971–972.

7 Deil S. Wright, *Understanding Intergovernmental Relations*, 3rd ed. (New York: Houghton Mifflin Harcourt, 1998); Timothy J. Conlan, *From New Federalism to Devolution: Twenty-Five Years of Intergovernmental Reform*, revised ed. (Washington, D.C.: Brookings Institution, 1998); David B. Walker, *The Rebirth of Federalism : Slouching toward Washington*, 2nd ed. (Chatham, N.J. : Chatham House, 1999); Laurence J. O'Toole, ed., *American Intergovernmental Relations: Foundations, Perspectives, and Issues*, 4th ed. (Washington, DC: CQ Press, 2007); Timothy J. Conlan and Paul L. Posner, eds., *Intergovernmental Management for the 21st Century*, (Washington, DC: Brookings Institution, 2008).

8 Edward S. Corwin, "The Passing of Dual Federalism," *Virginia Law Review* 36:1 (February,1950), 1–24; Morton Grodzins, "The Federal System" in *Goals for Americans: The Report of the President's Commission on National Goals* (Englewood Cliffs, New Jersey: Prentice-Hall, 1960), 265–266.

9 Timothy J. Conlan, *From New Federalism to Devolution: Twenty-Five Years of Intergovernmental Reform*, revised ed. (Washington, DC: Brookings Institution, 1998); Deil S. Wright, *Understanding Intergovernmental Relations*, 3rd ed. (New York: Houghton Mifflin Harcourt, 1998), 13–14; Laurence J. O'Toole, ed., *American Intergovernmental Relations: Foundations, Perspectives, and Issues*, 4th ed. (Washington, DC: CQ Press, 2007); Timothy J. Conlan and Paul L. Posner, eds., *Intergovernmental Management for the 21st Century*, (Washington, DC: Brookings Institution, 2008).

10 *Martha Derthick, "*Crossing Thresholds: Federalism in the 1960s," in *Integrating the Sixties: The Origins, Structures, and Legitimacy of Public Policy in a Turbulent Decade*, ed. Brian Balogh (University Park, PA: Penn State University Press, 1996), 64, 73, 77–78.

11 William H. Riker, *Federalism: Origin, Operation, Significance* (Boston: Little, Brown, 1964); "Federalism and Formal Theory," *Publius* 7:2 (Spring 2007), 135–261; Mikhail Filippov, Peter C Ordeshook, and Olga Vitalievna Shvetsova, *Designing Federalism: A Theory of Self-sustainable Federal Institutions* (Cambridge and New York: Cambridge University Press, 2004); Jenna Bednar, *The Robust Federation: Principles of Design* (Cambridge and New York: Cambridge University Press, 2009); Sean Nicholson-Crotty and Nick Theobald, "Claiming Credit in the U.S. Federal System: Testing a Model of Competitive Federalism," *Publius* 41:2 (Spring 2011), 232–256.

12 Craig Volden, "States as Policy Laboratories: Emulating Success in the Children's Health Insurance Program," *American Journal of Political Science* 50:2 (April 2006), 294–312; Graeme Boushey, *Policy Diffusion Dynamics in America* (New York and

Cambridge: Cambridge University Press, 2010); Todd Makse and Craig Volden, "The Role of Policy Attributes in the Diffusion of Innovations," *Journal of Politics* 73:1 (January 2011), 108–124; Brady Baybeck, William D. Berry and David A. Siegel, "A Strategic Theory of Policy Diffusion via Intergovernmental Competition," *Journal of Politics* 73:1 (January 2011): 232–247.

13  Harry N. Scheiber, "Federalism and the American Economic Order, 1789–1910," *Law and Society Review* 10:1 (Fall, 1975), 57–118, and "American Federalism and the Diffusion of Power: Historical and Contemporary Perspectives," *University of Toledo Law Review* 9 (Summer 1978), 619–680; Ballard C. Campbell, *The Growth of American Government: Governance from the Cleveland Era to the Present* (Bloomington, IN: Indiana University Press, 1995); William J. Novak, *The People's Welfare: Law and Regulation in Nineteenth Century America* (Chapel Hill, NC: University of North Carolina Press, 1996); Jon C. Teaford, *The Rise of the States: Evolution of American State Government* (Baltimore, MD: Johns Hopkins University Press, 2002); Brian Balogh, *A Government Out of Sight: The Mystery of National Authority in Nineteenth-Century America* (Cambridge and New York: Cambridge University Press, 2009).

14  Weissert, "Beyond Marble Cakes and Picket Fences." Examples include Jonathan A. Rodden, *Hamilton's Paradox: The Promise and Peril of Fiscal Federalism* (Cambridge and New York: Cambridge University Press, 2006); Kent Eaton, "Federalism in Europe and Latin America: Conceptualization, Causes, and Consequences" *World Politics* 60: 4 (July 2008), 665–698; Daniel Ziblatt, *Structuring the State: The Formation of Italy and Germany and the Puzzle of Federalism* (Princeton, NJ: Princeton University Press, 2006); Tulia Falleti, *Decentralization and Subnational Politics in Latin America* (New York: Cambridge University Press, 2010); Anand Menon and Martin A. Schain, eds, *Comparative Federalism: The European Union and the United States in Comparative Perspective* (Oxford and New York: Oxford University Press, 2006); Jan Erk and Wilfried Swenden, *New Directions in Federalism Studies* (Milton Park, Abingdon, Oxon, England, and New York: Routledge, 2009).

15  Karen Orren and Stephen Skowronek, *The Search for American Political Development* (Cambridge and New York: Cambridge University Press, 2004), 123.

16  Robert C. Lieberman, *Shifting the Color Line: Race and the American Welfare State* (Cambridge, MA: Harvard University Press, 1998), and *Shaping Race Policy: The United States in Comparative Perspective* (Princeton, NJ: Princeton University Press, 2005).

17  Suzanne Mettler, *Dividing Citizens: Gender and Federalism in New Deal Public Policy* (Ithaca, NY: Cornell University Press, 1998).

18  Kimberley S. Johnson, *Governing the American State: Congress and the New Federalism, 1877–1929* (Princeton, NJ: Princeton University Press, 2007).

19  John Dinan and Shama Gamkhar, "The State of American Federalism 2008–2009: The Presidential Election, the Economic Downturn, and the Consequences for Federalism" *Publius* 39:3 (Summer 2009), 369–407.

20  Rick Perry, *Fed Up!: Our Fight to Save America from Washington* (New York: Little, Brown, 2011).

21  Michael S. Greve, American Enterprise Institute webpage, http://www.aei.org/scholar/michael-s-greve/ (accessed December 26, 2011); Cato Institute, Federalism webpage. *http://www.cato.org/federalism* (accessed December 26, 2011); State Policy Network webpage, http://www.spn.org/, (accessed December 26, 2011).

22  Trip Gabriel, "G.O.P. Candidates Take an Anti-Federal Stance" *New York Times*, October 8, 2011.

23  U.S. Office of Personnel Management, "Historical Federal Workforce Tables," http://www.opm.gov/feddata/HistoricalTables/TotalGovernmentSince1962 (accessed November 23, 2010); U.S. Census Bureau, "Census Bureau Reports State and Local Government Employment Remains at 16.6 Million," http://www.census.gov/newsroom/releases/archives/governments/cb10-132.html (accessed November 23, 2010). Federal spending through grants-in-aid contributed to the state and local totals.

24  Paul Teske, *Regulation in the States* (Washington, D.C: Brookings Institution, 2004), 9; Barry G. Rabe, "Power to the States: The Promise and Pitfalls of Decentralization" in *Environmental Policy: New Directions for the Twenty-First Century*, ed. Norman J. Vig and Michael E. Kraft (Washington, DC: CQ Press, 2006), 35–36.

25  William L. Cary, "Federalism and Corporate Law: Reflections upon Delaware," *Yale Law Journal* 83:4 (March 1974), 663–705.

26  U.S. Department of Education, "Public Elementary and Secondary School Student Enrollment and Staff Counts From the Common Core of Data: School Year 2009–10," at http://nces.ed.gov/pubs2011/2011347.pdf, accessed January 8, 2012.

27  U.S Bureau of Justice Statistics, "Correctional Population in the United States, 2010," http://bjs.ojp.usdoj.gov/content/pub/press/p10cpu10pr.cfm (accessed December 26, 2011).

28  Andrew Karch, *Democratic Laboratories: Policy Diffusion among the American States* (Ann Arbor: University of Michigan Press, 2007). On the influence of state innovations on national policy, see Richard P. Nathan, "Updating Theories of Federalism," in *Intergovernmental Management for the Twenty-First Century*, ed. Timothy J. Conlan and Paul L. Posner (Washington, DC: Brookings Institution, 2008), 16.

29  Congressional Research Service, "National Guard Personnel and Deployments: Fact Sheet," January 17, 2008, http://www.fas.org/sgp/crs/natsec/RS22451.pdf (accessed November 23, 2010).

30  Gallup, "State of the States," http://www.gallup.com/poll/125066/State-States.aspx?ref=interactive (accessed March 4, 2012)

31  Source: Frank Newport, "Mississippi Most Conservative State, D.C. Most Liberal," Gallup website, February 3, 2012 http://www.gallup.com/poll/152459/Mississippi-Conservative-State-Liberal.aspx?utm_source=tagrss&utm_medium=rss&utm_campaign=syndication (accessed March 8, 2012).

32  Harry N. Scheiber, "Federalism and the American Economic Order, 1789–1910," *Law and Society Review* 10:1 (Fall, 1975), 57–118.

33  Aaron Wildavsky, "Federalism is About Inequality," in *The Costs of Federalism*, ed. Robert T. Golembiewski and Aaron Wildavsky (New Brunswick, NJ: Transaction Books, 1984), 66.

34  Paul Pierson, *Politics in Time: History, Institutions, and Social Analysis* (Princeton, NJ: Princeton University Press, 2004), 17–53.

35  David Brian Robertson, *Federalism and the Making of America* (Abingdon, UK, and New York: Routledge, 2011)

36  On the importance of sequence, see Paul Pierson, "Not Just What, but *When*: Timing and Sequence in Political Processes," *Studies in American Political Development* 14:1 (Spring 2000), 72–92.

37  Martin Shefter, *Political Parties and the State: the American Historical Experience* (Princeton, NJ: Princeton University Press, 1994), 61–97.

38  Robertson, *Federalism and the Making of America*, 41–49.

39  Theda Skocpol, *Protecting Soldiers and Mothers: The Political Origins of Social Policy in the United States* (Cambridge: Belknap, 1992), 424–479.

40   John D. Nugent, *Safeguarding Federalism: How States Protect Their Interests in National Policymaking* (Norman, OK: University of Oklahoma Press, 2009), 77–88.

41   Richard F. Weingroff, "The Federal Highway Administration at 100," U.S. Department of Transportation, http://www.tfhrc.gov/pubrds/fall93/p93au1.htm (accessed May 23, 2010).

42   Larry Cuban, "Enduring Resiliency: Enacting and Implementing Federal Vocational Education Legislation," in Harvey Kantor and David B. Tyack, *Work, Youth, and Schooling: Historical Perspectives on Vocationalism in American Education* (Stanford: Stanford University Press, 1982), 45–78.

43   Elizabeth Sanders, *Roots of Reform: Farmers, Workers, and the American State, 1877–1917* (Chicago: University of Chicago Press, 1999), 314–337.

44   Johnson, *Governing the American State*, 9.

45   Michael R. Fein, *Paving the Way: New York Road Building and the American State, 1880–1956* (Lawrence, KS: University Press of Kansas, 2008), 145–146.

46   Jess Gilbert and Carolyn Howe, "Beyond 'State vs. Society': Theories of the State and New Deal Agricultural Policies," *American Sociological Review* 56: 2 (April, 1991), 204–220; Grant McConnell, *The Decline of Agrarian Democracy* (New York: Atheneum [1953] 1969).

47   Robertson, *Federalism and the Making of America*, 110.

48   Alan Ware, *The American Direct Primary: Party Institutionalization and Transformation in the North* (Cambridge and New York: Cambridge University Press, 2002.

49   Thomas Goebel, *A Government by the People: Direct Democracy in America, 1890–1940* (Chapel Hill, NC: University of North Carolina Press, 2002); David D. Schmidt, *Citizen Lawmakers: the Ballot Initiative Revolution* (Philadelphia: Temple University Press, 1989).

50   U.S. Department of Commerce, National Economic Accounts, Table 3.2, "Federal Government Current Receipts and Expenditures," http://www.bea.gov/national/nipaweb/TableView.asp?SelectedTable=87&ViewSeries=NO&Java=no&Request3 Place=N&3Place=N&FromView=YES&Freq=Year&FirstYear=1929&LastYear=19 40&3Place=N&Update=Update&JavaBox=no#Mid (accessed June 13, 2010); U.S. Census Bureau, Government Employment & Payroll, http://www.census.gov/govs/apes/ (accessed June 28, 2010).

51   James T. Patterson, *The New Deal and the States: Federalism in Transition* (Princeton, NJ: Princeton University Press, 1969), 127, 171.

52   *N.L.R.B.* v. *Jones & Laughlin Steel Corp.*, 301 U.S. 1 (1937); *Wickard* v. *Filburn*, 317 U.S. 111 (1942).

53   William R. Childs, "State Regulators and Pragmatic Federalism in the United States, 1889–1945," *Business History Review* 75:4 (Winter 2001), 705.

54   Jon C. Teaford, *The Rise of the States: Evolution of American State Government* (Baltimore, MD: Johns Hopkins University Press, 2002), 195–230; Ann O'M. Bowman and Richard C. Kearney, *The Resurgence of the States* (Englewood Cliffs, NJ: Prentice-Hall, 1986), 47–106; David B. Walker, *The Rebirth of Federalism : Slouching toward Washington*, 2nd ed. (Chatham, N.J. : Chatham House, 1999), 264–277.

55   Stephen Gardbaum "New Deal Constitutionalism and the Unshackling of the States," *University of Chicago Law Review* 64:2 (Spring 1997), 483–566.

56   Budget of the United States Government, 2005, Historical Table 17.1 — Total Executive Branch Civilian Employees, 1940–2003, http://www.gpoaccess.gov/usbudget/fy05/sheets/hist17z1.xls (accessed June 13, 2010).

57   Walker, *The Rebirth of Federalism*, 124.

58 Source: U.S. Office of Management and Budget, *Fiscal Year 2013 Budget, Historical Tables*, http://www.whitehouse.gov/omb/budget/Historicals (accessed March 9, 2012)

59 David B. Walker, *Toward a Functioning Federalism* (Cambridge, MA: Winthrop, 1981), 193–196.

60 Walker, *The Rebirth of Federalism*, 124.

61 Ronald Reagan, "Remarks in Atlanta, Georgia, at the Annual Convention of the National Conference of State Legislatures," July 30, 1981, at John T. Woolley and Gerhard Peters, *The American Presidency Project,* http://www.presidency.ucsb.edu/ws/index.php?pid=44131 (accessed September 29, 2010).

62 Joseph F. Zimmerman, "Federal Preemption under Reagan's New Federalism," *Publius,* 21:1 (Winter, 1991), 7–28.

63 Timothy J. Conlan and John Dinan, "Federalism, the Bush Administration, and the Transformation of American Conservatism," *Publius* 37:3 (Summer 2007), 279; Paul L. Posner, "Mandates: The Politics of Coercive Federalism," in *Intergovernmental Management for the 21st Century*, ed. Timothy J. Conlan and Paul L. Posner (Washington, DC: Brookings Institution, 2008), 286–309.

64 J. Mitchell Pickerill and Cornell W. Clayton, "The Rehnquist Court and the Political Dynamics of Federalism," *Perspectives on Politics* 2:2 (June 2004), 240–241.

65 Linda Greenhouse, "5-to-4, Now and Forever; At the Court, Dissent Over States' Rights Is Now War," *New York Times,* June 9, 2002.

66 Guttmacher Institute, "States Enact Record Number of Abortion Restrictions in 2011," January 5, 2012, http://www.guttmacher.org/media/inthenews/2012/01/05/endofyear.html (accessed January 8, 2012).

67 Nathan, "Updating Theories of Federalism," 18–21.

68 Walker, *The Rebirth of Federalism*, 150.

69 Martha Derthick, *Up in Smoke: From Legislation to Litigation in Tobacco Politics,* 2nd ed. (Washington, DC: CQ Press, 2005), 71–92.

70 Colin Provost, "When is AG Short for Aspiring Governor? Ambition and Policy Making Dynamics in the Office of State Attorney General," *Publius* 40:4 (Fall 2010), 597–616.

71 Dale Krane, "The Middle Tier in American Federalism: State Government Policy Activism During the Bush Presidency," *Publius* 37:3 (Summer 2007), 453–477.

72 Human Rights Campaign, "Map of State Laws and Policies," http://www.hrc.org/about_us/state_laws.asp (accessed January 13, 2012); National Conference of State Legislatures, "Same-Sex Marriage, Civil Unions and Domestic Partnerships," July 14, 2011, http://www.ncsl.org/default.aspx?tabid=16430 (accessed December 23, 2011).

73 Ann O'M. Bowman, "Horizontal Federalism: Exploring Interstate Interactions," *Journal of Public Administration Research and Theory* 14:4 (2004), 535–546.

74 Walker, *The Rebirth of Federalism*, 156–171; Timothy J. Conlan and John Dinan, "Federalism, the Bush Administration, and the Transformation of American Conservatism," *Publius* 37:3 (Summer 2007), 279.

75 Kaiser Commission on Medicaid and the Uninsured, "The Role of Section 1115 Waivers in Medicaid and Chip: Looking Back and Looking Forward," March 2009, http://www.kff.org/medicaid/7874.cfm (accessed January 8, 2012).

76 Robert Pear, "Obama Signs Children's Health Insurance Bill," *New York Times* February 5, 2009.

77 John Dinan, "The State of American Federalism 2007–2008: Resurgent State Influence in the National Policy Process and Continued State Policy Innovation," *Publius* 38:3 (July 2008), 381–415.

79  Thomas Gais and James Fossett, "Federalism and the Executive Branch," in *The Executive Branch*, ed. Joel D. Aberbach and Mark A. Peterson (Oxford and New York: Oxford University Press, 2005), 486–522; Carol S. Weissert and William G. Weissert, "Medicaid Waivers: License to Shape the Future of Fiscal Federalism," in *Intergovernmental Management for the Twenty-First Century*, ed. Timothy J. Conlan and Paul L. Posner (Washington, DC: Brooking 2008), 158–165.

79  Winnie Hu, "10 States Are Given Waivers From Education Law," *New York Times* February 10, 2012; Sam Baker, "HHS Finalizes Over 1,200 Waivers Under Healthcare Reform Law," *The Hill*, January 6, 2012, http://thehill.com/blogs/healthwatch/health-reform-implementation/202791-hhs-finalizes-more-than-1200-healthcare-waivers (accessed March 2, 2012).

80  Martha Derthick, "Whither Federalism?", Urban Institute, The Future of the Public Sector, No. 2 (June, 1996), http://www.urban.org/uploadedPDF/derthick.pdf (accessed December 23, 2011).

# Chapter 2

# Reintroducing the Policy Process into Studying Congress

*Sean M. Theriault and JoBeth Surface Shafran*

Congress is perhaps the most studied branch of government and certainly the most studied legislature in the world. Scholars have made great strides understanding this institution by combining "formal models" of Members' behavior with quantitative analysis of their voting records. However, in explaining how Congress makes policy, Theriault and Shafran argue that scholars have become too reliant on ideological scores of individual members to predict how Congress will make laws. Scholars tend to like simple—or parsimonious—explanations of outcomes, and these ideological scores definitely simplify analysis of Congress. However, Theriault and Shafran believe contemporary approaches miss essential differences in policymaking across policy domains. To understand Congress, they urge us to lift the hood to see what is going on at various stages in the policymaking process. Congressional policymaking is more than the sum of individual member preferences. Theriault and Shafran suggest researchers return to an older tradition of scholarship that appreciates how context affects legislators' behavior. In some circumstances, Members consider seriously the concerns pushed by colleagues, interest groups, and party leaders. Identifying these circumstances is crucial to understanding the representative function of a legislature. This chapter shows how new research and data may help us learn about when and why legislators polarize into warring parties and when they appear likely to find common ground.

When members of Congress finally left town on December 22, 2010, for their long awaited Christmas recess, the *Bloomberg News* declared in its headline that "No Congress Since 1960s Has Impact on Public as 111th." The other major news outlets joined in by writing year-end reviews with plaudits for the work that had been accomplished. Not only had Congress passed a major health care reform; it passed the stimulus bill and an expansion of national and community service programs and brought an end to the "Don't Ask Don't Tell" policy that kept gays and lesbians in the closet during their military careers. Many scholars find these end-of-Congress reviews helpful for summarizing the work of Congress. David Mayhew uses them to develop his list of "Major Enactments." Other scholars use them to develop lists of major failures.[1] These lists provide a good summary of the rhythm of the legislative process.

Almost as soon as these lists are developed, the policy content is discarded, and they are reduced to numbers that can be used to ask questions about a Congress's productivity: How many major pieces of legislation were enacted into law? How big was the legislative agenda? Was the congress that is now ended one of the most productive (111th Congress, 2009–2010) or one of the least? What is lost in the quick transformation from issues to numbers is the actual *process of policy change*. Rather than studying how problems were defined, solutions chosen, legislation written, and coalitions formed, the focus of research is relegated to a content-free analysis of congressional decision making. Little attention is paid to words of the policy proposals or the process itself before or after the roll call vote.

Though the questions of productivity and decision making are important, this quick transformation leaves many questions about the policy process unanswered. Some of the most important questions that have been left unanswered include why does Congress act on some problems and not others? How does Congress decide which solutions to consider and which to ignore? What beside party or ideology determines how voting coalitions form in Congress? Does the legislative process work differently when Congress is addressing economic issues rather than social domestic problems? By addressing these puzzles, political scientists could help explain how Congress, the most powerful legislature in the world, represents citizens and shapes American public policy. Recently, congressional scholars have turned to the public policy literature to help answer these questions. This new direction in congressional research has already yielded fascinating answers to some of these big policy-related questions.

In this chapter, we explore this new direction in congressional research. We begin by highlighting some of the key findings from an earlier congressional literature that took questions of policy change seriously. In the second section, we explain how the congressional scholarship came to be dominated by the legislative process, which forced policy-specific considerations to the scholarly sidelines. The third section argues that such a narrow focus on the legislative process offers an inaccurate, at worst, or incomplete, at best, view of what it is that Congress does. In the penultimate section, we describe some of the more recent research that has begun to incorporate public policy theory. In the fifth section, we optimistically conclude this chapter by encouraging these new developments of reintegrating the policy process into the congressional research.

## Policy-Focused Congress Research

Those studying Congress have a long history of incorporating policies and the policy-making process into their scholarship. In this section, we outline some of these key contributions. Policy-focused Congress research has added to our understanding of congressional decision making, representation, and committee behavior.

One way in which the literature has integrated policy into the study of Congress is by differentiating between policy areas in the decision-making process (e.g., civil rights, social welfare, foreign policy). Previous studies have argued that we must understand congressional action in terms of policy because a single dimension of liberal-conservatism is too simple to describe legislators' decision-making processes across policies.[2] The sheer number of issues members of Congress face requires a complex understanding of individual and institutional decision making.[3] To understand policymaking that is occurring on multiple issues simultaneously, we must analyze the various *layers* of the decision-making process itself. First, members of Congress must decide which policy dimension best represents the policy *question* with which they are confronted. Then, they must rely on the policy *position* for that specific dimension to decide whether to support the initiative. Policy positions are based on a variety of individual characteristics of legislators, including party membership and region. These policy positions act like decision shortcuts, allowing legislators to make decisions without being fully informed.

Policy dimensions are one type of cue that members of Congress can use to inform their decisions. The cue-taking model of legislative decision making suggests that legislators seek to cut their information costs by considering several decision-related factors, including the policy dimensions of the issue, colleagues' preferences, and personal goals.[4] Issue-specific characteristics, such as the controversy surrounding the issue and issue salience, also provide cues to legislators on their best vote choice. If there is no controversy surrounding the issue, legislators will vote consistently with their environments (e.g., interest group preferences, colleague preferences, constituency preferences); they require no other information. When the issue is controversial, though, members consider their personal preferences, their constituents' preferences, and their parties' preferences. If there is no conflict among these actors, members, again, have an easy decision and vote consistent with the overall environment. If there is conflict among these actors, members must follow a set of decision rules to arrive at an appropriate decision. When the issue is highly salient, constituency considerations will overtake the others. For lower salience issues, legislators have more leeway to choose to focus on goals other than appeasing constituents.

Differentiating between policy areas has also enriched research on congressional representation. Congressional roll-call decisions are based both on legislators' personal preferences and their perceptions of constituencies' preferences. The likelihood that a legislator's vote is based on one preference set rather than the other varies by policy area, resulting in different policy areas' being characterized by different types of representation.[5] In civil rights policy, representatives base their decisions on their constituents' preferences, reflective of the instructed delegate mode of representation. Social welfare policy is best characterized by the responsible-party model of representation where shared party-based preferences drive decision making. Decisions on matters of foreign affairs are more reliant on outside information (usually the executive branch) than on individual legislator or constituency preferences, similar to the trustee model of representation.

Congressional committee behavior is also partially dependent on issues, varying by members' goals and the committees' policy environments.[6] Members request their committee assignments based on their goals.[7] The executive branch, clientele groups, political parties, and other House members set the policy environment for the committees by supplying them with policy information. Four categories of policy environments were identified based on the relative strength of the environment groups: executive-led, party-led, clientele-led, and House-led. The dominant coalition group of a committee will constrain its ability to make public policy, especially for those committees focused on good public policy and constituency benefits. For example, the House Education and Labor Committee is characterized by a party-led policy environment, which is derived from electoral politics. Conversely, the House Natural Resource Committee is characterized by a clientele-led environment. Though interior policy is not of much interest to the parties, it is of utmost importance to certain clientele groups. These clientele groups may be even more constraining than party-led coalitions because of their level of interest in the policy area and their ability to affect elections.

Congressional scholars have been making keen insights into the policy-making process. A major finding is that members of Congress make decisions dependent upon the policy domain under consideration. They do not simply provide the same decision criteria or representational style across policies. Lawmaking on military policy, for example, follows a much different route than lawmaking on education. The latter is usually much more contentious. pitting one set of actors against their perpetual opponents. On the former, forming consensus usually predominates the members' decision making. These behavioral and institutional nuances are critical for understanding how Congress and changes policies.

## Why Policy Got Dropped

Despite the advances made in understanding how policy change happens, congressional scholars, for the most part, lost interest in policy-specific and policy-making research. Two innovations in political science literature, which mutually reinforced each other, focused congressional research away from public policy. First, a complex analysis of voting scores suggested that the decision-making process in Congress could easily be reduced to a one-dimension ideological continuum.[8] Second, taking this continuum as a given, various law-making models analyzed the legislative process without regard to policy area.[9] These two innovations in the political science research combined with the real world phenomenon of party polarization to drive public policy from the congressional research agenda. In this section, we outline these three developments.

## One-Dimensional Voting

Keith Poole and Howard Rosenthal introduced the DW-NOMINATE algorithm in their 1997 book, *Congress: A Political-Economic History of Roll Call Voting*. This algorithm takes account of every roll call vote cast on the floors of the House and Senate since the beginning of the U.S. Congress. They range from −1 (extreme liberal) to 1 (extreme conservative) and are comparable across congresses, though the scores are most valid when comparing congresses in close proximity to one another. The scores they developed are highly correlated with ideology scores generated from rankings by interest groups: the Americans for Democratic Action and American Conservative Union. The DW-NOMINATE algorithm revealed that member voting on the various policy dimensions did not appreciably differ across those dimensions. The summary voting scores are reported for the first—or dominant—dimension but also higher-ordered dimensions. As it turns out, most roll call votes, whether they are increasing student loans or enacting trade barriers, collapse onto the first dimension, especially following the 1970s.[10] In fact, the first dimension, which has been largely defined as the government's intervention in the economy, can correctly classify nearly 90 percent of the votes correctly in the most recent congresses. When the second dimension, which in the modern political era has tapped a racial dimension, is added to the analysis, the percentage of correct classifications increases by just 1 percentage point.

The dominance of the first dimension is not uniform throughout history. Throughout the 1950s and 1960s, the second dimension would increase the correct classifications sometimes by as much as 5 percentage points. The dominance of a first dimension has encouraged scholars to ignore important distinctions across policy areas. For most congressional scholars, taking account of such distinctions seemed more trouble than it was worth, and they felt confident in assuming "unidimensionality" of congressional voting.

## Policy-Independent Models

Shortly after Poole and Rosenthal introduced their DW-NOMINATE innovation, scholars, perhaps even because of their innovation, started developing lawmaking models that could explain the broad sweep of the legislative process and legislator decision making. The models that gained the most currency were those that reduced legislative bargaining to a number line, which would place the move liberal member at one endpoint (usually the left) and the most conservative member at the other endpoint and all the other legislators in ideological order between the two endpoints.[11] These models reasoned that to understand policy making in Congress, scholars did not need to waste their time analyzing the legislators near the endpoints but rather only the members who were *pivotal* for deciding a policy's ultimate fate. In their models, it did not matter whether the policy was welfare reform or Israeli foreign aid: The only thing that mattered was who ultimately would be responsible for deciding whether the new policy could pass or would fail. The focus would be on the key legislators whose votes would ultimately determine whether the new policy had enough votes to pass. The veracity of these models rested upon the compelling evidence presented by Poole and Rosenthal. If legislators aligned themselves along a consistent and reliable ideological continuum, policy outcomes could be predicted, again, consistently and reliably.

These models quickly became the lens through which scholars studied congressional actions. While political science research was becoming less amenable to appreciating the differences in the policy process, political reality abetted this view because the political parties were, in fact, becoming more internally consistent and externally divided. One potential danger is that scholarship may fail to observe critical points of departure from this over-generalized approach to understanding Congress.

## Party Polarization

The development of uni-dimensional voting scores and the analytic leverage gained by considering the key players in the legislative game were combined with a trend in politics that propelled the focus away from policy development in Congress. That trend—polarization between the parties—is, perhaps, the most pronounced development in Congress over the last fifty years. The 2008 elections brought about the most polarized Congress since at least the early 1900s, and there is nothing happening in the 112th Congress (2011–2012) to suggest that it will be any less so. We analyze Poole and Rosenthal's DW-NOMINATE data in this section to describe how polarized the parties have become. The summary we provide is explored more systematically in the political science literature.[12]

The congresses after the 1964 election and into the 1970s were some of the least polarized in modern history. The mean House Democratic DW-NOMINATE during these congresses, which is depicted as the black line running through the black bars of Figure 2.1, was about 0.5 away from the mean Republican DW-NOMINATE, which is depicted as the black line running through the white bars. The black (white) bars show one standard deviation on either side of the mean for the Democrats (Republicans). Beginning in the mid-1970s, the parties' means started to separate. The partisan divergence was only slightly less pronounced in the Senate (see Figure 2.2).

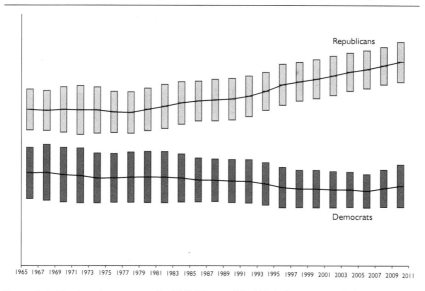

*Figure 2.1* Ideology by party in the U.S. House, 89–111th Congresses (1965–2010)

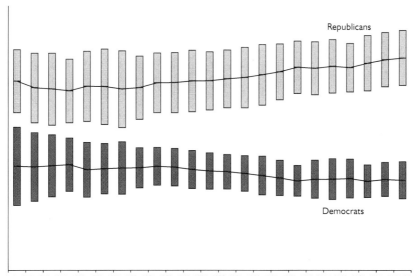

*Figure 2.2* Ideology by party in the U.S. Senate, 89–111th Congresses (1965–2010)

By the 111th Congress (2009–2010), the divergence between the parties had almost doubled in the House to 0.97 and increased by more than 50 percent to 0.82 in the Senate. Not only have the means separated, but the parties have become much more internally cohesive. The infusion of Tea Party members in the 112th Congress and the Blue Dog Democrat losses in 2010 will likely only exacerbate the divide between the parties.

The quantitative and analytic tools developed by political scientists in the 1980s and 1990s were perfect for analyzing the voting trends in Congress. As a result, the mechanics behind and the analysis of how members' cast roll-call votes dominated the literature. The politics reinforced the scholarship in driving attention away from the policies and the policy-making process within the study of Congress.

### Problems with Ignoring Policy

Using the tools of ideological scoring and pivotal actors, the analysis of how members cast votes became one of the most developed subfields in political science. Such scholarly concentration, however, did not come without the cost of focusing on only one part of a larger policy-making process. Before Congress can votes on legislation, several events must first happen. First, Congress must recognize a phenomenon and define it as a problem. Second, the problem must become salient enough to earn space on the policy agenda. Finally, policy is formulated and works its way through the legislative process. Only the most successful bills eventually become law. Keep in mind that even after passage, the process is not complete. Once a new law is formed, implementation must follow, which typically requires the federal bureaucracy to interpret what can be rather vague mandates in the law.

Roll-call voting, which has dominated studies of Congress, is just *one* stage in the entire process (Figure 2.3).[13] The highlighted boxes of formulation and passage are where the literature on Congress has flourished in recent years. It is important to consider how the stages before and after formulation and passage can affect legislation. It is not enough to know whether a bill passes but to understand *why* an issue is considered an important problem and *how* the law is ultimately implemented. The following section describes the problem definition, agenda setting, and implementation stages and their relevance to the study of Congress.

### Problem Definition

The first stage of the policy process is the means by which a phenomenon is labeled as a problem requiring government action. The definition of a problem will ultimately shape its solution. There are four main strands of research on the problem definition stage, each focusing on a different aspect of the process: actors, nature of the problem, language, and causal story.[14]

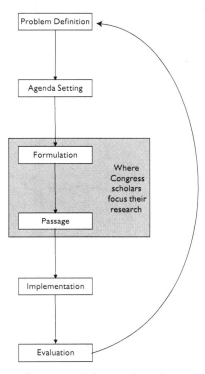

*Figure 2.3* Attention from Congress scholars on the policy process

The first strand of the problem definition literature focuses mainly on the role of political actors, including members of Congress and the president, in defining problems. Policy entrepreneurs must take advantage of political opportunities to define and highlight a problem.[15] According to this literature, successfully defining a problem is dependent on the resources and opportunities that are available to the policy entrepreneur. Others studying the problem definition stage tend to focus on the nature of the problem.[16] For these scholars, the ability to define a phenomenon as a problem is dependent on how pressing the issue is, whether it is an emerging issue or one that is reoccurring, whether the issue is seen as a long-term or short-term problem, and whether it is or is not an emergency. A third stream of literature looking at the process of problem definition is concerned mainly with the use of language and symbols.[17] The images and symbols used to describe a problem can change its definition drastically. Even when political actors have the opportunity and resources to define a problem, they must do so through the use of language and symbols.[18] The final strand of the literature on problem definition focuses on the importance of actors creating causal stories to define a problem in terms of cause, blame, and responsibility.[19] Members of Congress must create the stories in such a way as to gain support for their coalition.

All four strands of research are necessary for understanding the process of defining a problem and can foster new research in the study of Congress. Future research could focus on how problem definition occurs within the legislative branch. Possible research questions include which members or parties in Congress are most likely to succeed in defining a problem? Does success vary by policy area? How does the increased partisanship affect the problem definition stage? And, how do the images used by Democrats, Republicans and, most recently, Tea Party members differ?

## Agenda Setting

After an issue has been defined as a problem, it must then garner enough attention to gain a space on the government's agenda (issues that are actively discussed by Congress or other political institution).[20] Once the issue is on Congress's agenda, policy formulation and passage can take place.

According to the *punctuated equilibrium theory*, both political actors and institutions have a tendency to over-attend to some information or policy issues and under-attend to others.[21] Major policy change is able to occur only when attention is shifted to new issues via a change in the definition of the problem or as a result of an exogenous shock (e.g., an environmental disaster). Regardless of the mechanism behind the attention shift, reordering of priorities on the government's agenda is required. Once a new issue reaches the agenda, the possibility for change in that area dramatically increases.

The importance of agenda setting is more than just which policies are receiving attention, though. The order and way in which choices are presented to people can alter their decisions.[22] Agenda setters can decide not only what will or will not be discussed by Congress but the order in which individual initiatives and roll-calls are considered.

There are two major sources of power—the power to set the agenda and the power to decide.[23] The power to set the agenda is the power to decide what issues will be addressed and what issues will be ignored. The power to decide is the power to vote on policy solutions for those issues on the agenda. The ability to set the agenda is more powerful than the ability to decide on policy solutions.[24] This theory of power is also shared by members of Congress. As John Dingell famously remarked, "If you let me write the procedures and I let you write the substance, I'll [beat] you every time."[25]

Both scholars and members of Congress agree that a large amount of power lies in setting the institutional agenda. Because of the importance of this stage for formulation and adoption, future research should focus on connecting the agenda setting literature with congressional studies. Questions future studies could seek to answer include what strategies should majority leadership use for setting the agenda? Do these strategies differ by chamber? What opportunities do minority members have to set the agenda? How have factions within the parties (i.e., Tea Party Republicans) inhibited the ability of party leadership to set the agenda?

### Implementation

Thus far, we have focused on the policy process preceding the formulation and passage stages. How problems are defined and how the congressional agenda is set determines which policies are considered and, ultimately, which are passed. The way in which legislation is implemented determines how policy will become working law.[26]

A large area of work on implementation in regard to Congress has revolved around Congress's ability to control the bureaucracy and possible strategies for control. For example, previous research shows that Congress is more likely to use ex post controls of the bureaucracy.[27] Rather than engaging in costly oversight, Congress will wait for constituents to alert them to a problem.[28] This not only saves Congress valuable resources such as time but allows Members to claim credit for fixing a problem.

How much discretion bureaucrats should actually have when implementing policy is another dominant stand in the implementation literature. For some, the argument is a normative one: Does more or less discretion lead to better or worse policy. Responsive competence describes bureaucrats who respond quickly and without question to Congressional mandates, the epitome of democratic accountability. Some argue, however, that better public policy results from the neutral competence of bureaucrats, who are willing to combat bad (scientifically unsound) policy ideas with their expertise.[29]

Yet for others, the level of bureaucratic discretion in implementation is a direct result of the politics of the policy formulation and passage stages. Four basic factors determine the level of discretion bureaucrats will have when implementing public policy.[30] First, when there is conflict between members of Congress and the bureaucrats, bureaucratic discretion is less likely to be granted. Second, in policy areas where the costs of writing detailed legislation are high, we are likely to see increased bureaucratic discretion. Third, when we see increased political conflict between the House and Senate, we are more likely to see bureaucratic discretion granted because of the need for compromise between chambers. Finally, when legislators cannot rely on non-statutory factors to influence implementation, bureaucratic discretion will be limited. In short, the implementation process—how legislation becomes law—is highly dependent on how the policy was originally formulated (level of detail) and on the context in which it was formulated (type and level of conflict).

The implementation stage is when policy actually reaches the public. Without implementation, the previous stages have no meaning. As a result, future research should pay more attention to the role Congress plays in this area. For those scholars who are interested in polarization, this policy stage provides another venue for understanding how party conflict can affect policy. Has the implementation process changed as politics have become more polarized? What effect has this had on public policy, if any?

### Evaluation

When the policy is finally implemented, the process does not end. Rather, the effectiveness of the policy is evaluated. If the policy is effective, it is usually merely monitored to ensure that it remains effective. If it is ineffective, the process starts all over again as Congress considers changes to the policy in hopes of making it more effective.

The stages before and after formulation and passage have not received nearly the attention and energy that roll-call voting has. As such, questions about which matters make it to the floor and how legislation is ultimately implemented have been neglected. The literature presented in this chapter clearly suggests that the policy stages are interdependent. Problem definition, whether through the use of symbols or causal stories, will affect the agenda-setting process. Only those issues that reach Congress's agenda can be considered for passage. Earlier decision-making studies show that the issue characteristics, including salience, conflict, and policy dimension, affect legislators' vote choices.[31] The context and content of the decision-making process will directly impact the implementation process. Because of the interdependence of the stages, future research would greatly benefit from greater attention devoted to issues throughout the policy making process.

## Bringing Policy Back into Congressional Research

The empirical and theoretical models suggest that little is lost when the difference in policy areas is ignored. Even if information is lost, so the literature would suggest, the parsimony that is gained in these models (i.e., the ability to explain outcomes with just a few factors) more than compensates for the nuance that is not even considered. Some recent Congress literature, however, has been bringing the distinction in policy areas back into the analysis. Thus far, these advances suggest that policy dependent research is fertile ground for scholars to make insights into the legislative process that would be lost if the difference between policy areas were not explicitly considered. In this section, we highlight several of these advances.

### Competition for Power Varies across Policy Domains

In 2009, Frances Lee published *Beyond Ideology: Politics, Principles, and Partisanship in the U.S. Senate*. She argues that many of the partisan battles in the Senate are not so much rooted in the policy differences between the parties as they are in competition for power. As politics has been practiced since this book's publication, her argument has become even truer.

Lee posits that some of the divide between the parties is based in how expansive the government's role should be in solving problems, while another part of the division is based on competition for power. The only way she is able to gain leverage on the amount of discord that can be explained by these different roots is by breaking up Senate roll-call votes into five different categories or policy areas: economic issues, social issues, hawk-versus-dove issues, multilateralism versus unilateralism, and good-government issues. At other times, her analysis is divided into 19 different categories based on government function.[32]

Using these categories, Lee determines that much of the party conflict is "beyond ideology." In fact, 45 percent of the votes on issues that cannot easily be captured by the ideological dimension, nonetheless, divide the parties. Her analysis also shows that the Senate has become more polarized over time because they have consumed a larger part of their agenda with issues that are more divisive. She is able to make these determinations only by looking at the policy content of roll-call votes.

### Filibusters and Obstructionism Vary across Policy Domains

A year after Lee's important book, Gregory Koger published *Filibustering: A Political History of Obstruction in the House and Senate.* As with Lee's book, Koger purpose was not to explain the differences in policy areas,but rather to understand filibustering, a growing phenomenon particularly in the Senate. Koger (2010, 16) defines filibustering as "legislative behavior (or threat of such behavior) intended to delay a collective decision for strategic gain." The Senate's filibuster, of course, is the most well-known example of filibustering behavior but not the only one, which can also include dilatory motions and disappearing quorums.

In developing a theory of obstructionism, Koger shows that the number of filibusters, largely defined, has grown over time and that, most recently, it has grown at an increasing rate. Koger is able to delve more deeply into these interesting findings by classifying the filibusters according to different policy realms. Not surprising, the subject of filibusters varies with time and is not necessarily the same in both chambers. In the nineteenth century, for example, the lion's share of the Senate filibusters were on budget and regulation issues, whereas the House frequently also filibustered civil liberties and foreign policies.

By categorizing the filibusters into different policy areas, Koger is able to more deeply analyze the legislative process and the decisions that senators make. His case study of civil rights filibusters and those linked to electoral advantage help shed light on the motives behind filibusters. If Koger had not engaged in this policy-specific analysis, his study would still have been important, but it would have been less nuanced and less illuminating.

### New Sources of Data Reveal Variation across Policy Domains

The Policy Agendas Project allows scholars to track policy change across institutions and over time.[33] Researchers are able to achieve both institutional and temporal consistency using a content-coding scheme. The scheme codes each piece of data into one of 19 major policy areas (e.g., "1" indicates macroeconomics) and one of 225 specific policy topics (e.g., "107" indicates Industrial Policy). Even though the language describing a policy may change over time, the coding system remains consistent by focusing on content rather than on keywords. For example, a hearing investigating the construction of federal fallout shelters in 1964 would be coded as 1615 (Civil Defense and Homeland Security) in the Policy Agendas Project coding scheme. The same code would also be used to code a hearing in 2008 investigating the ability to share information on possible terror threats across multiple levels of government and the private sector.

The Policy Agendas Project offers several datasets that may be used to understand the connection between Congress and the public policy process:

- The Congressional Hearings Dataset currently provides scholars with information on all congressional hearings from 1946 to 2008. Each hearing is coded according to the Project's content-coding scheme. The dataset also provides a plethora of additional valuable information (e.g., committee and subcommittee and whether the hearing was legislative in nature).
- The Public Laws Dataset contains each law passed between 1948 and 2007. The laws, like the hearings data, have been coded according to policy content. The dataset provides the user with links to the full text of the law and to the bill summary.
- The *Congressional Quarterly (CQ) Almanac* dataset provides information on the articles contained in the main chapters of the *Almanac* from 1948 to 2007. Each CQ story is coded according to policy content and for a variety of variables, including relevant bill numbers, primary sponsors, and article length.
- The Most Important Laws Dataset includes the most important laws passed between 1948 and 1998 based on coverage in the *CQ Almanac*. The dataset provides policy codes for each law and the number of lines in the *CQ Almanac* and public law number among other variables.
- The Congressional Roll Call Voting Dataset currently provides users with all roll-calls from 1946 to 2004 coded according to the Policy Agendas Project's content coding scheme. In addition to providing policy information for each roll-call, the dataset also includes other valuable data, including the relevant bill and amendment sponsor (when applicable).

Another data project that uses the Policy Agendas' coding scheme is the Congressional Bills Project.[34] The Congressional Bills Project provides users with all bills introduced in Congress since 1947. The bills are coded for a number of different characteristics, including policy content, the committees to which they were referred, and various pieces of information on the bill sponsor.

Tracy Sulkin (2005) used the Policy Agendas Project data in her book, *Issue Politics in Congress*. By examining policy-specific activity in Congress, Sulkin is able to see whether congressional incumbents who win reelection co-opt their opponents' issues in the subsequent congress. In analyzing the process that she labels "Issue Uptaking," she finds a significant change in how members behave after their competitors focus on their legislative shortcomings. This critical development in the link between elections and governing was possible only by considering policy-specific legislation.

Some of the most recent work emerging from the Policy Agendas Project seeks to explain the increased polarization of Congress. Ashley Jochim and Bryan Jones (2012) use the Policy Agendas Congressional Roll Call Voting Dataset to show that partisan politics are much more prevalent in some policy areas (e.g., education policy) than others (e.g., foreign affairs policy). They also find that some policy areas have become more partisan over time (e.g., health care policy). Conversely, they find that other policy areas that many would assume have become more polarized (e.g., environment policy) have remained multidimensional. By simply accounting for the policy differences of roll-call votes, they show that even in roll-call voting studies, we cannot always assume that partisan politics will overwhelm policy differences and their effects on congressional action.

The Policy Agendas Project provides valuable resources for understanding a Congress that is not free of policy content. More important, the project provides data they needed to investigate policy stages other than formation/passage stage and important consequences of policy differences in the legislative process. For example, the hearings, bills, and roll calls have been previously used to investigate agenda setting (Baumgartner and Jones, 1993). The Policy Agendas Project has thrown open the doors to the reintegration of public policies into congressional scholarship.

## Conclusion

For more than ten years, roll-call voting analyses dominated the scholarship on Congress. By so doing, the Congress subfield became one of the most vibrant in all of American politics. The polarization of the political parties only reinforced the blending of quantitative analyses that tested the formal models of congressional decision making. This focus on roll-call votes, however, did not come without a cost. Crime bills, stimulus packages, and welfare reform were reduced to symbols on a number line as though the decision-making process underlying these different policy areas is all the same. Such assumptions flew in the face of what Congress scholars had learned in the 1960s and 1970s: that policy differences had important consequences on the legislative process.

Over the last few years, the distinction between policy areas has reentered the congressional scholarship. This new direction in the study of Congress has already provided insight into two of the most pronounced trends in Congress in the last ten years. The congressional scholars have suggested that party polarization and the rise of filibustering tactics happen as a matter of course in contemporary American politics without regard to the policies that are under examination. More recent scholarship shows that these trends vary greatly across policy domains. Political scientists ignore these differences at their own peril. The Policy Agendas Project facilitates the reintroduction of policy research back into Congress. With more scholarly attention, we feel confident that other segments of the decision-making process will be as understood as the causes and consequences of roll-call votes.

## Notes

1  See George C. Edwards III, Andrew Barrett, and Jeffrey Peake, "The Legislative Impact of Divided Government," *American Journal of Political Science* 41 (1987): 545–63; see also Sean M. Theriault, *Party Polarization in Congress* (New York: Cambridge University Press, 2008).

2  See Aage R. Clausen, *How Congressmen Decide: A Policy Focus* (New York: St. Martin's Press, 1973).

3  Clausen lists five policy dimensions: civil liberties, international involvement, agricultural assistance, social welfare, and government management. See Aage R. Clausen, *How Congressmen Decide: A Policy Focus* (New York: St. Martin's Press, 1973).

4  See John W. Kingdon, "Models of Legislative Voting." *Journal of Politics* 39 (1977): 563–95.

5  See Warren E. Miller and Donald E. Stokes, "Constituency Influence in Congress" *American Political Science Review* 57 (1963): 45–56.

6  See Richard Fenno, *Congressmen in Committees* (Boston: Little, Brown and Company, 1973).

7  Fenno defines three goals: deliver benefits to their constituencies, make good public policy, or gain power within the chamber. See Richard Fenno, *Congressmen in Committees* (Boston: Little, Brown and Company, 1973).

8  See Keith T. Poole and Howard Rosenthal, *Congress: A Political-Economic History of Roll Call Voting* (New York: Oxford University Press, 1997).

9  See Keith Krehbiel, *Pivotal Politics: A Theory of U.S. Lawmaking* (Chicago: University of Chicago Press, 1998), and David W. Brady and Craig Volden, *Revolving Gridlock: Politics and Policy from Carter to Clinton* (Boulder, Colorado: Westview Press, 1998).

10  To learn more about DW-NOMINATE and to access the scores going back to the First Congress (1789–90), see http://voteview.com/dwnomin.htm.

11  Keith Krehbiel, David Brady, and Craig Volden, became the scholars most associated with these models. See Keith Krehbiel, *Pivotal Politics: A Theory of U.S. Lawmaking* (Chicago: University of Chicago Press, 1998), and David W. Brady

and Craig Volden. *Revolving Gridlock: Politics and Policy from Carter to Clinton* (Boulder, Colorado: Westview Press, 1998).

12 See, for example, Nolan McCarty, Keith T. Poole, and Howard Rosenthal, *Polarized America: The Dance of Ideology and Unequal Riches* (Cambridge: MIT Press, 2008), Barbara Sinclair, *Party Wars: Polarization and the Politics of National Policy Making* (Norman: The University of Oklahoma Press, 2006), and Sean M. Theriault, *Party Polarization in Congress* (New York: Cambridge University Press, 2008)..

13 This figure proves a simplified illustration of the policy making process. In reality, multiple stages may be occurring at once.

14 See Deborah A. Stone, "Causal Stories and the Formulation of Policy Agendas" *Political Science Quarterly* 104 (1989): 281–300.

15 See John W. Kingdon, *Agendas, Alternatives, and Public Policies* (New York: HarperCollins College Publishers, 1984).

16 See Roger W. Cobb and C.D. Elder, *Participation in American Politics: The Dynamics of Agenda-Building* (Boston: Allyn & Bacon, Inc., 1972) and Roger W. Cobb and David A. Rochefort, "Problem definition, agenda access, and policy choice," *Policy Studies Journal* 21 (1993) 56–71.

17 See Frank R. Baumgartner and Bryan D. Jones, "Changing Image and Venue as a Political Strategy," paper presented at Midwest Political Science Association, Chicago, 1989, Frank R. Baumgartner and Bryan D. Jones, *Agendas and Instability in American Politics* (Chicago: University of Chicago Press, 1993), and John W. Kingdon, *Agendas, Alternatives, and Public Policies* (New York: HarperCollins College Publishers, 1984).

18 See John W. Kingdon, *Agendas, Alternatives, and Public Policies* (New York: HarperCollins College Publishers, 1994).

19 See Deborah A. Stone, "Causal Stories and the Formulation of Policy Agendas," *Political Science Quarterly* 104 (1989): 281–300.

20 See Roger W. Cobb and C.D. Elder, *Participation in American Politics: The Dynamics of Agenda-Building* (Boston: Allyn & Bacon, Inc., 1972).

21 See Frank R. Baumgartner and Bryan D. Jones, *Agendas and Instability in American Politics* (Chicago: University of Chicago Press, 1993).

22 See William H. Riker, *The Art of Political Manipulation* (New Haven: Yale University Press, 1986).

23 See Peter Bachrach and Morton Baratz, "Two Faces of Power," *American Political Science Review* 56 (1962): 947–52.

24 See Peter Bachrach and Morton Baratz, 1962, "Two Faces of Power," *American Political Science Review* 56 (1962): 947–52.

25 Quoted in Walter J. Oleszek, *Congressional Procedures and the Policy Process* (Washington, D.C.: CQ Press, 1986). The original Dingell quote reputedly contained spicier language than the one reported in Oleszek. John Jackley attributes a similar quote to Tony Coelho when he was Majority Whip: "Give me process and the other guy substance, and I'll win every time." See J.L. Jackley, *Hill Rat: Blowing the Lid Off Congress* (Regnery Gateway, 1992).

26 Mazmanian and Sabatier define implementation as "those events and activities that occur after the issuing of authoritative public policy directives, which include both the effort to administer and the substantive impacts on people and events." See Daniel Mazmanian and Paul Sabatier, *Implementation and Public Policy*, (Palo Alto, CA: Scott Foresman, 1983), 4.

27 See Mathew D. McCubbins and Thomas Schwartz, "Congressional Oversight Overlooked: Police Patrols versus Fire Alarms," *American Journal of Political Science* 28 (1984): 165–79.

28  McCubbins and Schwarts liken this type of control to fire alarms. See Mathew D. McCubbins and Thomas Schwartz, "Congressional Oversight Overlooked: Police Patrols versus Fire Alarms," *American Journal of Political Science* 28 (1984): 165–79.

29  See Bryan D. Jones and Walter Williams, *The Politics of Bad Ideas: The Great Tax Cut Delusion and the Decline of Good Government in America* (Washington: Center for American Politics and Public Policy, 2007).

30  See John Huber and Charles Shipan, *Deliberate Discretion? The Institutional Foundations of Bureaucratic Autonomy* (New York: Cambridge University Press, 2002).

31  See Aage R. Clausen, *How Congressmen Decide: A Policy Focus* (New York: St. Martin's Press, 1973); also see John W. Kingdon, "Models of Legislative Voting," *Journal of Politics* 39 (1977): 563–95.

32  These categories include macroeconomics, civil rights, health, agriculture, labor employment, education, environment, energy, transportation, social welfare, law/crime/family, community development, banking/finance, defense, space/science/technology, foreign trade, international affairs, government operations, and public lands/water.

33  For more information, see www.policyagendas.org. The Policy Agendas Project data were originally collected by Frank R. Baumgartner and Bryan D. Jones, with the support of National Science Foundation grant numbers SBR 9320922 and 0111611. The data are distributed through the Department of Government at the University of Texas at Austin.

34  E. Scott Adler and John Wilkerson, *Congressional Bills Project: (1947–2008)*, NSF 00880066 and 00880061.

## Chapter 3

# Presidential Authority in a Separated System of Governance

*Andrew Rudalevige*

The question of presidential power gripped the Framers and remains a source of intense debate to this day. How much power does he have? Pundits tend to attribute magical powers to the president and call him a weak leader if he fails to get what he wants. Andrew Rudalevige, however, reminds us that the presidency is constrained as part of a wider system of interlocking political institutions, even when it appears the president has authority to act unilaterally. Rudalevige traces how scholars typically study the presidency, which offers a special challenge because of the "small N" problem: Though there have been thousands of Members of Congress over the nation's history, when it comes to studying the presidency, n = 44 at most. To avoid reducing knowledge about presidential power to case studies of leadership, he urges that we "think institutionally rather than simply personally." This means looking systematically at how the presidents make policy decisions within and across institutions. Drawing on the insights of organizational economics, Rudalevige shows when presidents choose to centralize policy proposals in the White House rather than leave it to the bureaucracy, with important implications for policy success. His historical approach reveals how enduring institutions shape presidential power and how presidents, in turn, shape institutions. This chapter demonstrates that good research requires creative thinking, disciplined data collection, and well-conceived theories about the political process.

On June 1, 1787, James Wilson of Pennsylvania stood up at the Constitutional Convention and made a seemingly simple motion: that the presidency of the United States should be an office filled by a single person. The immediate response, as recorded by James Madison, was "a considerable pause." It took an intervening plea from the convention's elderly conscience, Benjamin Franklin, to prompt the delegates even to debate the idea.[1]

A simple motion, but what had cowed the assembled notables was the realization that its consequences would be quite profound. The new nation was, after all, seeking to avoid the "absolute despotism," "the history of repeated injuries and usurpations," assigned by the Declaration of Independence to the British monarchy. Yet, it also wanted to avoid governance by legislative committee and the aimlessness of the Articles of Confederation regime, and knew (as Alexander Hamilton would later put it) that "energy in the executive is a leading character in the definition of good government."[2] The goal was to create a presidency that was strong enough to do things *for* the people of the United States but too weak to do things *to* them.[3]

Striking that balance would require a resort to constitutional ambiguity that has been clarified only through the practice and precedent of 220-plus years of American history. In fits and starts, the American presidency has grown to fill the enormous demands placed upon it by American expansion, industrialization, and globalization. Even a quiet news day in the early twenty-first century might range across the president's approval rating, dealings with Congress or with foreign leaders, efforts to shape the public agenda, or choice of pet or White House décor. All in all, "the quantity and intensity of attention to the American presidency exceeds that devoted to any other political institution."[4] That attention both reflects the magnitude of the office and in turn serves to magnify it.

Still, the assigned powers in Article II of the Constitution are vague; and since they have barely been modified from the framers' work in 1787, there is no clear guidance as to how they are supposed to work. Consider examples drawn from just the last few years: Should presidents be able to remove terrorism suspects from the civilian courts and detain them, perhaps indefinitely—or kill them, by remotely controlled drone? Should they be able to use force (in Libya, say) without congressional authorization? Should they be able to cancel U.S. treaty obligations? Should they be able to issue regulations that legislators have opposed or block regulations that expert technocrats have proposed? Should they be able to place their appointees in place even without Senate confirmation, if the Senate is too polarized to take action?

The lure of studying the presidency is that these questions are both central to the field and also matter in the real world. The key lines of inquiry in the subfield date back to the Framers' instinctive nervousness: They center on presidential power—its definition, its extent, and its efficacy. Scholars seek to track the president's assigned powers, his or her ability to sway the public, to influence the other branches of government, and his or her ability to act alone to effect policy change. All of this takes place in the context of a Constitution that gives the president few explicit grants of authority. So both "old school" qualitative scholars and "new institutionalists" who prefer quantitative work are actually inspired by the same question: How can a president in a separated system of governance gain leverage over that system?[5] How can a weak presidency allow presidents to be strong leaders?

One point of this chapter, then, is to paraphrase the famous Watergate formulation: What can presidents do, and how can they do it? However, at least as a coda, we must add: What *should* they do?[6] There is always a risk that specialists in any field become "fans" of a sort, rooting for the institution they study. There is also a well-earned concern about treading into normative waters beyond where data can guide.

However, as students of political science, it is our job to gauge objectively not just the how and the what—but the "so what?" as well—to try to discern how the enduring consequences of presidential power might play out in our public life. After all, as Supreme Court Justice Robert Jackson noted sixty years ago, "Comprehensive and undefined presidential powers hold both practical advantages and grave dangers" to American governance. The reason to study the presidency is to understand that enduring balance in theory and to be part of the debate over its proper calibration in practice.

## The Powers of the Presidency

Few aspects of the text of the Constitution would win points from professors grading on specificity, but Article II, dealing with the presidency, is perhaps its "most loosely-drawn chapter,"[7] and mostly about the electoral college to boot. This begins with the very first sentence of Article II: "The executive power shall be vested in a President of the United States of America." However... what *is* "the executive power?" It is left undefined.

That ambiguity helped the document win ratification, but it makes for uncertain guidance when trying to analyze presidential power.

One thing that *is* clear is the limited nature of the presidential office, at least in terms of its enumerated powers. The president was given a handful of specified powers, some of them rather unimpressive on paper ("he may require the opinion, in writing, of the principal officer in each of the executive departments...") and most of the rest further constrained by a sort of Congressional asterisk. For instance, the president can finalize treaties, or appointments, only with Senate approval; the execution of the law assumes its legislative passage; no money can be spent that is not first appropriated by Congress. How these shared powers might work was not clarified either: As Madison wrote in *Federalist* #51, inter-branch interaction would allow institutional "ambition... to counteract ambition." As elsewhere in the Constitution, the key was to separate authority, to provide checks and balances. Thus, the framework of presidential power was left largely in outline form, to be worked out in practice. Justice Oliver Wendell Holmes once observed that "a page of history is worth a volume of logic."[8] He was not talking about presidential power—but he might as well have been.

That history began almost immediately, when Treasury Secretary Alexander Hamilton and Congressman James Madison argued over the scope of President Washington's unilateral authority. Reduced to its essence, the dispute was—and still is—relatively straightforward: Is a president limited to the specific powers affirmatively listed in the Constitution or granted in statute, or can he take whatever actions he deems in the public interest so long as those actions are not actually prohibited by the Constitution? Theodore Roosevelt argued, "My belief was that it was not only [the President's] right but his duty to do anything that the needs of the Nation required unless such action was forbidden by the Constitution or by the laws." William Howard Taft claimed instead that

> the President can exercise no power which cannot be fairly and reasonably traced to some specific grant of power or justly implied within such express grant as proper and necessary to its exercise. There is no undefined residuum of power which he can exercise because it seems to him to be in the public interest.[9]

Whatever the Framers' true intentions—and the Taft side of things is probably closer to them—the Hamilton/TR position won out over time. Indeed, to that side of the ledger must be added the more recent expansive claims of some presidential "unitarians": that the president has unilateral powers that can be exercised even if they are *forbidden* by law.[10] The growth in the size and scope of government during and after the Great Depression, and national security apparatus built during World War II and the Cold War effectively settled the argument. H. L. Mencken noted in 1926 that "No man would want to be President of the United States in strict accordance with the Constitution."[11] However, people do want to be president, for the powers of the modern presidency go beyond anything the framers foresaw.

## Studying the Presidency: Topics, Methods, and Problems

Over time, presidents acquired many tools to work around their constitutionally mandated weakness, sometimes by their own initiative and sometimes by congressional delegation. They used their formal powers strategically and proactively. They built an executive branch in their own image, with an extensive presidential staff to oversee and control it. And they continually and creatively interpreted Constitutional vagueness in their favor to reshape the policy landscape—extending and relying on a direct connection with the public to legitimize their actions. Arguably a new framework for American government was created along the way, crystallized in a "modern presidency" starting with Franklin D. Roosevelt's administration and institutionalized by his successors.[12]

Presidents have always received public attention, of course and, as early as the 1860s, former presidents had begun putting out self-justifying memoirs (James Buchanan, who had a lot to justify, was first.)[13] However, sustained scholarly attention was far slower in arriving. Hugh Heclo notes that in the 1950s there was only one undergraduate course on the presidency offered at any major college—Clinton Rossiter's class at Cornell—and that the political science literature on the topic could squeeze into a single large satchel.[14]

However, as the outlines of the modern presidency became clearer, that new framework prompted both new work and a new organization of presidency studies around these broad presidential strategies. A group of substantive subfields has arisen that seeks to make sense of the president's place in a separated system and each incumbent's efforts to maximize influence in that system. My purpose here is not to replicate the very useful detailed handbooks to presidency studies that already exist.[15] Instead, I will suggest four broad groupings that attempt to summarize the research areas prominent in the field. We might call these (1) the constitutional presidency, (2) the institutional presidency, (3) the public presidency, and (4) the unilateral presidency.[16]

These categories do not cover everything of interest—such as presidents' relationships with the judiciary, for instance (which begin, but do not end, with the appointments of individual judges). Further, they contain numerous smaller specializations within them; and even so, they frequently overlap. Most prominently, perhaps, the large literature on the "legislative presidency" analyzing how presidents seek to influence Congress draws on research conducted under all four headings. Studying the "war presidency"—a literature revived in the 2000s, for obvious reasons—involves all four areas as well. And analyzing presidents and the media requires thinking about presidential messaging and rhetoric but also the growth of an institutional apparatus within the executive office of the president. Presidential elections obviously link to public, parties, and policymaking, but the study of elections is most often hived off into a wholly separate field, and I will not discuss it in detail here (see instead Chapter 7 of this volume).

With these caveats, however, these groupings usefully sum up presidents' use of power and the research issues this has inspired. They can be discussed briefly in turn.

The "constitutional presidency" tracks the development and use of the enumerated powers given presidents in the constitution. These are not in themselves overly impressive, as noted earlier, but, used cleverly and strategically, they can give the president standing and leverage in a wide number of areas. One part of this subfield is a public law approach to understanding what each power means, to presidents, under the law, and as interpreted by the courts.[17] This is essential to understanding the legal boundaries of presidential authority. Consider the one short sentence in the Constitution that allows presidents to make appointments without Senate approval, when the Senate is in recess. But what counts as a recess? President Obama's controversial appointment of Richard Cordray to head the Consumer Financial Protection Bureau brought that question into the headlines in early 2012 (and into the courts shortly thereafter).

Indeed, studying these questions is important for understanding how presidents have learned over time to exploit the vantage points the enumerated powers give them in the policy process. Early presidents, for instance, used the veto only when they felt a bill enacted by Congress was unconstitutional. Now, we assume that presidents will sign or veto bills based largely on their policy preferences. The veto, combined with the constitutional invitation to the president to recommend to Congress "such measures as he shall judge necessary and expedient," gives presidents a foothold at both ends of the legislative process. We might also consider how presidents have made more effective use of the appointment power, seeking to install personal (as opposed to party) loyalists in key positions across the government. Or how they have interpreted the title of commander-in-chief to build up their influence in foreign policy, even in peacetime.

The "institutional presidency," in turn, centers on the growth of what we might call the "presidential branch": the personal staff built up by presidents over time to serve as a "counter-bureaucracy" that allows them to extract information from, and seek to control the actions of, the wider executive branch.[18] As the government grew, managing that government became a more important part of the president's job but, at the same time, one that was nearly impossible. As early as 1937, the Brownlow Commission observed that "the president needs help"; over time, he got it.[19] There are now at least 1,500 substantive aides to the president within the executive office of the president (EOP), on the White House staff proper, and within such ongoing units as the Office of Management and Budget, National Security Council, and Office of Policy Development. Presidents have developed new staff institutions devoted to functions ranging from communications and congressional liaison to intergovernmental relations and AIDS policy. This has enabled presidents to bring functions that used to be performed in the Cabinet departments into the closer reaches of the EOP (this is often termed "centralization" and is discussed at greater length as part of the research case study following). They have also sought to rework advising processes and reorganize extant agencies to make them more responsive to presidential—not congressional or interest group—preferences. One controversial result has been the creation of White House "czars" by a succession of presidents seeking to coordinate and control the overlapping policy areas otherwise spread out across a number of departments.[20]

The "public presidency" (sometimes termed the "rhetorical presidency")[21] studies how presidents have sought to forge, exploit, and expand their relationship with the American people—and with those people's organizational manifestations, such as interest groups and political parties. The philosophical underpinnings here date back to the Framers' discussions over how elections should be conducted and certainly to Andrew Jackson's populist conception of the office as the "tribune of the people." However, presidential strategies to "go public" are tied to technology, too, and have been intertwined with developments that made mass—and then tightly targeted—communication ever easier. From the age of party newspapers to the rise of broadcast TV and now through the Internet and social networking, presidents have sought to get their message heard despite heavy competition for the public's attention and an increasingly polarized media environment. Speechwriting, travel, and other efforts to connect the president directly with voters (or a sympathetic subset of them) are now staples of the White House schedule and staff. In one typical week in mid-February 2012, aside from DC duties that included meeting with the heir-apparent to the Chinese presidency and delivering his fiscal year 2013 budget to Congress, President Obama traveled to events in Virginia, Wisconsin, California, and Washington state, giving speeches, raising money, and pushing his agenda as he went.[22]

Scholars study both the outputs and the outcomes involved in this frenetic activity. They examine how presidents relate to the media, how they choose to elevate issues or frame them rhetorically, the words they use and the places they deliver them and, of course, how the public responds to all of this. Public approval of the president is also studied as an independent variable: as a resource for influencing other political actors to do the president's bidding.

That, of course, is often an uphill battle. So the "unilateral presidency" involves presidents' attempts to avoid the problems of a separated system by doing an end-run around it—imposing their preferred policy outcomes without legislative or judicial approval and sometimes in the face of those branches' opposition. As George W. Bush once put it, having tried to achieve something legislatively, he "got a little frustrated in Washington because I couldn't get the bill passed out of the Congress.... Congress wouldn't act, so I signed an executive order. That means I did it on my own."[23] Acting "on my own" involves tools such as executive orders, proclamations, signing statements (that guide or constrain execution of a given law), executive agreements (that bypass the treaty ratification process), and a wide array of military directives. Presidents also seek to protect themselves from prying eyes by claiming executive privilege or invoking the state-secrets doctrine that prevents judicial consideration of controversial cases.[24]

Such tools are often justified by an expansive interpretation of "the executive power" granted by (but not defined in) Article II, in conjunction with the presidential role as commander-in-chief. However, they are partly, even largely, extra-constitutional. A unilateral strategy is grounded in the structural advantages a single actor has over a collective body such as a legislature (Hamilton summed these up in *Federalist* #70 as "activity, decision, secrecy, dispatch.") It also draws on broader notions of executive "prerogative"—what the philosopher John Locke called "to act according to discretion, for the publick good, without the prescription of the Law, and sometimes even against it."[25]

Reliance on unilateral authority is not new—think of the Louisiana Purchase or the Emancipation Proclamation—but as recently as the mid-1970s, a leading text on the presidency could exclude "executive orders" and "signing statements" from its index.[26] These days, not so much; this area is a growth industry of sorts within the discipline, inspired in part by contemporary presidential behavior in everything from the war on terror to President Obama's 2012 "we can't wait" campaign of administrative dictate designed to spotlight congressional inaction. Indeed, mounting polarization likely means more presidential efforts to go it alone. (It also makes it harder for Congress to act in a unified way to *stop* presidents from doing so, no small development.)

## Methods and Problems

These, in rough outline, are the "what" of presidency studies. They suggest the range of the different audiences and actors over whom a president wants to exercise influence. We still need to consider the "how."[27]

The problem of presidential power was addressed in the first instance by cataloging it. For instance, Edward Corwin's *The President: Office and Powers*, which appeared in multiple editions beginning in 1940, laid out a detailed history of the constitutional and statutory duties of the president—as interpreted by presidents, legislators, and especially by the judiciary.[28] Clinton Rossiter, in his 1956 book *The American Presidency*, instead looked at this list of powers and sought to organize them by function. He noted "the staggering number of duties we have laid upon" the occupant of the Oval Office and divided them into a series of "hats" worn by the president.[29] For example, the president was chief of state; chief executive; chief diplomat; commander in chief; chief legislator; chief of party; Voice of the People—and even, for good measure, Leader of a Coalition of Free Nations.

To be sure, Rossiter realized that all these roles were interactive, indeed intertwined into the job description of a single incumbent. However, it was Richard Neustadt's *Presidential Power* in 1960 that most prominently sought to fuse them into the practical realities of being president. His book argued that "one must try to view the Presidency from over the President's shoulder, looking out and down with the perspective of his place," rather than from outside his office, looking in.[30] Neustadt focused the book on the president's effort to gain personal sway: He defined power as influence over governmental outcomes. Thus, issuing an order in itself did not constitute power unless that order was implemented as desired, but, as noted, presidents' *formal* grants of authority were often insufficient to the task. That meant the president had to bargain, constantly, with a wide array of "Washingtonians."[31] His own resources included his constitutional powers, certainly, but also his professional reputation for "skill and will" and the prestige he accumulated through his ability to communicate with—really, to teach—the mass public.

The ideas that the field should focus on the realities of wielding power and that effective presidential power was grounded in successful persuasion rather than command proved immensely influential. Five decades on, Neustadt's work has sold more than 1 million copies and remains the most cited work on the presidency. Substantial scholarly efforts ensued in all substantive areas of the subfield devoted to testing the premises of the book—for instance, examining presidents' abilities to influence Congress and communicate with the public.

Not all scholars have been enthused by Neustadt's influence. They argued that his approach encouraged a research agenda that focused on a given incumbent's abilities and influence—in short, on the personal qualities of the president rather than on the institution of the presidency. "Here is the irony," wrote the most prominent critic of the latter approach. "At precisely the same time that Neustadt's work was reorienting scholarly thinking around the concept of the personal presidency, the presidency itself was becoming highly institutionalized. Indeed, the hallmark of the modern presidency is its growth and development as an institution."[32]

This critique, though not entirely convincing as applied to *Presidential Power* itself,[33] did identify an important issue. Personal accounts—even efforts to analyze presidents psychologically—are certainly prominent in the field.[34] To some extent, this is unavoidable. After all, there is only one president at any one time. Who that person is must matter.

One can see this through simple counterfactual questions. For instance, would the New Deal and Second World War have played out the same way if the assassination attempt on Franklin D. Roosevelt on February 15, 1933 had succeeded and John Nance Garner taken office instead of FDR three weeks later? Had butterfly ballots fluttered the other way in Florida's presidential election in 2000 and Al Gore instead of George W. Bush succeeded Bill Clinton as president, would the American policy reaction to the terrorist attacks of September 11, 2001 have been the same? There is, as Fred Greenstein has argued, a "presidential difference."[35]

So far, so good. Indeed, "the prominence of the presidency as a topic of commentary lies, to some extent, in its ability to be personalized."[36] Yet, this is a double-edged sword for political scientists, if not for biographers or journalists. Exploring all aspects of the individual who serves as president explains a lot— but only about that president. This can make it difficult to develop testable hypotheses that could be generalized across different presidencies. It can lead to reliance on personality-driven anecdotes and case studies, at best producing a sequence of summaries detailing developments across a short span of postwar administrations. Important, too, is that it overstates presidents' centrality to the separated system in which they seek to operate. "The president is not the presidency."[37]

For some time, partly as a result, the presidency subfield was quite self-critical, even as its volume of scholarship exploded. Even adding presidencies together did not guarantee systematic study, because of the same simple fact about the presidency noted earlier: There is only one at a time. Thus, even in the aggregate—all the way from George Washington to Barack Obama—a researcher using presidents as the unit of analysis could have no more than forty-four observations. In a mischievous moment, the Harvard methodologist Gary King pointed out that we will not have a sufficient population of presidents to achieve statistical significance until 2193—and that more robust results would have to wait for the fifth millennium AD.[38] For a long while, presidency scholars were prone to envious glances at their colleagues studying Congress or the electoral process. They had so many things to count!: hundreds of legislators, thousands of roll call tallies, millions of voters. Thus, sustained attention to quantitative or formal work (i.e., game theory) came relatively late to the presidency.

Yet, the field has developed rather dramatically, to the extent that even longtime critic Terry Moe hails "a revolution in presidency studies."[39] What has distinguished good recent work is a sophisticated approach to the institutional focus noted earlier and a transcendence of the "$n = 1$" problem—obtained by shifting the research focus away from individual presidents and onto behaviors and strategies common to all modern presidents. All presidents make decisions, of all sorts, within action-forcing streams of information. They send legislation; ponder budget recommendations; make appointments; review regulations; give speeches; deal with their political parties; build advising structures. In short, as noted, they act within an institutional framework—and all presidents can be expected to behave, well, like presidents. Regardless of their party or their personalities, they are actors facing similar incentives and limits. To take one example, George W. Bush was notable in acting aggressively to expand his office's powers vis-à-vis other political actors; but Barack Obama, while disavowing some of his predecessor's rationales for those tactics, has acted in a similar manner in a number of areas.[40]

Studying repeated behavior by and around presidents allows the number of observations available to the scholar to rise dramatically, but an institutional focus does not have to inspire statistical analysis. The growth in the historical study of the presidency under the rubric of "American Political Development" is all about the evolution of large-scale institutions over time. This is not quantitative, but it is rigorous. That is, it derives clear hypotheses and tests them against the relevant evidence. It allows scholars to draw general rules of presidential behavior given certain institutional conditions—but does not rule out presidents' entrepreneurial manipulation of those institutions in ways that can change history.[41]

Best yet, perhaps, is a combination of qualitative work and quantitative analysis. Coding, and the analysis it makes possible—as it translates qualitative research into quantitative summary—can be only as reliable as the research that underlies it. If we are to expand the reach of our general conclusions about presidential behavior and the conditions under which it is effective, substantive rigor must be married to careful modeling. Our knowledge of presidential behavior, both in grand strokes and in its nuances, benefits when archival research and large-$n$ work are determinedly and reciprocally cumulative.

### Applying the Approach: One Research Agenda

To show this, it may be useful to trace the development of one research project as an extended case study of one effort at approaching the study of the presidency. At worst, it may serve as a sort of step-by-step guide to conceiving and conducting such a project.

The example here is drawn from the research that became my book *Managing the President's Program: Presidential Leadership and Legislative Policy Formulation*, which is about the president's legislative program: how it is created within the executive branch, how it is received by Congress, and whether the two things are connected.[42] As one of Lyndon Johnson's staffers responded, when asked, "How do you twist an arm?" to get a member of Congress to vote the president's way—"If you're talking about persuasion, we initiate by proposing."[43]

Studying presidents' *legislative* success was, of course, hardly a new idea. A surge of research had been conducted in the late 1980s and early 1990s on the contexts that conditioned presidential efforts to pass desired bills through Congress. One notable finding was that presidential "skill" seemed to have far less impact than factors less under his control, such as the relative strength of the two parties.[44]

However, linking legislative achievement to *executive* success was novel. If legislating had become crucial to presidents—and it had—surely the creation of that legislation should be crucial too. This raised the potential for a cruel irony. As presidents have to act in many overlapping arenas at once—foreign and domestic, public and backroom, executive and legislative, fiscal and social— actions that advance presidential preferences in one arena can have unintended but damaging consequences in another. So it was here: Might effective action in one important realm of presidential action (executive management) have negative ramifications in another key area (legislative success)?

What we knew about policy formulation tended to follow a clear conventional wisdom: that policy making had centralized. (Again, this simply means that, over time, presidents had shifted a series of substantive duties from the wider executive branch to the relatively new White House staff.) That made some sense. After all, presidents—like any managers—surely sought responsiveness, which was more likely to be found in aides who worked with and reported to them directly than out in the Cabinet departments. A rational president, facing the separated system mandated by the Constitution, would bring as much as possible under his direct control.

If this was right, what were the observable implications? To start with, an increasing proportion of policy should be made in the White House, with little centralization at the start of the presidential program timeline, under President Truman, and lots of it by the end (at the time of writing, under President Clinton). Certainly the White House staff, and the EOP more generally, had grown substantially during that period. Yet, we did not have much information about how legislation was discussed or drafted inside the executive branch. (Indeed, there was not even a commonly accepted definition of what the presidential program actually comprised.)

Further, the logic of centralization struck me as very much contingent. That is, bringing materials "in house" in this way had costs and benefits as a management instrument. If so, we should expect rational presidents to use it under certain circumstances and not others. If so, it would vary bill by bill and not presidency by presidency, an important shift of the unit of analysis that allowed the project to escape the "$n = 1$" problem.

If all this was right, centralization was not simply a matter of time; it was a question less of evolution than of expedience.[45] To think about the conditions under which it would be used, I drew on the insights of organizational economists such as Ronald Coase and Oliver Williamson, who had thought about what was termed the "make or buy?" question in the context of individual firms. They had asked whether a firm should make its own product or buy it elsewhere: The answer depended on cost, naturally, but that in turn depended on the insight that (beyond dollars and cents) there were "transaction costs" that applied to both internal and external production. I extended the analogy, imperfectly to be sure, to the presidential context: Should the president "make" legislation inside the EOP or "buy" it from the departments? The transaction costs involved, as with firms, would vary depending on specific aspects of the legislation involved and on the wider political environment presidents occupied at the time.

The puzzle, then, was both theoretical and empirical but, first, it required new data.

## Data Gathering

Indeed, the first step was to discover what presidents had actually proposed to Congress over fifty years or so. It became clear this would require something that only a bored graduate student had the time for: reading the *Public Papers of the President* page by page from 1949 forward and counting the messages presidents sent to Congress along with the individual proposals therein. At the time, this required many hours in a basement cubicle. (However, a decade later, automated word searches and coding are very feasible, and much used.[46])

This task yielded nearly 2,800 messages, containing more than 6,900 proposals. This population was too large for detailed study of each item, so I utilized a methodology common in other parts of political science and drew a representative random sample. This yielded about 380 messages, or slightly more than thirty observations per presidential term.[47]

At that point, another hard job awaited: discovering where in the administration each of those 380 items had been formulated, so that it could

CLEARED ADMINISTRATION-SPONSORED LEGISLATION - 105TH FINAL

| Title | Legislative History | Bill No | Comments |
|---|---|---|---|
| **African Development Foundation** | | | |
| Authorize Appropriations for the African Development Foundation | CLEARED In Accord on 03/21/97; TRANSMITTED to Congress on 03/24/97; REFERRED to Senate Foreign Relations Ctte. 04/14.97 -- House International Relations Ctte. 04/09/97 | No | |
| **AGRICULTURE** | | | |
| Agriculture Marketing Order Fees (Title I - Subtitle C of the Balanced Budget Act of 1997) | CLEARED In Accord on 03/10/97 | No | |
| Agriculture Reform and Improvement Act of 1998 | CLEARED In Accord on 03/18/98; TRANSMITTED to Congress on 04/02/98; REFERRED to House Agriculture Ctte, House Commerce Ctte, House Ways & Means Ctte. 05/11/98 -- Senate Agriculture Nutrition & Forestry Ctte. 04/20/98 | No | |
| Child Nutrition and WIC Reauthorization Amendments of 1998 | CLEARED In Accord on 03/10/98; TRANSMITTED to Congress on 03/10/98; REFERRED to Senate Agriculture Nutrition & Forestry Ctte. 03/23/98 -- House Education & Workforce Ctte, House Government Reform & Oversight Ctte. 03/23/98 | Certain provisions enacted as part of P.L. 105-336 (H.R. 3874) on 10/31/98. |
| Consolidated Farm and Rural Development Act Amendments | CLEARED In Accord on 03/10/98; TRANSMITTED to Congress on 03/10/98 | No | |
| Department of Agriculture Fee Act | CLEARED In Accord on 04/13/98; TRANSMITTED to Congress on 05/14/98; REFERRED to House Agriculture Ctte. 06/05/98 -- Senate Agriculture Nutrition & Forestry Ctte. 06/04/98 | No | |
| Farm Safety Net Improvements (Title I - Subtitle A of the Balanced Budget Act of 1997) | CLEARED In Accord on 03/10/97; TRANSMITTED to Congress on 36/28/97; REFERRED to Senate Agriculture Nutrition & Forestry Ctte. 09/17/97 | No | |
| Food Assistance (Title XII - Subtitle A of the Balanced Budget Act of 1997) | CLEARED In Accord on 03/07/97 | Similar provisions enacted as part of P.L. 105-33 (HR 2015), signed 8/5/97. |
| Food Safety and Inspection Service Fees (Title I - Subtitle D of the Balanced Budget Act of 1997) | CLEARED In Accord on 03/14/97; TRANSMITTED to Congress on 06/26/97; REFERRED to Senate Agriculture Nutrition & Forestry Ctte. 07/10/97 -- House Agriculture Ctte. 07/09/97 | No | |
| Fund for Rural America Technical Correction | CLEARED In Accord on 03/10/97 | This bill will be transmitted as Title I, subtitle 8 of the Balanced Budget Act of 1997. |
| Grain Inspection Fees (Title I - Subtitle F of the Balanced Budget Act of 1997) | CLEARED In Accord on 03/10/97 | No | |
| Housing Act of 1949 Amendment to Prohibit Moratorium Assistance on Accelerated Loan | CLEARED In Accord on 03/25/97 | No | |
| Housing Act of 1949 Amendments to Refinance 502 Loans | CLEARED In Accord on 03/25/97; TRANSMITTED to Congress on 05/13/97; REFERRED to Senate Agriculture Nutrition & Forestry Ctte. 05/22/97 | No | |
| Livestock Dealer Trust Act | CLEARED In Accord on 07/25/97; TRANSMITTED to Congress on 08/11/97; REFERRED to House Agriculture Ctte. 09/09/97 -- Senate Agriculture Nutrition & Forestry Ctte. 09/02/97 | File brought forward to 106th Congress see file #120 |
| Packers and Stockyards Licensing Fee Act of 1997 (Title I - Subtitle G of the Balanced Budget Act of 1997) | CLEARED In Accord on 03/10/97 | No | |

*Figure 3.1* Final report of cleared administration-sponsored legislation, 105th Congress

be coded properly for further analysis. Doing so required the usual literature search—combing news stories, memoirs, scholarly accounts of different presidencies—but it also relied on exploring the archival record. The American presidency, if nothing else, has generated an awful lot of paperwork. Each incumbent since Hoover has created a presidential library (often paired with a museum, or foundation, or both) to house those records. Further, the National Archives and Records Administration holds millions of documents generated by executive branch agencies.[48]

Among those agencies is the Office of Management and Budget (OMB), which has existed in different forms since 1921. The OMB has long been assigned by presidents to conduct "central clearance"—that is, to keep track of the policymaking efforts of the executive branch, whether conducted through budgeting, congressional testimony, proposed regulations, or (luckily) proposed legislation. This in itself is an important example of presidents' seeking to gain leverage over their political environment. The OMB's Legislative Reference staff kept track of administration-sponsored bills and compiled individual files on the formulation and legislative progress of each bill. Figure 3.1 shows the first page of the final OMB report for the 105th Congress in 1997–1998—the first of twenty-three similar pages, listing affected departments A to Z.

To be sure, these files were scattered and were coded using a decimalized system that made sense when it was created (one assumes) but was not obviously intuitive to a late–twentieth century researcher. Still, deciphering

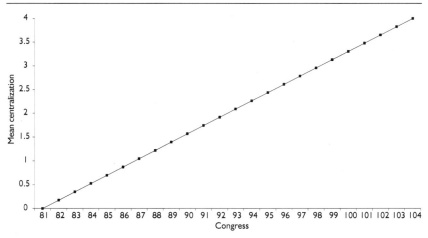

*Figure 3.2a* Estimated mean level of centralization of legislative policy formulation, by Congress, using "linear centralization" hypothesis

various finding aids in various archives paid off by (1) helping to confirm the reliability of the *Public Papers* database itself; (2) filling in, sometimes in rich detail, internal debates over the role of the presidential staff in the policy formulation process; and (3) providing relatively comprehensive bill histories for most of the items in the project's sample. In the end, I was able to determine whether a particular proposal was "decentralized" (created in the wider executive branch), centralized (in the EOP), or resulted from some mix of the two. This in turn allowed a five-part coding index of zero through four to be applied to each item.

For example, in March of 1971, President Richard Nixon sent Congress a Message on Special Revenue Sharing for Manpower, justifying the Manpower Revenue Sharing Act of 1971. (Revenue sharing generally was designed to send money from the federal government to the states—in this case, to help with job creation and training programs.) The departments of Labor and Treasury had a good deal of input shaping the bill, but the process, and the final specifications of the proposal, were driven by OMB staffers working with the staff of the White House Domestic Council directed by Nixon aide John Ehrlichman. Eventually, Ehrlichman wrote to the Secretary of Labor that he had met with the president to review the "several policy issues which my staff and OMB have discussed with the Department." In each instance, the president decided against Labor's position.[49]

A proposal such as this, then, would be coded as "2"—a mixed process but with the White House in the lead. (One calibrated the other way, toward the departments, would be coded a "1.") Figure 3.2b presents the actual mean level of centralization for each two-year Congress in the study (the 80th Congress served in 1947–1948, the 104th in 1995–1996.) Remember, though, the conventional wisdom we are trying to test empirically—that centralization

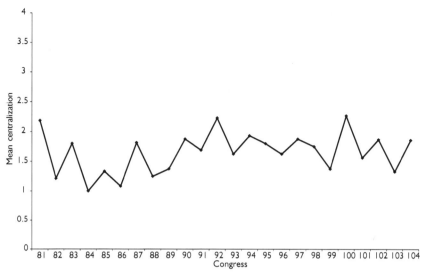

*Figure 3.2b* Actual mean level of centralization of legislative policy formulation, by Congress

increased in a more or less linear fashion over time. This might itself be graphed: It would look something like Figure 3.2a.

Comparing the two graphs allows a quick hypothesis test. As it shows at a glance, centralization did not increase in a linear fashion over time. So clearly, the next question was: Under what conditions did it occur?

As a result, other coding was added based on hypotheses derived from the transaction cost literature noted earlier, designed to tease out which contextual factors would make centralization "cheaper" and which would make assigning policy development to the departments more attractive. This allowed me to translate archival research into quantitative analysis, namely an "ordered probit" technique that helped predict the relative impact of each factor on the likelihood of centralization.[50] It turned out that the most important variables included whether a given bill had a reorganizational impact; the number of departmental jurisdictions that bill cut across; the president's ideological distance from a median member of Congress (the farther away from Congress, the more likely centralization would occur); and the bill's substantive complexity (the more complex, the less likely its formulation would be centralized.)

Importantly, these results were consistent with the theoretical predictions resulting from applying the insights of the "transaction costs" literature noted earlier about presidents' managerial costs. For example, presidents would presumably be unwise to trust departments to give unbiased advice about their own reorganizations. With a large number of departments involved, the costs of coordination should be lower for presidents if they centralize the formulation process. Or, when examining presidents' ideological "distance" from Congress, remember that both the president and Congress have control over the bureaucracy. Thus, presidents who are "far away from" (i.e., have more profound disagreements with) Congress will likely trust the bureaucracy less as well to act unsupervised, as its denizens may be listening to Congress rather than to the Oval Office. Thus, the more distant a president from Congress, the more centralized his policy formulation should be. And so the analysis suggested.

This was half the battle; the next question was whether centralization mattered to legislative success. My hypothesis was that more centralized proposals should do less well in Congress, partly because of the informational economics involved—legislators were far more informed about the formulation process if the departments were taking the lead.

### More Data

However, now another data problem arose. Legislative "success" is a familiar concept but one that is tricky to measure precisely. Early cuts at the question relied solely on roll-call votes: Did members of Congress vote in the way the president had asked them to vote? *Congressional Quarterly*'s longitudinal database of roll calls and presidential position taking has been invaluable.

Such a measure enables us to infer (though not directly observe) how much influence presidents have had on the decisions of legislators. This is critical but, depending on the question at hand, it might not be everything we want to know. After all, roll-call votes make up a minority of congressional actions. Items might be passed by voice vote or get rolled into an omnibus package. The key decision might come in committee, not on the floor, or through negotiation of a rule or unanimous consent agreement—all without ever coming to a recorded vote.[51] Further, votes can be misleading. They can be gamed, for one thing, by presidents who take positions on votes they expect to pass, in order—as Kennedy aide Ted Sorensen put it—"to fatten [their] 'batting average.'" Or they can be transient. In 2005, for instance, George W. Bush lost a number of roll-call votes on a series of budget amendments but, thanks to a sympathetic conference committee, the version of the budget eventually enshrined in law reflected Bush's preferences, not those of the original roll-calls.[52]

In the project traced here, the unit of interest was the president's proposal itself—the bill sent by the president to Congress—and whether it became law. Discerning that outcome required scouring various primary and secondary sources to track legislative action on presidential requests. In the end, this was coded on an index, from "failure" to "success," with intermediary stops along the way. In this sample, at least, about 40 percent of presidents' proposals failed outright, and slightly less than 30 percent were passed more or less in the form the president desired. The remainder passed but at some distance from the president's preferences.[53]

*More Testing*

Checking whether the process used to produce a proposal mattered for that bill's success in Congress meant another round of statistical analysis. This in turn meant thinking about control variables—that is, other possible causes of legislative success or failure, so that one could isolate the impact of the centralization variable accounting for other important influences. For instance, how many seats in Congress were held by the president's co-partisans (and how polarized they were) would obviously matter to an item's legislative reception. Would centralization matter, even accounting for that—or for other factors such as presidential approval, policy type, or whether the item was proposed during a crisis situation?

The short answer was that all these obvious controls mattered—but, even independent of them, so did centralization. Indeed, moving from the least centralized to the most centralized formulation process increased the chances that a program item would fail outright by some 16 percentage points, all else equal.

## Conclusions—but Not Concluded!

The research helped to tease out, then, what conditions led presidents to rely on some advisers rather than others in developing their legislative policy proposals. And it sought to lay out the costs and benefits of that tactic: Simply put, what helps presidents manage the executive branch may hurt them in leading the legislative.

All this seems like a lot of work. And, in the end, good research is the same in any field: Theorizing leads to hypotheses, which lead to collecting the right data, which leads to the appropriate probing tests, which lead to conclusions. Yet, there are some specifics, too, for presidency research of any scope. Think institutionally, not simply personally. Identify processes and flows of behavior, not individual quirks. However, beware of oversimplifying: Even if the short answer is "it depends," the interesting part is the longer answer, detailing *on what* it depends.

Just as important, this was not the end of the line. Doing one project can lead to another. One question that *Managing* raised concerned the relationship of centralization to another topic, presidential appointments. As noted, presidents have sought to politicize this process by installing their loyalists across the executive branch. So, if a president were able to effectively politicize a given department or agency, did that mean he would "trust" it more—and, thus, be less inclined to centralize proposals within its jurisdiction?[54]

A second follow-up project comes from the recent stress on the field on presidential unilateralism. Having studied presidential legislation stirred up another question: What about when presidents do *not* send legislation? Studying executive orders is one obvious next step. The legislative program project went from the qualitative to the quantitative. However, the executive order literature suggested going in the opposite direction—taking a quantitative literature and filling it in with archival nuance.

One side of the data picture here, after all, is easy enough: Scholars have a nice record of all the executive orders issued since the late 1930s, courtesy of the *Federal Register*.[55] To that, we can add some context to help explain the timing of order issuance and some idea of the systemic factors that explain what makes an order more likely to be issued. Many of those factors are legislative in nature, such as unified versus divided government. Others are more systemic or contextual: Have we seen a shift in administration between presidents of different parties? Is it an election year? Is the president particularly popular or unpopular?[56]

Even so, looked at this way—with the unit of analysis being the simple fact of an order's issuance—orders tend to spring from a sort of immaculate conception. And though this would not matter for all purposes, it does if we want to explore the question of unilateral action by presidents. Can we assume that the presidency and the executive branch can be treated as a single, unitary actor? Unlike Congress, some scholars suggest, "presidents are not hobbled by these collective action problems and, reigning supreme within their institution, can simply make authoritative decisions about what is best."[57] A recalcitrant department is told to shape up and fly right, perhaps to enforce integrated housing policies or to submit their proposed regulations for White House scrutiny. Policy is unified and perfectly reflects presidential preferences.

Yet my work on the advising process that led to legislative program formulation did *not* suggest a perfectly unified executive branch. Most of the history of public administration is, in fact, predicated on the difficulties of managing, not on the ease of authoritative decisions.[58] Nixon aide William Safire called the executive branch a "lethargic behemoth" that presidents struggle to control: "The so-called Chief Executive," he added, "can tug and haul all day and never rip up the bureaucracy."[59] In a branch that collects nearly 3 million persons within its purview, we can expect collective action problems. Recall Bill Clinton's 1993 struggle to end the ban on gays' open service in the military or George W. Bush's program of domestic surveillance (including a dramatic showdown between Department of Justice and White House staff in Attorney General John Ashcroft's hospital room).[60]

Untangling this unleashes yet more empirical work, more trips to the archives. However, even an early version of the analysis suggests a good deal of complexity hiding behind the label of "unilateralism." Close examination of an executive order issued by Bill Clinton in 1997, requiring that federal agencies formally assess the impact of their regulations on children's health, shows that it came not from the White House but the Environmental Protection Agency (EPA). Its deliberation brought together some seventeen departments and executive staffs over a four-month series of negotiations aimed at lessening bureaucratic resistance to the idea. Even the draft sent to the president, which EPA complained was "redone to address concerns" and "weakened already," shifted further to the departmental vantage when the president scrawled on the memo that staff "might want to ease burden a bit."[61] A more systematic archival analysis of nearly 300 executive orders issued between 1947 and 1987 found that the Clinton order's experience was not an anomaly. Nearly two-thirds of presidential orders originated in the wider bureaucracy rather than the White House, and even those driven by the latter normally receive wide discussion and, often, revision. In short, "unilateral" does not have to mean "unitary" or even "unified."

One last question arises. What about the flip side of these orders? As the focus of the literature to date has been on the issuance of a unilateral order, it has not assessed how well the orders worked once issued. As Clinton told an interviewer after leaving office, "One of the things that I was frustrated about when I was president, was that … I'd issue all these executive orders, and then you can never be 100 percent sure that they were implemented."[62] That gap surely ties into the broader theme of presidential power, especially if that is defined as a president's influence over governmental outcomes. Indeed, what if, as suggested, executive orders often come from the agencies without much presidential forethought? If Actor B says, "Tell me to do X"; Actor A says, "Do X"; and B does X. Is that power? Defining it will take more work, and thought. In so doing, we will have come full circle to return to the key questions with which we started this chapter. How much power do presidents really have? How can they get more? And… do we really want them to?

## Judging Presidents in a Separated System

Studying the presidency matters, because presidents matter. Yet, the study of the presidency both benefits and suffers from the prominence of its chief protagonist. On the one hand, scholars of the presidency will rarely lack for relevance or raw material. However old or new one's choice of media, it is likely to be full of the doings and failings of the nation's chief executive. On the other hand, as Charles O. Jones puts it, "The presidency is not the government. Ours is not a presidential system."[63]

This is a simple fact but one too often ignored by pundits and even practitioners. If nothing else, studying the presidency should provide a sense of presidential weakness as much as presidential power. The means presidents have used to gain influence in a system not designed to give them much independent sway need careful documentation and assessment.

Indeed, scholars can provide a systematic, institutional view, grounded in historical context, countering the never-ending demand for instant rankings and ratings—and the demands of those who alternate their opinion of presidential authority depending on which party happens to hold that office.[64] Justice Robert Jackson, cited at the start of the chapter, observed that

> the opinions of judges, no less than executives and publicists often suffer the infirmity of confusing the issue of a power's validity with the cause it is invoked to promote, of confounding the permanent executive office with its temporary occupant. The tendency is strong to emphasize transient results upon policies… and lose sight of enduring consequences upon the balanced power structure of our Republic.[65]

Resisting that tendency allows us to judge presidents more fairly. Understanding the presidency as part of a wider set of interlocking institutions helps us understand, in turn, important realities. For instance, why presidents' approach to key elements of executive power and foreign policy is so consistent over time. Why presidents who say they will change policy "with a stroke of a pen" find it so hard to take up that pen. Why it is never right to say "President X passed Law Y"—no matter how winning a negotiating technique he or she may have. Why the decisions the president makes about who staffs the White House take first priority, even above those named to the Cabinet. Why presidents must structure other actors' choices, not simply order them to act, if they want to successfully lead.

In short, the study of the presidency aims to build an accumulating body of knowledge that will help us explain presidential behavior, assess it—and guide it. Understanding contingency requires an "$n$" large enough to see contrasts; understanding process and nuance requires grounding in the internal history of a given administration. Understanding today's American politics requires both.

## Notes

1   James Madison, *Debates on the Adoption of the Federal Constitution*, ed. Jonathan Elliot (Philadelphia: J.B. Lippincott & Co., 1876), 140. Wilson would later serve on the U.S. Supreme Court.
2   Alexander Hamilton, "Federalist #70," in *The Federalist Papers*, ed. Clinton Rossiter (New York: Mentor, 1961), 423.
3   Thanks to Prof. Morris Fiorina for this formulation.
4   George C. Edwards, III, and William G. Howell, "Introduction," in *The Oxford Handbook of the American Presidency*, eds. George C. Edwards, III, and William G. Howell (New York: Oxford University Press, 2009), 3.
5   Richard E. Neustadt argued that the American system was one of "separated institutions sharing powers." See Neustadt, *Presidential Power and the Modern Presidents* (New York: Free Press, 1990), 29; see also Charles O. Jones, *The Presidency in a Separated System*, 2nd ed. (Washington, DC: Brookings Institution Press, 2005).
6   For an excellent discussion of this theme see Hugh Heclo, "Whose Presidency is This Anyhow?", in *The Oxford Handbook of the American Presidency*, eds. George

C. Edwards, III, and William G. Howell (New York: Oxford University Press, 2009). Taking a similar tack with regards to undergraduate teaching is Louis Fisher, "Teaching the Presidency: Idealizing a Constitutional Office," *PS: Political Science and Politics* 45 (January 2012): 17–31.

7  Edward S. Corwin, *The President: Office and Powers,* 5th rev. ed., with Randall W. Bland, Theodore Hinson, and Jack W. Peltason (New York: New York University Press, 1984), 3.

8  Majority opinion in *N.Y. Trust Company v. Eisner,* 256 U.S. 345 (1921).

9  Theodore Roosevelt, *An Autobiography* (1913; reprint, New York: Da Capo Press, 1985), 372; William Howard Taft, *Our Chief Magistrate and His Powers* (1916), quoted in Christopher H. Pyle and Richard M. Pious, eds., *The President, Congress, and the Constitution: Power and Legitimacy in American Politics* (New York: Free Press, 1984), 70–71.

10  "Unitarians" are those who press for a strong version of "unitary executive" theory. For a real-life example see the Working Group Report on Detainee Interrogations in the Global War on Terrorism: Assessment of Legal, Historical, Policy, and Operational Considerations, U.S. Department of Defense, April 4, 2003, 21, which argued that "in order to respect the President's inherent constitutional authority to manage a military campaign, 18 U.S.C. §2340A [the prohibition against torture] as well as any other potentially applicable statute must be construed as inapplicable to interrogations undertaken pursuant to his Commander-in-Chief authority."

11  H.L. Mencken, *Notes on Democracy* (New York: Alfred A. Knopf, 1926), 185.

12  Fred I. Greenstein, "Toward a Modern Presidency," in Greenstein, ed., *Leadership in the Modern Presidency* (Cambridge, MA: Harvard University Press, 1988), 3. Not all scholars agree with this sort of periodization – see especially Stephen Skowronek, *The Politics Presidents Make* (Cambridge, MA: Harvard University Press, 1993).

13  James Buchanan, *Mr Buchanan's Administration on the Eve of the Rebellion* (New York: D. Appleton, 1866).

14  Heclo, "Whose Presidency is This Anyhow?", 771.

15  Students seeking further depth in any of the research areas discussed herein are referred to, among other recent useful compendia, Joel Aberbach and Mark A. Peterson, eds., *The Executive Branch* (New York: Oxford University Press, 2005); George C. Edwards, III, and William G. Howell, eds., *The Oxford Handbook of the American Presidency* (New York: Oxford University Press, 2009); and Lori Cox Han, ed., *New Directions in the American Presidency* (New York: Routledge, 2011).

16  These are not official subfield names, but I think they will be generally accepted. See, for instance, the slightly different but certainly compatible groupings provided by Richard J. Ellis in an excellent recent textbook: Ellis, *The Development of the American Presidency* (New York: Routledge, 2012).

17  Louis Fisher, "Political Scientists and the Public Law Tradition," in *The Oxford Handbook of the American Presidency,* eds. George C. Edwards, III, and William G. Howell (New York: Oxford University Press, 2009).

18  John Burke, *The Institutional Presidency,* 2nd ed. (Baltimore, MD: Johns Hopkins University Press, 2000); John Hart, *The Presidential Branch,* 2nd ed. (Chatham, NJ: Chatham House, 1995); Richard Nathan, *The Administrative Presidency* (New York: Macmillan, 1983).

19  See Matthew J. Dickinson, *Bitter Harvest* (New York: Cambridge University Press, 1997); Justin S. Vaughn and Jose D. Villalobos, "White House Staff," in Han, ed., *New Directions.*

20  See Mitchel A. Sollenberger and Mark J. Rozell, *The President's Czars* (Lawrence: University Press of Kansas, 2012), for a strongly critical review of this development.

21  Two seminal works here are Samuel Kernell, *Going Public: New Strategies of Presidential Leadership*, 4th ed. (Washington, DC: CQ Press, 2006); Jeffrey Tulis, *The Rhetorical Presidency* (Princeton, NJ: Princeton University Press, 1987).

22  February 12–18, 2012. See http://www.whitehouse.gov/schedule/complete/2012-W7

23  "President's Remarks at Faith-Based and Community Initiatives Conference," Office of the White House Press Secretary (March 3, 2004). More generally, see Kenneth R. Mayer, *With the Stroke of a Pen: Executive Orders and Presidential Power* (Princeton, NJ: Princeton University Press, 2001), 11; William G. Howell, *Power without Persuasion: The Politics of Direct Presidential Action* (Princeton, NJ: Princeton University Press, 2003).

24  For bibliographies, see Kenneth R. Mayer, "Going Alone: The Presidential Power of Unilateral Action," and Richard Pious, "Prerogative Power and Presidential Politics," both in *The Oxford Handbook of the American Presidency*, eds., George C. Edwards, III, and William G. Howell (New York: Oxford University Press, 2009); for a recent review specific to secrecy issues see Robert M. Pallitto and William G. Weaver, *Presidential Secrecy and the Law* (Baltimore, MD: Johns Hopkins University Press, 2007).

25  John Locke, *Second Treatise of Government,* ed. C. B. Macpherson (Indianapolis: Hackett, 1980 [1690]), 84. See also Michael A. Genovese, *Presidential Prerogative* (Stanford, CA: Stanford University Press, 2011).

26  Louis Koenig, *The Chief Executive*, 3rd ed. (New York: Harcourt Brace Jovanovich, 1975).

27  Again, what follows is much simplified. For more detail, and vigorous argument, see the essays in George C. Edwards, III, John H. Kessel, and Bert A. Rockman, eds., *Researching the Presidency: Vital Questions, New Approaches* (Pittsburgh: University of Pittsburgh Press, 1993), and more recently the various contributions to the "Symposium on the Future of Presidential Studies" in the December 2009 issue of *Presidential Studies Quarterly*.

28  Edward S. Corwin, *The President: Office and Powers* (New York: New York University Press, 1940). The last edition written entirely by Corwin appeared in 1957, though a revised and updated fifth edition was issued in 1984, twenty-one years after his death.

29  Clinton Rossiter, *The American Presidency* (New York: Harcourt Brace, 1956), 4, 62.

30  Neustadt, *Presidential Power*, xxi. Cites are to the 1990 edition of Neustadt's book, entitled *Presidential Power and the Modern Presidents* (New York: Free Press, 1990), which appends newer chapters to the 1960 text. The first edition was published by John Wiley & Sons.

31  Defined not as residents of Washington, but rather as anyone interested and potentially influential in the doings of the national government – these included academics, local politicians, and foreign governments.

32  Terry M. Moe, "Presidents, Institutions, and Theory," in *Researching the Presidency: Vital Questions, New Approaches*, eds., George C. Edwards, III, John H. Kessel, and Bert A. Rockman (Pittsburgh: University of Pittsburgh Press, 1993), 340.

33  For a spirited rebuttal, see Matthew J. Dickinson, "We All Want a Revolution: Neustadt, New Institutionalism, and the Future of Presidency Research," *Presidential Studies Quarterly* 39 (December 2009): 736–70.

34  See, e.g., James David Barber, *The Presidential Character* (Englewood Cliffs, NJ: Prentice-Hall, 1972).

35  Fred I. Greenstein, *The Presidential Difference*, 3rd ed. (Princeton, NJ: Princeton University Press, 2009).

36  George C. Edwards, III, John H. Kessel, and Bert A. Rockman, "Introduction," in *Researching the Presidency: Vital Questions, New Approaches*, eds., George C. Edwards, III, John H. Kessel, and Bert A. Rockman (Pittsburgh: University of Pittsburgh Press, 1993), 3.

37  Jones, *Separated System*, 1.

38  Gary King, "The Methodology of Presidential Research," in *Researching the Presidency: Vital Questions, New Approaches*, eds., George C. Edwards, III, John H. Kessel, and Bert A. Rockman (Pittsburgh: University of Pittsburgh Press, 1993), 406.

39  Moe, "Revolution in Presidency Studies."

40  To take just three examples: the assassination of American citizens acting with al-Qaeda in Yemen; the evasion of the War Powers Resolution in Libya; the use of the state secrets doctrine in fending off judicial inquiry.

41  The most influential work here is probably Skowronek, *Politics Presidents Make*; see also Skowronek and Matthew Glassman, eds., *Formative Acts: American Politics in the Making* (Philadelphia: University of Pennsylvania Press, 2008).

42  Andrew Rudalevige, *Managing the President's Program: Presidential Leadership and Legislative Policy Formulation* (Princeton, NJ: Princeton University Press, 2002).

43  Quoted in Rudalevige, *Managing*, 113.

44  Among others, see Jon Bond and Richard A. Fleisher, *The President in the Legislative Arena* (Chicago: University of Chicago Press, 1992); George C. Edwards, III, *At the Margins* (New Haven, CT: Yale University Press, 1989); Mark A. Peterson, *Legislating Together* (Cambridge, MA: Harvard University Press, 1990).

45  Rudalevige, *Managing*, 11.

46  These days the Public Papers are available on-line, via the Government Printing Office or The American Presidency Project at the University of California, Santa Barbara. See http://www.presidency.ucsb.edu/. John Woolley and Gerhard Peters deserve special commendation for their pioneering work in bringing presidential records of all stripes on-line. For an example of a coding program used successfully for analysis, see B. Dan Wood, *The Myth of Presidential Representation* (New York: Cambridge University Press, 2009).

47  See Rudalevige, *Managing*, 165–79.

48  See http://www.archives.gov and, for direct links to the presidential libraries, http://www.presidency.ucsb.edu/libraries.php.

49  See Rudalevige, *Managing*, 79, and 78–79, notes 56–59, for the archival references utilized.

50  Much more than you will want to know about probit may be found in Rudalevige, *Managing*, 99–109, or (for those who truly want to ingratiate themselves with their professor) Tim Liao, *Interpreting Probability Models* (Thousand Oaks, CA: Sage, 1994).

51  An "omnibus" package rolls several bills, sometimes substantively unrelated to one another, together into a single measure – making it hard to determine what a "yes" vote is really for. A unanimous consent agreement is a mechanism utilized in the Senate to limit debate and forestall a filibuster, rendering the vote on the measure itself something of an afterthought.

52  For a fuller discussion see Andrew Rudalevige, "The Executive Branch and the Legislative Process," in *The Executive Branch*, ed. Joel Aberbach and Mark A. Peterson (New York: Oxford University Press, 2005), 429–31.

53  The index ran 0–3, so if a president had perfect success in Congress, his or her score would be 3.00. The actual mean, between from 1949 and 1996, was 1.38.

54  The answer seems to be 'yes.' For a preliminary analysis, see Andrew Rudalevige and David E. Lewis, "Parsing the Politicized Presidency: Centralization and

Politicization as Presidential Strategies for Bureaucratic Control," presented at the Annual Meeting of the American Political Science Association, September 2005.

55  Note that this does not contain the text of classified orders, which are usually given an identifier that does not interrupt the numerical sequence of orders.

56  For a more detailed review, see Andrew Rudalevige, "Executive Orders and Presidential Unilateralism," *Presidential Studies Quarterly* 42 (March 2012): 138–60.

57  Terry M. Moe, "The Presidency and Bureaucracy: The Presidential Advantage," in *The Presidency and the Political System*, 4th ed., ed. Michael Nelson (Washington, DC: CQ Press, 1995), 417.

58  Graham Allison and Philip Zelikow, *Essence of Decision*, rev. 2nd ed. (New York: Longman, 1999); Hugh Heclo, *A Government of Strangers* (Washington, DC: Brookings Institution Press, 1977); Harold Seidman and Robert S. Gilmour, *Politics, Position, and Power*, 4th ed. (New York: Oxford University Press, 1986).

59  William Safire, *Before the Fall: An Inside View of the Pre-Watergate White House* (New York: Da Capo Press, 1975), 246–47.

60  See, respectively, Elizabeth Drew, *On the Edge: The Clinton Presidency* (New York: Touchstone, 1995), 43–47; Barton Gellman, *Angler: The Cheney Vice-Presidency* (New York: Penguin, 2008), Ch. 12.

61  The Clinton order was E.O. 13045, issued April 21, 1997. See Rudalevige, "Executive Orders and Presidential Unilateralism," 142–44 and 153–55.

62  Quoted in Andrew Rudalevige, "The Administrative Presidency and Bureaucratic Control," *Presidential Studies Quarterly* 39 (March 2009), 18.

63  Jones, *Presidency in a Separated System*, 1.

64  To take a semi-frivolous example from broader work by Charles Franklin, in 2006, 75% of Democrats, but only 45% of Republicans, thought the pump price of gasoline was "something a president can do a lot about." But in 2012, more than 60% of Republicans though this was true – and fewer than a third of Democrats. The only difference was, presumably, that partisan respondents wanted to blame, or absolve from blame, "their" president in each case. See http://pollsandvotes.com/PaV/2012/04/gas-prices-and-partisan-filters/ (accessed April 20, 2012.)

65  Justice Jackson, concurring opinion in *Youngstown Sheet and Tube v. Sawyer*, 343 U.S. 579 (1952).

# Chapter 4

# The Supreme Court and Political Regimes

## "Great Tides" in Politics and Law

*Cornell W. Clayton*

In theory, judges should be neutral arbiters of the law. However, many Americans might easily believe that judges are political when they make decisions. In this view, judges decide law based on ideological preferences and, indeed, much of political science research has demonstrated exactly this. This finding raises a troubling question about the rule of law: Can we have justice if interpreting the law depends on the ideological whims of individual judges? Cornell Clayton provides a conceptual framework to reconcile the two views about how the Supreme Court justices make decisions. Judging is a political process, but judges strive for norms of objectivity in deciding cases. We can understand this if we see the courts as shaped by the wider politics of an era—what he calls "regime politics". Rather than evaluate judges as if they are merely legislators, Clayton urges us to take seriously that judges seek objectivity, but that they unavoidably bring to the bench their experiences, which are shaped by the wider political environment. Clayton's research is a good example of using historical analysis to provide a broader and integrated view of political institutions in the United States. This approach tends to challenge the traditional 'behavioral' approach that reduces institutional outcomes to the sum of individual preferences.

In September 2005, a crowded Senate Caucus Room of the U.S. Capitol listened to John G. Roberts Jr. testify during his confirmation hearings to become the seventeenth Chief Justice of the United States Supreme Court. Roberts had earlier served as a partisan advocate in the administration of George H.W. Bush and he was widely viewed as a leading conservative judge on the court of appeals in the District of Columbia. Hoping to assuage concerns about his political views, Roberts explained that, if confirmed, he would have "no agenda" and no "political platform." Justices should be humble "servants of the law" he said, like "umpires" at a baseball game whose role is "calling balls and strikes and not to pitch or bat."[1]

Roberts' analogy to umpires is an iconic depiction portraying judges as neutral, apolitical oracles of the law. Today, the phrase "judges calling balls and strikes" receives more than 7 million hits from a Google search. Yet, this depiction flies in the face of much of what we know about judging and especially about the work of justices who serve on the Supreme Court. Indeed, it is common today for media accounts of the Court to describe justices as voting with liberal or conservative blocs and for judicial confirmation battles to be fought out largely on partisan lines.[2] In fact, just four years after Roberts promised to be a neutral servant of the law, he sat a few feet in front of Barack Obama during the President's 2010 state of union address. Obama blasted the Court for overturning a "century of law" in a case entitled *Citizen's United v. FCC*. The case, which struck down restrictions on corporate spending in political campaigns, was decided by a familiar vote; five conservative justices voted with the majority, the four more liberal justices dissented.[3] Roberts had written a concurring opinion in the case trying to reconcile his role as "umpire" with his vote to ignore a long line of legal precedent. He sat stoically through the president's speech but later complained about the Court's being criticized in such a political setting.[4]

The Court *is* a political institution, and the justices *are* political actors. Since the early days of the twentieth century, when legal realist debunked the idea that law and politics can be neatly separated, no serious student of American courts has believed that judges can serve as neutral oracles of the law. Judges in the United States are political actors because they are appointed through a highly political process and because it is impossible to interpret the law, especially constitutional law, without some reference to underlying political values. In fact, building on the insights of legal realism, political scientists have produced more than a half-century of empirical research predicting how judges will decide cases based on their personal political attitudes. To extend Roberts' analogy, judges might call balls and strikes, but what counts as the strike zone is a political choice that judges also make. The question is not *whether* judges are political actors but *how* they are political actors.

What explains the disparity between the highly political role of the Supreme Court and the persistence of the myth about Solomon-like, apolitical judges? And, if judging is just another political process, if judges decide cases in the same ways that, say, members of Congress make choices when legislating, what becomes of the ideal of the rule of law?

This chapter discusses efforts within political science to address these two interrelated questions by placing judicial decision making within the broader context of the electoral-political system or political regime. In contrast to prevailing political science models of Supreme Court behavior, which for most of the past fifty years have tended to treat the Court as little more than a collection of individuals pursuing their personal policy preferences, the "regime politics" approach seeks to explain how law and legal institutions are shaped by the interests and agendas of elected elites. The idea of "political regimes" refers to the notion that American political history can be thought of in terms of a series of political party and interest group coalitions or party systems that dominate electoral politics over extended periods (i.e., the New Deal Democratic regime dominated between the 1930s and 1970s or the New Right Republican regime predominated since 1980). The basic insight of this approach—that broad shifts in electoral politics will shape the work of the Supreme Court by changing the way judges and others think about the law and constitutional values—was captured nearly a century ago by Justice Benjamin Cardozo, who wrote that "the great tides and currents which engulf the rest of men, do not turn aside in their course, and pass the judges by."[5]

By exploring the various ways that law and legal institutions are constructed by politics in the elected branches, this research holds out the promise of better integrating the study of courts and judges into the mainstream of political analysis. Equally important, it also provides a way of thinking about the rule of law in a post–legal realist perspective and can explain how judging is both a political process while also remaining a commitment to the rule of law.

## The Supreme Court and the Legal Realist Legacy

Unlike organizations discussed in other chapters in this volume, the Supreme Court is both a legal and a political institution. It and its members are steeped in a profession that has its own sense of mission and purpose and whose norms differ from those that drive politics in the elected branches, administrative agencies, or elsewhere. Thus, it is important to begin by saying something about the legal profession and how it understands courts and judges before considering how political science has come to understand and study these subjects.

The philosophical realism of the early twentieth century profoundly influenced both the legal academy and the social sciences. In the legal academy, legal realists such as Oliver Wendell Holmes, Benjamin Cardozo, and Karl Lewellyn criticized formalist models of jurisprudence that had sought to distinguish law from politics. In the formalist view, politics was the process through which discretionary policy choices were made and codified into statutes, ordinances, constitutions, or other legal codes. The practice of law and judging, conversely, was viewed as a mechanistic practice through which law was discovered and applied to facts in cases. Judges did not *make* policy choices, they simply applied cannons of interpretation to *discover* the choices made by political actors and then applied those to facts in individual cases.

By contrast, the realists insisted that judging required resolving policy questions that the framers of the original law never considered or could even comprehend. Asking a judge to discover the choices made by the framers of the Fourth Amendment with regard to whether the police need a warrant before using electronic wiretaps or GPS tracking devices, for instance, missed the point of how judging actually works. Those who wrote and ratified the Fourth Amendment in 1789 could not have conceptualized, let alone decided the policy questions around, electronic surveillance that would emerge a century later. The realists understood that judges were forced to make such choices to decide cases; and the only way they could make those choices was in light of their own experiences and understanding of the times within which they lived. Holmes's famous statement that "(t)he life of the law has not been logic; it has been experience" reflected this view. Law required more than mastering certain cannons of interpretation; it required studying social, economic, and political history.[6] In other words, law was no longer an insular science but was intimately tied to politics and social history.

In undermining the autonomy of law, realism also led to the emergence of a new field within political science. What allowed political scientists to say something interesting about the law that could not be said more authoritatively by law professors was that the discussion at some level now took place on the terrain of politics, something over which political science presumably had unique insight. Early political scientists such as Charles Grove Haines, Robert Cushman, and Edward Corwin were all legal realists. Although they used the same methods of doctrinal and historical analysis employed by law professors of their day, their goal was to understand how judicial decisions were related to the political and social contexts that gave them meaning. No clearer statement of this view can be found than in the preface of one of the first political science textbooks in the field, Cushman's 1925 *Leading Constitutional Decisions*:

> The Supreme Court does not do its work in a vacuum. Its decisions on important constitutional questions can be understood in their full significance only when viewed against the background of history, politics, economics, and personality surrounding them and out of which they grow.

From the very outset, then, the subfield of public law adopted a realistic view of law that saw judicial decisions and political values as intimately connected. Law was an evolving set of professional norms and customs that was only *relatively independent* from the political and social forces within which it was embedded.

Yet if realism influenced both the legal academy and political science, it had different consequences for how the two came to teach and think about law and courts. Because the core function of law schools was to train legal practitioners, the legal academy was more impervious to the changing conception of law and its new linkage with politics. Indeed, the law school curriculum to this day continues to rely largely on traditional, formalist models to teach students how to practice law. Ideas about precedent, *stare decisis*, and cannons of textual construction continue to be the way most lawyers learn their craft and the way most judges describe what they do. Typical of this perspective is Justice Scalia's opinion in *American Trucking Assns v. Smith* (1990), wherein he objects to any view of judicial "decisions as creating the law, as opposed to declaring what the law already is. Such a view is contrary to that understanding of the 'judicial power' ... which is not only the common and traditional one, but which is the only one that can justify courts." When the Court declares a statute unconstitutional, Scalia proclaimed, it does "not to announce that we forbid it, but that the *Constitution* forbids it."[7]

Elite academic lawyers and sophisticated jurists like Justice Scalia recognize that realism had long ago undermined such formalist theories of jurisprudence, and raised important questions about judicial review and the very idea of the rule of law. Indeed, contemporary legal theorists have created a cottage industry debating how to limit the influence of politics over the law in a post-realist world.[8] That debate includes books with evocative titles such as Alexander Bickel's *The Least Dangerous Branch: The Supreme Court at the Bar of Politics* and Robert Bork's *The Tempting of America: The Political Seduction of Law*. It also included more radical post-realist critiques of the law by scholars associated with critical legal studies, law and economics, feminist jurisprudence, and other movements, arguing against the possibility of judging as anything other than the exercise of political power.[9]

Nevertheless, legal practitioners such as Scalia continue to insist that the practice of the law can be separated from debates surrounding its theoretical conceptualization. Indeed, such debates, though central to elite legal academic scholarship, are remarkably compartmentalized within the legal academy and are usually confined to an occasional course on jurisprudence or legal theory, but they remain curiously detached from the processes of professionalization and practice of the legal craft.[10] This schizophrenia between academic theories of law and the training of legal practitioners is not difficult to understand: If most lawyers and judges think of their craft in terms of traditional or formalist approaches, then it would make little sense for law schools to change the way they educate lawyers.

In fact, the traditional legal model accurately describes most of what takes place in the practitioner community. Realism suggested that the law—as a system of professional norms about precedent and textual interpretation—became indeterminate and a part of politics only at some level. Most cases in the judicial system are easily resolvable by appealing to traditional or agreed-upon legal criteria. It is only in "hard cases," where the agreed-upon legal criteria do not provide clear answers, that judges must make essentially political choices. Such cases are relatively rare in trial courts and other lower courts but by design they make up the majority of cases in the U.S. Supreme Court. Since the vast majority of cases in the judicial system are resolved by appeal to traditional legal criteria and the vast majority of judges and lawyers work in this ordinary legal world, it makes sense that law schools should continue to train and professionalize lawyers that way.

Political science, by contrast, was never interested in the practice of law as such but rather in how it becomes part of politics at some level. In other words, political scientists were interested in the very small number of cases, usually in the Supreme Court, where traditional legal criteria failed to generate clear answers and judicial discretion came to the fore. Indeed, early political science scholarship about law and courts differed from law school scholarship not in its methods of research but rather in the scope or focus of study. Law schools taught the entire practice of law, both private law (i.e., torts, contracts, family law) and public law (administrative law, constitutional law, etc.), whereas political science was interested mainly in a very limited area of judicial decision making, usually in courts of last resort, where political choice was required. And though some legal academics shared this research interest, it was never at the core of the legal academy or central to understanding the practice of law as a profession.

## Supreme Court Behavior and Judicial Attitudes

A watershed in studying law and courts in political science came with the behavioral revolution that swept across the social sciences in the mid–twentieth century. In contrast to earlier political science, behavioralists emphasized positivist (largely quantitative) methods of inquiry over historical and interpretive ones, and they shifted the focus of investigation away from the institutions of government toward a focus on the individual-level behavior of political actors. The seminal work reflecting this new approach was C. Herman Pritchett's *The Roosevelt Court*, published in 1948.[11] Adopting the realist's insight that Supreme Court justices make political choices, Pritchett ignored the Court's institutional product—its written opinions—and focused instead on the individual voting patterns of the justices, analyzing their votes in cases according to whether they supported liberal or conservative policy outcomes. His research demonstrated that the justices tended to form voting blocs on the Court, with some justices consistently voting for liberal policy outcomes while others voted conservatively. As the members of the Court disagreed with one another systematically over time, Pritchett concluded that the justices were basing their decisions on their *ideological attitudes* or policy preferences rather than on the law or legal norms.

Following Pritchett's lead, political scientists over the next fifty years developed increasingly sophisticated ways to measure the influence of the justices' attitudinal preferences over the Court's decisions. Methodological techniques such as Guttman scaling and factor analysis were used to show that Supreme Court voting could be ideologically scaled and that individual justices were ideologically consistent in their voting behavior (at least within certain areas of the law such as civil liberties cases or economic regulatory cases).[12] The mature fruits of this "attitudinal" approach came in the 1993 publication of Jeff Segal and Harold Spaeth's *The Supreme Court and the Attitudinal Model*. Analyzing Court decisions during a thirty-year period, the authors found that the justices' voting patterns remained relatively consistent over time and correspond closely to their *a priori* policy preferences. In short, Justice "Rehnquist vote(d) the way he (did) because he (was) extremely conservative; Marshall vote(d) the way he (did) because he (was) extremely liberal," and neither voted on the basis of legal criteria.[13] Attitudinal scholarship since has demonstrated convincingly that the relationship between the justices' ideology at the time of their appointment, and their decision making behavior while on the Court, is very strong.[14]

Segal and Spaeth were quick to note that the *attitudinal model* explained Supreme Court behavior because the Court is a unique institution with distinctive features not shared by most other courts. The justices enjoy life tenure and operate in a system that effectively insulates them from removal or retaliation for unpopular decisions. They also sit at the top of a judicial hierarchy that weeds out easy cases and leaves them to decide the "hard cases" where judicial discretion, and hence ideology, play a larger role. Finally, the justices also know that they are free from being overturned by a higher court. Thus, in contrast to other judges, Supreme Court justices were free to vote according to their sincere policy preferences and were unconstrained by law or other institutional limitations on their power.

As the standard approach for studying Supreme Court behavior, the attitudinal model also spawned a secondary line of research adopting a *strategic choice approach*. Based on assumptions that the justices want to maximize their individual policy preferences but also must interact with other power holders to do so, scholars using this approach focus on the strategic choices that justices must make. The seminal work adopting this approach was Walter Murphy's *The Elements of Judicial Strategy*, first published in 1964.[15] Murphy argued that the justices make strategic calculations about the views of other actors, both on and off the Court, who were in a position to impede or advance their policy goals. Building on that insight, a theoretically sophisticated literature about strategic judicial behavior has emerged. Some scholars who adopt this approach focus on whether the justices' decision-making behavior is influenced by the views of members of Congress, presidents, or other elected officials. These so-called separation-of-powers models posit that the justices are sometimes prevented from voting their sincere policy preferences out of a fear that Congress or the executive will override their decisions or refuse to enforce them. Other scholars adopting the strategic approach focus on the dynamics of decision making inside the Court. These "internal strategic approach" scholars examine how the collegial nature of the Court keeps justices from voting their sincere policy preferences—for instance, exploring how justices interact with one another to attract a majority or to avoid dissenting opinions.[16]

Attitudinal and strategic choice scholarship has gone a long way toward creating a more systematic understanding of Supreme Court behavior. It allows scholars and commentators to speak authoritatively about voting blocs on the Court and to describe the justices and their decisions as ideologically conservative or liberal. Nevertheless, this research has important limitations. First, the attitudinal model is specific to the unique institutional features of the U.S. Supreme Court and it is not well adapted to study other courts. Lower court judges, for instance, know that their decisions will be reversed by higher courts if they stray too far from established precedent or norms. Similarly, in many countries, courts issue *per curiam* or unsigned opinions for the entire court, in which the votes and views of individual judges are not revealed. Because the attitudinal model focuses on the differences in the voting behavior of individual judges, it can offer us little about the behavior of such courts. Moreover, even in the Supreme Court, such models are useful only for some cases. For example, nearly one-third of the Court's decisions each year are decided unanimously, and the attitudinal model once again has nothing to say about these cases because there are no differences in individual votes to observe. Moreover, in many of the remaining cases decided by the Supreme Court, the questions presented involve areas of law, such as contract disputes, patent cases, or technical procedure questions, that cannot be readily defined as having either "liberal" or "conservative" outcomes. It is difficult to know, for example, whether upholding the right to patent a newly isolated human gene is either politically conservative or liberal.

The most important problem with attitudinal and strategic approaches of Supreme Court behavior however is the core assumptions made about judicial motivations. These models assume that the justices are motivated by personal policy preferences in cases rather than by law or legal norms. Such an assumption flies in the face not only of how judges and lawyers are professionalized but also how they describe and explain what they do. It also ignores much of the justices' observed behavior. Justices do not simply vote in cases, they write lengthy opinions that explain and justify their decisions in terms of law and prevailing professional norms. Indeed, justices often agree about the outcome of a case but disagree about the appropriate interpretation of law or legal doctrine and will write lengthy concurring opinions explaining why. On average, there is one or more concurring opinion written in each case decided by the Court. In short, justices act as if the law matters a great deal. If attitudinalist assumptions are correct, these judges are either engaged in an elaborate charade or these sophisticated and highly trained professionals are self-deluded.[17] Moreover, if justices simply seek to advance their policy preferences when deciding cases, then the rule of law is also a deception, a chimera used to mask the justices' exercise of brute power when advancing their own personal predilections.

There are many reasons to think that attitudinal assumptions about judicial motivation are wrong. Not only is there a difference between the practice of law and its academic characterizations but there is also no reason to believe that judicial attitudes are uni-dimensional or focus solely on policy outcomes. Indeed, unlike the early legal realists who argued that judicial attitudes about law and politics were intertwined and inseparable, attitudinal, and strategic models of Supreme Court behavior try to separate them and claim that only politics motivates the justices' behavior. In short, such models make a leap from the empirical evidence that the justices vote in ideologically consistent ways to an unfounded conclusion that they do so only because of their policy preferences. That conclusion is neither compelled by the evidence nor plausible in light of the professional and institutional milieu in which the justices are immersed.[18]

This latter point reflects a broader critique of behavioralism made by "new institutional" scholars.[19] According to this critique, behavioralism misconceptualizes institutions as mere shells or arenas within which individual behavior takes place. New institutionalists argue that institutions are better thought of in terms of the organizational "missions" or shared normative purposes and goals around which they are organized rather than as collections of autonomous individuals. Courts, for example, are not simply buildings or physical places (courts can meet anywhere). A court is defined by ideas about what judges ought to do.[20] Just as a university is not really characterized by the physical campus it occupies, but by the shared understanding of what professors and students do in that space, the Supreme Court is not really constituted by the neo-classical building that sits across from the U.S. Capitol but by the shared understanding of what the justices are supposed to do there. In this sense, institutional identities generate their own values, preferences, and senses of duty, and the individuals within them. Just as university professors are motivated to behave as good educators, judges are motivated to behave as good jurists. If this is true, it is less likely that Supreme Court justices see themselves as engaged in the game of advancing their policy preferences as much as they see themselves acting as stewards of the Court's "institutional mission" and promoting the rule of law. It would be odd, indeed, if the justices—who are trained in the legal profession, read legal briefs, listen to legal arguments, write lengthy legal opinions, and go through all the motions required of the judicial vocation—simply turned around and decided cases based on which policy outcome they personally preferred.

Why does it matter what the justices *think* (as opposed to what their observable actions or votes are)? The question of motivations is critical not just for adequately explaining the meaning of judicial behavior but also for assessing normative questions about the possibility of the rule of law in American democracy. In the post-realist era, the rule of law cannot be defined in terms of whether justices decide cases correctly (in hard cases there are no "correct" answers to be had). Instead, at the level of the Supreme Court, the rule of law turns on what the justices *believe* they do when they decide cases. If the law cannot be defined as a fixed set of rules that produce correct answers in cases—but rather is seen as a historically evolving set of professional practices and norms—the rule of law is simply when judges adhere to their best interpretation of those norms and practices irrespective of the outcomes produced. In other words, in the post-realist world, the rule of law is a frame of mind rather than a set of correct principles or outcomes in cases.[21]

Although there is no reason to take issue with the observation that the behavior of judges is shaped by their attitudes, understanding their attitudes and motivations requires a more complete understanding of the professional and institutional context of that behavior, not just a count of their votes. It requires attention to how they explain their decisions in written opinions and to the shifting professional norms and practices that define the legal profession and the Court's institutional role over time. Important for political scientists, it requires attention to the various political forces that shape these contexts. Elected political elites appoint justices to the Court, control its jurisdiction and authority, shape its agenda, enforce its decisions, and influence the broader legal profession in a myriad of ways. These political elites have their own agendas and views about law and legal institutions that they also seek to advance. Understanding how the Court is both shaped by these, and in turn can influence such political forces is thus the focus of a growing body of research in political science that adopts the regime-politics approach.

## The Supreme Court and Political Regimes

The regime-politics approach seeks to situate the Supreme Court within the broader political system to understand how electoral politics structures judicial attitudes about law and legal institutions. It begins with two basic observations. First, judges and justices behave as if the law and professional legal norms matter a great deal when deciding cases. They are professionalized into the practice of law and the judicial role, they write lengthy opinions explaining the legal rationales for their decisions, and their solicitude to professional norms explains why the vast majority of cases in the judicial system (including more than one-third of cases before the Supreme Court cases decided unanimously) are easily decided in the same way by judges who hold very different ideological views. Second, commonly held views about the law, the legal profession, and the judicial role have changed over time as a result of broad shifts in electoral politics. This was the key insight of the legal realists—that the law (as a set of professional practices) was contingent on the same forces shaping the nation's political life.

The political regime approach also draws upon political science research about American electoral history, especially scholarship that has identified broad periods of electoral change marked by the rise and fall of "party systems" or "electoral regimes." Electoral regimes, such as the Jacksonian party system that existed from the 1820s though the Civil War or the New Deal Democratic regime that was in place from the 1930s though 1970s, consist of rival coalitions of political parties and groups with more or less coherent governing philosophies and policy agendas dominating electoral politics for a generation or more at a time. The political agendas and governing philosophies of these partisan regimes will invariably include views about constitutional values and about specific legal and judicial doctrines.

Consider New Deal Democrats who came into office in the 1930s who held views about the federal government's constitutional authority to regulate the economy. Their views differed substantially from both Republican and Democratic political elites before them, and they also differed from the views held by justices on the Court who had been appointed by those earlier elites. When early New Deal legislation was struck down by the Court as violating existing legal doctrines restricting federal power, New Deal Democrats also advanced new doctrines and views about judicial restraint and deference to legislative policymaking. These views and understandings about the Constitution and the role of judges eventually came to dominate the courts and the legal system as a result of processes of judicial appointment, government and interest group litigation, and other forms of legal mobilization by political leaders. For example, in *Wickard v. Filburn* (1942), the Court upheld Congress's authority to regulate how much wheat a farmer could grow even though the wheat was for the farmer's personal use and not sold in interstate commerce. This decision required the Court to overturn established doctrines that previously limited federal regulatory power to products that were sold in interstate commerce. What motivated the justices in this case to do so? Was it because they preferred higher wheat prices or less liberty for farmers, or simply wanted to support the president's policies? More likely it was a sincere belief that the Constitution, properly understood, allowed Congress to regulate the interstate market for wheat and that it was not the proper role of the Court to second-guess Congress's choice of how. In fact, many of the justices who heard that case were appointed by President Roosevelt because they held that view of the law. Previous justices would have disagreed with that interpretation of the Constitution. Subsequent justices appointed by New Right Republican presidents after 1980 may also disagree with this view of the Constitution.[22] However, the fact that judicial attitudes about the law change over time does not lead to the conclusion that the justices vote simply on the basis of policy preferences; it means only that judicial attitudes about the law are themselves politically constructed. Thus, the central insight of the regime-politics approach is that the law and politics are inseparable in the judicial mind and both are shaped by the broader political forces that also shape electoral institutions.

Once we recognize the inseparability of law from politics, it becomes clear that attitudinal analyses of judicial behavior had always assumed but just never made explicit a political regimes framework all along. Judicial ideology is not a free-standing concept. Labels such as "liberal" or "conservative" can derive meaning only from the political contexts in which they are used. For example, consider attitudinal scholarship examining civil liberties cases which has in the past coded decisions favoring an individual rights claim as "liberal" and decisions upholding the government's regulation as "conservative." In the context of the New Deal political regime this coding scheme may have made sense, but how should the Court's decision in the *Citizen's United* case (discussed at the beginning of this chapter) be coded? Surely it would be wrong to describe this as a liberal decision, even though it struck-down a government regulation and upheld a claim to free speech rights? The only way to code this decision as having anything meaningful to say about political ideology is to contextualize it within the politics of the current New Right regime, in which case it would be coded as a "conservative" outcome.

The primary goal of the regime-politics approach is, thus, to understand how the rise and fall of electoral-political regimes influence Supreme Court behavior, both by shaping the ideological terrain of politics and by shaping views about law and judicial institutions. Figure 4.1 depicts a simple model of how the approach conceptualizes the relationship between the formation of a regime's values and the decision-making behavior of the Supreme Court. Important is that the model depicts a feedback loop, recognizing that Court decisions can also have unexpected consequences for political mobilizations and the reorganization of electoral politics.

The idea that the Supreme Court's behavior is tied to electoral politics is not new. Early public law scholars recognized how political developments influenced the Court and shaped judicial doctrines. Like the legal academics of their day, however, they relied upon doctrinal analysis, interpretive history, and other traditional methods of legal scholarship. The first political scientist to bring the more rigorous empirical methods of modern social sciences to bear on these relationships was Yale political scientist Robert Dahl. In a path-breaking study in 1957, Dahl analyzed cases in which the Court struck down federal statutes, and found that the Court rarely invalidated laws favored by

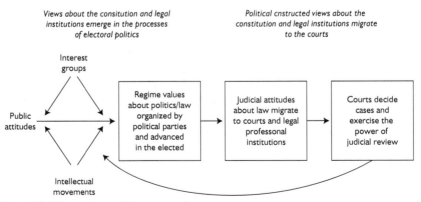

*Figure 4.1* The regime politics approach

current governing majorities. In nearly every case, he found that the law struck down by the Court had either been passed during a previous electoral regime or was unimportant to current elected elites. Dahl's explanation was simple: Since justices are appointed by party leaders to the Court, and party leaders tend to appoint individuals who share their general attitudes and views, the Court would never be out of step very long with the prevailing views and values that dominate the elected branches. Except for "short-lived transitional periods," the Court "is inevitably a part of the dominant national alliance… (and) supports the major policies of the alliance."[23]

Dahl's insight led to a surge of research focusing on the Court's role relative to "critical elections" and major party realignments in American history. Much of this first wave of regime-politics research was consistent with attitudinalist assumptions of Supreme Court behavior. In fact, much of this work characterized the justices as acting as simple *agents* of the policy preferences of the elected elites who appointed them.[24] More recent regime politics research however adopts the insights of new institutionalism, which takes more seriously the role of legal norms and professional role obligations in shaping judicial motivations. Thus, this newer research tends to explore more seriously the role of electoral politics in shaping conceptions about the law itself and also the various ways that the Court might interact with the electoral regime other than as an agent of its policy agenda.[25]

Scholars adopting this approach often focus on the legal views and constitutional values held by political elites and how they seek to advance these through strategies of judicial selection, litigation, and public persuasion or by empowering and disempowering courts. For example, Lucas Powe's award-winning study of the *Warren Court and American Politics* demonstrated how the justices of the Warren Court worked in concert with Great Society liberals to advance a progressive view of the law greatly expanding federal protection of civil liberties and rights.[26] Howard Gillman similarly demonstrated how the post-Reconstruction era Republican Party's policy agenda required a more active role for a judiciary to promote economic nationalism, so they empowered federal courts through such things as the Judiciary Act of 1875, which expanded federal jurisdiction over economic activity.[27]

A key insight emerging from the regime-politics research is that far from begrudging the Court's exercise of judicial review, elected elites often welcome it and channel certain kinds of political disputes into courts in order to build or maintain their electoral coalitions. Mark Graber's work demonstrating what he called the "nonmajoritarian difficulty," for example, demonstrated how governing political elites welcomed judicial intervention into slavery politics in the mid–nineteenth century, antitrust policy at the turn of the twentieth century, and abortion politics in the early 1970s, all in efforts to avoid confronting divisions within their own electoral coalitions.[28] Kevin McMahon's study of Franklin Roosevelt shows how the president set out to reform race relations using a judicial strategy rather than a legislative one, both out of a fear of alienating southern Democratic support for the New Deal but also in an effort to reform the Democratic Party.[29] Similarly, Keith Whittington's *The Political Foundations of Judicial Supremacy: The Presidency, the Supreme Court, and Constitutional Leadership in U.S. History*, persuasively shows how past presidents of all political parties utilized judicial power to advance their policy agenda and overcome blockages in legislative politics, manage ideological cleavages in their electoral coalitions, or to entrench policies that were becoming electorally vulnerable.[30]

Though the regime-politics approach recognizes that judicial attitudes about law and the role of courts are politically constructed, it also recognizes that such attitudes do not simply mirror partisan policy preferences. For example, justices who share the New Right Republican Party's commitment to constitutional federalism and limited federal regulatory authority may vote to invalidate specific federal statutes, such as the Religious Freedoms Restoration Act of 1993, which the Republican Party supported as a matter of policy.[31] In other words, judicial attitudes about law and constitutional principles, though politically constructed and generally in sync with the regime's governing philosophy, are different from the regime's specific policy preferences. Moreover, because justices are influenced by their institutional identities as members of a legal profession, one would expect them to be more resistant to abrupt changes in the law than their fellow partisans in the elected branches and more sensitive to protecting judicial prerogatives and institutional powers. Thomas Keck's book, *The Most Activist Court in History: The Road to Modern Judicial Conservatism*, for example, demonstrates that the Rehnquist Court's high level of activism was the result of the combination of the justices' solicitude to judicial prerogatives, their embrace of new conservative economic rights favored by New Right Republicans, and their hesitancy to abandon existing Supreme Court doctrines that had established liberal social rights in an earlier period.[32]

In previous work, Mitch Pickerill and I have explored the various ways that the Court interacts with electoral politics by focusing specifically on the rise of the New Right Republican regime since the 1960s and its construction of conservative legal and constitutional values during this period. In addition to its effort to advance broad conservative constitutional views such as constitutional originalism, we trace the Republican Party's development and advancement of specific legal doctrines that subsequently shaped the Court's decision making. For instance, we have shown how the Republican Party's commitment to federalism and devolution of federal authority emerged first in presidential platforms, Justice Department litigation policies, and in Republican judicial appointment strategies beginning in the 1960s, prefiguring the new federalism jurisprudence that emerged in Court decisions in the early 1990s.[33] Similarly, we traced the Republican Party's use of criminal justice as a political wedge issue in electoral politics beginning in the 1960s, and how the Party's views regarding the rights of the accused and police power eventually migrated to the Court in the late 1980s and 1990s.[34] Our work also seeks to explain how the Court's decisions can in turn influence electoral politics in unexpected ways. For example, the Court's embrace of New Deal views about individual rights in church-state relations and the right to privacy helped to mobilize evangelical conservatives and Catholic voters, both of which became important parts of the New Right electoral coalition that supplanted it.[35]

By taking the Court's various contexts more seriously, the regime-politics approach allows a more complete picture of the justices' voting behavior and their motivations. This in turn permits scholars to address the normative questions surrounding the rule of law. Indeed, contrary to the attitudinalist view, a shift in the Court's decision-making behavior based on the politics of appointment does not necessarily call into question the rule of law or the commitment to decide cases on the basis of legal criteria. We should expect justices appointed by an emerging electoral regime to reflect that regime's constitutional values and legal views and decide cases differently than their predecessors. In other words, we should expect John Roberts in 2005 to hold different views about the Constitution, the law, and the role courts than did his predecessor, Earl Warren, in the 1950s. The critical question for assessing rule of law is not whether legal change occurs on the Court, or whether that change is related to politics in the elected branches, but rather whether individual justices consistently apply the principles and professional norms they embrace and profess. In this sense, the legal and constitutional views and values of the dominant political regime, serves as the interpretive framework within which judicial behavior and motivations can be understood and critiqued.

## Conclusion: Some Thoughts on Future Study of the Supreme Court

Cardozo's statement that judges are influenced by the "great tides and currents that engulf the rest of men" reflected his recognition that the judicial mind is constituted by the very same forces that shape electoral politics. The regime-politics approach is heir to this legal realist tradition. Unlike attitudinal or strategic models of Supreme Court behavior, it assumes that legal and political values are intertwined and inseparable. However, it also draws upon recent political science efforts to model Supreme Court behavior by adopting more rigorous empirical methods and the insights from political science scholarship about electoral politics.

The approach, however, is not without critics. For example, Thomas Keck studied the Court's decision making over a twenty-five-year period and found only mixed support for Dahl's argument that the Court rarely strikes down federal laws favored by current governing majorities.[36] Indeed, Keck and others are correct to argue that much of the regime-politics literature has focused too heavily on the role of the courts as *agents* of regime values and not enough on the other roles courts play relative to the agendas of political elites. Future research for example should do more to explain not only how the Court advances the policy agenda of the elected elites but also how its role may be complicated by divisions within the governing coalition, how it sometimes acts to entrench previous regime values, or protect its own institutional prerogatives.

A second criticism of the regime-politics approach concerns whether it is able to produce falsifiable hypothesis and predictive models of judicial behavior similar to those produced by attitudinal or strategic approaches. In other words, does it meet rigorous "scientific" standards for inquiry? After all, if legal and professional norms change over time, and those norms may or may not reflect specific policy preferences of the regime, how can we draw any inferences about judicial motivation? There is a suspicion that the Court's behavior can always be interpreted as reflecting regime politics whatever decisions it reaches. Here, too, future research must do more to develop rigorous ways to map the regime's legal views and positions. For example, this can be done by systematically analyzing presidential electoral platforms, executive branch litigation positions, or partisan debates during Senate confirmation hearings through content analysis. Scholars using the approach will also have to think about how to better measure judicial adherence to a more sophisticated version of the "legal model," one that recognizes that legal and professional commitments evolve with emerging and declining partisan regimes. One promising way to do this is to employ new computer-aided technologies to systematically analyze the content of judicial opinions. Another may be to focus attention on what Mark Richards and Burt Kritzer have called "jurisprudential regimes" in Supreme Court decision making, which seek to show how discrete doctrinal changes structure the justices' voting behavior.[37]

A more complete answer to this criticism, however, will lead to deeper questions about the philosophy of social science and whether the goal of social scientific inquiry is to explain the meaning of human behavior or simply to predict it. Such questions are beyond the scope of this chapter, but, without engaging such debates, it is not hard to understand the advantages of the regime-politics approach over alternatives to studying the Supreme Court. Not only does the regime-politics approach allow scholars to more fully integrate the study of courts into the study of other political institutions and the political system generally, it is an approach that, unlike the attitudinal or strategic models, can explain behavior in other courts as readily as it can the Supreme Court. Though the Supreme Court may be at the epicenter of politically constituted shifts in law and legal norms, those shifts affect all courts and legal practitioners.

The regime-politics approach also allows scholars to bridge the divide between political science research that has focused on empirical aspects of judicial behavior with legal academic research that has tended to focus on the development of legal doctrines and professional norms. Surely common sense should tell us that judges, steeped in a profession with its own institutional identities and commitments, will behave as if these mattered (rather than assume that judges are duplicitous or self-deluded when explaining their own behavior). Recognizing that judicial motivation may be grounded in a judge's commitment to legal and professional norms, even when those norms have been politically constructed and reconstructed over time, also allows political science to take seriously the idea of rule of law in a post-realist age. Do judges *believe* they are adhering to the best understanding of constitutional and legal values when they decide cases? If so, regardless of *how* they decide cases, there is reason to retain faith in the idea of rule of law even as a courts' interpretations of law changes over time as a result of politics. This in turn, allows political scientists to tie empirical study of judicial behavior back to the central normative concern regarding the role of the courts in American politics.

When Chief Justice Roberts characterized judges as umpires enforcing the legal rules of the game, he was simply suggesting that some ways of thinking about the law and the Constitution are more consistent with his particular professional understandings and legal views. The fact that political science seeks to explain how those were politically constructed by the same force that drive electoral politics simply recognizes that the great tides that engulf the rest of men do not turn aside and pass the judges by.

## Notes

1 Linda Greenhouse, "An Opening Performance Worthy of an Experienced Lawyer," *The New York Times*, September 13, 2005, accessed February 12, 2012, http://www. nytimes.com/2005/09/13/politics/politicsspecial1/13roberts.html.
2 Roberts was confirmed by the full Senate on September 29, by a margin of 78–22. All Republicans and one Independent voted for Roberts; but half of Democrats voted against confirmation, splitting their vote evenly 22–22.
3 Alan Silverleib, "Gloves come off after Obama rips Supreme Court ruling". *CNN.com*, January 28, 2010, accessed April 3, 2012, http://www.cnn.com/2010/ POLITICS/01/28/alito.obama.sotu/index.html?hpt=Sbin.
4 Jay Reeves, "John Roberts: Scene at State of the Union was 'Very Troubling," *Huffington Post*, March 9, 2010, accessed April 10, 2012, http://www.huffingtonpost. com/2010/03/09/john-roberts-scene-at-oba_n_492444.html.
5 Benjamin Cardozo, *The Nature of the Judicial Process* (New Haven: Yale University Press, 1921), 168.
6 Oliver Wendell Holmes, *The Common Law* (Boston: Little Brown, and Company, 1881), I.
7 *American Trucking Assns v. Smith*, 110 L. Ed 2d 148, at 174.
8 Alexander Bickel, *The Least Dangerous Branch: The Supreme Court at the Bar of Politics* (New York: Bobbs-Merrill, 1962); John Hart Ely, *Democracy and Distrust: A Theory of Judicial Review* (Cambridge: Harvard University Press, 1980); Robert Bork, *The Tempting of America: The Political Seduction of Law* (New York: Touchstone, 1990); Ronald Dworkin, *A Matter of Principle* (Oxford: Oxford University Press, 1985).

9   For a general discussion of this view see Michael Louis Seidman and Mark V. Tushnet, *Remnants of Belief: Contemporary Constitutional Issues* (Oxford: Oxford University Press, 1996).

10   See Richard Posner, "The Decline of Law as an Autonomous Discipline: 1962–1987," *Harvard Law Review 100* (1987): 761–80; Posner, *The Problems of Jurisprudence* (Cambridge: Harvard University Press, 1990).

11   C. Herman Pritchett, *The Roosevelt Court* (New York: Macmillan, 1948).

12   Examples of this kind of work include Glendon Schubert, *Judicial Decision-Making* (New York: Free Press, 1964); David W. Rohde and Harold J. Spaeth, *The Supreme Court* (San Francisco: W.H. Freeman, 1976).

13   Jeffrey A. Segal and Harold J. Spaeth, *The Supreme Court and the Attitudinal Model* (Cambridge University Press, 1993), 65.

14   For an overview of attitudinal research see Jeffrey A. Segal, "Judicial Behavior" in *The Oxford Handbook of Law and Politics*, eds., Keith E. Whitington, R. Daniel Kelemen, and Gregory A. Caldeira (Oxford: Oxford University Press, 2008), 19–33.

15   Walter F. Murphy, *Elements of Judicial Strategy* (Chicago: University of Chicago Press, 1964).

16   For an overview of both strands of research adopting the strategic approach see Pablo T. Spiller and Rafael Geley, "Strategic Judicial Decision-making," in Whittington, Kelemen and Caldiera, *Handbook of Law and Politics*, 34–45.

17   Indeed scholars in both political science and the legal academy have asserted that the justices must be acting in a "disingenuous" or "self-deceptive" if they say legal institutions and professional norms shape their behavior. See, for example, Richard A. Posner, *The Federal Courts* (Cambridge: Harvard University Press, 1985; Segal and Spaeth, *The Attitudinal Model*.

18   For a general discussion of this see Cornell W. Clayton, "The Supreme Court and Political Jurisprudence: New and Old Instituitonalisms" in *Supreme Court Decision-Making: New Instituitonalist Approaches*, eds., Cornell W. Clayton and Howard Gillman (Chicago: University of Chicago Press, 1999); and Howard Gillman, "What's Law Got to do with it? Judicial Behavioralists Test the 'Legal Model' of Judicial Decision Making," *Law and Social Inquiry* 26 (2001): 465.

19   For an overview of the new institutionalist approaches to the courts see Rogers Smith, *Historical Institutionalism and the Study of the Law*, in Whittington, Kellmen and Caldeira, *Oxford Handbook of Law and Politics*, 47–59. See also Clayton and Gillman, *Supreme Court Decision-Making*; Howard Gillman and Cornell W. Clayton, eds., *The Supreme Court in American Politics: New Institutionalist Interpretations* (Lawrence, Kansas: University of Kansas Press, 1999).

20   See Howard Gillman, "The Court as an Idea, Not a Building (or a Game): Interpretive Instituitonalism and the Analysis of Supreme Court Decision-Making," in Clayton and Gillman, *Supreme Court Decision-Making*, 65–90.

21   See Gillman, "What's Law Got to do with it?"

22   At the time of this writing the Court is considering a challenge to the Affordable Care Act (or HR 3962) of 2009. The act, which reforms the U.S. healthcare system, was opposed by Republicans in Congress and challenged by a coalition of Republican state attorneys general who argued that the law exceeds Congress' authority under the interstate commerce clause.

23   Robert Dahl, "Decision-Making in a Democracy: the Supreme Court as a National Policy-Maker," *Journal of Public Law* 6 (1957): 291–93.

24   See for example, Richard Funston, "The Supreme Court and Critical Elections," *American Political Science Review* 69 (1975): 795–811; Martin Shapiro, *Law and Politics in the Supreme Court: New Approaches to Political Jurisprudence* (New York:

Free Press, 1964); David Adamany, "The Supreme Court's Role in Critical Elections," in Richard J. Trilling, ed., *Realignment in American Politics* (Austin: University of Texas Press, 1980).

25 See Cornell Clayton and David D. May, "The New Institutionalism and Supreme Court Decision Making: Toward a Political Regimes Approach, *Polity* 32 (1999): 233–52. For a more general overview of this second wave of work see Gillman, "Courts and the Politics of Partisan Coalitions," in Whittington, Kelemen and Caldiera, *Handbook of Law and Politics*, 644–662.

26 Lucas A. Powe, Jr., *The Warren Court and American Politics* (Cambridge, Mass: Belknap, 2001).

27 Howard Gillman, "How Political Parties Can Use Court to Advance Their Agendas: Federal Court in the United States 1875–1891," *American Political Science Review* 96: (2002): 511–524.

28 Mark A. Graber, "The Non-Majoritarian Difficulty: Legislative Deference to the Judiciary," *Studies in American Political Development* 7 (1993): 35–73.

29 Kevin McMahon, *Reconsidering Roosevelt on Race: How the Presidency Paved the Road to Brown* (Chicago: University of Chicago Press, 2003).

30 Keith Whittington, *The Political Foundations of Judicial Supremacy: The Presidency, the Supreme Court, and Constitutional Leadership in U.S. History* (Princeton: Princeton University Press, 2007).

31 See *City of Bourne v. Flores*, 521 U.S. 507 (1997).

32 Thomas Keck, *The Most Activist Supreme Court in History: The Road to Modern Constitutional Conservatism* (Chicago: University of Chicago Press, 2004).

33 J. Mitchell Pickerill and Cornell W. Clayton, "The Rehnquist Court and the Political Dynamics of Federalism" *Perspectives on Politics* 2 (2004): 233–48.

34 Cornell W. Clayton and J. Mitchell Pickerill, "The Politics of Criminal Justice: How the New Right Regime Shaped the Rehnquist Court's Criminal Justice Jurisprudence," *Georgetown Law Journal* 94 (2006): 1385–1425.

35 J. Mitchell Pickerill and Cornell W. Clayton, "The Supreme Court's Abortion and Privacy Jurisprudence and the New Right Regime" (paper presented at the annual meeting of the American Political Science Association, Toronto, Canada, September 3, 2009); Cornell W. Clayton and J. Mitch Pickerill, "The Rehnquist Court's Establishment Clause Jurisprudence and the Political Regime," (paper presented at the annual meeting of the American Political Science Association, Philadelphia, Sept. 1, 2006).

36 Thomas M. Keck, "Party, Policy, or Duty: Why Does the Supreme Court Invalidate Federal Statutes?" *American Political Science Review*, 101 (2007): 321–338.

37 Jurisprudential regimes are judicial constructs used by the justices during an identifiable period of time to identify relevant case factors and/or set the level of security for deciding cases in a given area of law. For example, analyzing how the Court's content-neutrality" doctrine in free speech cases, or the Court's *Lemon test* used to decide Establishment Clause cases, are connected to electoral branch politics is perhaps one promising way to more systematically explain the Court's relationship to the political regime. See Mark J. Richards and Herbrt M. Krizer, "Jurisprudential Regimes in Supreme Court Decision-Making," *American Political Science Review* 96 (2002): 305–20.

# Part II

# Influencing Politics

# Chapter 5

# The Networked Party
## How Social Network Analysis Is Revolutionizing the Study of Political Parties

*Seth Masket*

What is a political party? This is not a simple question, particularly in the United States, where parties appear more amorphous and varying than elsewhere. In particular, it has frequently been difficult to understand who belongs to them and who has influence within them. Gaining knowledge about political parties has been central to political science scholarship because of their fundamental role in making mass democracy possible. Traditional analyses that focus exclusively on the formal party organization often fail to capture the range of players and activities that shape the partisan character of politics. Seth Masket describes a novel approach to understanding parties through a technique called social network analysis (SNA). This approach does not assume that parties are hierarchical organizations but rather organic clusters of groups that coordinate activities to achieve partisan goals. The party can be "seen" by mapping the network of activities among activists, interest groups, and officeholders to nominate candidates, raise money, mobilize voters, and pass laws. By observing the network of interactions, scholars can identify which players appear especially vital or powerful. SNA can be applied to other kinds of questions, and Masket explains its descriptive power and its limits in understanding causal relationships.

The Republican Party had a problem. It was late August, just two months prior to the 2008 presidential election, and their presumed presidential nominee had just picked someone almost completely unknown to Republican voters as his running mate. And what little people did know about Alaska Governor Sarah Palin suggested that, though she could possibly provide some energy and enthusiasm for the Republican ticket, she had some potential negatives. Notably, she was politically inexperienced (undermining one of the main arguments against Democratic nominee Barack Obama), and she had a pregnant unmarried teenage daughter; these things could easily be exploited by the Democrats if Republicans did not define her quickly.

And define her they did. Bill O'Reilly used his Fox News platform to explain that, so long as the Palins were not drawing federal welfare funds to help their expectant daughter Bristol, her pregnancy was none of the nation's business.

Karl Rove argued that Palin's executive experience as Alaska's governor and Wasilla's mayor was better training for the presidency than Barack Obama's few years in the U.S. Senate. Republican consultants and McCain campaign staffers took to the airwaves and op-ed pages to defend Palin and portray her critics as sexist and elitist.

The response could be construed as just a group of conservative media figures independently defending their party's choices, but it gave the impression of a coordinated effort, with different actors across different platforms echoing the same talking points with virtual simultaneity. What's more, the response did not appear to be directed by the McCain campaign, the White House, the Republican National Committee, Fox News, or any other single source. Rather, it seemed to emerge nearly spontaneously from many sources at once.

Is this activity evidence of a political party? It certainly does not match up with traditional views of parties. That is, it did not involve a coalition of legislators working to advance an agenda in Congress.[1] We did not see a traditional hierarchical "boss"-dominated organization along the lines of Tammany Hall or Mayor Richard J. Daley's Chicago machine.[2] Yet, we nonetheless observed some of the key activities of parties: a varied group of individuals operating in concert to protect their candidate and to try to get her elected for the purpose of molding public policy.

One of the most vexing questions in political science remains, "What is a party?" In this chapter, I argue that we are due for a new answer to that question. Hierarchies and legislative coalitions simply no longer explain the bulk of what we would consider parties today in the United States. Party activity is as likely to be conducted by those outside the government as by those inside it, and the vast majority of party activities appear to be conducted by those who do not work for the party in any official capacity. It has become very challenging to determine just where on a party organizational chart different people fit. A party thus has many potential leaders and an undefined membership at any given moment; it is "a polycephalous creature with ambiguous boundaries."[3]

Social network research, I argue, presents a compelling model for both the conceptualization and the study of modern American political parties. It provides an answer to the elusive question of what parties are and offers us tools to determine their strengths and weaknesses. I begin this chapter by reviewing some of the competing theories about the nature of parties and explain why the social network model offers a considerable advancement for political science. I review research that demonstrates how studying the party through network analysis allows scholars to answer vital questions about the nature, behavior, and membership of parties. I conclude with some cautionary notes about the over-use and misinterpretation of network analysis.

## Seeing Parties as Networks

SNA has a venerable history in mathematics and has been adopted by the social sciences over the past few decades, but it has really taken hold only within political science since the late 1990s. In general, SNA examines the relationships between individual actors, relying upon links (or "edges") between individuals (or "nodes") to reveal hidden but important patterns in behavior. For example, education researchers have heavily used SNA to study the social patterns of school children. Students may be asked to "nominate" classmates as friends, and researchers then detect important patterns in, for example, racial and gender segregation, bullying, and social status. Parker and Asher,[4] for example, noted the decline in cross-gender friendships between third and fifth grade and also made discoveries about the basis and consequences of loneliness among young children. Some of these results are presented graphically in Figure 5.1. Though asking grade-schoolers about such issues directly would likely yield few useful results, the application of SNA to simple questions about their friends makes for a highly powerful tool in the study of group behavior.

Political parties make an ideal venue for such research methods. Parties are, after all, very poorly defined entities, in several senses. First, we have no real scholarly consensus on what a party is. Definitions range from a collection of like-minded individuals[5] to groups devoted to winning office[6] to conspiracies of policy demanders.[7] This is less a function of political scientists' being unable to commit to a definition than it is a reflection of the fact that parties have changed forms numerous times in American history. Political parties of the

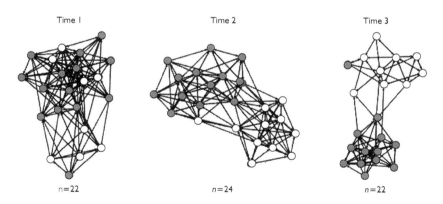

Time 1          Time 2          Time 3

n=22            n=24            n=22

*Figure 5.1* Decline in cross-gender friendships in grade-schoolers, as measured by Parker and Asher (1993)[8]

Each node represents an elementary school student. Shaded nodes are boys; white nodes are girls. Ties between the nodes indicate that one has indicated the other as a friend in Parker and Asher's survey. Times 1, 2, and 3 are grades 3, 4, and 5, respectively. Graphs compiled by Carter Butts (2011) nineteenth century, following the model pioneered by Andrew Jackson and Martin Van Buren, were largely fueled by patronage and run at the state and local level. They took on a more ideological tone and centralized, hierarchical structure around the turn of the twentieth century, often appearing to serve the needs of their officeholders.[9] Over the past few decades, they have lost some of their rigid structure but seem ever more national in scope and ideological in nature, sometimes even to the detriment of their officeholders. The model one has of parties can depend strongly on when those parties are being observed.

A second reason that parties are poorly defined is that it is not always clear just which political actors are members of parties and which are not. Are interest groups part of the party?[10] Are voters?[11] If a nominally independent senator caucuses with a party and tends to vote with it, is he or she a member or not a member of that party?

Beyond their poorly defined nature, parties, particularly American parties, have an organizational structure today that can more accurately be characterized as a network than as hierarchy. Party machines with rigid hierarchies once dominated politics in places such as New York, Boston, Chicago, and Baltimore.[12] Bosses maintained unilateral control over hundreds or thousands of patronage positions, paying loyal party workers and providing them with a *cursus honorum* for a stable career in politics. Such organizations, for the most part, simply do not exist any longer. The Shakman decrees[13] by the Supreme Court and federal crackdowns on these sorts of organizations largely drove them from the scene. This hardly means, however, that strong parties are gone. Rather, they have taken on a different form.

Much of the labor and energy in parties is now provided by ideological activists rather than salaried party staffers.[14] Their less-regular appearances and mixed motives for showing up to work for a party make it considerably more difficult to determine the party's structure. Compounding this problem is that it is often unclear just who the leaders of a party are. With official bosses such as William Tweed and Richard Daley no longer in charge, the torch has been passed in some cases to small groups of people. In research I conducted in Southern California,[15] I found that Orange County Republicans maintained an organization dominated by land developers, whereas South Los Angeles Democrats called home an organization run largely by Rep. Maxine Waters and an inner circle of donors, club leaders, union bosses, and church officials. The "boss" in these organizations may vary frequently, even if the same basic organizational structure and ideological agenda remain intact.

To add another wrinkle, one of the ways that traditional party bosses were able to keep their officeholders in line was by ensuring a steady stream of campaign funds. Democratic aldermen, state legislators, and members of Congress from mid–twentieth-century Chicago could count on lawn signs, flyers, and radio ads appearing on cue as long as they voted in a way that kept Mayor Daley happy. Today, campaign finance restrictions make such generous direct or in-kind contributions impossible; benefactors instead channel their largesse via 527s, Super PACs,[16] and other complex legal inventions. Thus, the party might encompass a more diffuse set of party supporters whose decisions might be tracked by following the money.

Finally, related to the foregoing, much of the work that modern parties do is necessarily secret. Party leaders do not readily admit to conspiring to fix a primary election or to limit voters' choices, and evidence of collusion on things such as campaign finance can actually be used by a prosecutor. As Cohen et al.[17] note, party insiders since 1980 have generally picked favorites in presidential races and sought to communicate this information to party activists. It is difficult for outside observers, however, to determine when and whether party insiders have made such a choice. We must rely on publicly observable data, such as endorsements, to detect such behavior.

That all these changes have occurred while parties appear to be as strong as, if not stronger than, they were during the age of the bosses suggests that the old models do not apply anymore. A hierarchical flowchart will simply fail to describe the structure of modern American parties and the behavior of their members.

In the remainder of this chapter, I examine how social network research techniques can help us understand modern political parties. I focus on what political scientist V. O. Key[18] described as the three main parts of the party: the party organization (those workers and activists who try to get people elected under a party banner); the party in government (the coalitions of legislators and other government employees who work to enact a party's agenda); and the party in the electorate (the voters who identify themselves with and vote for a party). I devote somewhat more attention to the study of party organizations where, in my opinion, SNA can provide the greatest help and where our current understanding is the weakest. The chapter concludes on a note of caution, however. Just because something can be studied as a network does not make it a network, and just because political actors are networked does not make them a party.

## The Networked Party Organization

Early political science research on the nature of parties tended to focus on formal party organizations or "traditional party organizations."[19] Even at their peak, these organizations probably represented fewer than half of the types of party organization existing in American politics.[20] There were certainly other types in use, as chronicled in Ehrenhalt,[21] but it was the formal hierarchy that caught the attention of political scientists.

Late-twentieth-century scholarship on parties tended to focus more on legislatures as the source of party genesis.[22] Arguing that the more formal machines with their legions of patronage workers had atrophied, these scholars viewed party organizations, to the extent they existed, as lying in service to ambitious politicians rather than to a political boss. To the extent that a network was conceptualized, it was one of *egonets*: Powerful politicians were the prominent nodes, connected to a host of pollsters, consultants, and party workers who served their needs, turning out voters and providing expert advice that kept them in office. "The major political party," writes Aldrich, "is the creature of the politicians, the ambitious office seeker and officeholder."[23]

A more recent strain of the parties' literature has taken a new turn, arguing that strong party organizations are back and have their own sets of interests that occasionally run counter to those of the politicians who bear their label, but these new party organizations do not quite look like their machine forebears. With party leaders generally unable to rely on patronage positions to staff their organizations, they are increasingly reliant on those whom J. Q. Wilson[24] referred to as "amateurs"—volunteers far more motivated by ideological than material rewards.

Some of the pioneering research in this subfield draws on the network as a concept if not a methodological tool. The recent work by Cohen et al., *The Party Decides*, for example, focuses on modern presidential nominations, arguing that a collection of party insiders (defined as intense policy demanders within a major party) determines the presidential nominee usually well in advance of the first caucuses and primaries. They do so by conveying vital campaign resources essential to winning those caucuses and primaries (money, endorsements, expertise) upon a preferred candidate who is perceived to be capable both of winning in the general election and of providing policies those party insiders desire once in office. However, how do those insiders decide upon a nominee in advance? Cohen et al. describe the process as an extended conversation. Candidates meet with activists and others across the country, and those activists have discussions with one another about candidates' relative strengths and weaknesses and, usually, are able to coordinate on one they feel is the strongest. The language used here is that of a network:

> [M]ost serious candidates for presidential nomination do a great deal of traveling – an amount that journalists routinely denominate in the hundreds of thousands of miles. At this level of effort, candidates can make personal contact with tens of thousands of people, a number that may constitute a substantial fraction of their party's most important officials, donors, interest-group leaders, and campaign workers. These party insiders are in turn connected with one another, whether through personal relationships, organizational membership, fax, or, nowadays, the Internet.[25]

Here, the authors have built on the work of Steger,[26] who argues that "elite party elected officials appear to have a potent signaling effect on the partisan electorate as to which candidate should be supported." As a recent example of such coordination, nearly every sitting Republican governor in 1999 had endorsed George W. Bush for president after extensive discussions with political activists and their counterparts in other states, sending a signal to other prospective Republican candidates that this was simply not the year to run. The result is as though a single boss has anointed a candidate, but the process is much more in the style of a network.

It is certainly possible in some cases that little signaling is necessary. Just as two people seeking each other out in New York City may end up coordinating on Penn Station, so might active Republicans looking for a presidential nominee in 1999 converge on George W. Bush—a popular big-state governor with strong name recognition—without requiring much instruction. However, in most scenarios, coordination points are not obvious. Why did Republican insiders in 2012 converge on one relatively moderate Mormon governor (Mitt Romney) but not another (Jon Huntsman)? It might be obvious that a party will either support or oppose a president's nominee for the Supreme Court or his signature piece of legislation, but it is not obvious what arguments to use. This requires active coordination.

Such coordination is hardly limited to presidential politics. Dominguez[27] examines patterns in congressional primaries and finds evidence of elite networks coordinating to aid preferred candidates before the voters even have a say, particularly when they estimate that the general election will be competitive. My own research on California politics[28] demonstrates some of this style of network coordination occurring in state and local elections as well. Through a combination of quantitative analysis of endorsements and campaign donation records and extensive interviews with local political elites, I find, for example, a collection of conservative land developers in Orange County using money, personal influence, and intimidation to advantage some candidates and deter others from entering races.

Other studies have taken the network concept beyond metaphor and used it as a research method, demonstrating how some notoriously clandestine party activity may be observed and measured. Noel,[29] for example, employs a network analysis of the endorsement data utilized in the Cohen et al. book and finds persistent factions within each party over time. Schwartz's[30] and Monroe's[31] studies of state and local elected officials and staff, meanwhile, revealed the existence and coordination of networked parties in Illinois and southern California, respectively. Other innovative work along these lines has found that political consultants, long alleged to be operating independent of or even against the parties' interests, are in fact highly integral to party networks, facilitating coordination[32] and even aiding with the dissemination of campaign techniques throughout a party.[33] Other studies have demonstrated coordination patterns among elite party donors[34] and 527s.[35]

The advantages of using network analysis techniques can be seen in work I conducted with Gregory Koger and Hans Noel.[36] Interested in uncovering patterns of coordination among like-minded party actors, we sent small

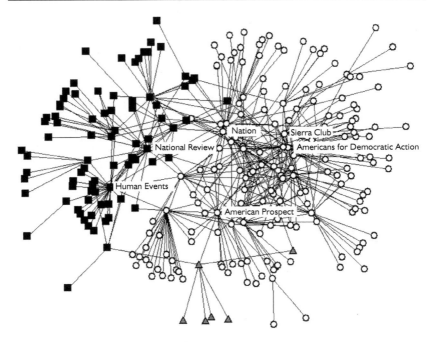

*Figure 5.2* Extended party networks[37]

The extended party networks, as described in Koger et al. (2009). Factional analysis reveals two main communities and one smaller one, with little interaction across communities. Democratic actors are depicted as hollow circles, Republicans as black squares. The third faction is depicted as gray triangles.

donations and subscription fees to a group of presidential candidates, interest groups, and political magazines in 2003 and 2004, listing our return address (a post office box) slightly different for each. This specification allowed us to keep track of how these organizations traded or sold our address to allies within the party network. After donating to the Sierra Club, for example, we received solicitations from John Kerry's presidential campaign and the Democratic National Committee using the exact same address. After contributing more money to the second wave of solicitors, we were able to use SNA methods to draw out networks of party actors who cohered strongly within ideological boundaries. Figure 5.2 shows a network diagram of the results, with some of the better-connected nodes labeled. The data and a factional analysis algorithm provided solid evidence of a sharply polarized extended party network system, where journals and interest groups provide exclusive assistance to the candidates and parties with which they are tied ideologically.

One central function of parties is to nominate candidates for office. Most scholars acknowledge that the nomination is not simply won or lost on the day of a primary election. Network analysis helps reveal coordination among party actors designed to winnow the field of candidates before voters get to choose. Even though the 2003 California gubernatorial recall election lacked an official primary, for example, Republican elites used endorsements, funding, and personal influence to advantage Arnold Schwarzenegger and pressure other candidates out of the race.[38] Network analysis has also proven useful in analyzing the differences between parties' national convention delegates. Heaney et al.[39] analyze the results of interviews with delegates during the summer 2008 conventions, finding that Democrats tended to belong to a greater number of interest groups and that Republicans seem to have a more hierarchical party organizational style. This may tend to indicate greater difficulty among Democrats in settling on presidential nominees, as the greater number of interest groups may form factions that make coordination more challenging. Indeed, the 2008 presidential nomination processes across the two parties offer a persuasive data point along these lines.

It seems fair to say that we have only scratched the surface of the utility of social network research in uncovering structures and patterns within American political parties. These methods are already helping to bring a level of understanding to a notoriously intractable subject.

## Members of Congress Have Friends

Even if parties are more than simply legislative coalitions, those legislative coalitions are clearly important, determining which ideas get converted into laws and which do not. Much scholarship on legislative partisanship tends to treat the ideological positions of individual legislators as fixed over time.[40] Thus legislative parties are a function of the preferences their members bring with them. The network approach, however, allows us to see the importance of social influences on legislators' votes. It reminds us that members of a party do not simply agree or disagree on things; sometimes, they learn from one another.

Keith Poole and Howard Rosenthal[41] revolutionized the study of Congress with the development of their nominal multidimensional estimates (NOMINATE) of members' "ideal points," or numerical approximations of members' ideological proclivities. Previous efforts to analyze the behavior of individual members of Congress depended on limited measures of roll-call behavior, such as interest group ratings, which drew from a small and usually biased sample of votes. This created challenges for scholars attempting, for example, to compare legislative partisanship across different chambers or years or to detect the influence of lobbying on elected officials. It also made it hard to assess the dimensionality of voting. For example, if a southern Democrat were observed voting with his or her Republican peers, was that because the southerner was an economic conservative, because of racial concerns, or something else?

Even if a researcher could have collected complete records of roll-call votes, it was not clear what she or he could do with them, as computing power was often too limited. (The voting agreement patterns detected by Truman[42] and Buchanan[43] are notable exceptions.) Poole and Rosenthal's method, conversely, calculated ideal points based on entire roll-call voting records. It was suddenly possible to see who voted with whom over an entire session and in multiple dimensions, allowing scholars to distinguish between ideological proximity on economics, race, and regional issues. Through the extensive measurement and generous sharing done by Poole and Rosenthal, many other scholars have been able to examine important long-term trends in Congressional history, such as party polarization.[44]

NOMINATE scores and other similar item response theory (IRT) methods of determining legislator ideal points[45] have thoroughly pervaded the literature on American legislatures. Their convenience and relatively straightforward interpretation has made them extremely attractive to a wide range of scholars. Often lost, however, is discussion of some important assumptions that these models make.[46] For example, votes are treated as isolated events, when in fact legislators likely vote differently based on the knowledge that their vote on one day may influence future options.[47] We additionally know that logrolling is a common phenomenon in legislatures, resulting in members' voting against their own preferences in exchange for a future payoff.[48] Finally, we have substantial evidence of members' being influenced by things other than their ideology, constituents, and party, such as roommates,[49] desk-mates,[50] and friends and colleagues.[51]

To understand this complexity, scholars have chosen to use network tools to investigate legislative behavior. Koger[52] and Fowler[53] have looked into patterns in the co-sponsorship of legislation, with the latter taking an explicitly network approach to the study. Fowler generates a network by linking any member of Congress to another member whose bill the first sponsored. In doing so, he develops measures of connectedness for members and charts out social networks in the House and Senate. In a similar vein, Victor and Ringe[54] perform a network study of the hundreds of informal congressional caucuses, tying members based on their shared caucus memberships. The authors find that these caucuses serve to reinforce the relationships formed by more formal institutions, including parties and standing committees. Nyhan,[55] meanwhile, uses a network approach to examine the use of Clinton-era scandal references in floor speeches by Congressional Republicans. This work nicely maps the contours of what Hillary Clinton dubbed the "vast right wing conspiracy."[56] These studies help us to understand the nature of influence within a legislative party setting. Rather than seeing legislators as atomistic individuals who voted their fixed preferences and go home, we see them as connected members of a network, learning from and influencing one another, affecting their votes, their approach to lawmaking, and the very language they use to describe politics.

I further examined such influences in work I conducted with Betsy Sinclair, Jennifer Victor, and Gregory Koger,[57] exploring the use of "agreement scores" in the study of congressional voting patterns. Such scores simply measure the frequency with which any given member of Congress votes identically to another member.[58] This is a conceptually and methodologically simple approach to studying congressional behavior that avoids some of the assumptions of item response theory methods while allowing for network influences. It also can help us identify the most influential and most polarizing members of a legislature. And it yields useful findings, as demonstrated in Figure 5.3. Here, we see that the average roll-call voting agreement within parties has increased since the 1960s, whereas agreement across parties has decreased over the same time period. Again, using this simple, yet networked, approach, we can observe the rise of two important aspects of polarization—intraparty homogeneity and interparty heterogeneity—without making unnecessary and unrealistic assumptions about members' behavior. The analysis in Figure 5.3 confirms earlier findings that the parties are growing more polarized, and it shows us that they are doing so because members within the same party are voting in greater agreement with their co-partisans and in greater disagreement with those in the opposing party.

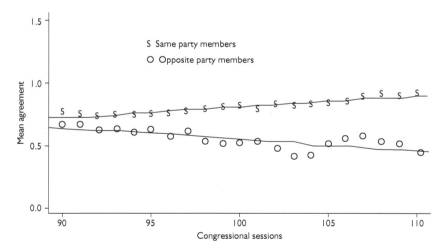

*Figure 5.3* Agreement scores in Congress[59]

Observations above are average agreement scores in the U.S. House of Representatives between the 90th (1967–68) and 110th (2007–08) Congresses. Agreement scores are calculated for same-party pairs (labeled as "S") and opposite-party pairs (labeled as "O").

## The Party in the Electorate: Our Networks, Ourselves

Party leaders and members of Congress are hardly the only people with potent political social networks. It turns out that the people with whom we associate can have a powerful impact on our vote choice and partisan affiliations. While earlier scholarship on political behavior often treated voters as atomistic individuals (e.g. Do we vote with our pocketbooks or our expectations? How much does our race or class affect our vote? Do we evaluate our ideological proximity to the candidates?), network scholars have examined the nature of our own social networks and the effect they can have on our political decisions. Again, this gives us greater purchase on the concept of political parties. That is, though there is legitimate debate over whether lay voters should be considered members of parties, there is broad agreement that voters' partisan attachments matter to electoral and legislative outcomes. Network research helps us see how those attachments form and how malleable they are.

As it turns out, conversation is vitally important in shaping citizens' vote choices and their partisan attachments. David Knoke did some important early work on this topic, examining the characteristics of voters' egocentric networks (the people to whom they are directly connected). Discussion of politics within these networks was found to be strongly related to increased interest and participation in political activities, and the partisan nature of these networks was found to be particularly important.[60] Huckfeldt and Sprague[61] also find that individuals construct their own political information networks and that these networks can abet the misperception of new political information. Beck[62] analyzed voters' social networks in the 1992 election, finding that conversations with supporters of Ross Perot that year could undermine voters' party attachments and encourage a vote for the third party candidate. Scott McClurg[63] pursues this line of research further, finding that political discussion networks can affect the awareness, sophistication, and participation of their members, allowing individuals to behave politically in a way that goes beyond their own resource limitations. That is, the political sophistication of our social networks may have a greater effect on our participation than our own individual understanding of politics does.[64]

Diana Mutz,[65] meanwhile, looks at the nature of political disagreement within a social network, finding that individuals may actually be less likely to participate politically if they experience cross-pressure from their network of friends. Not only does such cross-pressure make potential voters feel politically ambivalent, but it raises fears of repercussions within a social network by the loss of friends. Huckfeldt, Johnson, and Sprague,[66] conversely, challenge some of these findings with their own study, noting that most Americans are already cross-pressured within their social networks and that such pressures are helpful in compelling people to reexamine their political views. They do find that cross-pressure modestly decreases interest in politics, although they detect no important reduction in voter turnout.

Social networks research is also helping to shed light on participation in more demanding forms of political participation, such as partisan activism and protest. Klandermans and Oegema,[67] for example, surveyed participants at the 1983 peace demonstration at the Hague, discovering that "recruitment networks" are vital for individuals' participation in a social movement. The "epistemic communities" of pre–World War I Europe functioned as just such recruitment networks, bringing many leaders scholars, policy experts, and politicians into the International Labor Organization in 1919.[68] Heaney and Rojas,[69] meanwhile, use network analysis to understand the ties of antiwar activists in the early 2000s to established antiwar groups and to the major political parties.

As with other areas of partisan behavior, it is becoming increasingly clear that we cannot fully understand the behavior of voters and activists without considering the social networks to which those individuals belong. As we seek to understand just what caused people to gather in Tahrir Square in Cairo, to occupy Zuccotti Park in New York, or to join a Tea Party gathering in Washington—and what caused other people not to do these things—SNA is lighting the way.

## Some Notes of Caution: Is It a Network? Is It a Party? What Is Causing What?

SNA techniques are undoubtedly important and useful, but they are also seductive. A novice can learn a software package such as UCInet or one of the related R packages and, within just a few hours, map out and measure a social network. Just because they have mapped something out and measured it, though, does not mean that it was a network in the first place. One could analyze the first 100 names in a phone book and connect individuals based on the number of shared digits in their phone numbers, but that does not mean they are observing actual network behavior. Similarly, one may be observing a social network, but just because it consists of political actors does not make it a party.

Hans Noel explained this challenge in his paper "Toward a Network Theory of Political Parties," methodically comparing accepted definitions of parties and networks. Political actors bound together due to shared ideologies or political environments may well comprise a network, but it is not necessarily a party. A party, rather, presumably involves political actors *influencing* one another. For example, the Democratic Party of the 1950s could hardly be said to be an ideologically coherent organization, as it contained both liberals and conservatives, integrationists and segregationists. However, prominent party leaders were nonetheless able to coordinate on presidential nominees, compile and enact a congressional agenda, and so on. Presumably, influence occurred in such activities. Influence, however, is notoriously difficult to demonstrate empirically.[70]

The recent network debate over some of the findings of Christakis and Fowler[71] is emblematic of this problem. The authors examine the idea of social contagion across a network, finding that people who are divorced tend to have divorced friends, and their friends' friends tend to be divorced as well. Similarly, people who lose weight tend to have friends who lose weight, as do those friends' friends. Does this mean that we are indirectly influencing people through our social networks? Or is this homophily, the tendency of people with similar interests to cluster together?[72] Distinguishing between these two causes of a correlation is extremely daunting, but it is essential for understanding how a network—or a party—functions.

This is vitally important for party research. As mentioned earlier, political actors can sometimes converge on a candidate or a policy idea with little effort. At other times, though, convergence points are not obvious, and party elites must attempt to influence one another if they are going to maintain a united front. Though a good deal of social network research is descriptive in nature, not lending itself well to tests of causality or influence, some researchers have developed tools that allow for hypothesis testing and causal interpretations. Such techniques allow network analysis to go well beyond mere description.

Issues of causality and influence nonetheless remain serious for the use of SNA in understanding parties, although they are not insurmountable, and they are hardly more serious than those affecting other approaches, such as rational choice or political psychology. Despite its notable limitations, SNA offers opportunities to study some important remaining questions about aspects of parties. For example, how do parties adapt to institutional rules changes, such as campaign finance reform or term limits? We have a sense that parties can evolve to meet such new challenges, but network research allows us to map out what a party does when some key individuals or transactions are removed. How do interest groups and 527s interact and fit in within a party system? How do unofficial groups influence legislative partisanship? How can voters be enticed into voting or not voting for a party? And just what is a party, after all? SNA offers us new ways to address these vital current questions where previous methods simply could not. It is hoped that scholars who are new to this subfield will be taught the limits of such methods as they learn the many possibilities SNA offers for the understanding of parties, one of the most challenging subjects in the social sciences.

## Notes

1  Aldrich, John H. 1995. *Why Parties?* Chicago: University of Chicago Press. Schwartz, Thomas. 1989. "Why Parties?" Unpublished Manuscript. Cox, Gary W.,

and Mathew D. McCubbins. 1993. *Legislative Leviathan: Party Government in the House*. Berkeley: University of California Press.

2  Mayhew, David R. 1986. *Placing Parties in American Politics*. Princeton: Princeton University Press.

3  Masket, Seth E., Michael T. Heaney, Joanne M. Miller, and Dara Z. Strolovitch. 2009. "Networking the Parties: A Comparative Study of Democratic and Republican National Convention Delegates in 2008." Presented at the the annual meeting of the American Political Science Association, Toronto, Ontario.

4  Parker, Jeffrey G., and Steven R. Asher. 1993. "Friendship and Friendship Quality in Middle Childhood: Links with Peer Group Acceptance and Feelings of Loneliness and Social Dissatisfaction." *Developmental Psychology* 29 (4): 611–621.

5  Burke, Edmund. 1839. "Thoughts on the Cause of the Present Discontents (1770)." In *The Works of the Right Honorable Edmund Burke*. Boston: Little, Brown & Company. 425–426.

6  Schattschneider, E. E. 1942. *Party Government*. Westport, CT: Greenwood Press.

7  Bawn, Kathleen, Marty Cohen, David Karol, Seth Masket, Hans Noel, and John Zaller. 2012. "A Theory of Political Parties: Groups, Policy Demands and Nominations in American Politics." *Perspectives on Politics* 10 (3): 571–97.

8  Source: Packer and Asher, 1993.

9  Klinghard, Daniel. 2010. *The Nationalization of American Political Parties, 1880–1896*. New York: Cambridge University Press.

10  Bawn et al. 2012.

11  Schattschneider 1942. Rosenblum, Nancy L. 2008. *On the Side of the Angels : An Appreciation of Parties and Partisanship*. Princeton: Princeton University Press.

12  Mayhew 1986.

13  The Shakman decrees refer to a series of court decisions related to independent candidate Michael Shakman's battles against political patronage in Chicago in the 1970s. Courts ultimately determined that public employees (with the exception of some policy advisors) could not constitutionally be hired or fired for political reasons.

14  Wilson, James Q. 1966. *The Amateur Democrat: Club Politics in Three Cities*. Chicago: University of Chicago Press. McGirr, Lisa. 2001. *Suburban Warriors: The Origins of the New American Right*. Princeton: Princeton University Press.

15  Masket, Seth E. 2009. *No Middle Ground: How Informal Party Organizations Control Nominations and Polarize Legislatures*. Ann Arbor: University of Michigan Press.

16  527s are tax-exempt organizations that can fund electioneering activities so long as they don't expressly advocate for or against a specific candidate. Super PACs are organizations that can spend on campaign communications as long as they don't directly coordinate with a campaign.

17  Cohen, Marty, David Karol, Hans Noel, and John Zaller. 2008. *The Party Decides : Presidential Nominations before and after Reform*. Chicago: University of Chicago Press.

18  Key, Jr., V. O. 1952. *Politics, Parties, and Pressure Groups*. New York: Thomas Y. Crowell Company.

19  Mayhew 1986.

20  Ostrogorski, M. 1921. *Democracy and the Party System in the United States: A Study in Extra-Constitutional Government*. New York: The MacMillan Company.

21  Ehrenhalt, Alan. 1991. *The United States of Ambition: Politicians, Power, and the Pursuit of Office*. New York: Times Books.

22  Aldrich 1995. Cox and McCubbins 1993. Cox, Gary W. 1987. *The Efficient Secret: The Cabinet and the Development of Political Parties in Victorian England*. Cambridge:

Cambridge University Press. Kiewiet, D. Roderick, and Mathew D. McCubbins. 1991. *The Logic of Delegation: Congressional Parties and the Appropriations Process.* Chicago: University of Chicago Press.

23  Aldrich 1995, 4.

24  Wilson, James Q. 1966. *The Amateur Democrat: Club Politics in Three Cities.* Chicago: University of Chicago Press.

25  Cohen et al. 2008, 249.

26  Steger, Wayne. 2007. "Who Wins Presidential Nominations and Why: An Updated Forecast of the Presidential Primary Vote." *Presidential Research Quarterly* 60: 91–97.

27  Dominguez, Casey Byrne Knudsen. 2005. "Before the Primary: Party Participation in Congressional Nominating Processes." Doctoral Dissertation University of California.

28  Masket 2009.

29  Noel, Hans. 2010. "It's Not Personal; It's Strictly Business: A Social Networks Analysis of Internal Party Cleavages, 1972–2008." Presented at the the annual conference of the Southern Political Science Association, Atlanta, Georgia.

30  Schwartz, Mildred A. 1990. *The Party Network: The Robust Organization of Illinois Republicans.* Madison: University of Wisconsin Press.

31  Monroe, J. P. 2001. *The Political Party Matrix : The Persistence of Organization.* Albany: State University of New York Press.

32  Bernstein, Jonathan. 1999. "The Expanded Party in American Politics." Doctoral Dissertation University of California. Doherty, Joseph William. 2006. "The Candidate-Consultant Network in California Legislative Campaigns: A Social Network Analysis of Informal Party Organization." Ph.D. Dissertation University of California.

33  Montgomery, Jacob, and Brendan Nyhan. 2010. "The Party Edge: Consultant-Candidate Networks in American Political Parties." Presented at the the third annual Political Networks Conference, Durham, NC.

34  Bernstein, Jonathan, and Casey B. K. Dominguez. 2011. "Democratic Donors During the 2007–08 Invisible Primary." Presented at the the annual conference of the American Political Science Association, Seattle, Washington.

35  Skinner, Richard M., Seth E. Masket, and David A. Dulio. 2012. "527s and the Political Party Network." *American Politics Research* 40 (1): 60–84. Skinner, Richard, Seth E. Masket, and David Dulio. 2011. "527 Committees, Formal Parties, and the Party Networks." In *the annual conference of the Midwest Political Science Association.* Chicago.

36  Koger, Gregory, Seth E. Masket, and Hans Noel. 2009. "Partisan Webs: Information Exchange and Party Networks." *British Journal of Political Science*, 39: 633–53.

37  Created by the author with data from Koger et al. 2009.

38  Masket, Seth E. 2011. "The Circus That Wasn't: The Republican Party's Quest for Order in the 2003 California Gubernatorial Recall." *State Politics and Policy Quarterly* 11 (2): 124–148.

39  Heaney, Michael, Seth Masket, Joanne Miller, and Dara Strolovitch. 2012. "Polarized Networks: The Organizational Affiliations of National Party Convention Delegates." *American Behavioral Scientist* (forthcoming).

40  Poole, Keith T. 1998. "Changing Minds? Not in Congress!" In *Working Paper #1997-22*: Carnegie-Mellon University.

41  Poole, Keith T., and Howard Rosenthal. 1997. *Congress: A Political-Economic History of Roll Call Voting.* New York: Oxford University Press.

42  Truman, David B. 1959. *The Congressional Party: A Case Study.* New York: John Wiley and Sons.

43  Buchanan, William. 1963. *Legislative Partisanship: The Deviant Case of California*. Berkeley: University of California Press.

44  McCarty, Nolan, Keith T. Poole, and Howard Rosenthal. 2006. *Polarized America: The Dance of Ideology and Unequal Riches*. Boston: MIT Press. Theriault, Sean M. 2008. *Party Polarization in Congress*. Cambridge; New York: Cambridge University Press.

45  Jackman, Simon. 2001. "Multidimensional Analysis of Roll Call Data Via Bayesian Simulation: Identification, Estimation, Inference, and Model Checking." *Political Analysis* 9 (3): 227–241.

46  Sinclair, Betsy, Jennifer Nicoll Victor, Seth E. Masket, and Gregory Koger. 2011. "Agreement Scores, Ideal Points, and Legislative Polarization." Presented at the the annual meeting of the American Political Science Association, Seattle, Washington.

47  Penn, Elizabeth Maggie. 2009. "A Model of Farsighted Voting." *American Journal of Political Science* 53 (1): 36–54.

48  Calvert, Randal L., and Richard F. Fenno. 1994. "Strategy and Sophisticated Voting in the Senate." *The Journal of Politics* 56 (2): 349–76.

49  Bergemann, Patrick, and Paolo Parigi. 2011. "Living Together and Voting Together: The Impact of Congressional Boardinghouse Networks on Voting Patterns, 1815–1841." Presented at the the fourth annual Political Networks Conference, Ann Arbor, Michigan. Young, James Sterling. 1966. *The Washington Community, 1800–1828*. New York: Columbia University Press, although see Bogue, Allan G., and Mark Paul Marlaire. 1975. "Of Mess and Men: The Boardinghouse and Congressional Voting, 1821–1842." *American Journal of Political Science* 19 (2): 207–230. Rogowski, Jon, and Betsy Sinclair. 2011. "Socializing in Session: Congressional Networks and Legislative Behavior." Presented at the the fourth annual Political Networks Conference, Ann Arbor, Michigan.

50  Masket, Seth E. 2008. "Where You Sit Is Where You Stand: The Impact of Seating Proximity on Legislative Cue-Taking." *Quarterly Journal of Political Science* 3 (2008): 301–311.

51  Matthews, Donald R., and James A. Stimson. 1975. *Yeas and Nays: Normal Decision-Making in the U.S. House of Representatives*. New York: Wiley. Kingdon, John W. 1973. *Congressmen's Voting Decisions*. New York: Harper & Row.

52  Koger, Gregory. 2003. "Position Taking and Cosponsorship in the U.S. House." *Legislative Studies Quarterly* 28 (2): 225–246.

53  Fowler, James H. 2006. "Connecting the Congress: A Study of Cosponsorship Networks." *Political Analysis* 14 (2006): 456–87.

54  Victor, Jennifer Nicoll, and Nils Ringe. 2009. "The Social Utility of Informal Institutions Caucuses as Networks in the 110th U.S. House of Representative." *American Politics Research* 37 (2009): 742–66.

55  Nyhan, Brendan. 2009. "Strategic Outrage: The Politics of Presidential Scandal." Ph.D. Dissertation Duke University.

56  Squitieri, Tom. 1998. "First Lady: Prosecutor Part of Plot." *U.S.A. Today*, January 28, 1A.

57  Sinclair, Betsy, Jennifer Nicoll Victor, Seth E. Masket, and Gregory Koger. 2011. "Agreement Scores, Ideal Points, and Legislative Polarization." Presented at the the annual meeting of the American Political Science Association, Seattle, Washington.

58  Truman 1959.

59  Source: Betsy Sinclair, Jennifer Nicoll Victor, Seth E. Masket, and Gregory Koger. 2011. "Agreement Scores, Ideal Points, and Legislative Polarization." Presented at the the annual meeting of the American Political Science Association, Seattle, Washington, p. 30.

60   Knoke, David. 1990. "Networks of Political Action: Towards Theory Construction." *Social Forces* 68: 1041–63.
61   Huckfeldt, Robert, and John Sprague. 1987. "Networks in Context: The Social Flow of Political Information." *The American Political Science Review* 81 (4): 1197–1216.
62   Beck, Paul A. 2002. "Encouraging Political Defection: The Role of Personal Discussion Networks in Partisan Desertions to the Opposition Party and Perot Votes in 1992." *Political Behavior* 24: 309–337.
63   McClurg, Scott D. 2003. "Social Networks and Political Participation: The Role of Social Interaction in Explaining Political Participation." *Political Research Quarterly* 56 (4): 448–465. McClurg, Scott D. 2006. "The Electoral Relevance of Political Talk: Examining Disagreement and Expertise Effects in Social Networks on Political Participation." *American Journal of Political Science* 50: 737–754.
64   Rolfe, Meredith. 2012. *Voter Turnout: A Social Theory of Political Participation*. New York: Cambridge University Press. Sokhey, Anand Edward, and Scott McClurg. 2012. "Social Networks and Correct Voting." *Journal of Politics* (forthcoming).
65   Mutz, Diana C. 2002. "The Consequences of Cross-Cutting Networks for Political Participation." *American Journal of Political Science* 46: 838–855.
66   Huckfeldt, Robert, Paul E. Johnson, and John Sprague. 2004. *Political Disagreement: The Survival of Diverse Opinions within Communication Networks*. New York: Cambridge University Press.
67   Klandermans, Bert, and Dirk Oegema. 1987. "Potentials, Networks, Motivations, and Barriers: Steps Towards Participation in Social Movements." *American Sociological Review* 52: 519–531.
68   Van Daele, Jasmien. 2005. "Engineering Social Peace: Networks, Ideas, and the Founding of the International Labor Organization." *International Review of Social History* 50: 435–466.
69   Heaney, Michael T., and Fabio Rojas. 2007. "Partisans, Nonpartisans, and the Antiwar Movement in the United States." *American Politics Research* 35 (4): 431–464.
70   Noel, Hans. 2012. "Toward a Theory of Parties as Networks." Presented at the conference on American Political Parties: Past, Present, and Future, Charlottesville, VA, October 8.
71   Christakis, Nicholas A., and James H. Fowler. 2009. *Connected: The Surprising Power of Our Social Networks and How They Shape Our Lives*. New York: Little, Brown and Co.
72   Lyons, Russell. 2011. "The Spread of Evidence-Poor Medicine Via Flawed Social-Network Analysis." *Statistics, Politics, and Policy* 2 (1): 1–27. Noel, Hans, and Brendan Nyhan. 2011. "The 'Unfriending' Problem: The Consequences of Homophily in Friendship Retention for Causal Estimates of Social Influence." Unpublished manuscript.

## Chapter 6

# The Influence of Interest Groups in American Politics
## Myth versus Reality

*Matt Grossmann*

The American public often demonizes special interests for subverting the common good. As Matt Grossmann points out, however, the preponderance of research indicates that interest groups do not easily shape public policy by their political activities. Grossmann's work suggests that the story is complex as he highlights just how difficult it is for any group to affect policy. The system is heavily biased toward the status quo, and most interest groups are unlikely to have much influence no matter what they do. Grossmann's work, however, reveals some findings that challenge conventional expectations about who has power. The strength of his research, like others in this volume, is its multi-pronged approach to analyzing the question. He draws on news archives, hundreds of historical accounts, and legislative outcomes to assess the effectiveness of groups. In discussing his research design, he explains why it remains so hard for political scientists to establish causal links between interest group activity and policy outcomes. His account pushes us to think clearly about what might constitute genuine evidence of interest group power. The findings of "minimal influence" raise puzzling questions about what interest groups expect from all their expensive efforts.

American business wants to make it much harder for you to steal music and movies on the Internet. Reducing the online theft of intellectual property through strict regulations is a top political priority of some of America's largest corporations, not only movie studios and the recording industry but book publishers, media networks, and drug companies. During 2011, it looked as if Congress was likely to assent to their wishes and pass the Stop Online Piracy Act (SOPA), which would impose severe penalties on Internet services that made it easier to access illegal movies, music, video games, and generic drugs. SOPA had the support of America's largest lobbying group, the U.S. Chamber of Commerce, along with its major unions, law enforcement officials, and local governments. The organizations that favored SOPA spent millions of dollars lobbying the federal government and gave millions in contributions to political candidates. What did all of this buy them? After a public uproar, Congress did what it does best: nothing at all. Some major American industries lost their most important political battle.

This outcome is somewhat at odds with the myth that interest groups dominate our politics. Citizens, reporters, and politicians repeatedly claim that interest groups are able to easily alter legislative outcomes, usually as a result of hiring lobbyists and buying votes with campaign contributions. We are told that corruption is rampant and that Washington is a city of legalized bribery. So, it may come as a surprise that political science has accumulated little definitive evidence that interest group influence is overpowering or common. Scholars have even failed to show that interest group activity on behalf of legislation reliably changes any legislators' votes, much less that interest groups find an unobstructed path to getting their way on public policy.

Yet, attempting to evaluate interest group influence from the outcome of the SOPA debate raises the same difficulties that scholars confront. As organizations such as Google, Facebook, and the American Civil Liberties Union opposed the legislation, how do we know that these interest groups did not turn the tide against it? Because the vast bulk of legislation fails, how do we know that interest groups were to blame? How can we differentiate among the many reasons that legislation fails to become law? Political science research attempts to investigate these questions by studying the relationships between interest group activities and policy outcomes across a broad range of issues, organizations, and political contexts. The research has been able to disconfirm the popular claim that interest groups control government, but that is hardly the end of the story.

After all, there are good reasons to expect interest group influence. Collectively, interest groups spend approximately $3 billion per year lobbying the U.S. Congress and millions more donating to political campaigns.[1] Politicians regularly credit interest groups for their involvement in the legislative process. President Obama, for example, thanked several interest groups when he signed his economic stimulus bill and health care bill into law.[2] Long-time observers of government often claim that interest groups have fundamentally changed the process of how a bill becomes a law. How can these perceptions of great influence be reconciled with the research? When studies failed to confirm an easy path from interest group resources to policy change, political scientists responded by subdividing their investigations of influence; they seek to determine the groups most likely to be influential, the activities they undertake that could produce influence, and the likely times and places of influence.

In this chapter, I appraise the state of research on interest group influence and then tackle the topic using three different strategies from my own research. First, I look at group *capacity* for influence based on which interest groups are most often quoted by the media and invited to share their views in government. My second approach provides a test of whether interest group activity is independently *associated* with legislative success, in terms of bills becoming law (even if this association falls short of demonstrable proof that the interested group caused this outcome). Third, I look at the judgments of policy historians to assess which interest groups have been *credited* with federal policy changes in fourteen different issue areas since 1945. Each of these three approaches makes some progress, but together they still suffer from the fundamental problems of causal inference that make it difficult to pinpoint the power of interest groups. Nonetheless, comparing how scholars investigate interest group influence with how politicians and pundits portray their role shows how far off the myth is from the reality.

## Research on Interest Group Influence

Competition between interest groups has long seemed central to politics and government. In *The Federalist Papers*, the American founders warned of the "mischiefs of faction," by which they meant groups motivated by their own interests or passions rather than the best public policy. Early political scientists such as Arthur Bentley and David Truman produced theories meant to explain the entire political process as the product of interest group competition.[3] In their view, government just provided a forum for social and economic groups to fight for their desired policies. In response to these accounts, Mancur Olson argued that many large groups have no incentive to mobilize politically; as a result, small self-interested groups would dominate politics.[4] E. E. Schattschneider argued that any type of group competition was likely to benefit the wealthy at the expense of the poor.[5] Yet, all of these scholars agreed that when one interest group mobilized much more than another, their greater influence on public policy was a given. Mobilizing more organizational resources was taken as tantamount to getting your way more often.

More recent political science scholarship has focused on the population of interest organizations in Washington and their activities. Businesses and their associations account for the vast majority of national interest groups and spend the most resources on lobbying and campaign contributions, but organizations motivated by single issues or political ideology are the fastest growing segment of the population.[6] Scholars study where all of these organizations obtain their resources, which legislators they attempt to influence, and whether they ally with other groups. Political scientists have learned that interest groups often generate resources directly from government or foundations rather than raising money from members.[7] Surprisingly, interest groups also discuss policy most often with the legislators who already agree with them, rather than trying to convince their opponents.[8] In addition, interest groups often work alone rather than with others that support their cause.[9] Scholars now know quite a bit about what interest groups and their lobbyists do: They talk directly to policymakers and the media, they mobilize their supporters to contact legislators, they produce research for use in policy debates, and they attempt to raise the profile of their causes. Although this shows how interest groups attempt influence, however, it does not assess whether or when interest groups succeed in influencing policy.

Scholarship that directly addresses the question of influence shows that groups are much less influential than commonly assumed and lack any guaranteed route to translating resources into the policies that they support. The influence of interest groups on legislation is commonly investigated by assessing whether members of Congress who receive Political Action Committee (PAC) campaign contributions vote the way their contributors would like. A PAC is an organization, usually affiliated with a business or nonprofit organization, that contributes money to candidates for federal office. Research finds quite limited evidence of PAC influence.[10] If they are influential, campaign contributions do not secure enough votes to determine whether bills pass Congress or approach the scale of influence that popular commentators assume they do.[11]

Studies of the impact of lobbying resources, the money spent to pay staff and build organizations to talk directly to policymakers, have also failed to demonstrate consistent influence. Assessments of lobbying influence usually take the form of comparing the winning and losing sides in interest group battles. Yet, the amount of resources used for lobbying on each side of a debate has no consistent effect on who wins and loses.[12] Many other factors unrelated to interest groups better predict policy success and failure, and no change in policy is always the most likely outcome. Interest groups are usually on the winning or losing side because of factors unrelated to their activities. Other studies of group influence use surveys of group leaders to ask directly for their self-reports of success, finding that some tactics and groups are thought to be more influential.[13] Yet, this tells us only about perceptions of influence, not whether group actions lead to different policy outcomes.

Do we know that interest groups influence public policy at all? If influence means changing the votes of legislators or whether bills are signed into law, we have surprisingly little evidence that interest groups exert influence. Research that has generated consistent evidence of influence tends to focus on narrow policy goals rather than significant legislation. Groups with non-ideological or uncontroversial causes, for example, may influence policy with campaign contributions.[14] Business interest groups are most likely to achieve policy goals when they have little public or interest group opposition.[15] Resources spent to procure earmarks, specialized spending programs directed by Congress, can be effective.[16] Studies that demonstrate influence tend to show small effects that are conditional on other political factors, often on minor policy outcomes.

Given these research findings, why is so much money and effort directed to group influence? First, groups may pursue their goals in a straightforward manner, without knowing whether they will be successful. Many people voice their opinions or stage protests even when they are unlikely to be influential. Second, interest groups may need to have their names attached to the ideas they support to maintain constituency support and help with fundraising. Third, the professional firms that carry out most lobbying on behalf of far-away clients may convince their clients that they are influential. Fourth, the potential influence of a government decision on an interest group may justify a large expenditure even if there is only a small chance of influence. It is worth spending $1 million in the hopes of influencing who wins a government contract if that contract would provide $1 billion for your business. Fifth, interest groups may be most interested in small changes to policy, where research does show their influence. Interest groups can win support, for example, for spending small amounts of government money or gaining a specific exemption to pay fewer taxes.

Nevertheless, political scientists are not giving up in their quest to assess wider interest group influence on public policy. We know that money does not easily buy votes and that the amount of money spent on each side does not determine policy results, but that does not mean that influence is an illusion. After all, we do have examples of legislative language taken directly from interest group writings and courtroom sagas that demonstrate some explicit bribery.[17] Scholars have also shown that lobbying may raise the level of legislator involvement in legislation supported by an interest group.[18] Although they do not generally change legislators' votes, interest group contributions and lobbying efforts may thus lead legislators to pay more attention to issues that they might not otherwise address. Interest group influence may also occur only for specific types of organizations or in specific political environments. Scholars have many examples of cases that look like interest group influence but are still investigating when and how it occurs.

### Interest Group Prominence and Involvement

In my book, *The Not-So-Special Interests: Interest Groups, Public Representation, and American Governance*, I study several precursors to influence rather than trying to determine whether group actions independently change policy.[19] After all, there are important intermediary steps in the process of organizing political interests to influence policy outcomes. Many interest groups survive, but few become prominent players in political debate and regularly involved actors in national policymaking. The prominence of organizations in political debates in the news media and the involvement of organizations in policymaking venues can be thought of as measures of the *potential* for influence, though they fall short of it. Assessing prominence and involvement has the advantage of differentiating the various levels of success associated with a multitude of organizations. Two organizations may each be able to obtain a meeting with an administrator or member of Congress, for example, but those meetings are unlikely to be equally important if one organization is much more prominent and more regularly involved.

To measure organizational prominence, I use data on the number of times that each group is mentioned in major news reports. I count the number of references to each organization in Washington print media and in national and local television news broadcasts. Television news broadcasts are the primary political information source for the public, whereas Washington print publications are the main source of information for political elites and government insiders. I also use an indicator of each organization's prominence in new media. I count the number of links provided by other Web publishers to each organization's site on the World Wide Web.

To analyze organizational involvement in national policymaking, I use indicators of involvement in four different venues. I measure (1) the number of times that each organization testified in congressional committee hearings, (2) the number of times that they were mentioned in the writings, press releases, executive orders, proclamations, and other materials issued by the White House, (3) the number of times they were mentioned in the final rules and administrative decisions issued by executive branch agencies, and (4) the number of times they were mentioned in federal court proceedings. Although these indicators provide only crude estimates of the involvement of each group in each policymaking venue, they can be compiled across a broad range of groups to provide a basis of comparison.

Table 6.1 reports descriptive statistics on the distributions of all of these indicators of prominence and involvement across the interest group community. In all cases, the standard deviation is much larger than the mean. This indicates that the distribution is skewed, with most organizations scoring as not prominent or involved; a small subset of organizations score much more highly. Another way to see this is to line up all of the interest groups in order from highest to lowest on each indictor. Table 6.1 reports several indicators based on this sorting: The median reports the score on each indicator for the middle organization, the range reports the highest and lowest scores across all organizations, and the middle 50 percent reports the range between the scores of the organization that scores lower than all but 25 percent of organizations and the organization that scores higher than all but 25 percent of organizations. For example, the least prominent interest group receives zero mentions in the Washington print media per year, but the most prominent receives 533 mentions per year. The majority of organizations receive only a little more than one mention per year or less. The same types of skewed distributions show up on every indicator.

The bottom line is that most interest groups have very few, if any, opportunities to share their views with policymakers. A small number of organizations dominate appearances in the news media and participation in Congress, the administration, and the courts. Asking whether the average interest group has influence over policy is not the same as asking whether interest groups, in general, have influence. The average interest group is almost never quoted in the news and is ignored by policymakers. A few major players, conversely, are involved annually in all branches of government and regularly quoted by all types of media. This does not necessarily mean influence is this concentrated, but it makes it more likely.

*Table 6.1* Distributions of indicators of advocacy group prominence and involvement

| Indicator | Mean | Standard Deviation | Median | Middle 50% | Range |
|---|---|---|---|---|---|
| Washington print media mentions per year | 8.5 | 28.4 | 1.3 | 0.3–5.4 | 0–533 |
| Television news media mentions per year | 46.3 | 240.4 | 2.1 | 0.2–13.6 | 0–4301 |
| Web links | 615 | 1347 | 176 | 46–575 | 0 –15700 |
| Congressional testimony appearances per year | 0.5 | 1.3 | 0.1 | 0–0.4 | 0–24 |
| Mentions in the papers of the President per year | 0.0 | 0.1 | 0 | 0–0 | 0–8 |
| Mentions in administrative agency decisions per year | 4.1 | 30.1 | 0.1 | 0–0.7 | 0–882 |
| Mentions in Federal Court documents per year | 3.2 | 17.8 | 0.1 | 0–0.7 | 0–313 |

The table reports descriptive statistics regarding the distribution of prominence and involvement across the interest group advocacy community.

I also predict which kinds of groups will be prominent and involved. As it turns out, the same organizational characteristics—age, staff size, membership, and breadth of issue agenda—predict prominence in all types of media and involvement in all branches of government. The oldest, largest, and broadest organizations are the most prominent and involved everywhere. These organizations have developed reputations for representing constituencies and offering informed policy commentary. They are taken for granted as the obvious players in Washington, and they nearly always get a seat at the policymaking table. Making campaign contributions or hiring lobbyists, in contrast, make almost no difference for an organization's level of prominence or involvement in any media outlet or venue. This provides some sense of why the previous literature may not have found consistent influence for these expenditures of resources.

## Lobbying and Bill Advancement

Another way of assessing interest group influence is to look directly at whether group activity is associated with final results. How does a group's lobbying correspond with the advancement of corresponding legislation through Congress? Do bills with more lobbying move further in the legislative process? To investigate, my colleague Kurt Pyle and I study more than 17,000 bills introduced in the House and Senate of the 106th and 107th Congresses, including more than 3,500 bills with reported lobbying. We analyze whether each bill makes it out of committee and whether they pass each chamber to try to assess whether interest groups play a role.[20]

To identify lobbying on Congressional bills, we rely on the lobbying reports submitted to the Senate Office of Public Records. Lobbyists are required by law to register with this office if they are paid, make a significant number of contacts to influence policy, and devote at least one-fifth of their time to lobbying activities. Though not all lobbying reports include specific bills, lobbyists are instructed to mention bill numbers where appropriate. Where bill number information is included, the Center for Responsive Politics collates the reports and produces a database of bills with associated lobbying reports. We aggregate these data, creating a measure of the number of lobbying reports filed on each bill.

To get a sense of how many bills generate lobbying and how many bills advance through each stage of the legislative process, Figure 6.1 illustrates the path from bill introduction to passage. We report the number of bills that move from stage to stage and the number of bills with reported lobbying. As is evident, the traditional tale of how a bill becomes a law does not always match the true process; not all bills that pass are first reported from committee.[21] Unsurprisingly, a higher percentage of bills reported from committee pass in the House than in the Senate, most likely due to the Senate's supermajoritarian rules, such as the sixty-vote requirement to end debate.

Lobbying is reported on a significant minority of bills in both the House and the Senate. In the House, lobbying reports covered 18.9 percent of bills introduced, 34.5 percent of those reported from committee, and 30 percent of those that passed. In the Senate, lobbying was reportedly associated with 23.7 percent of bills introduced, 28.1 percent of those reported, and 22.8 percent of those passed. Reported lobbying is thus limited to a minority of bills introduced in both houses of Congress, but the subset is not small. The same is true of bills that make it out of committee and those that survive to final passage.

Of course, interest groups may not be the only, or the most important, factor in whether bills become laws. We assess interest group influence in combination with the many other factors that may affect whether bills advance. For example, bills introduced by members of the majority party, especially a committee chair, are more likely to pass. Bills with more cosponsors are also more likely to succeed. The issue area of a bill also influences its likelihood of advancement.

We are able to assess whether bills associated with lobbying activity are more likely to advance through the legislative labyrinth, independent of the congressional factors that typically predict bill advancement. As it turns out, bills with more lobbying are more likely to advance from committee and pass each chamber, even accounting for the characteristics of bill sponsors, cosponsors, and issue areas. Bills with ten lobbyists working on them are 27 percent more likely to pass in the House and 12 percent more likely to pass in the Senate than

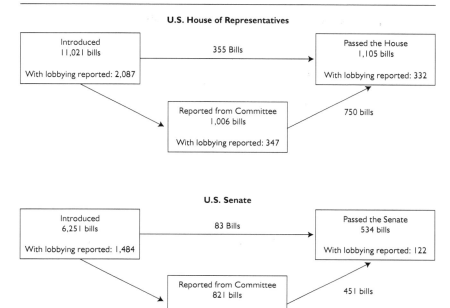

**U.S. House of Representatives**

Introduced
11,021 bills

With lobbying reported: 2,087

355 Bills

Passed the House
1,105 bills

With lobbying reported: 332

Reported from Committee
1,006 bills

With lobbying reported: 347

750 bills

**U.S. Senate**

Introduced
6,251 bills

With lobbying reported: 1,484

83 Bills

Passed the Senate
534 bills

With lobbying reported: 122

Reported from Committee
821 bills

With lobbying reported: 231

451 bills

*Figure 6.1* Lobbying and bill advancement

The figure reports the number of bills that make it to each stage of the legislative process in each chamber, along with the number that feature interest group lobbying.

bills with no lobbyists working on them. Yet, the vast majority of bills, with and without lobbying, fail to make it out of committee, and even fewer pass the House or Senate. Lobbyists appear to work on many specific bills with little chance of passing, but each additional lobbyist working on a bill increases the chance that a bill will pass.

We were unable to confirm, however, that the bills endorsed by lobbyists advanced farther in the legislative process because of interest group lobbying in favor of the bills. Both lobbying in favor and against a bill are associated with passage. This dual association may result because lobbying brings attention to bills or provides information for policy debates to move forward. More likely, lobbyists assess which bills have a chance of success and focus their lobbying on these bills, which tend to move further in the legislative process regardless of the amount of lobbying.

The results place the failure of SOPA, the online intellectual property legislation mentioned at the beginning of the chapter, in perspective. A bill is always much more likely to go nowhere than to pass. Bills associated with lobbying are more likely to pass than those with no lobbying, but they are still unlikely to advance much beyond introduction.

## Reported Influence in Policy History

The third approach draws on expert observers to assess interest group influence in all branches of government over a much longer period. I look at all significant policy changes enacted by the American federal government since 1945 in fourteen broad domestic policy areas.[22] I aggregate the explanations for policy change offered by historians of particular policy areas. There are substantial scholarly literatures about the policymaking process in areas such as the environment, education, health, housing, and science. I use 268 of these historical accounts, each covering ten years or longer of post-1945 policy history, as the raw materials for my analysis. I aggregate explanations for 790 specific U.S. landmark federal policy enactments that were considered significant by policy historians, including laws passed by Congress, executive orders by the President, administrative agency rules, and federal court decisions.

Although these authors did not set out to prove or disprove interest group influence, I find substantial evidence for interest group influence in their accounts. Based on their collective assessments, factors related to interest groups are important in 48.7 percent of all policy enactments. More than 300 interest groups are specifically credited with helping to produce a policy enactment. Table 6.2 lists the organizations credited for the most significant policy changes since 1945, as judged by policy historians. The most reportedly influential groups include representatives of labor, business, governments, and ethnic and religious groups and several single-issue concerns. In total, interest groups were partially credited with 279 new laws passed by Congress, 31 executive orders, 29 administrative agency rules, and 46 judicial decisions. Policy historians credit interest group factors with playing a role in policymaking in every type of federal policymaking venue.

Interest group influence is reportedly more common in some issue areas than in others. Figure 6.2 shows the percentage of policy changes involving interest groups by major policy domain (as established by the Policy Agendas Project). Interest groups were most frequently involved in policy changes in the environment and civil rights and liberties, where they were partially credited with more than two-thirds of policy changes. Groups were least commonly credited with policy change in criminal justice, but they still reportedly played a role in more than 30 percent of significant enactments. Reported interest group influence thus varies widely across issue areas but is never absent.

Of course, it is possible that the policy historians are too generous in assigning credit to interest groups. Yet, historical analysis of policy change points toward the importance of a small number of central groups with reputations for constituency representation. Most interest groups were infrequently or never credited with policy enactments. Despite the relative consensus among policy historians that interest groups play an important role in landmark policy changes, there is little evidence that they do so unilaterally. Instead, policy enactments are almost always credited to specific legislators or the president in addition to interest groups.

*Table 6.2*  Interest groups credited most often with policy change since 1945

| Ranking | Name |
| --- | --- |
| 1st | AFL-CIO (American Federation of Labor—Congress of Industrial Organizations) |
| 2nd | NAACP (National Association for the Advancement of Colored People) |
| 3rd | U.S. Conference of Mayors |
| 4th | American Civil Liberties Union |
| 5th | National Association of Manufacturers |
| Tied-6th | Sierra Club |
| | American Farm Bureau |
| 8th | U.S. Chamber of Commerce |
| Tied-9th | National Organization for Women |
| | National Urban League |
| | National Farmers Union |
| Tied-12th | American Medical Association |
| | American Municipal Association |
| | Leadership Conference on Civil Rights |
| | National Association of Home Builders |
| | United Auto Workers |
| Tied-17th | American Cancer Society |
| | Americans for Democratic Action |
| | National Council of Churches |
| | National Education Association |

The table lists the organizations credited with the most significant policy changes since 1945 by policy historians, almost always alongside other actors such as members of Congress. The AFL-CIO and the NAACP are also listed by their former names; both organizations are now known only by their initials.

### Remaining Problems of Causal Inference

Political science still faces several fundamental problems in evaluating the causal influence of interest groups on public policy. Scholars are increasingly concerned about the difficulty of proving causal relationships, especially when lots of factors influence an outcome such as public policy choices. This is leading political scientists to back away from our broadest claims about what factors are responsible for policy outcomes and instead to focus on the circumstances under which groups might be influential. The problem in the traditional literature was that scholars assumed that we could expect influence

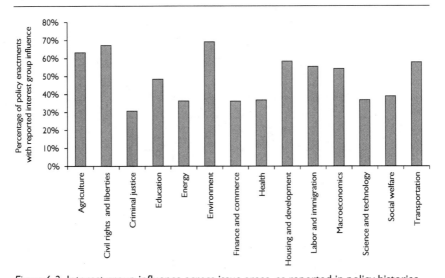

*Figure 6.2* Interest group influence across issue areas, as reported in policy histories

The graph reports the percentage of significant policy enactments reportedly involving interest groups by issue area based on a content analysis of policy histories in each issue area.

to consistently follow resource advantages, such as the amount of money spent on lobbying or campaign contributions. The measure of influence was also relatively direct—usually changes in votes on the final passage of legislation. The results of these investigations were ambiguous at best, with most pointing in the direction of little or no influence. Even if scholars had found evidence of a strong relationship between money spent to influence politicians and their votes, they would still need to evaluate two alternative possibilities: that interest groups dedicated resources to those that already supported their cause or that another characteristic of a politician (such as their partisanship or their ideology) caused both their votes and their pattern of interest group support. To successfully rule out these other possibilities, scholars generally need to know the complete set of factors that predict both interest group activity and policy change. Unfortunately, this knowledge is usually unavailable.

The three approaches I have outlined here provide new evidence about the likely patterns of interest group influence. By researching the distribution of prominence and involvement across interest groups, I demonstrate that the capacity for influence is likely to be highly concentrated among a small number of groups. In other words, most interest groups are unlikely to have much influence no matter what they do. By looking at the role of lobbying in how a bill becomes a law, I find that the amount of interest group activity is consistently related to how far a bill makes it in the process. Bills that generate more interest group activity are more likely to advance toward becoming law.

By drawing on the collective wisdom of policy historians, I generate qualitative evidence in support of widespread interest group influence on policy change but show that a small subset of groups is reportedly responsible for policy enactments alongside government officials.

Yet, none of these conclusions solve the fundamental problems of assessing causality. From the first study, scholars still do not know for sure that policy influence follows reliably from involvement. The idea that rarely involved groups are unlikely to influence outcomes is an untested assumption. The study of congressional bills permits comparison of legislation that generates interest group lobbying with legislation that does not. Unfortunately, the direction of causality is difficult to assess. If bill advancement and lobbying are associated, bill advancement could cause lobbying rather than the reverse. The third study, meanwhile, relies on the judgments of policy historians. We can conclude that most close observers of the history of public policy in many different issue areas regularly see interest group influence, but their assessments could be wrong. They may just see interest group activity associated with policy change; the policy changes may have happened with or without the support of interest groups.

Nevertheless, the studies provide some reason to suspect that scholars may be looking in the wrong places for interest group influence. If prominence and involvement are best predicted by organizational age and staff size rather than campaign contributions and the use of lobbying firms, influence may be less likely to follow directly from these typical tactics. Even though interest group influence is reportedly common, the chance that any one attempt by an interest group to influence policy is successful might still be low. We often blame interest groups when legislation such as SOPA fails to pass, but we should not lose sight of the general bias in favor of the status quo; regardless of whether interest groups get involved, betting that nothing will change is usually a safe bet.

## Applications to Current Controversies

Given what political scientists know about interest group influence on public policy, scholars can provide better context for ongoing public debates about interest groups and the political process. Claims that one group holds overwhelming power, for example, should be held to a high standard. Since the 2010 Republican gains in Congress, many media outlets have been highlighting the role of Grover Norquist's Americans for Tax Reform (ATR) and its pledge to oppose tax increases that was signed by many first-year members of Congress. The group coaxed these members into signing the pledge, the story goes, and so they have opposed all efforts to raise taxes. This is too simplistic. Most of the people who signed the pledge already opposed tax increases, and most votes against taxes are driven by ideology and partisanship rather than adherence to the pledge. The pledge also generally favors the status quo, and that comes with quite an advantage. Once we incorporate the many factors influencing final votes on tax legislation in Congress, we are unlikely to find much of a role for ATR's pledge.

Yet, this hardly means that we can conclude that ATR lacks influence. Indicators of prominence and involvement show that it is repeatedly active in policymaking and considered a major player. Over many years, ATR helped remind Republicans of the importance of the tax issue and built a coalition of voters to oppose candidates who raise taxes. It helped change the debate about the definition of a tax increase, categorizing any closure of a tax loophole without a decline in tax rates as a tax increase. Furthermore, it provided an obvious signal that helps voters and the media select conservative candidates: willingness to sign the tax pledge. Even if ATR did not unilaterally change any votes in Congress, a policy historian would likely conclude that it played an important role in the increasingly strident positions of Republicans in Congress on taxes.

Interest group lobbying also comes up in the news when it is the subject of criminal investigations. In 2006, the lobbyist Jack Abramoff was convicted of conspiracy for his efforts to defraud Native American tribes and bribe public officials. The charges arose after the Senate Indian Affairs Committee began looking into the tribes' efforts to legalize casino gambling on their reservations. Many elected and appointed public officials were also investigated, and some faced criminal penalties. The public saw it as another in a long line of cases proving that American politics is corrupt. Most of the specific evidence accumulated in the Abramoff trial and related investigations, however, indicated that it was not that easy for the tribes to win permission from officials via lobbying and campaign contributions. Instead, Abramoff appears to have extorted millions of dollars from the tribes without delivering much in return.

After his release from jail, Abramoff appeared with a new book on the culture of corruption in Washington, arguing that public policy is for sale. Political science research suggests that these may not be the best lessons to learn from his actions. Based on my measures of prominence and involvement, American Indian tribes are among the many interest groups that rarely obtain a hearing from officials in Washington, no matter how much they spend on lobbyists and campaign contributions. The groups that do influence policy are more likely to be large and well known, such as the AFL-CIO, the AARP, and the U.S. Chamber of Commerce. They mostly use their internal staff, rather than hired lobbyists, to make their pitches to policymakers. When American Indian interest groups compete to influence policy, they do so on a narrow range of issues and sometimes have to compete with more established players. They may be convinced by charlatans such as Abramoff to hand over big bucks for little in return, but that does not mean that policy is easily bought or sold.

## Correcting Public Perceptions and Developing Alternatives

Political science research on interest group influence has accumulated only limited evidence that interest groups can successfully use their resources to change policy outcomes. Where scholars do find evidence, it tends to cover a narrower range of groups, issues, and venues than most people would expect. That does not mean interest groups lack any influence or that scholars will not continue to look in new places for additional evidence. The research presented in this chapter shows that bills with more lobbying make it farther in the process; that close observers of policy history tend to find indications of interest group influence across many different policy areas; and that a small portion of the interest group community takes up most of the regular opportunities to share their views in the news media and with policymakers.

There is still much to learn about interest group influence, but we know enough to conclude that it does not seem to match the public's pessimistic assumptions or the regular pronouncements of breathless pundits. There is little evidence that campaign contributions or lobbying dollars regularly buy legislative outcomes. Scholars have not failed to find the evidence for lack of trying. The reasons are straightforward: Many different factors affect the policy process, only some of which involve interest groups, and few attempts to change public policy succeed, by interest groups or by anyone else. Most complaints about interest groups may be better conceived of as complaints about the political system as a whole, usually boiling down to the idea that public policy often does not follow public opinion or the public interest.

The limited evidence of interest group influence certainly does not mean that the policy process is optimal or that interest groups are blameless for the nation's ills. For many people, any evidence of interest group influence is too much, and any one instance of lobbying dollars making a difference is confirmation of corruption. Knowing that a small number of interest groups dominate opportunities for influence, however, might stimulate Americans to seek to broaden interest group participation in policymaking rather than eliminate it.

The lesson from research is that the realities of politics often do not match the assumptions of the American public. Even evidence that seems to support our myths, such as the association between lobbying and bill passage, needs scrutiny before we can conclude that there is a reliable and causal relationship. Any explanation of policy outcomes that relies on only one factor is unlikely to be telling the full story. Interest groups are an important component of the policymaking process, but they are hardly its unilateral directors.

## Notes

1   These data are compiled by the Center for Responsive Politics from the Senate Office of Public Records. Updated data is available online at <http://www.opensecrets.org>.
2   An online transcript is available at <http://www.gpoaccess.gov/presdocs/2009/DCPD200900087.htm>. Accessed 2/2/11.
3   Bentley, Arthur. 1908. *The Process of Government: A Study of Social Pressures.* Chicago: University of Chicago Press; Truman, David. 1951. *The Governmental Process: Political Interests and Public Opinion.* Westport, CT: Greendwood Press.
4   Olson, Mancur 1965. *The Logic of Collective Action: Public Goods and the Theory of Groups.* Cambridge: Harvard University Press.
5   Schattschneider, E. E. 1975. *The Semisovereign People: A Realist's View of Democracy in America.* Hinsdale, IL: Dryden Press.
6   Schlozman, Kay Lehman and John T. Tierney. 1986. *Organized Interests and American Democracy.* New York: Harper & Row; Berry, Jeffrey. M. 1989. *The Interest Group Society,* 5th ed. New York: HarperCollins Publishers.
7   Walker, Jack. 1991. *Mobilizing Interest Groups in America: Patrons, Professions, and Social Movements.* Ann Arbor: University of Michigan Press.
8   Hojnacki, Marie and David C. Kimball. 1998. "Organized Interests and the Decision of Whom to Lobby in Congress." *American Political Science Review* 92(4): 775–90.
9   Hojnacki, Marie. 1997. "Interest Groups' Decisions to Join Alliances or Work Alone." *American Journal of Political Science* 44(1): 61–87.
10  Frank R. Baumgartner and Beth L. Leech. 1998. *Basic Interests: The Importance of Groups in Politics and Political Science.* Princeton: Princeton University Press.
11  Gregory Wawro. 2001. "A Panel Probit Analysis of Campaign Contributions and Roll-Call Votes." *American Journal of Political Science* 45(3): 563–579.
12  Frank R. Baumgartner, Jeffrey M. Berry, Marie Hojnacki, David C. Kimball, and Beth L. Leech. 2009. *Lobbying and Policy Change: Who Wins, Who Loses, and Why.* Chicago: University of Chicago Press.
13  Thomas T. Holyoke. 2003. "Choosing Battlegrounds: Interest Group Lobbying Across Multiple Venues." *Political Research Quarterly* 56 (3): 325–36; Michael T. Heaney. 2004. "Outside the Issue Niche: The Multidimensionality of Interest Group Identity." *American Politics Research* 32 (6): 611–51.
14  Witko, Christopher. 2006. "PACs, Issue Context, and Congressional Decisionmaking." *Political Research Quarterly* 59 (2): 283–95.
15  Smith, Mark A. 2000. *American Business and Political Power: Public Opinion, Elections, and Democracy.* Chicago: University of Chicago Press.
16  De Figueiredo, John M. and Brian S. Silverman. 2006. "Academic Earmarks and the Returns to Lobbying." *Journal of Law and Economics* 49 (2): 597–626
17  Dara Z. Strolovitch. 2007. *Affirmative Advocacy: Race, Class, and Gender in Interest Group Politics.* Chicago: University of Chicago Press.
18  Richard L. Hall and Frank W. Wayman. 1990. "Buying Time: Moneyed Interests and the Mobilization of Bias in Congressional Committees." *American Political Science Review* 84 (3): 797–820.
19  Matt Grossmann. 2012. *The Not-So-Special Interests: Interest Groups, Public Representation, and American Governance.* Stanford: Stanford University Press. The book only addresses a subset of interest groups, those that claim to represent public interests or concerns. It does not include an analysis of business policy offices or trade associations. Some descriptions used in this chapter are taken from the book.

20 Matt Grossmann and Kurt Pyle. Forthcoming. "Lobbying and Congressional Bill Advancement." *Interest Groups & Advocacy*. Some descriptions used in this chapter are taken from the article.
21 In the House, passage without moving through committee is most often achieved via suspension of the rules. The Rules Committee also has the power to extract bills from committee. In the Senate, bills can bypass committee action via a unanimous consent agreement.
22 Matt Grossmann. 2012. "Interest Group Influence on U.S. Policy Change: An Assessment Based on Policy History." *Interest Groups & Advocacy* 1(2): 171–192. Some descriptions used in this chapter are taken from the article.

## Chapter 7

# The Reach of the Partisan Media

## How Choice Affects the Political Influence of Sean Hannity and Rachel Maddow

*Kevin Arceneaux and Martin Johnson*

Scholars have challenged simplistic notions that the media radically change how people think about politics. However, the rise of highly partisan and shrill news programs raises the concern that one-sided coverage might distort how citizens view politics and further polarize America into warring camps. Kevin Arceneaux and Martin Johnson design intriguing experiments using college students to assess the impact of the partisan news media. One experiment allows subjects to use a TV remote to pick what they want to see from a range of programs. Their findings challenge conventional wisdom and caution us against thinking of citizens as passive "blank slates." In an era of abundant programming, citizens are highly selective in choosing what they want to watch, which dampens the impact of partisan news shows. Arceneaux and Johnson's research raises important questions about other ways partisan media might impact citizen views and what happens to a democracy when people can opt out of watching news altogether. Their work also generates insights about why people do not like or trust the media. This chapter, in particular, explains what it means to create experiments with internal and external validity to ensure that scholars identify causal relationships that can then be applied to the real world.

The mass media in the United States have changed dramatically during the last twenty years. Starting in the 1990s, cable and satellite television offer an ever-expanding choice of programming to viewers. Figure 7.1 shows just how dramatic this change has been. In 1980, the average home had access to fifteen television channels. This figure doubled by 1990, with the average American household, typically a home subscribing to cable television, having about thirty-three television channels available. By 2008, that had increased fourfold to 130 channels.[1] The array of choices is quite fantastic, and this is just what is on television. We are not even considering the myriad choices of information and entertainment available to people via the Internet. How does the growth in these viewing choices affect what people watch? Does it affect politics?

There has certainly been a proliferation of television channels, but the more interesting thing is the programming these channels carry. There seems to

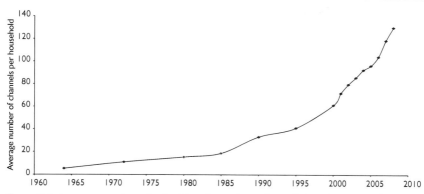

*Figure 7.1* Average number of television channels per household, 1960–2010

be something for everyone, from shows centered on the exploits of colorful young people, such as the denizens of the *Jersey Shore*, to programs that follow sympathetic and nurturing pet trainers, such as *The Dog Whisperer*. Of course, there is a wealth of celebrity gossip, cooking competitions, and sporting events to watch. Researchers who study political communication and many politicians themselves are more interested in the increasing number of twenty-four-hour cable television news channels.

Some of these cable news channels are well known for mixing political commentary with the reporting of political news. The Fox News Channel presents much of its news and commentary from a conservative political perspective and MSNBC has news anchors and talk show hosts who adopt a more progressive, left-of-center approach to the news.[2] Many observers—no less astute than President Obama and esteemed broadcast journalists such as Ted Koppel (who hosted ABC's Nightline news program for twenty years)—express concerns about the availability of partisan news. Many associate the ideological division on television and the apparent growing polarization of the American public.[3] Yet, the expansion of choice in the media environment does more than just allow for selective exposure to like-minded news sources. It also allows people to selectively expose themselves to *anything* they like.

We study the influence of mass media given the tremendous choice available to viewers. Scholars and other observers have been concerned that the media are too influential on people and their political viewpoints for a very long time, at least since the founding of the American republic. Our particular concern is with the extent to which people's ability to select from among all of these different options affects the influence of mass media, which we refer to as *selective exposure*.[4] With the tremendous technological and programming changes afoot in today's media environment, many puzzles remain. Will the emergence of partisan news shows have a powerful impact on voter attitudes? We look specifically at how the abundance of programming choices for

Americans affects the impact of such shows. In short, we find that the presence of choice mutes the impact and reach of partisan news shows. This leads us to conclude that selective exposure limits the influence of the mass media.

Our research offers an alternative to the conventional view that the partisan news media on cable television are responsible for undermining democratic comity and, in the process, threatening the viability of American democracy. We agree that the shows on partisan news networks can be shocking. People on these shows often say and do outlandish things. However, it is important to keep the novelty and reach partisan news media in perspective. First, this is not the first time in American history that news media outlets have exhibited clear partisan biases, and democracy in the United States survived its initial experience with the partisan press. Second, the surfeit of entertainment choices limits the reach of the partisan press. All of this is not to say that the partisan news media have no effects on the health of American democracy, but we must look beyond the simplistic model implicit in the conventional wisdom that partisan news shows have massive negative effects on a large swath of Americans.

In this chapter, we discuss the rise, fall, and rise of partisan news media in the United States, considering the span of American history, and review complementary concerns about the influence of mass media. Then we discuss contemporary approaches to the study of media effects and our own approach. Our laboratory-based experimental research focuses on studying how the choices people make affect the influence of news media. We present an example of these studies and discuss their implications for how we understand the influence of political communication in the era of cable and satellite television.[5]

## Partisan Media in the United States

Partisan media are nothing new in U.S. history, although it seems novel today given the journalistic values of objectivity and partisan balance that dominated broadcast television news and major daily newspaper reporting throughout most of the twentieth century.[6] At an earlier time, however, partisanship pervaded the presentation of news. In the late eighteenth century, two factions developed a fierce competition over how strong the federal government should be.[7] The first system of U.S. party politics arose during the presidency of George Washington, and newspapers were exploited as an essential tool for promoting the platforms of these new political parties.

The first political party leaders were Treasury Secretary Alexander Hamilton, who advocated a strong federal government and, among other things, a central national bank, and Secretary of State Thomas Jefferson, a proponent of a limited federal government. Hamilton and Jefferson facilitated the growth of a political press not dissimilar in its ethics or practice from today's partisan cable news talk shows. Hamilton helped finance and contribute commentary to a newspaper edited by businessman John Fenno, the *Gazette of the United States*, which adopted the ominous motto, "He that is not for us, is against us."[8] Via this publication, Hamilton defended Washington and his *Federalist* policies.

To communicate an alternative *Republican* perspective (i.e., to personally and politically criticize Hamilton), Jefferson used a patronage appointment to support Philip Freneau's publication of the *National Gazette*.[9] This arrangement underscored the deep connection between American media and party organizations. One historian describes the establishment of an opposition newspaper as "the first overtly partisan act by a United States government official, and the first concrete act of party building...the partisan press and American political parties began life as one."[10]

Publications such as these gave voice to intense early conflicts during "the passionate decade" of the 1790s.[11] To be sure, these newspapers addressed fundamental political questions—the size and role of the federal government and what kind of leaders should serve Americans and administer their government—but they also preoccupied themselves with the salacious, by debating the private behavior of officials and publicizing scandals, such as Hamilton's extramarital affair.[12] Political talk show hosts such as Sean Hannity and Bill O'Reilly on Fox News and Ed Schultz and Rachel Maddow on MSNBC are not far from the mark set by the Founders and their partisan press.

Already at the founding, political observers were concerned that the public was vulnerable to harm from the ideas presented in news media. A Pennsylvania state court judge named Alexander Addison, a Federalist, expounded upon theories of republican government and his views on freedom of speech in an essay he address to grand jurors but circulated as a pamphlet, too, defending the Sedition Act. The 1798 law made it illegal to publish false, scandalous, or malicious false writing against the U.S. government.[13] He was particularly concerned about the power of the press to manipulate public opinion: "Give to any set of men the command of the press, and you give them the command of the country; for you give them the command of public opinion, which commands every thing."[14] He considered the words themselves to be influential because "Speech, writing, and printing are the great directors of public opinion, and the public opinion is the great director of human action."[15]

The news industry changed dramatically over the ensuing decades. By the end of the nineteenth century, partisan newspapers gave way to a more neutral press. Technological and social changes made it better business for publishers to become independent. During the era of the partisan press, publishers were often able to stay afloat financially because of government contracts. For example, the patronage appointment in the State Department Jefferson used to help support Freneau's publication of the *National Gazette*. Other newspapers were supported through the award of government printing contracts. By the late nineteenth century, many of these opportunities for partisan publishers were disappearing with the expansion of the federal government and the establishment of in-house printing capabilities, such as the Government Printing Office.[16]

More important, perhaps, newspapers were increasingly financed through advertising sales. As a consequence, publishers faced pressure to moderate the political views expressed in their newspapers to attract larger audiences. Why? If a newspaper espoused an explicitly Republican Party perspective at this time, it risked alienating readers affiliated with the Democratic Party and political moderates. Adopting standards, such as objectivity and balanced coverage of news, or attempting to represent the views of multiple sides of a political controversy helped broaden a newspapers' appeal, earned it more readers, and generated greater advertising revenue.[17] Newspapers also became even more sensational in their coverage of military conflict, public scandals and, of course, consumer safety in the late nineteenth and early twentieth centuries to expand their appeal to readers.[18]

## Classic Research on Media Effects

Even as the news media in the United States became more procedurally objective, Americans have continued to express concerns about their influence on people. Consequently, *social scientists* have been interested in media effects, especially in the realm of politics since at least the turn of the twentieth century. In the 1920s and 1930s, researchers were just beginning to use tools such as survey research to understand public opinion and political psychology, but these were not yet as widespread as they are today. The earliest research on media effects was driven by a focus on the content of mass media and anecdotes about the influence of media on people.

Communication scholar Harold Lasswell paid close attention to the efforts of politicians to sway public opinion during World War I. In his book *Propaganda Technique in the World War*, Lasswell famously described the political rhetoric used by President Woodrow Wilson and the U.S. Committee on Public Information to communicate propaganda about World War I at home and abroad. His claims about the influence of mass media provide an intuitive model of media effects, which is widely known among media scholars as the "hypodermic model" or "magic bullet theory."[19] This theory promoted the view that Wilson had "brewed a subtle poison" of propaganda that he "injected into the veins of a staggering people, until the smashing powers of the Allied armies knocked them into submission" and convinced the American public to go to war.[20] Like Addison more than 100 years earlier, Lasswell described a direct influence of mass media on members of the audience.

Just a few decades later, research informed by more direct observation of people and their views found that this was a greatly exaggerated perspective on the influence of mass media. Studies conducted by Paul Lazarsfeld and his colleagues at the Columbia University Bureau for Social Research found that people were far less influenced by "propaganda," especially political campaign messages, than Lasswell and others had envisioned. One of their most compelling findings was that *most* voters have made up their mind about which presidential candidate to support far before the start of the campaign (typically Labor Day in September). Instead, voters appear guided by their long-standing identification with a particular political party and other reference groups related to ethnicity or social class. Consequently, voters interpret the events of the campaign and candidate appeals though the filter of these group identifications and make political choices that are strongly informed by these group ties rather than propaganda.

Much of the research calling into question the "hypodermic model" was synthesized by Joseph Klapper in a 1960 book, *The Effects of Mass Communication*. As Klapper explains, the influence of mass media is limited by the tendency of people to *selectively* expose themselves to information, *selectively* perceive the messages contained in their chosen sources of information, and *selectively* remember things.[21] The important insight here is that people are not nearly as passive as many of us envision. Think about your own use of television and the Internet today. You may sometimes surf from channel to channel or from Web site to Web site, but you are looking for something—the latest news on some topic of interest, or a particular kind of entertainment. This is selective exposure: You choose to expose yourself to the kinds of information and entertainment that you like to watch. Other people do this, too.

These processes of selective exposure, perception, and memory do not mean media have no influence at all. For example, the news media play an important role in establishing political priorities, called *agenda setting*. Bernard Cohen observed that mass media "may not be successful much of the time in telling people what to think, but it is stunningly successful in telling its readers what to think about."[22] One particularly important study in 1972 suggested that by reporting on some issues and not others, the newspapers of Chapel Hill, North Carolina, affected what issues voters found important during the 1968 U.S. presidential election. They analyzed the content of newspaper and broadcast campaign coverage and found a strong relationship between the attention the news paid to a given issue and the rank of issues people said they found important when surveyed. Hundreds of studies have replicated this finding.[23]

It is also clear that news media can affect how people think about political issues, through a process called *framing*. In addition to not being able to present all possible news stories, news organizations inevitably make choices about how to cover issues and what aspects of a public controversy to focus on in news coverage. For example, one study shows that how a problem is framed substantially influences how people think about an issue and, therefore, what solutions they deem appropriate.[24] News organizations often frame crime episodically, focusing on specific criminals and criminal acts, rather than thematically exploring the structural roots of crime. The implication is that people who see coverage of crime want to punish individual criminals more severely because they bear responsibility for their actions. However, this is only part of the story, of course. If news coverage of crime focused on the economic and social forces that affect criminal behavior, people might support different approaches to law enforcement.

The mass media may also serve to *reinforce existing attitudes* rather than necessarily changing minds about issues or their prior beliefs. If people selectively expose themselves to information that is already consistent with their worldview, it may make them more resistant to future attempts at persuasion.[25] If people actively screen out oppositional or mainstream news and only consume like-minded news, it could create a "reinforcing spiral" in which positive feedback loops allow individuals to maintain their preexisting attitudes even in the face countervailing facts on the ground.[26] For example, even though the Bush Administration conceded that there was no evidence for the pre-Iraq War claim that Saddam Hussein possessed weapons of mass destruction (WMDs), many rank-and-file Republicans continued to hold the belief that he did. It's possible that partisan news outlets helped Republicans continue to believe WMDs existed in Iraq by providing plausible rationales (e.g., the unsubstantiated claim that Hussein removed WMDs just before the American invasion). In this way, like-minded news may encourage viewers to interpret facts incorrectly so that the narrative remains consistent with desired outcomes.[27] Earlier students of media effects did not necessarily consider this to be a particular problem, because they were interested in how people's attitudes about things might change.[28] In contrast, many scholars today see attitude reinforcement as an aspect of persuasion.[29]

## How Do Scholars Study Media Influence?

Social scientists have been interested in media effects for some time. Today, most research in this area adopts one of two major approaches: public opinion surveys, often combined with knowledge about the types of media people might consume, and experiments. We will briefly describe both of these approaches and our new direction in media effects research, which draws on the strength of both kinds of research.

Studying public opinion and media effects using surveys seems like an intuitively reasonable approach to the problem. If you want to know whether Fox News viewers are somehow different from MSNBC or CNN viewers, or newspaper readers (e.g., if they are more conservative, less knowledgeable), it seems quite sensible to find some people who attend to each one of these potential sources of information and explore how different they are. After all, we know that the content of these news sources expresses important differences.[30] If we see differences between MSNBC and Fox News viewers, as we do, it seems plausible that it is due to differences between the media outlets, right? Maybe, but we are not convinced.

The problem with this approach is that it possesses weak *internal validity*, which refers to the extent to which we are able to infer that the media messages really cause the differences between the groups of people we sample or whether it was something else. The major threat to internal validity of the survey research design here is the fact that people *select* the programming they view. So, if conservatives prefer Fox News and liberals prefer MSNBC, we cannot conclude that watching partisan news shows causes people to adopt the viewpoints espoused on those shows. Instead, all we can say is that Fox News viewers are different from MSNBC viewers, and it could have nothing at all to do with the fact that they watch different news networks.

Survey research allows us to observe only the *correlation* between news viewing behavior and political attitudes. This kind of analysis alone cannot conclusively tell us whether watching Fox News causes viewers to become conservative. As the adage goes, correlation does not equal causation. A common example of the flaw in associating correlation with causation is that both ice cream consumption and homicides tend to increase in the summer months. It would be ridiculous to claim this association provides evidence that eating ice cream causes people to become more violent. Because we know people select news on the basis of their political views,[31] we should also be skeptical of claims that news shows *cause* viewers to think or behave in a particular way based on a correlation.

Randomized experiments provide a better strategy for isolating causal effects. In a randomized experiment, the researcher randomly assigns individuals to *treatment conditions* she or he believes to cause an attitude or behavioral change. These treatments differ only on the hypothesized causal factor. So, in the current example, we might design an experiment where we assign people at random to watch Fox News, MSNBC, or CNN or to read the newspaper.[32] By making assignment to these different treatments at random, by rolling a die or flipping a coin to decide which news source the person will receive, we can be sure that the treatment that people receive is not affected by some other factor that may also affect the outcome we are interested in studying, such as their political beliefs, economic circumstances, or level of education.

Random assignment gives us a way to answer the fundamental question underlying all causal inference: What would happen if the same people experienced different treatments? Actually observing this is impossible because each person can do only one thing: We cannot simultaneously observe the effects of watching MSNBC and *not* watching MSNBC for the same person. All we can do is ask this person to either watch or not watch MSNBC. When we use random assignment, we create (at least) two groups of people who are highly similar in terms of their demographic and social characteristics, allowing us to simulate a world in which we simultaneously expose the same person to different treatments. Because the people in our randomly assigned treatment groups are highly similar to one another, we can infer that any differences between these groups after the experimental treatment is administered are caused by the treatments rather than the preexisting characteristics of the people in the study.

It sounds great, but there are limitations here, too. Political communication researchers have learned a great deal about the effects of media on opinions using randomized experiments. However, these experiments rely on the assumption that people in the study would actually watch the shows being studied. In fact, we know people do choose what to watch and may avoid shows they do not want to watch because such shows may actually challenge their opinions. It is hard to imagine that a very liberal person would choose to watch a conservative talk show host such as Sean Hannity on Fox News other than out of sheer curiosity or to get their blood boiling. More generally, many laboratory-based experiments trade strong internal validity for weak *external validity*, which refers to how well a study demonstrates something that happens in the real world. Many laboratory experiments rely on narrow samples (e.g., college sophomores) who may react to news programs differently than the average Joe.

It is important to recognize that we are not making wholesale critiques of previous research. We have a lot to learn from survey research projects, especially creatively designed research such as the paper by McCombs and Shaw[33] or the analysis of survey data collected over time.[34] Similarly, we have learned a great deal about potential effects of messages from randomized experiments that assign subjects to treatments at random.[35] These studies isolate the causal effects and capture maximal effects. However, we also recognize there are lessons to learn from more explicitly engaging viewers on their terms and seeing what happens *when people have the ability to choose what they view*.

Our research also reflects the fact that technology is changing rapidly, offering media audiences more and more choice daily. Until quite recently, scholars could reasonably assume people would be exposed to content broadcast on the mainstream media due to the relatively small number of viewing options available as late as the early 1990s. During the broadcast television era, many people were exposed to political news whether they wanted to watch it or not because at multiple times of the day, news was the only thing on television.[36] The expansion of channels on cable and satellite television and the plethora of options on the Internet has forced political communication researchers to reconsider experimental designs and develop new approaches to study media effects. We have developed alternative research strategies that allow us to take advantage of the benefits of experiments and simultaneously consider the opportunities for choice viewers have.

## New Directions in the Study of Selective Exposure to Media

In a traditional political communication experiment studying the effects of television, viewers are assigned to watch a particular television show, an alternative television program, or potentially nothing at all. In a sense, research participants are forced to watch a given program. It sounds strong to say it this way, but this is how we would learn whether a given television show affected the viewers somehow—by forcing them to watch it or not allowing them to watch it. Viewers were given few choices in these kinds of experiments, really only the choice to participate or not. This is a problem for the external validity of traditional political communication experiments: When people watch television, they usually are not forced to watch something they do not want to, unless their roommate is in control of the remote. To address this problem, we modify this forced exposure design by assigning subjects at random to forced viewing treatment conditions or alternatively to a choice condition in which participants are given a remote control and allowed to flip among the television programs showcased in the forced conditions.[37] Similar to sitting on the couch at home, with remote control in hand, participants were allowed to spend as much time on each program as they liked and could flip back and forth as much as they wanted. In our studies, these viewing sessions for people assigned to forced viewing or choice conditions lasted between five and twenty minutes. By comparing posttreatment outcomes in the choice condition to those in the control and forced treatment conditions, it is possible to gauge how people assigned to the choice were different after the experiment from people in the forced viewing conditions and, thus, *how self-selection influenced media effects.*

Although the selective exposure design stimulates conditions that are slightly more natural than the convention laboratory study, it does not *perfectly* replicate viewing at home. However, we think this research design does improve the external validity of our experiments while maintaining their internal validity. The selective exposure design is no different. Subjects assigned to the choice condition are not watching television at home, and they do not have access to the 130 channels or so that they could watch at home. They are in a laboratory on a college campus, and they know we are studying them. As a result, the inference we can draw from these studies is limited, albeit slightly less so, in the same way traditional laboratory studies are limited. We learn about the maximal effect of television programs news when a limited number of choices are available.

## Applying the Selective Exposure Experiment: Reactions to Partisan News

As the news media on cable have become more partisan, we are interested in whether this has changed how people view the news. Interestingly, if we go back to a time when the news was ostensibly "objective" and journalist followed norms of providing equal time to both sides on controversial issues, you find that people nonetheless often perceived bias in news reporting. One prominent study asked participants to watch television news segments chronicling the

1982 massacre of civilians in refugee camps in Sabra and Shatila, Lebanon.[38] Christian militiamen had carried out the horrific slaughter of Arab refugees over the course of two bloody days. Many people faulted the Israeli military for failing to intervene. Even though they watched the same newscast, pro-Israeli participants overwhelming viewed the stories and the news organizations that generated them as biased against Israel, whereas pro-Arab participants came to the opposite conclusion. They thought that the stories were overly favorable to Israel.

This phenomenon is called the *hostile media effect*, and other scholars have documented it in various political contexts.[39] Why would people believe that news stories and organizations are biased against their side when these news reporters are following norms of journalist objectivity by telling both sides of the story? The answer, in part, lies in the fact that the journalists are telling both sides. If people strongly believe that one side (theirs) is the right side, it would be inaccurate to suggest that the other side might be correct. It would be akin to suggesting that maybe the world is flat.

Enter partisan news media. These shows *are* biased. They tend to present only one side of the story and, in the process, require us to refine the hostile media effect thesis. For those who expose themselves to like-minded media, it creates the possibility of a *friendly media effect* in which viewers say, "Finally these guys are getting the stories right!"[40] At the same time, if people are exposed to oppositional media, they may reach the opposite conclusion: "How could anyone believe that!"[41] In our study, we called this *oppositional media hostility*—the possibility that the mere presence of oppositional news media causes viewers to believe that the news media, in general, really are biased against their side.[42]

Of course, this entire discussion about the effect of the partisan news shows on media perceptions makes the implicit assumption that people tune into these shows. In fact, we know that many people do *not* watch partisan news shows. Indeed, the ratings of programs such as *The O'Reilly Factor* on Fox News or *The Rachel Maddow Show* on MSNBC are actually quite small relative to other programming. For example, in the week of January 2, 2012, the week of the Iowa presidential caucuses, the first run of O'Reilly's telecast—the most popular show on Fox News—drew an average of 2.8 million viewers each night, peaking with almost 3.3 million each of the two days after the Iowa caucuses.[43] Maddow, who tends to just edge out host Ed Schultz most evenings on MSNBC, had an average of slightly more than 1 million viewers each night that week. The most popular nightly broadcast news show is the NBC Nightly News, which enjoyed an average of 8.9 million viewers[44] each night that week—more than three times O'Reilly's viewership and almost nine times more than Maddow's.

Furthermore, viewership for these news shows pales in comparison to entertainment programs. The most popular scripted drama the week of January 2–8 was *NCIS* on CBS with 19.8 million viewers, whereas the most popular comedy, *Modern Family* on ABC, had 14 million total viewers.[45] In short, with many more popular shows and hundreds of channels available, people who *do not* watch partisan news are a very large majority of television viewers. We argue that this fact alone should blunt the effects of partisan news shows.

## The Evidence

We began our study by first demonstrating that exposure to partisan news shows engenders oppositional media hostility. We exposed participants to either like-minded or oppositional news shows, and we found that those exposed to oppositional news shows left the study with a bad taste in their mouth. Not only did they believe these shows were horrible, but these negative perceptions spilled over into their judgments of the news media as a whole.

With this baseline established, we then investigated what happens when you give study participants the option to change the channel with the aid of two selective exposure studies. As we described earlier, participants in these studies were randomly assigned to one of four groups. Some were forced to watch a like-minded show, some were forced to watch an oppositional show, and some were placed in a "control" group where they were asked to watch nonpolitical entertainment shows. The fourth group was given a remote control and allowed to flip the channel among these options. Just as in natural settings, they could watch as much of or as little of partisan news media as they wanted.

The first selective exposure study was conducted in winter 2009 with the help of 167 undergraduate students recruited from the University of California, Riverside. To simplify matters, we simulated a sort of one-sided information environment in which the only partisan news available came from a liberal viewpoint: a segment drawn from the *Hardball with Chris Matthews* show on MSNBC. This particular segment aired in November 2008 and featured a tendentious discussion about the positive qualities of then president-elect Barack Obama. For the entertainment shows, we selected *Dirty Jobs*, a Discovery Channel show about performing undesirable jobs, and a show about vacations in log cabins that aired on the Travel Channel.

The second selective exposure study was conducted in the fall 2009 with the help of 117 University of California, Riverside students. We made this study a bit more realistic by featuring partisan news shows drawn from liberal and conservative news outlets. The conservative segment aired on *The O'Reilly Factor*, and the liberal segment aired on *The Rachel Maddow Show*. Both of these shows focused on the debate about health care reform, taking diametrically opposed positions and bashing the other side in the process. The entertainment shows were *The Dog Whisperer* (National Geographic Channel), which features a dog trainer helping people train their dogs, and *Dhani Tackles the Globe* (Travel Channel), which follows former professional football player Dhani Jones on his various trips.

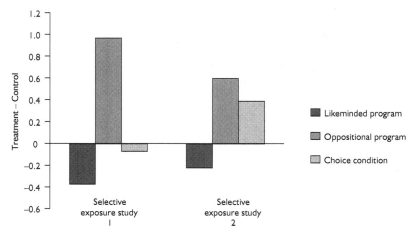

*Figure 7.2* The effects of partisan news and choice on hostile media perceptions

After watching television, we administered a *posttest survey* in which we asked subjects various questions about the news media. Using these questions, we created a *hostile media* index in which larger values on the scale correspond with perceptions that the news media, in general, are biased. Figure 7.2 summarizes our findings from these two studies. The bars in this figure represent the difference in hostile media perceptions between the treatment groups and the control group. A positive value indicates that the subjects assigned to a particular condition left the study believing that the media are more hostile than subjects assigned to the control group did. Conversely, a negative value indicates that subjects assigned to the treatment group left the study believing that the news media are less hostile than subjects assigned to the control group.

As we found in the baseline studies, individuals forced to watch an oppositional news show were more likely to perceive hostility in the news media. We also uncovered suggestive evidence that isolated exposure to like-minded news programs may cause individuals to develop less hostile views toward the news media. However, once we move beyond the confines of the forced exposure treatment and allow people to choose what they want to watch, we discover two things. First, giving people choices tends to blunt the effects of partisan media. Second, even though the effects of partisan news media are smaller in the world of choices, we find in the second study that the presence of like-minded and oppositional news shows may erase the friendly media effect. Knowing that the other side is out there bloviating against one's side may generate an oppositional media effect.

Although we will not go into the details here, we took the extra step in our study to understand why choice blunts the effect of partisan news media. The simplest explanation is that fewer people are watching. This is undoubtedly the case. However, we also found evidence that partisan news media tend to have a smaller impact on those who choose to watch these shows than it does on those who would rather watch something else. People who seek out partisan news, it appears, are different from those who seek out other forms of entertainment. Partisan news seekers enjoy these shows. They watch them regularly. They know what to expect and are not surprised by it. Those who seek out other forms of entertainment do not watch these shows regularly and, when someone in a lab coat forces them to do so, it has a dispiriting effect.

## Discussion

We find that the effects of partisan news are blunted by the choices audience members make. People who are forced to watch shows with a different ideological perspective from their own perceive a great deal of hostility from the media, whereas participants we assigned to watch shows from their own point of view see them as friendlier. Neither of these findings should seem all that surprising and are quite consistent with other traditional experimental research on political communication that limits the choices people have available in a laboratory context. However, historically, researchers such as us have known far less about what happens when people actually are allowed to choose what they view. We show that choice mutes the effects of media in this instance—especially when political programs available reflect only one side of the ideological spectrum. Also in the full research article, we are able to isolate the effects of oppositional news to people who would prefer not to watch the political shows in the first place. These people make political judgments and have opinions but would rather watch shows about dog trainers and athletes. By selecting out of watching political news, people dilute its potentially negative effects.

Clearly, partisan news *can* have a great deal of influence on people, consistent with the concerns of so many scholars and observers. Nonetheless, these greater effects are conditional on people being somehow forced to view partisan news. The far greater concern, in our view, is the tendency of people to self-select out of news at all. Not too long ago, many people tuned into the evening news on broadcast television because it was the only thing on after they got off work. This large inadvertent audience of news watchers meant that lots of folks were at least exposed to the news, meaning they would have a basic understanding of the major political events that made it on the 6:00 news. The presence of ample entertainment choices has changed all of that. Now, people watch the news mostly because they actually want to watch the news. Paradoxically, this means that as the news has become more shrill and has greater power to provoke, its reach has become diminished. Even though people have more reasons to be hostile toward the news than once before, they may not actually be more hostile simply because they choose to change the channel.

Though we see less of a role for contemporary cable news to harm or divide viewers, we do see a greater tendency for people to remove themselves from news, becoming less informed and less likely to participate in public life.[46] This means that the implications that increasing choice and the emergence of the partisan news media have for democracy are more complicated than it first seems. Choice diminishes the negatives that accompany partisan news, but it does so at the risk of shrinking the informed citizenry.

Future research should move beyond simple models of media transmission. In a world with 130 channels, we cannot expect partisan news shows to have massive direct effects. Yet, that does not mean that partisan news shows have no effects. After all, these shows still might influence people indirectly through opinion leaders who tune in and then discuss politics with their friends and family. Moreover, political elites, such as politicians and pundits, regularly tune into partisan news shows. Consequently, these shows may have important effects on influential people. And doing so, partisan news shows with small audiences may still be able to shape the public discourse. These indirect and mediated effects of the partisan news media could prove to be more consequential than the imagined massive direct effects that have captivated the attention of contemporary political observers.

## Notes

1 Joe Mandese, "T.V. Universe Expands, Share of Channels Tuned Does Not," *Media Daily News*, July 21, 2009. Accessed December 16, 2011, http://www.mediapost. com/publications/article/110159/. PRNewswire, "Average U.S. Home Receives a Record 104.2 T.V. Channels, According to Nielsen," March 19, 2006. Accessed December 16, 2011, http://www.prnewswire.com/news-releases/average-us-home-now-receives-a-record-1042-tv-channels-according-to-nielsen-52170292.html. Nielsen Media Research Group, *Nielsen Report on Television* (New York, 1981).

2 Natalie J. Stroud, *Niche News: The Politics of News Choice* (New York: Oxford University Press, 2011).

3 Kathleen Hall Jamieson and Joseph N. Cappella, *Echo Chamber: Rush Limbaugh and the Conservative Media Establishment*, (New York: Oxford University Press, 2008). Diana C. Mutz, *Hearing the Other Side: Deliberative versus Participatory Democracy*. (New York: Cambridge University Press, 2006). Natalie J. Stroud, "Polarization and Partisan Selective Exposure," *Journal of Communication* 60 (2010): 556–76.

4 Joseph T. Klapper, *The Effects of Mass Communication*. (Glencoe, IL: The Free Press, 1960.)

5 Kevin Arceneaux, Martin Johnson, and Chad Murphy, "Polarized Political Communication, Oppositional Media Hostility, and Selective Exposure," *The Journal of Politics* 74 (2012).

6 Michael Schudson and Susan E. Tifft, "American Journalism in Historical Perspective," in *The Press*, ed. Geneva Overholser and Kathleen Hall Jamieson (New York: Oxford University Press, 2005), 17–47.

7 John H. Aldrich, *Why Parties? The Origin and Transformation of Political Parties in America*, (Chicago, IL: University of Chicago Press, 1995).

8  Eric Burns, *Infamous Scribbles: The Founding Fathers and the Rowdy Beginnings of American Journalism*, (New York: Public Affairs, 2006), 264.
9  Timothy E. Cook, *Governing with the News: The News Media as a Political Institution*, (Chicago, IL: University of Chicago Press, 1998). Jeffrey L. Pasley, *"The Tyranny of Printers": Newspaper Politics in the Early American Republic*, (Charlottesville, VA: University Press of Virginia, 2001).
10  Pasley, *"Tyranny,"* 78.
11  Burns, *Infamous Scribblers*, 225–45.
12  Burns, *Infamous Scribblers*, 312–14.
13  Burns, *Infamous Scribblers*, 356.
14  Addison *Liberty of Speech*, 19.
15  Addison *Liberty of Speech*, 18.
16  Cook, *Governing*, 32.
17  James T. Hamilton, *All the News That's Fit to Sell: How the Market Transforms Information into News*, (Princeton, NJ: Princeton University Press, 2004). Maria Petrova, "Newspapers and Parties: How Advertising Revenues Created the Independent Press," *American Political Science Review* 105 (2011):790–808.
18  Jeremy D. Mayer, *American Media Politics in Transition* (Boston, MA: McGraw-Hill, 2007).
19  Elizabeth M. Perse, *Media Effects and Society*, (Mahwah, NJ: Erlbaum, 2001), 33.
20  Harold D. Lasswell, *Propaganda Technique in the World War* (New York: Alfred A. Knopf, 1927; reprint, New York: Garland Publishing, 1972).
21  Klapper, *Effects*, 64.
22  Bernard C. Cohen, *The Press and Foreign Policy*, (Princeton, NJ: Princeton University Press, 1963), 13.
23  Maxwell E. McCombs, *Setting the Agenda: The Mass Media and Public Opinion* (Malden, MA, Blackwell Publishing, 2004).
24  Shanto Iyengar, *Is Anyone Responsible? How Television Frames Political Issues*, (Chicago, IL: University of Chicago Press, 1991).
25  Carl Hovland, "Effects of Mass Media of Communication," in *Handbook of Social Psychology*, ed. Gardner Lindzey, (Cambridge, MA: Addison-Wesley, 1954).
26  Michael D. Slater, "Reinforcing Spirals: The Mutual Influence of Media Selectivity and Media Effects and Their Impact on Individual Behavior and Social Identity," *Communication Theory* 17 (2007): 281–303.
27  Brian Gaines, James H. Kuklinski, Paul J. Quirk, Buddy Peyton, and Jay Verkuilen, "Same Facts, Different Interpretations: Partisan Motivation and Opinion on Iraq," *Journal of Politics* 69 (2007): 957–74.
28  Klapper, *Effects*.
29  R. Lance Holbert, R. Kelly Garrett, and Laurel S. Gleason, "A New Era of Minimal Effects? A Response to Bennett and Iyengar," *Journal of Communication* 60 (2010), 17, emphasis added.
30  Lauren Feldman, Edward W. Maibach, Connie Roser-Renouf, and Anthony Leiserowitz, "Climate on Cable: The Nature and Impact of Global Warming Coverage on Fox News, CNN, and MSNBC," *The International Journal of Press/Politics* 17 (2012): 3–31. Stroud, *Niche News*.
31  Stroud, *Niche News*; Shanto Iyengar and Kyu S. Hahn, "Red Media, Blue Media: Evidence of Ideological Selectivity in Media Use" *Journal of Communication* 59 (2009): 19–39.
32  Lauren Feldman, "The Opinion Factor: the Effects of Opinionated News on Information Processing and Attitude Change," *Political Communication* 28 (2011):163–81.

33  Maxwell E. McCombs and Donald L. Shaw, "The Agenda-Setting Function of Mass Media," *Public Opinion Quarterly* 36 (1972):176–87.

34  Stroud, *Niche News*

35  Shanto Iyengar and Donald R. Kinder, *News that Matters: Television and American Opinion*, (Chicago, IL: University of Chicago Press, 1987).

36  Markus Prior, *Post-Broadcast Democracy: How Media Choice Increases Inequality in Political Involvement and Polarizes Elections*, (New York: Cambridge University Press, 2007).

37  Communication scholar Dolf Zillmann and his colleagues used a similar research design during the late 1970s to study how children are affected by educational television. Jacob J. Wakshlag, Raymond J. Reitz, and Dolf Zillmann, "Selective Exposure to and Acquisition of Information from Educational Television as a Function of Appeal and Tempo of Background Music," *Journal of Educational Psychology* 74 (1982): 666–77. Dolf Zillmann, Richad T. Hezel, and Norman J. Medoff, "The Effect of Affective States on Selective Exposure to Televised Entertainment Fare," *Journal of Applied Social Psychology* 10 (1980): 323–39. Dolf Zillmann and Jennings Bryant, "Selective-Exposure Phenomena," in *Selective Exposure to Communication*, eds. Dolf Zillmann and Jennings Bryant, (Hillsdale, NJ: Lawrence Erlbaum Associates, 1985).

38  Robert P. Vallone, Lee Ross, and Mark R. Lepper, "The Hostile Media Phenomenon: Biased Perception and Perceptions of Media Bias in Coverage of the 'Beirut Massacre,'" *Journal of Personality and Social Psychology* 49 (1985):577–85.

39  Russell J. Dalton, Paul A Beck, and Robert Huckfeldt, "Partisan Cues and the Media: Information Flows in the 1992 Presidential Election," *American Political Science Review* 92 (1998): 111–26. Albert C. Gunther and Kathleen Schmitt, "Mapping Boundaries of the Hostile Media Effect," *Journal of Communication* 54(2004): 55–70. Tien-Tsung Lee, "The Liberal Media Myth Revisited: An Examination of Factors Influencing Perceptions of Media Bias," *Journal of Broadcasting & Electronic Media* 49 (2005):43–64.

40  Seth K. Goldman and Diana C. Mutz, "The Friendly Media Phenomenon: A Cross-National Analysis of Cross-Cutting Exposure," *Political Communication* 28 (2011): 42–66.

41  Kevin Coe, David Tewksbury, Bradley J. Bond, Kristin L. Drogos, Robert W. Porter, Ashley Yahn, and Yuanyuan Zhang, "Hostile News: Partisan Use and Perceptions of Cable News Programming," *Journal of Communication* 58 (2008): 201–19.

42  Political scientist Jonathan Ladd shows that political elites on the left and the right over the past 20 years have undermined trust in the news media by accusing it of bias. Jonathan M. Ladd, "The Neglected Power of Elite Opinion Leadership to Produce Antipathy toward the News Media: Evidence from a Survey Experiment," *Political Behavior* 32 (2010): 29–50.

43  Bill Gorman, "Cable News Ratings for Monday, January 2, 2012." *TV by the Numbers*, January 4, 2012. Accessed January 16, 2012, http://tvbythenumbers. zap2it.com/2012/01/04/cable-news-ratings-for-monday-january-2-2012/ 115237/. Bill Gorman, "Fox News Tops Iowa Caucuses Coverage – Cable News Ratings for Tuesday, January 3, 2012." *TV by the Numbers,* January 5, 2012. Accessed January 16, 2012, http://tvbythenumbers.zap2it.com/2012/01/05/fox-news-tops-iowa-caucuses-coverage-cable-news-ratings-for-tuesday-january-3-2012/115424/. Bill Gorman, "CNN's Iowa Caucus Ratings Boost Deflates; Cable News Ratings for Wednesday, January 4, 2012." *TV by the Numbers*, January 5, 2012. Accessed January 16, 2012, http://tvbythenumbers.zap2it.com/2012/01/05/cable-news-ratings-for-wednesday-january-4-2012/115426/. Bill Gorman, "Cable News Ratings for

Thursday, January 5, 2012." *TV by the Numbers*, January 6, 2012. Accessed January 16, 2012. http://tvbythenumbers.zap2it.com/2012/01/06/cable-news-ratings-for-thursday-january-5-2012/115575/. Robert Seidman, "Cable News Ratings for Friday, January 6, 2012." *TV by the Numbers*, January 9, 2012. Accessed January 16, 2012. http://tvbythenumbers.zap2it.com/2012/01/09/cable-news-ratings-for-friday-january-6-2012/115839/.

44  Chris Ariens, "Evening News Ratings: Week of January 2." *TVNewser*, January 10, 2012. Accessed January 16, 2012. http://www.mediabistro.com/tvnewser/ category/evening-news-ratings.

45  Robert Seidman, "TV Ratings Broadcast Top 25: Lions-Saints Wildcard, 'Modern Family,' 'NCIS' Top Week 16." *TV by the Numbers*, January 10, 2012. Accessed Janaury 16, 2012. http://tvbythenumbers.zap2it.com/2012/01/10/tv-ratings-broadcast-top-25-lions-saints-wildcard-modern-family-ncis-top-week-16/115915/.

46  Prior, *Post-Broadcast*.

# Chapter 8

# Why Tough Campaigns Are Good for Democracy

*Keena Lipsitz*

Many Americans say they dislike political campaigns because of mudslinging between candidates, but Lipsitz explains why campaigns are so important for representative democracy. Scholars have long argued that hard-fought, competitive elections yield more information to voters about candidates, but Lipsitz wants to know whether this information is substantively "good." By good she means whether the information actually promotes democratic values such as free choice, equality, and deliberation. The conventional wisdom is that negative advertising produces useless, even harmful information for voters. Lipsitz shows otherwise. Using unique data on campaign ads, she measures how the substance of congressional campaigns varies at different levels of competition. Remarkably, she finds that even slight improvements in competition yield substantial gains in providing quality information to voters. Yet, few elections for Congress are competitive, which means many voters are not benefiting from the rich information that elections potentially provide. The research raises important questions about what kinds of reforms might improve the competitiveness of elections. Lipsitz's work also shows how scholars try to measure complex concepts such as political equality or deliberation and how to use straightforward statistics to predict outcomes.

> I know nothing grander, better exercise, better digestion, more positive proof of the past, the triumphant result of faith in human kind, than a well-contested American national election.
>
> —*Democratic Vistas*, Walt Whitman

In a January 2012 *Daily Show* segment, Jon Stewart checked in with his correspondents in South Carolina, the state with the third contest of the Republican Primary season where Mitt Romney was expected to have his toughest fight yet. His correspondent in Columbia, South Carolina, Aasif Mandvi, reported that the primary "had not hit yet," but residents were "preparing for the worst." "They're boarding windows shut, collecting canned food. The flood of negativity is expected to reach at least chest high," says

Mandvi. Stewart asks, "What should people in the direct path of the campaign do?" To which, Mandvi replies in a stricken tone, "Head for the high moral ground. Hug your loved ones close. And, for goodness sake, stay away from TVs and radios!"

There is a long history of comparing hard-fought elections to violent events, such as hurricanes. For instance, the word *campaign* itself is from the Latin word *campus*, meaning *field*, and originally referred to the period of time when an army was doing battle. Alexis de Tocqueville offered another metaphor, describing American campaigns as periods during which the entire nation is gripped by a "feverish state." Most Americans would probably find these metaphors apt as many fail to see the benefit of competitive elections. In fact, when asked in a 2006 national survey what the effect of facing a tough election is for a politician, 62 percent of respondents said tough campaigns make politicians, "focus too much on fundraising and campaigning instead of being a good representative." Only 22 percent said that they make representatives "work harder to represent their district better."[1] These findings suggest that most Americans believe competitive elections do more harm than good and that they would find the declining number of closely contested elections in the United States to be a welcome trend.

In this chapter, I challenge this dim view of competitive elections. Like Walt Whitman, I believe well-contested elections should be celebrated and promoted. Though most scholars believe that competitive elections enhance the accountability of elected officials by forcing them to respond to challengers' charges, I argue competitive campaigns have an added value: They are better than uncompetitive ones at providing voters with the kinds of information they need to make an informed electoral decision.[2] Yet, many elections are far from competitive. For example, in the ten election cycles from 1992 to 2012, on average only 8 percent of House races were considered competitive.[3] This should be worrisome to anyone who cares about the health of American democracy. However, just how competitive do elections need to be to create informational benefits for citizens? Using new data on television advertising in campaigns, I show it does not take much. In fact, most of the benefits accrue when elections are just slightly more competitive than usual.

Some basic values of democratic theory—free choice, equality, and democratic deliberation—give us a good place to start thinking about what characteristics campaign information should have to help promote a healthy democracy. Data about campaign advertising help us see that competitive elections expose voters not only to more information but *better* information. In fact, most of the benefits accrue when elections become just slightly more competitive than the usual safe House district. I end with a brief discussion of reforms for enhancing electoral competitiveness and the obstacles that lay ahead for reformers.

## What Kinds of Information Do Voters Need?

Most Americans would agree with James Madison's description of the tactics and strategies used by politicians to win elections as the "vicious arts." Yet, just imagine an election without a campaign. There would be no television and radio advertisements, no phone calls from campaign volunteers, and no direct mail. If there was no campaign, you would never see a candidate making a speech, debating an opponent, shaking a voter's hand, or kissing a baby. Under such circumstances, only the most politically engaged citizens would be aware that there was even an election going on. And only the most motivated of those citizens would actually visit their polling station. Those who did would know little about their choices, so they would vote for the most-familiar candidates, irrespective of their qualifications or issue positions. Without campaigns, challengers would have virtually no chance against incumbent politicians or celebrity candidates.

This exercise illustrates the importance of campaigns and the information they provide to voters; they educate them, persuade them, and encourage them to turn out on Election Day. Yet, it is plainly clear that the quality of campaign information can range wildly. Before making any claims about reforms that would improve elections, we need to establish standards for evaluating the information provided to voters in campaigns. The following discussion does this by asking what kinds of information voters need if elections are to promote the values of free choice, political equality, and public deliberation.

### Free Choice

In a representative democracy, such as the United States, elections allow citizens to choose who will represent them in government. By definition, a choice involves selecting one of a number of alternatives. This means voters must be allowed to choose between at least two parties or candidates. Otherwise, if an election is uncontested, voters have no real choice. Yet, even when this minimal requirement has been met, problems can still arise. For example, a voter can be coerced into voting a particular way through intimidation or threats. Their vote can also be manipulated through more subtle and artful means. When voters have been coerced or manipulated, their vote is no longer free or autonomous, which undermines the democratic value of sovereignty. In a democracy, the people are supposed to be sovereign; in other words, all political power is supposed to originate with them. If they are being coerced or manipulated, the democratic credentials of a polity must be questioned.

### Political Equality

As the Declaration of Independence suggests with its solemn assertion that "all men are created equal," political equality is a central value in the American political system. The principle of one-person-one-vote is a natural extension of the belief in the intrinsic equality of citizens. Yet, some scholars have pointed out that inequalities can arise during the campaign period before a vote is even cast. In *A Preface to Democratic Theory*, Robert Dahl argues that the preservation of equal political influence and citizen sovereignty requires that voters possess identical information about the choices confronting them on Election Day. Dahl explains that meeting this condition, allows us to say that voter choice has not been ". . .manipulated by controls over information possessed by any one individual or group."[4] By "identical," Dahl means that candidates should be able to disseminate similar amounts of information to voters, as he is chiefly concerned about any one candidate or party being able to monopolize the airwaves in a campaign.[5] Another scholar, Ronald Dworkin, has arrived at the same conclusion by pointing out that political candidates are citizens, too. He argues that citizens are equals not only as voters but as candidates for office as well.[6] In fact, Dworkin argues we should be just as concerned about the equality of candidates for office as we are about the equality of voters. At minimum, his argument suggests that all citizens—including elected officials, candidates for office, and organized groups—should have a fair and equal opportunity to publish, broadcast, or otherwise command attention for their views. Thus, Dahl and Dworkin agree that if one candidate controls the flow of political communication, she or he will be able to manipulate the opinions of citizens and, as a consequence, her or his viewpoint will carry more weight than those of other candidates. Such an outcome obviously undermines equality.

### Deliberation

Like the value of political equality, the value of deliberation has roots that run deep within the Western democratic tradition. For example, in his eulogy of Athens, Pericles called the period of discussion preceding a political decision in a democracy "an indispensable preliminary to any wise action at all." Democratic theorists who value deliberation often compare it to the way decisions are typically made in democracy: A vote is held, and the side or candidate with the most votes win. Although this manner of making a decision is democratic in the sense that there has been a free vote, it also suggests that "might makes right." Those who believe our political institutions and processes should involve more debate and discussion point out that this form of decision making offers little to those who are on the losing side of a vote. The only explanation they are given for their loss is that they are too few in number. If the process had involved more deliberation, however, those in the minority might better understand the opinions and beliefs of the majority. They might also feel better about the process simply because it provided them with an opportunity to offer arguments and express their concerns. Some scholars even argue that opportunities for deliberation would promote more harmony and agreement among citizens.

Aside from creating opportunities for citizens to deliberate, one can also use deliberative principles to evaluate the information that voters receive in campaigns.[7] First, citizens need a high volume of information to ensure that at least a portion of it is actually received by them. Second, deliberation requires that voters be exposed to information from a diverse range of sources in a campaign to ensure that they are exposed to a variety of arguments about which candidate is superior. Such sources might include interest groups, in addition to the candidates and political parties. The reason why citizens need to be exposed to diverse information is that it helps them develop more thoughtful opinions and attitudes. Finally, deliberation requires candidates to engage one another's arguments and to refrain from "talking past" one another. From a voter's perspective, it is difficult to compare candidates when they are talking about different issues and refusing to respond to one another's arguments. When two candidates address the same issue, scholars refer to this as either "issue convergence" or "dialogue." A final point needs to be underscored: Deliberation does not require candidates to refrain from criticizing one another. Because deliberation requires candidates to be honest, we should be concerned when candidates are lying or trying to mislead voters, but we must differentiate such deceitful attacks from valid criticisms. Research has demonstrated that negative advertisements are far more informative than positive ads in which the candidates avoid talking about their opponent.[8] Scholars have also shown that voters also learn more from negative advertisements than positive ones.[9] Although one might find positive advertisements more appealing than negative ads, keep in mind that politics inevitably involves disagreement, and it is more helpful for citizens if candidates make the differences between themselves and their opponents clear in a negative advertisement than for them to make voters feel good with a positive advertisement that features images of waving flags and smiling children.

## Do Competitive Elections Provide Voters with Better Information?

Many studies have found that competitive elections generate a higher volume of information for voters. Studies of House elections have found that "hard-fought" congressional races generate more news coverage and television advertising.[10] Researchers have found that the same is true of news coverage and television advertising in Senate elections.[11] In presidential elections, it has long been recognized that electoral competitiveness at the state level shapes the behavior of presidential candidates, encouraging them to allocate their resources to states that could potentially swing toward either party.[12] In terms of the specific features of the information environments generated by competitiveness at the state level, many studies have found that residents of swing states are exposed to more television and radio advertising.[13] Research also shows that candidates are more likely to travel to competitive states[14] where their visit is likely to generate local news coverage.[15] In terms of the other features of the campaign information environment, there is little research on how competitiveness affects direct mail, phone banking, and canvassing, although it is probably safe to assume that competitiveness drives them as well. Thus, one might say that there is something of a consensus in the literature that voters receive more information when elections are competitive than when they are not. The question, however, is whether the information provided has characteristics that promote the democratic values discussed earlier or whether citizens are simply being inundated by useless or—at worst—harmful information.

Less attention has been given to how competitiveness affects the substantive content of campaign information. Conventional wisdom has it that closely contested races generate more negative information and some research confirms this. One study has found that advertising in competitive House races is substantially more negative than in noncompetitive races,[16] and a handful of others have shown that this is true of Senate races as well.[17] The one study that has compared the proportion of attack advertising in competitive House and Senate races observed that competitiveness has a much stronger relationship with negativity in the former than in the latter. When comparing the proportion of ads featuring attacks in competitive and noncompetitive races, it found that nearly half (45 percent) of the ads in competitive House races featured attacks, whereas only 21 percent of the ads in noncompetitive races did. In Senate campaigns, those numbers were 31 and 20 percent, respectively.[18] The one study that has examined how electoral competitiveness affects negativity in presidential elections has examined its effect at the national level; that is, how the closeness of a race nationally affects the general tone of advertising and finds no relationship. John Geer speculates that the reason is that

> presidential elections are always "competitive" by the standards employed by congressional scholars. …There is, in short, not as much variance as we see in races for the House of Representatives or the Senate. Even in the most lopsided presidential contests, there is a degree of competition that is still absent in most congressional races.[19]

Perhaps a similar logic explains why competitiveness is a stronger predictor of negativity in House than in Senate races. Senate races are usually more competitive than House races. Thus, one might argue, to use Geer's language, that even the most lopsided Senate race has a degree of competition that is absent in most House races.

Recently, scholars have turned their attention to exploring electoral competitiveness' effect on dialogue (i.e., when two candidates discuss the same issue, with mixed results). One study of dialogue in Senate campaigns, which coded candidate statements in newspaper accounts, found little evidence of a relationship[20] as did another that examined television advertising in 1998 House and Senate races.[21] Yet, two studies, one of Senate television advertising and another of presidential candidate statements in newspapers, found a strong relationship between competitiveness and dialogue.[22] The inconclusiveness of the findings in this area suggests more research is needed.

## What We Don't Know

Based on existing literature, we are fairly confident that competitive elections encourage candidates to provide more information to voters and that this information tends to be more negative. However, we have a conflicting set of findings regarding the effect of competitiveness on negativity or the likelihood of candidates discussing the same issues. In terms of the known unknowns, it is less clear how electoral competitiveness is related to information equality and diversity. In competitive races, it is natural to expect a wide range of voices to speak because they are responding to the same incentives that candidates are. In other words, because interest groups and parties also have finite resources, they will spend those resources as efficiently as possible, which means they will target elections where their efforts have the greatest potential to affect the outcome of a race, that is, close elections. As a result, competitive elections should generate information environments with more sources of information. In terms of the equality of information about candidates, we know that candidate spending differences are much smaller in competitive elections, which suggests that the volume of information should be more balanced as well.

Although some of these hypotheses, such as the relationship between advertising diversity and equality, seem straightforward enough, it is unclear what the relationship between competition and each of these information characteristics looks like. A goal of my research is to understand just how competitive an election needs to be to give political elites enough of an incentive to provide voters with better information. Studies that examine the effects of electoral competitiveness typically use one of two types of measures: a linear measure, such as the margin of victory in a previous election, or a dichotomous measure, which classifies a race as "hot" or "cold." The linear measure assumes that each unit increase in the measure of competitiveness yields the same increase in whatever variable is being explained, which is a strong assumption. For example, a 5 percent reduction in the margin of victory, from, say, 10 percentage points to 5 percentage points is likely to yield a bigger change in the information environment than a reduction in the margin from 25 to 20 points. Using a dichotomous measure assumes that no races are "lukewarm." Yet, not only are there plenty of lukewarm races out there but we need to know whether they generate information environments that are substantially better than cold races or substantially worse than hot ones. These are important questions for reformers because the answers to these questions will indicate the difficulty of the task that lies ahead for them. Our electoral laws would have to be drastically reformed to make a significant number of Senate and House races highly competitive. Yet, there are a number of more modest reforms that might increase the number of marginally competitive elections. Thus, it is important to understand exactly what the relationships between electoral competitiveness and dialogue, information diversity, and information equality look like.

## The Data: Analyzing Campaign Ads to Assess the Information Environment

To assess the impact of competitiveness on campaign information environments in this chapter, I use House television advertising data from 2000 to 2004 that were collected by the Campaign Media Analysis Group (CMAG).[23] CMAG uses sophisticated technology to "capture" ads as they air and store information about when and where they appeared. It tracked ad airings in seventy-five of the country's largest media markets in 2000 and one hundred of the largest media markets in 2002 and 2004. A media market is a county or group of counties whose residents tend to watch the same television stations, and there are more than 200 in the United States. The unit of analysis in the CMAG dataset is the ad airing as opposed to the ad itself. If one simply examined the content of a single ad as many studies have done, one might get a skewed sense of what a voter's campaign environment looks like because one would have no sense of how often that ad was aired or where it was aired.[24] The CMAG data provide this important information.

Despite the strengths of the CMAG data, using them to analyze House campaign ads poses a problem that researchers seldom acknowledge. Because CMAG monitors only about half of the media markets in the country and media market boundaries are not congruent with congressional districts, it is possible that the CMAG monitoring area only partly covers a congressional district. This raises a problem. If the CMAG dataset has no ad airings for a congressional race but monitors a media market that serves only a small portion of that district, we might mistakenly conclude that no ads were aired in the race when in fact the candidates and their supporters might have done all their advertising in a neighboring media market that serves more of the district but is not monitored by CMAG.

To address this issue, I used a geographic information system to determine what portion of a given media market's population lies in each congressional district. By doing this, I was able to identify which congressional districts are completely monitored by CMAG, which are partly monitored, and which lie totally outside the CMAG monitoring areas. Districts that fell completely outside of CMAG monitoring areas were not included in the following analysis. To determine whether a partly covered district should be included in the analysis, I examined districts that fell completely within the CMAG monitoring area but were served by at least two media markets. I found that candidates and their supporters usually air at least a handful of ads in a media market if it serves more than 40 percent of the district's population. Based on this, I concluded that I could fairly code districts that had more than 40 percent of their population living in CMAG-monitored media markets but had no ads in the dataset as having no ads overall. If a congressional district had less than 40 percent of its population residing in CMAG-monitored media markets, I did not include it in my analysis regardless of whether the CMAG dataset indicated there was or was not advertising in the district.

One might ask whether political ads are the best measure of the overall campaign information environment that a voter is experiencing. After all, a voter's campaign information environment includes the news broadcasts of local, network, and cable television stations. It also includes the articles voters read in newspapers and magazines and what they hear on the radio about the races in their area. Aside from these more obvious purveyors of information, an individual's information environment also consists of the information conveyed by family, friends, and coworkers in conversation. Although television ads are clearly just one element of a voter's information environment, I would argue they are a central component of it. Television advertisements have become an increasingly important element of political campaigns for both candidates and interest groups. Even candidates in House elections spend the bulk of their money budgeted to communications on television advertising. For example, a candidate in a typical House campaign spends 22 percent of his or her budget on television ads, 12 percent on radio ads, 8 percent on direct mail, 8 percent on campaign literature, and less than 5 percent on other forms of communication.[25] Although the bulk of television advertising is sponsored by candidates and parties during campaigns, interest groups rely more heavily on it with each campaign cycle. Clearly, television advertising has become the most important means of communication for politicians and their supporters during campaigns, which makes them a key source of campaign information for voters.

In the following analysis, I examine the effect of a race's competitiveness on five dependent variables that measure different aspects of a voter's campaign information environment and reflect the political values discussed earlier: (1) the total number of ads aired during the campaign; (2) the diversity of the information as determined by the number of unique advertising sponsors in the race; (3) the ratio of the incumbent or favored candidate's ad airings to the challenger's; (4) the amount of dialogue in the advertising; and (5) the proportion of the total ads aired that attack a candidate. To create the first measure, I counted the total number of ads aired during the general election campaign between Labor Day and Election Day. For the diversity measure, I counted all the individuals and organizations sponsoring ads in the campaign as identified by CMAG. In the number of total sponsors, I included candidates and party organizations, but I did not allow for more than one party committee to be represented in the total number. Thus, if the Republican National Committee and the Republican state party committee sponsored ads, I added only one sponsor to the total number of ad sponsors in the campaign. This is because it is unlikely that the two party committees speak with distinct voices.

The equality or balance of information measure reflects the ratio of ad airings in favor of one candidate to the number of ad airings in favor of the other. Specifically, I created this measure by dividing the number of ad airings supporting the candidate with the fewest number of ad airings (usually the challenger) by the number of ad airings supporting the candidate with the greatest number (usually the incumbent). This method yields a continuous measure ranging from 0 to 1, with "0" indicating that only one candidate was supported in the advertising and "1" indicating that they were equally represented. If a race did not feature any ads, it was excluded from the analysis.

For the dialogue measure, I created an issue attention profile for each Republican and Democratic candidate by determining the percentage of their advertisements that mentioned a particular issue.[26] For instance, a Democratic candidate might mention jobs in 30 percent of his or her ads, education in 40 percent, and the environment in the other 30 percent. A Republican might mention taxes in 40 percent of her or his ads, defense in 30 percent, and jobs in the remaining 30 percent.[27] To determine the amount of dialogue in the campaign I calculated the amount of overlap there was in these issue attention profiles by summing the absolute differences across all the issues. This number was then divided by two and then subtracted from one to yield a dialogue measure ranging from 0 to 1. Interpreting this measure is straightforward; if a race received a dialogue measure of .40, it means that there was a 40 percent overlap in the issue attention profiles of Republican and Democratic advertising sponsors. I took the additional step of coding cases in which there was no advertising or only one side advertising as "0," as no candidate dialogue could occur in such situations.

Instead of measuring the absolute number of attack ads in a campaign, I measured the proportion of ads in which a candidate or one of his or her supporters attacked an opponent. Most studies that examine the effect of negative advertising simply use a measure of negative advertising volume, such as the total number of ad airings. Yet, when average Americans or political observers talk about a campaign's negativity, they usually mean that it is more negative than positive. In other words, they consider the level of negativity in relation to how many positive things are being said. To create this measure, I determined whether each ad was intended primarily to promote a candidate, contrast the two candidates, or attack a candidate. For each race, I divided the total number of attack ad airings by the total number of ads aired overall to create the dependent variable, which ranges from 0 to 1. If there were no advertising in a race, it was excluded from the analysis of negativity.

In the analyses that follow, I use a variety of methods to analyze the effect of competitiveness on my dependent variables of interest.[28] All the analyses control for standard demographic characteristics of the congressional districts I analyze. Specifically, I include variables that might also predict my outcome variables, which enables me to isolate the independent effect of competiveness on the outcome variables. Thus, I include measures for the median age in the district, percentage of the population with a bachelor's degree, percentage of the population that is white, and median income. I also control for the average cost of an ad airing in the particular congressional race and whether the race features an incumbent representative or is open. I do not control for factors such as candidate spending in the election, because such measures are *intervening* variables.[29] The competitiveness of an election, as reflected in polls and previous electoral margins, drives how much money the candidates spend in a campaign. As a result, including such variables in the models risks masking the effect of electoral competitiveness and wrongly concluding that it does not matter.

All of the following analyses use a measure of competitiveness supplied by the Cook Political Report. Each election year, Cook codes House races using four categories. "Safe" districts are uncompetitive and are expected to be safe for the party that has controlled the seat for the previous term. The second least competitive category features those that are "likely" to favor the party in power. Moderately competitive districts "lean" toward one party but are still relatively competitive, whereas the most fiercely contested districts are labeled as "toss ups".

## The Results: Competition Generates More and Better Information for Voters

The findings are clear but nuanced. They show that although the relationship between electoral competitiveness and the *quantity* of information that voters receive in House races is largely linear (i.e., it increases steadily as the competitiveness of the race increases), the relationship between competitiveness and the *quality* of that information is of a different nature. Specifically, there are diminishing returns to competitiveness. This is good news for people who want to improve campaigns because it means that the road ahead is not so steep; modest improvements in competiveness make a significant difference in both the quantity and quality of information that voters get. And since most House elections in this country are "safe," many people would benefit from such reforms. The findings, which I describe next, also suggest that although voters might receive *more* information in highly competitive contests, the *quality* of that information is no better than it would be in only moderately competitive races.

## Information Volume

I analyzed the effect of competitiveness on the volume of information provided by House incumbents and challengers separately to see whether they respond differently to electoral threats. Most races feature an incumbent, so this will give us a sense of what happens in a typical House race. Figure 8.1 shows how incumbents and challengers respond to heightened electoral threats by showing the number of ads that we would expect them to air at each level of competition. The figure provides the reader with predicted probabilities, which were calculated from regression models that controlled for the variables discussed earlier. As it is often difficult to interpret coefficients provided by regression models, I report the predicted probabilities, which simply indicate the expected outcome on the dependent variable for each level of change in the key independent variable, when other independent variables (e.g., controls) are held at their mean. The figure reveals that incumbents and challengers in safe districts do not typically air many ads but that the predicted number of ad airings rises steeply as the level of competition increases. For incumbents, the predicted number of ad airings is 34 in safe districts, 602 in likely districts, 1,272 in leans districts, and 2,086 in toss-up districts, respectively. Similarly, for challengers, the predicted number of ad airings are 9 in safe districts, 446 in likely districts, 966 in leans districts, and 1,781 in toss-up districts.

Overall, one might describe this relationship as being nearly linear for both incumbents and challengers, with a slightly steeper rise for incumbents. Previous research suggests that incumbents tend to overreact to electoral threats because they are "running scared" and do not want to risk the chance of sending a signal to future challengers that they are vulnerable to losing a race.[30] Reduced margins might invite an even stronger challenger in the next election.

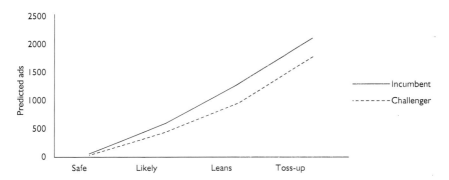

*Figure 8.1* Effect of competitiveness on advertising volume in House elections[31]

The vertical axis indicates the number of advertisements that the regression model predicts incumbents and challengers will air in the race.

The steeper line for incumbents might also reflect the fact that incumbents usually have more campaign money lying in reserve, so they can buy ads more easily than a challenger with fewer resources.

### Information Diversity

Information diversity is measured by the number of sponsors of TV ads in each House race. In most cases, if there is any television advertising in a district at all, it has a single sponsor: the incumbent. In terms of the effect of competitiveness on information diversity, the biggest gains appear to occur well before an election becomes a toss-up. For example, in races that have some modest competition, the expected number of sponsors is 1.7, which means voters are much more likely to be exposed to ads by both candidates, compared to races with a safe seat where voters are lucky to see ads by the incumbent. Many safe districts feature no ads at all, which is why the point on the graph dips below 1 to .3. The increase in sponsorship more than doubles again when the race moves from the likely to leans categories (from 1.4 to 2.6 sponsors). At the upper end, when the contest is a toss-up, sponsorship increases to just over 3 (3.2). However, given the limits of my data, I am not confident that the difference between the two highest levels of competitiveness is different from 0. The vertical lines bifurcating each black square indicate the plausible range of outcomes around the point-estimate. When the confidence intervals of two predictions—in this case, of the number of sponsors—overlap, we cannot be confident that these two situations will generate genuinely different outcomes. More important, even if the outcomes are different, the substantive increase of .5 sponsors is rather small, which suggests that most of gains in sponsorship arrive before a race becomes a toss-up (Figure 8.2).

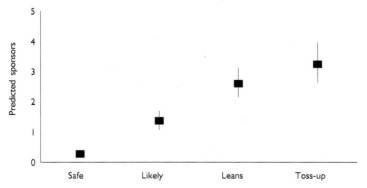

*Figure 8.2* Effect of competitiveness on information diversity in House elections[32]

The vertical axis indicates the number of advertising sponsors that the regression model predicts that will air advertisements in the race. Vertical lines indicate upper and lower bounds of 95 percent confidence intervals.

Just who are these sponsors adding to the information diversity in competitive races? In addition to the national and state party committees, some of the most frequent advertising sponsors in the campaigns from 2000 to 2004 were groups such as the Chamber of Commerce and the Business Roundtable, which typically supported Republican pro-business candidates, and the American Federation of Labor, which backed Democrats. The group that sponsored by far the most advertisements in the 2000 and 2002 elections, however, was a 527 committee that called itself Citizens for Better Medicare (CBM), which was funded primarily by the pharmaceutical industry to fight adding a drug benefit to Medicare. Although one might argue that the pharmaceutical industry has a right to air its views as much as other groups, CBM was criticized for claiming to be a grassroots organization and using an innocuous name to hide the real identity of its backers. Thus, even though competitive elections might draw more sponsors, there is no guarantee that the sponsors will present their views in a candid and truthful fashion. Still, these findings do suggest that modest increases in district competitiveness can result in substantially more information diversity in a campaign. At the very least, both candidates will air ads, which is a better situation than in safe districts where voters may not see any ads at all.

## Information Equality

Democratic theorists who promote the political value of equality emphasize the importance of candidates' having equal opportunity to make their case to voters. Moreover, for a voter's choice to be truly free, the citizen must be aware and informed about all the options. On a scale of 0 to 1, with "0" indicating unequal and "1" indicating equal, the mean equality ratio for House races in which ads were aired was .58. Put another way, for every ad aired by a challenger, the incumbent typically airs 1.7 ads or nearly twice as many. The graph in Figure 8.3 shows that the relationship between competitiveness and a House campaign's equality ratio is nonlinear. Once again, the biggest gains come from levels of competition just short of a toss-up race. The largest increase in equality occurs between safe districts (almost no competition) and those that are modestly competitive, with the predicted equality ratio tripling from .12 to .43. It then increases to .67 in lean races, and .69 in toss-up races, a difference that is not statistically significant. In sum, modest improvements in the competitiveness of a race significantly improve the equality of information provided to voters.

## Candidate Dialogue

Candidate dialogue refers to the amount of overlap in the issue attention profiles of the candidates during the campaign season. As Figure 8.4 shows, the most significant increase in House candidate dialogue occurs when a

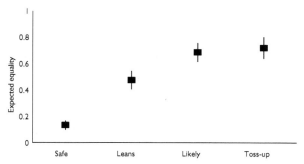

*Figure 8.3* Effect of competitiveness on information equality in House elections[32]

"0" indicates that only one candidate was supported with advertisements and "I" indicates that two candidates were equally represented. Vertical lines indicate upper and lower bounds of 95 percent confidence intervals.

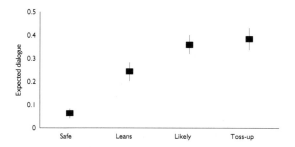

*Figure 8.4* Effect of competitiveness on dialogue in House elections[33]

"0" indicates no overlap in the issues discussed by the candidates during the campaign and ".5" indicates a 50 percent overlap in the issue attention profile of the candidates. A "I" (not shown) would indicate that the candidates gave the same amount of attention to the same issues. Vertical lines indicate upper and lower bounds of 95 percent confidence intervals.

district moves from being a safe contest to being likely to favor a party with the predicted level of dialogue increasing from .05 to .21. In other words, the percent of time that rival candidates are giving similar amounts of attention to the same issues in the campaign quadruples with just a modest increase in the level of competition (from 5 percent to 21 percent). House races that are moderately competitive receive an additional boost as the expected level of dialogue increases to .33. Toss-up races do not feature significantly more dialogue, however, demonstrating once again that there are diminishing returns to competition. In 2000 to 2004, candidates spent the most time discussing health care, especially Medicare, in their ads and education, social security, and taxes—all issues that are typically among the most important for American voters. Increased competition then, appears to force candidates to focus on a handful of issues, making it easier for voters to compare and contrast them.

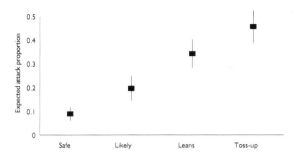

*Figure 8.5* Effect of competitiveness on negativity in House elections[34]

"0" indicates the candidates aired no negative ads and ".5" indicates that 50 percent of all the ad airings were negative. A "1" (not shown) would indicate that all of the ads were negative. Vertical lines indicate upper and lower bounds of 95 percent confidence intervals.

## The Share of Attack Ads

One of the main concerns about competitive elections is that they encourage candidates to be more negative. The first chart in Figure 8.5 leaves no doubt about the truth of this relationship. The expected share of attack ads starts out at just .10 in safe contests but increases to .20 and .33 in modestly and moderately competitive contests, respectively. The proportion of ads that are expected to be negative in toss-up contests is .48 or nearly half. The question then is how does all of this negativity affect voters? The common perception is that negative ads harm voters by manipulating and deceiving them, but political scientists have found that exposure to more negative ads, as measured by the total number of them, actually helps voters learn.

To extend this line of research, I used the proportional measure of negativity and found that in House elections, the edifying nature of negative ads is even more impressive. Figure 8.6 illustrates how the degree of negativity in ads is directly related to the ability of voters to rate House candidates on a *feeling thermometer*—a common measure of political knowledge in House races because it indicates whether voters know enough about candidates to have attitudes about them.[35] The y-axis is the predicted probability that the respondent knows enough about the candidates in a race to be able to rate both of them on a scale of 1 to 100. The three lines indicate the effect on a respondent's knowledge at high, medium, and low levels negativity. The top line shows that voters learn when the proportion of negative advertising is high. By high, I mean approximately 60 percent of the advertising is negative. The middle line indicates that a medium level of negativity (where approximately 30 percent of the ads are negative) has a slightly negative effect on knowledge, although the effect is so small that we are not confident it is substantively different from having no effect. The bottom line indicates that a low proportion

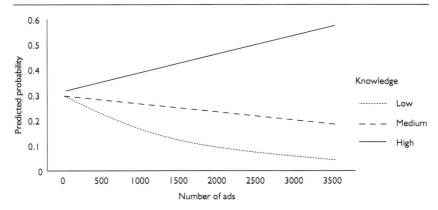

*Figure 8.6* Effect of levels of negativity on knowledge of House candidates[36]

The y-axis indicates the predicted probability that the respondent will be able to rate both candidates on a scale of 1–100.

of negative ads—or, to put it another way, a high level of *positive* advertising— actually harms the ability of respondents to rate the candidates. This is the first study to show that a high volume of positive television advertising is harmful for voters. Although it is beyond the scope of this study to explain why, the culprit may be the lack of substantive content in such ads. It is also possible that positive ads make voters feel more ambivalent—meaning of two minds— about the candidates and therefore, less capable of rating them. Clearly, more research is required to confirm the negative effect of positive advertisements and to explore what explains it.

## Conclusion

The analysis shows that competitive elections are more likely to provide voters with the information they need to make their decision on Election Day. By *need*, I mean information that promotes the key democratic values of free choice, equality, and deliberation. The findings should also be heartening for reformers because it shows that even a modest improvement in the competitiveness of a House race can yield substantial gains in terms of the quantity and quality of information that voters receive.

Yet, many questions remain. One can ask whether the findings of a study about House races apply to other kinds of contests, such as municipal, state- wide, or even state-level presidential races. In other words, do voters derive the same benefit from increasing competitiveness in those kinds of elections? Studies of campaign advertising often focus on one type of election, but it is difficult to draw broad conclusions about the effect of such advertising on voters, regardless of the type of election. Moreover, the emergence of new campaign strategies might also make it difficult to generalize the findings. For example, the findings in this study are based on data from 2000 to 2004. However, recently, new organizations have formed called "super PACs" that can raise unlimited funds from contributors and spend unlimited funds to endorse or defeat a candidate.[37] As research shows that advertising by outside groups—as opposed to candidates—is more negative, the quality of voters' campaign information environment may be adversely affected by the deluge of super PAC–funded advertising that will occur in highly competitive elections in the wake of this ruling. Further research will be necessary to see whether the findings of this study hold in this brave new world.

In addition, television advertising captures the dynamics for just one element of political campaigns. To be sure, television ads are an enormously important way for House candidates and interest groups to communicate with voters, but competitiveness might affect other forms of communication differently. For example, one important form of communication in campaigns is direct mail: the glossy postcards and brochures that turn up in voters' mailboxes during the campaign season. Unlike television ads, most direct mail goes unnoticed by news organizations and, as a result, candidates often reserve their nastiest attacks for them. The same can be said for campaign phone calls. As the competitiveness of an election increases, it is quite possible that direct mail and the content of these phone calls become more misleading and deceptive. This might mitigate some of the beneficial effects of television ads.

Finally, I want to turn to the issue of measurement, particularly with respect to the concepts of dialogue and negativity. Social scientists try to measure such concepts, which can have a variety of meanings and understandings. In this study, the concepts also reflect key political values I discussed at the beginning of the chapter: free choice, equality, and deliberation. For example, I measured the concept of deliberation by determining the amount of issue convergence there is in campaign advertising—what I call "dialogue." This measure of dialogue is a standard way for political scientists to obtain a partial measure of the much larger concept of deliberation. However, one might fairly ask whether it is an appropriate measure of the concept. Normally, one associates political deliberation with town hall meetings and debates, not with the back and forth of candidates through television advertising. Though it is true that candidates often respond to each other's ads in their own ads, some could argue that calling such exchanges deliberation is a stretch.[38]

The analysis also shows that negativity, another concept, is a by-product of competition. Political scientists typically call an advertisement in which a candidate focuses primarily on an opponent "negative" and one that focuses primarily on the sponsoring candidate "positive." Defining negativity in this fashion (and as I do earlier), most researchers find that negative ads help voters learn more about the candidates than positive ads because they are more likely to contain substantive information. This definition of negativity is "directional" because it simply refers to which candidate is being discussed in an advertisement. Yet, the average American or journalist might define *negativity* as some combination of directional and the degree to which the ad appears deceptive. One can imagine that deceptive ads would be less helpful for voters than truthful ones, but it is difficult to measure the veracity of an ad as candidates who criticize opponents are likely to argue that their criticisms are "true" from a certain perspective. I underscore this point to suggest that concepts used by political scientists may not always carry the same meaning for average Americans. Though I believe negative ads are, on balance, helpful for voters, political scientists must dissect them more carefully to identify which elements of them benefit citizens and which elements might be harmful.[39]

## Reforming Elections

If competitive elections appear to generate rich information for voters, what can be done to increase competition? One way is to adopt reforms that help challengers and weaken the many advantages that incumbents enjoy. For example, the former might include providing challengers with a reasonable level of public financing,[40] whereas the latter might involve reforming the franking privilege, which allows members of Congress to advertise themselves by sending mail to constituents without postage.[41] Most challengers are woefully underfunded compared to incumbents, and the results of this study suggest that even modest increases in challenger funding could improve citizen knowledge about candidates and issues. To the degree that the campaign finance system provides incentives to support challengers, American political campaigns will do a better job giving voters real choices, promoting equality, and enhancing public deliberation.

Conventional wisdom also points to redistricting as a major source of incumbents' advantage because it allows sitting legislators to literally pick and choose voters, drawing district lines in a way that virtually ensures victory. This would suggest that reforms taking redistricting out of the hands of legislators would benefit competition. Yet, though some scholars argue gerrymandering has a substantial effect on competition, others argue its effects are quite small.[42] Studies of states that have adopted independent redistricting commissions also offer mixed findings with respect to whether they increase competition.[43] Many also advocate term limits as a way of increasing the number of competitive elections (in statewide elections, as they are unconstitutional for members of Congress) because they would more frequently create open contests that do not feature an incumbent. Yet, a study of state legislative term limits shows that although term limits do create more open seats, these open seats are less competitive than those that occur naturally.[44] In short, even though the benefits of competitive elections—even just modestly competitive ones—for voters might be clear, the path for reformers is not.[45]

As I discussed at the beginning of the chapter, citizens often fail to see the benefit of closely contested elections, so they do not pressure elected officials to reduce the number of uncompetitive races in this country. Some advocates of reform have looked to the courts for help, arguing that they should help create a healthier political "marketplace."[46] Yet, the courts have provided little relief, in part because it is difficult to determine what is a healthy level of political competition. If elected officials and the courts will not help, the responsibility falls to those who, like Walt Whitman, recognize the worth of closely contested elections and who might educate voters to cease viewing them as hurricanes, fevers, or wars but rather as the very heart of democratic accountability and participation.

Portions of this chapter first appeared in *Competitive Elections and the American Voter* by Keena Lipsitz (Philadelphia, PA: University of Pennsylvania Press, 2011).

## Notes

1 Pew Research Center for People and the Press. 2006. "Lack of Competition in Elections Fails to Stir Voters." http://people-press.org/reports/pdf/294.pdf.
2 Some scholars disagree, arguing instead that uncompetitive elections are preferable to competitive ones. See Justin Buchler. 2011. *Hiring and Firing Public Officials: Rethinking the Purpose of Elections.* Oxford Univerity Press; Thomas L. Brunell. 2008. *Redistricting and Representation: Why Competitive Elections are Bad for America.* Routlege; Justin Buchler. 2005. "Competition, Representation and Redistricting: The Case Against Competitive Congressional Districts." *Journal of Theoretical Politics* 17, 5: 431–463. These scholars argue that uncompetitive elections may produce legislators and legislative bodies that are more responsive to citizen preferences (Buchler) and that voters are more satisfied with the outcomes of uncompetitive elections (Brunell).
3 Cook Political Report. Calculated based on ratings in report immediately preceding election. 2012 ratings based on report dated March 23.
4 Robert Dahl. 1956. *A Preface to Democratic Theory.* Chicago: The University of Chicago Press, 70.
5 Keena Lipsitz. 2011. *Competitive Elections and the American Voters.* Philadelphia, PA: University of Pennsylvania Press.
6 Ronald Dworkin. 2002. *Sovereign Virtue: The Theory and Practice of Equality.* Cambridge: Harvard University Press.
7 Lipsitz. 2011.
8 John Geer. 2006. *In Defense of Negativity: Attack Ads in Presidential Campaigns.* Chicago: University of Chicago Press; Darrell M. West. 2005. *Air Wars: Television Advertising in Election Campaigns 1952-2004.* Washington, D.C.: CQ Press; Jamieson, Kathleen Hall. 1992. *Dirty Politics: Deception, Distraction and Democracy.* Cambridge, UK: Oxford University Press.
9 Michael M. Franz, Paul B. Freedman, Kenneth M. Goldstein, and Travis N. Ridout. 2007. *Campaign Advertising and American Democracy.* Philadelphia, PA: Temple University; Geer. 2006.
10 Kenneth Goldstein and Paul Freedman. 2002. "Lessons Learned: Campaign Advertising in the 2000 Elections." *Political Communication* 19: 5–28.; Edie N. Goldenberg, and Michael W. Traugott. 1984. *Campaigning for Congress.* Washington, D.C.: CQ Press.

11  Goldstein and Freedman. 2002; Kim Fridkin Kahn and Patrick J. Kenney. 1999. *The Spectacle of U.S. Senate Campaigns*. Princeton, N.J.: Princeton University Press; Mark C. Westlye. 1991. *Senate Elections and Campaign Intensity*. Baltimore: Johns Hopkins University Press.

12  Taofang Huang and Daron Shaw. 2009. "Beyond the Battlegrounds? Electoral College Strategies in the 2008 Presidential Election." *Journal of Political Marketing* 8, 4: 272–91; Daron Shaw. 1999. "The Methods Behind the Madness: Presidential Electoral College Strategies, 1988–1996." *Journal of Politics* 61: 893–913; Daron Shaw. 2006. *Race to 270: The Electoral College and the Campaign Strategies of 2000 and 2004*. Chicago: University of Chicago Press; Larry M. Bartels. 1985. "Resource Allocation in a Presidential Campaign." *Journal of Politics* 47: 928–36; Mark Lake. 1979. "A New Campaign Resource Allocation Model." In *Applied Game Theory*, ed. Steven J. Brams, Andrew Schotter, and Gerhard Schwodiauer. Wurzburg, FRG: Physica-Verlag; Claude S. Colantoni, Terrence J. Levesque, and Peter C. Ordeshook. 1975. "Campaign Resource Allocation Under the Electoral College." *American Political Science Review*, 69(1), 141–154.

13  Shaw 1999, 2006; Richard Johnston, Michael G. Hagen, and Kathleen Hall Jamieson. 2004. *The 2000 Presidential Campaign and the Foundations of Party Politics*. New York: Cambridge University Press.; Goldstein and Freedman 2002; Marion R. Just, Ann N. Crigler, Dean E. Alger, Timothy E. Cook, Montague Kern, and Darrell M. West. 1996. *Crosstalk: Citizens, Candidates, and the Media in a Presidential Election*. Chicago: University of Chicago Press; Bartels 1985.

14  Emily Jane Charnock, James A. McCann, and Kathryn Dunn Tenpas. 2009. "Presidential Travel from Eisenhower to George W. Bush: An 'Electoral College' Strategy." *Political Science Quarterly* 124, 2: 323–39; Brendan J. Doherty. 2007. "Elections: The Politics of the Permanent Campaign: Presidential Travel and the Electoral College, 1977–2004." *Political Science Quarterly* 37, 4: 749–73; Shaw 1999; Stanley Kelley, Jr. 1961. "The Presidential Campaign." In *The Presidential Election in Transition, 1960–1961*, ed. Paul T. David. Washington, DC: Brookings Institution Press; Stanley Kelley, Jr. 1966. "The Presidential Campaign." In *The National Election of 1964*, ed. Milton C. Cummings, Jr. Washington, DC: Brookings Institution Press.

15  Andrew W. Barrett and Jeffrey S. Peake. 2007. "When the President Comes to Town." *American Politics Research* 35, 1: 3–31.

16  Goldstein and Freedman. 2002

17  Goldstein and Freedman. 2002; Kahn and Kenney. 1999; Jon F. Hale, Jeffrey C. Fox, and Rick Farmer. 1996. "Negative Advertisements in U.S. Senate Campaigns: The Influence of Campaign Context." *Social Science Quarterly* 77, 2: 329–43.

18  Goldstein and Freedman. 2002, 10.

19  Geer. 2006, 40.

20  Adam F. Simon. 2002. *The Winning Message: Candidate Behavior, Campaign Discourse, and Democracy*. Cambridge: Cambridge University Press..

21  John Sides. 2006. "The Origins of Campaign Agendas." *British Journal of Political Science*, 36, 3: 407–36.

22  Noah Kaplan, David K. Park, and Travis N. Ridout. 2006. "Dialogue in American Political Campaigns? An Examination of Issue Convergence in Candidate Television Advertising." *American Journal of Political Science* 50, 3: 724–36; Lee Sigelman and Emmett H. Buell, Jr. 2004. "Avoidance or Engagement? Issue Convergence in U.S. Presidential Campaigns, 1960–2000." *American Journal of Political Science* 48, 4: 660650–51661.

23  Some readers might think this data is "old" but CMAG did not share its data with the Wisconsin Advertising Project in 2006 and has placed a four-year moratorium on the use of CMAG advertising data by scholars to prevent them from studying the

strategies of advertisers in the previous election cycle. As a result, the 2008 data have only recently become available. This illustrates how research is often limited by the availability of data.

24 Markus Prior. 2001. "Weighted Content Analysis of Political Advertisements." *Political Communication* 18: 335–345.

25 Paul Herrnson. 2004. *Congressional Elections: Campaigning at Home and in Washington.* Washington D.C.: CQ Press: 83.

26 For previous uses of this measure of dialogue, see Sigelman and Buell 2004 and Kaplan *et al.* 2006.

27 In reality, it is not uncommon for an ad to mention several issues, but I am simplifying here for the purposes of illustration.

28 In the models that examine what accounts for the number of ad airings and unique advertising sponsors in an election, I use a negative binomial regression model because the dependent variable involves count data. Because the measures of information equality and dialogue range from 0 to 1, I use a generalized linear model with a logit link (for a binomial distribution) and robust standard errors for my analysis of each measure. This approach is recommended by Papke and Wooldridge (1996) for modeling proportional data (measures with a range of 0 to 1) because, in contrast to ordinary least squares models, such an approach produces predicted values that fall between zero and one.

29 An intervening variable provides a causal link or explains the relationship between other variables. In the case of the relationship between electoral competition and campaign information, candidates facing a stiff competitor usually attract and spend more money during the campaign than those in safe contests. Candidates who raise more money typically buy more ads, in addition to spending more on staff and other expenses. Thus, the amount of money candidates spend during a campaign is an intervening variable that explains part of the relationship between competitiveness and a candidate's advertising volume. This means that if I were to include a variable for candidate spending in my explanatory model of advertising volume, the effect of competitiveness would appear to be much smaller than it actually is because the candidate spending variable would "soak" up much of competition's effect.

30 Anthony King. 1996. *Running Scared: Why America's Politicians Campaign Too Much and Govern Too Little.* New York: Free Press.

31 Goldstein, Kenneth, Michael Franz, and Travis Ridout. 2002. "Political Advertising in 2000." Combined File. Final release. Madison, WI: The Department of Political Science at The University of Wisconsin-Madison and the The Brennan Center for Justice at New York University; Goldstein, Kenneth, and Joel Rivlin. 2005. "Political Advertising in 2002." Combined File. Final release. Madison, WI: The Wisconsin Advertising Project, The Department of Political Science at The University of Wisconsin-Madison; Goldstein, Kenneth, and Joel Rivlin. 2007. "Presidential advertising, 2003–2004" Combined File. Final release. Madison, WI: The University of Wisconsin Advertising Project, The Department of Political Science at The University of Wisconsin-Madison.

32 Goldstein et al. 2002; Goldstein and Rivlin. 2005, 2007.

33 Goldstein et al. 2002; Goldstein and Rivlin. 2005, 2007.

34 Goldstein et al. 2002; Goldstein and Rivlin. 2005, 2007.

35 Specifically, the question on the National Election Study says, "I'd like to get your feelings toward some of our political leaders and other people who are in the news these days. I'll read the name of a person and I'd like you to rate that person using something we call the feeling thermometer. Ratings between 50 and 100 mean that you feel favorably and warm toward the person; ratings between 0 and 50 degrees mean that you don't feel favorably toward the person and that you don't care too

much for that person. You would rate the person at the 50 degree mark if you don't feel particularly warm or cold toward the person." The respondents were then asked to rate the candidates running in their district. Political scientists use this as a measure of political knowledge because a respondent's inability to rate their district's candidates suggests they are not very informed about politics.

36  Goldstein et al. 2002; Goldstein and Rivlin 2005, 2007.
37  They arose as a consequence of the 2010 Supreme Court ruling in *Citizens United v. Federal Election Commission.*
38  Keena Lipsitz. "Dialogue is Not Deliberation." Paper presented at the American Political Science Association, September 2011.
39  John Geer and Keena Lipsitz. "Making Sense of Negativity." Paper to be presented at the Midwest Political Science Association, April 2012.
40  Kenneth R. Mayer, Timothy Werner, and Amanda Williams. 2006. "Do Public Financing Programs Enhance Competition?" In *The Marketplace of Democracy,* ed. Michael P. McDonald and John Samples. Washington, D.C.: Brookings Institution Press. 245–67.
41  Its use during campaigns is quite restricted but research suggests its use does increase significantly in election years.
42  Nolan McCarty, Keith T. Poole, and Howard Rosenthal. 2006. "Does Gerrymandering Cause Polarization?" Manuscript; Michael P. McDonald. 2006a. "Drawing the Line on District Competition." *PS: Political Science and Politics* 39, 1: 91–94; Michael P. McDonald. 2006b. "Re-Drawing the Line on District Competition" *PS: Political Science and Politics* 39, 1: 99–102; Michael P. McDonald. 2006c. "Redistricting and Competitive Districts." In *The Marketplace of Democracy,* ed. Michael P. McDonald and John Samples. Washington, D.C.: Brookings Institution. 222–44. Bruce E. Cain, Karin MacDonald, and Michael McDonald. 2005. "From Equality to Fairness: The Path of Political Reform." In *Party Lines: Competition, Partisanship, and Congressional Redistricting,* ed. Thomas E. Mann and Bruce E. Cain. Washington D.C.: Brookings Institution Press. 6–30; Mark Monmonier. 2001. *Bushmanders and Bullwinkles: How Politicians Manipulate Electronic Maps and Census Data to Win Elections.* Chicago: University of Chicago Press; Michael Lyons and Peter F. Galderisi. 1995. "Incumbency, Reapportionment and U.S. House Redistricting." *Political Research Quarterly* 48, 4: 857–71; Tufte, Edward R. 1973. "The Relationship Between Seats and Votes in Two-Party Systems." *American Political Science Review* 67, 2: 540–55.
43  McDonald 2006; Jamie L. Carson and Michael H. Crespin. 2004. "The Effect of State Redistricting Methods on Electoral Competition in United States House of Representative Races." *State Politics and Policy Quarterly* 4, 4: 455–69.
44  Bruce E. Cain, John Hanley and Thad Kousser 2006. "Term Limits: A Recipe for More Competition?" In *The Marketplace of Democracy,* ed. Michael P. McDonald and John Samples. Washington, D.C.: Brookings Institution Press. 199–221.
45  Cherie D. Maestas, Sarah A. Fulton, L. Sandy Maisel, Walter J. Stone. 2006. "When to Risk It? Institutions, Ambitions, and the Decision to Run for the U.S. House." *American Political Science Review* 100, 2: 195–208; L. Sandy Maisel, Walter J. Stone, Cherie D. Maestas. 2001. "Quality Challengers to Congressional Incumbents: Can Better Candidates Be Found?" Paul Herrnson, ed., *Playing Hardball: Campaigning for the U.S. Congress.* Prentice Hall, pp. 12–40; L. Sandy Maisel and Walter J. Stone. 1997. "Determinants of Candidate Emergence in U.S. House Elections: An Exploratory Study." *Legislative Studies Quarterly.* February 22, 1: 79–96.
46  Samuel Issacharoff and Richard H. Pildes. 1998. "Politics as Markets: Partisan Lockups of the Democratic Process." *Stanford Law Review* 50: 643–717.

# Chapter 9

# Polarized Populism
## Masses, Elites, and Ideological Conflict

*Paul J. Quirk*

With the nation's politics seemingly divided, scholars have spent considerable effort trying to discover sources of intensifying polarization. An ongoing controversy persists about whether elites are foisting extreme choices on moderate Americans or whether these elites simply respond to American voters who are sorting into parties that reflect ideological preferences. Paul Quirk posits a new way to think about the dynamic. He argues that highly engaged mass constituencies in both parties are pushing politicians to take extreme positions, while moderate voters remain passive. The result is what he calls "polarized populism"—a process in which elites feel compelled to respond to a disproportionately influential mass of voters who see legislative compromise and pragmatic politics as selling out. The dynamic is abetted by new media technology that makes it easier for engaged citizens to acquire information about politics and act on it (see Chapter 7). Quirk's ideas are conceptual and formed through a critical analysis of existing studies. The chapter illustrates the importance of re-conceptualizing research before collecting new evidence as a way to guide future empirical work. His analysis raises important questions about what it means to be a "model citizen" and points to institutional reforms that may increase the participation of less extreme voters in the political process.

Observers of American politics in the last few years have become increasingly alarmed about the future of the country. A Google search in June 2012 on the exact words "Is America in Decline?" yielded 80,000 Web pages—with links to leading think tanks, media organizations, and magazines high on the list.[1] The main cause of the anxiety has been a widely perceived failure of policymaking institutions to deal with critical policy challenges—above all, a vast gulf between long-term spending obligations and expected revenues. Confronted by undisputed evidence that the country is on a path to fiscal disaster, the president and Congress have failed to take significant action to correct the imbalance—not just for a brief period but for more than a decade.[2]

At least on the surface, the central political cause of this failure of policymaking has been the intense ideological conflict between Democrats and Republicans in Washington. On the one hand, Democrats, taking strong liberal positions, have resisted cuts in Social Security, Medicare, food stamps, and other entitlement programs. On the other hand, Republicans, insisting on conservative positions even more rigidly, have refused to consider increases in taxes—even as part of a balanced package of deficit-reduction measures. Indeed, in the face of severe long-term fiscal deficits, Republicans have pushed for additional tax cuts.[3]

What causes the destructive ideological conflict between the parties in Washington? In particular, what, if anything, do ordinary citizens or public opinion have to do with it? Have elected officials ignored the wishes of a moderate, pragmatic public and indulged their own hard-line ideological convictions? Or have they mostly responded to extreme policy demands from the public itself or from certain parts of it?

Largely through a critical analysis of existing literature, I make a case for a form of ordinary citizens' influence on policymaking that I call *polarized populism*.[4] In this sort of politics, the conduct of policymakers on major, publicly salient issues is driven largely by attitudes and responses of ordinary citizens. However, it is not simply the majority of the public—or the fabled *median voter*—who shapes policymaking. Rather, various, much narrower and more ideologically extreme groups of citizens—some on the left, some on the right—exert disproportionate influence. In the end, polarized populism reflects the interacting influences of both majority opinion and these more extreme groups.

Although my argument draws mainly on existing research, I depart in important ways from the standard interpretations. In particular, I make broader claims for the role of ordinary citizens in polarized politics than other scholars have entertained. In concluding, I consider the implications of polarized populism for the future of American politics.

## Perspectives on Polarization

The ideological polarization of the political parties—Democrats becoming more liberal, Republicans more conservative, and thus party differences growing increasingly severe—has been the most important development of the last three decades in American politics.[5] The magnitudes of this polarization, in Congress and in the electorate, have been carefully measured and documented.[6] In addition, some consequences of this polarization—such as harshness in political discourse and a tendency toward gridlock—have been widely discussed.[7]

Yet, scholars and commentators offer differing accounts of how polarization developed, what sustains it, and precisely how it shapes policymaking. In particular, they present conflicting views about the respective roles played by political elites, such as presidents and members of Congress, on the one hand, and ordinary citizens, on the other.

One view, associated especially with Morris Fiorina, argues that political elites have polarized—adopting more sharply opposed ideological positions—on their own, without encouragement by ordinary citizens.[8] Fiorina points to a "disconnect" between elite policymakers and the public, with elites drifting toward more extreme ideological positions while most citizens have stayed put in the center. Jacobs and Shapiro call this "elite-driven polarization" and present an even more dramatic claim: that politicians in this era simply pay little or no attention to the public in making policy decisions.[9] Rather, they adopt positions that reflect their own ideological beliefs and policy preferences.

Challenging the elite-driven account, in part, another approach acknowledges political elites as the first movers in polarization and yet also attributes a major role to ordinary citizens in later stages of the process. Abramowitz relates the development of polarization in Congress to an increase in ideological and partisan consistency in a key part of the electorate.[10] Other scholars have shown that citizens have sorted themselves into more strongly Democratic or Republican states and districts, creating what Jacobson calls an "electoral basis for polarization."[11]

Others observers reject the elite-driven view in a different way—describing powerful influences of ordinary citizens on policy decisions under polarized politics. Conservative columnist David Brooks writes, "Leaders today do not believe their job is to restrain popular will. Their job is to flatter and satisfy it.... Congress is capable of passing laws that give people benefits with borrowed money, but it gridlocks when it tries to impose self-restraint."[12]

My notion of polarized populism largely rejects the central claims of elite-driven polarization. I argue that polarization is at bottom caused by the attitudes and dispositions of certain groups of citizens—what I call *ideologically mobilized mass constituencies* (for short, *mobilized groups*). And I suggest that it results in an enlarged influence of those citizens and their ways of thinking on policymaking institutions and policy outcomes. (Bumper-sticker version: Your opinionated uncle is causing gridlock.)

## Who Are the Masses? Who Are the Elites?

To sort out the roles of masses and elites in polarized politics and policymaking, we need to be clear about who counts as an *elite* and what we mean by the *mass public* or *mass constituencies*. In my view, the most useful concept of political *elites* refers to people who hold influential positions in politics, government, or related fields and who engage in politics or government as a *day job*—not merely as a leisure-time or volunteer activity.[13] The main elites in national politics are elected policymakers (presidents, members of Congress) and high-level appointed officials (department secretaries, White House staff, senior congressional aides).

So defined, policymaking elites tend to have some broadly identifiable, characteristic perspectives. Of course, Congress members, in particular, come from a wide range of backgrounds. In Washington, however, they are constantly exposed to serious, informed discussion about public policy. They have access to specialized sources of policy and political information, and they have enough at stake to invest time and effort in making decisions. Some members may tune out most of the substantive policy information, but Congress members and other elites, especially when not under political constraints, often act on more informed and realistic understanding of issues.[14]

Members of the mass public are then those who participate in politics, if at all, as a leisure activity. The mass public ranges from those who never read the news or show up to vote to so-called *activists* who spend many of their evenings and weekends doing volunteer work in political campaigns.[15] A crucial issue, however, is how to deal with the mass public in political analysis—which groups or categories to consider separately. Jacobs and Shapiro, as for the most part Fiorina, focus attention on the entire public as a collective entity.[16] In assessing the influence of mass opinion, they look for policymakers' responses to "median national opinion, as measured by polls."[17]

In contrast, the notion of polarized populism draws attention to the role of more narrowly based mass constituencies. These include the core constituencies or party base (that is, the normally reliable, strong supporters) of each party, both at the level of the entire country and in particular states and districts. They also include a variety of other ideological or issue-oriented groups: politically active religious groups, especially the Christian Right; labor unions; citizens' groups representing environmental, gay and lesbian, or taxpayers' interests, among others; veterans and the elderly; political movements (the Tea Party, the Occupy movement); party activists; and small financial contributors to political campaigns.

The largest of these categories—the core constituencies of the two parties—represent perhaps 30 percent to 50 percent of each party's vote in a general election. At least a few tens of millions belong to one or another politically oriented citizens' group; about 10 million to 12 million make contributions to federal political campaigns. And probably a few million are active in one of the parties at the local, county, or state levels or volunteer to help in political campaigns.[18]

Unlike elites, members of any of these mass constituencies get their information mainly from mass media (TV, radio, newspapers, and Internet sources) using whatever sources they find interesting. Having no direct responsibility for decisions, they have little incentive to make judgments deliberately.[19] They thus respond primarily to the more easily grasped aspects of policy issues—tangible benefits or costs, short-term effects, symbolic or emotional appeals, *sound* bytes and slogans. The main implication of polarized populism is that the wide array of low-information, mass constituencies—whether moderate or ideologically extreme—are a major force in policymaking.

## The Development of Polarization

As we will see, two points about polarized party conflict are clear. First, the parties in Congress have grown farther apart ideologically—the Democrats more liberal, the Republicans more conservative—in recent years than at any previous time since the late nineteenth century. Second, the general public has also become more polarized but far less dramatically than Congress. The main question for research is how this polarization developed and the respective roles of masses and elites—or citizens and politicians—in that development.[20]

### Origins of Polarization: of Chickens and Eggs

Scholars assume a reciprocal relation between polarization at the elite and the mass levels: That is, in sorting themselves into liberal Democrats and conservative Republicans, politicians follow voters as a matter of electoral strategy, and voters follow politicians to make their policy attitudes and voting decisions more consistent.[21] The important question for the literature, however, was in effect which came first: the chicken or the egg—polarization of elites or of ordinary citizens?

In its simplest form, this question was easily answered. As various authors have shown, Democrats and Republicans in Congress, starting from an all-time low in party ideological differences in the 1970s, began to become more distinct ideologically by the early 1980s, the first years of the Reagan Administration. Democratic and Republican voters, trailing behind, did not show evidence of a similar trend until about a decade later and even then remained much more moderate than elected officials. In a recent book, Morris Fiorina compares changes in the distribution of ideological positions in Congress and among the public, from the 1960s and 1970s to the 2000s. The congressional graphs show the Democratic and Republican distributions overlapping each other considerably in the 1960s but with the moderate center shrinking drastically by the 2000s (Figure 9.1.) The graphs for ordinary citizens (with measurements on a much cruder scale) show far subtler changes—with only small increases in the numbers of self-identified liberals and conservatives, and with moderates holding nearly steady and remaining the largest part of the distribution (Figure 9.2.)

In terms of the chicken-or-egg question, it is as if someone found photographs from an earlier period that showed a barnyard full of chickens with no eggs. The apparent implication is that elected officials drove polarization. In Fiorina's view, the politicians are "disconnected" from the voters, staking out extreme positions that most voters reject.[22] In the following sections, I discuss three issues to challenge the claims of mass-elite disconnect and suggest a central role for mass constituencies in the development of polarized conflict.

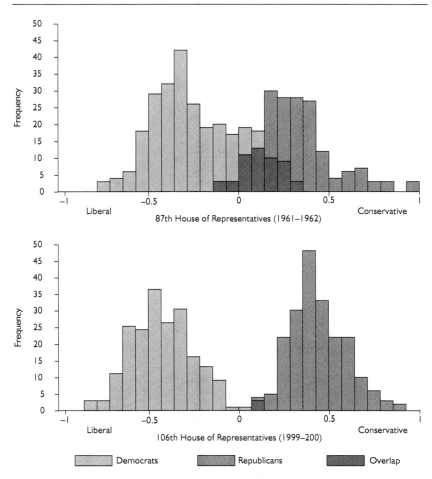

*Figure 9.1* Polarization of Congress since the 1960s[23]

## A Later Look: Emerging Electoral Foundations

The first issue concerns how the electoral and constituency support for polarized elite positions have changed over time. Several authors have shown that even if political elites started the trend toward polarized political conflict during the 1980s, strong electoral foundations for polarized conflict in Congress had emerged by the 1990s and 2000s.[24] Using American National Election Survey data from 1984 to 2004 and a finer scale of measurement than Fiorina, Abramowitz shows that the electorate, taken as a whole, has indeed shown only marginally increased partisan-ideological consistency (that is, consistent liberal attitudes with Democratic identification or conservative

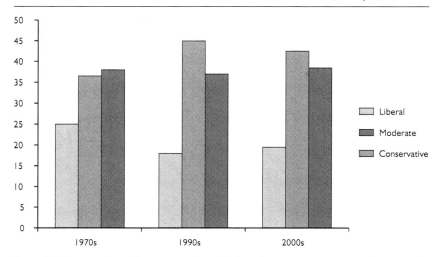

*Figure 9.2* Proportion of Americans who self-identify as conservative, moderate, and liberal[25]

attitudes with Republican identification). Yet, those who are "engaged" with politics, as evidenced by their self-reported participation in the current campaign, have become significantly more polarized. (For a comparison of all voters and the engaged voters in 2004, see Figure 9.3.) The politically engaged overwhelmingly are either liberal Democrats or conservative Republicans. In passing, Abramowitz remarks that these engaged citizens are the ones who best fit democratic norms of citizen participation.

Moreover, Jacobson shows that House districts and even the states have become far more homogeneous in partisan terms—that is, mostly either solidly Republican or solidly Democratic—and, thus, far less competitive in congressional elections.[26] As one indicator, in the mid-1970s, voters in the average House district won by a Democratic candidate had voted for the Democratic presidential candidate, in the most proximate presidential election, only about 7 percent to 10 percent more often than voters in the average district won by a Republican candidate. By 2008 and 2010, that difference had more than doubled, to about 18 percent to 22 percent (Figure 9.4). In other words, taking the presidential vote as the indicator, the average Congress member recently has had a roughly twenty-point advantage in party support. As a result, most Congress members have been able to win reelection with merely solid support from ideologically orthodox party regulars.

Abramowitz argues that the increased level of polarization among the more engaged citizens and the increased state and district partisan homogeneity are enough to give elected officials, such as members of Congress, significantly stronger incentives to abide by their respective partisan ideologies.[27] In his view, it accounts for a good deal of the continuing elite polarization of the late

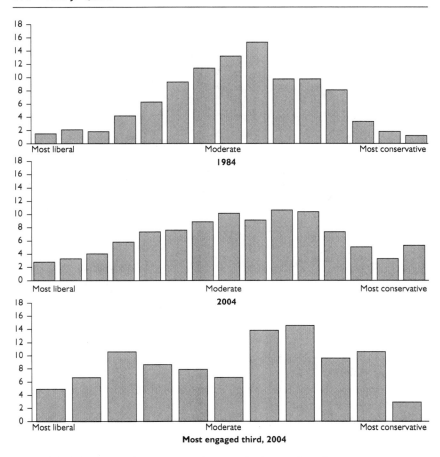

*Figure 9.3* Polarization of voters on multi-item ideology scales, all voters versus engaged voters, 1984 and 2004[28]

1990s and 2000s. In Jacobson's (2012) words, there is now a strong "electoral foundation" for party polarization in Congress.[29]

In short, the claims of elite-driven polarization overlook the development of strong constituency and electoral foundations for polarized elite conflict during the last two decades. On this evidence, polarization has been at least partly populist—driven by mass constituencies—at least after the initial stages.

## A Closer Look: How Citizens Polarize Politicians

A second issue in assessing the elite-driven account of polarization concerns what characteristics of the electorate have induced elites to become polarized— not just in the later stages of that trend but from the beginning in the early

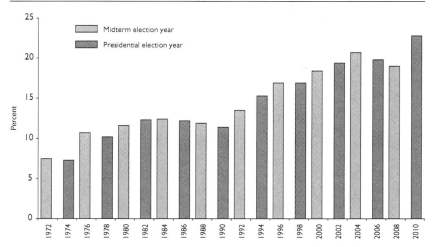

*Figure 9.4* Difference in the Democratic presidential vote between House districts won by Democratic and Republican representatives, 1972–2010[30]

1980s. I argue that we cannot understand the role of ordinary citizens in the development of polarized party conflict by focusing simply on which kind of polarization, mass or elite, preceded the other.[31] Rather, political elites will take strong ideological positions in response to conditions among mass constituencies that are merely, in effect, precursors of electoral polarization.

Politicians think about their constituencies in sophisticated, strategic ways.[32] For one thing, they gather information about voters' attitudes and dispositions to anticipate future responses and take positions intended to attract new supporters. Depending on the specific issues and groups involved, those positions may increase ideological consistency.

An important such case is well known. The Republican "Southern Strategy" in the 1968 presidential election campaign recognized that Southern Democratic voters had ideological and policy attitudes, especially on racial issues, that conflicted with positions of the national Democratic party.[33] As a result, Republicans were able to take increasingly conservative positions on racial issues—increasing elite polarization—to challenge the Southerners' ideologically anomalous Democratic identification. In short, politicians will sometimes take ideologically consistent, polarized positions to exploit a vulnerable *absence* of polarization among voters.

For another thing, politicians will take cues from relatively small numbers of ideologically committed citizens. In keeping track of opinion in their constituencies, politicians do not simply read polls and follow broad trends among large categories of voters; they attend carefully to the small numbers of politically active citizens—for example, those who show up at their "town-hall" meetings, send e-mails to their offices, or make contact in other ways.

Just as engaged voters are more ideologically consistent and polarized than the electorate as a whole, these *very* engaged voters are even more consistent and polarized. In fact, the most active sliver of constituents—the party activists who volunteer time and effort in political campaigns—have gradually become more ideologically extreme since at least the late 1950s.[34] The more extreme views of the most politically active citizens are essentially undetectable in standard opinion polls,[35] and yet, for several reasons, they will matter considerably to a Congress member.

First, the small numbers of active, ideologically mobilized citizens will often play a role in nomination politics. Their support may affect a member's likelihood of facing a primary-election challenge or ability to defeat such a challenge. A study by Seth Masket of party activists in California state politics demonstrates the polarizing effect of ideologically mobilized mass constituencies in nomination politics.[36] Using cases studies in both parties, he demonstrates that much of the ideological rigidity of Democrats and Republicans in the state legislature reflects the influence of what he calls *informal party organizations* at the local level. That is, operating outside the official Democratic or Republican organizations, informally organized networks—including party activists, membership organizations (labor unions, religious groups), financial contributors, and other participants—select candidates for nomination, dominate primary election campaigns, and provide crucial support in general elections.

These informal party organizations enforce ideological purity. One local Republican organization defeated a Republican incumbent state legislator for renomination solely because he had supported a bipartisan compromise budget with a modest increase in tax revenues. Although these organizations are often headed by a powerful boss, the ideological litmus tests they impose on party candidates obviously reflect the preferences of the available troops—the activists and constituency groups who campaign and vote for the favored candidates.[37] Apart from California, other areas of the country have seen an increase in organized, ideologically motivated participation in nomination contests, especially from the Christian Right and the Tea Party on the Republican side.

Second, aside from the possibility of a primary-election challenge, the more active, ideologically committed citizens are also important for general elections.[38] Some will contribute money or volunteer to work in the campaign. Their enthusiasm also will affect turnout. Of course, a liberal Democratic voter, disappointed with the moderate voting record of a Democratic member, will not defect to the Republican candidate, but he or she may lose interest in the campaign and fail to turn out on Election Day.

Finally, a consideration neglected by scholars: Ideologically mobilized citizens can make life difficult for Congress members in ways that do not depend on electoral clout—such as by criticizing them in face-to-face meetings and public gatherings.[39] Members often mention the aversive experience of explaining an unpopular vote to hostile constituents. A Congress member, thus, may feel pressure to please these ideologically intense, active citizens even beyond the incentives to do so for strictly electoral reasons. And, in fact, according to the best available evidence, members' voting records are typically, if anything, a bit more extreme (Democrats more liberal, Republicans more conservative) than their ideal strategies for winning elections.[40]

I am inclined, then, to reject the standard view that political elites initiated ideological polarization on the basis of their own ideological preferences, even in the early stages. In my view, political elites responded to strategically important conditions in the mass public that I have called *precursors* of broadly based electoral polarization. The racial attitudes of Southern voters; the issue demands of labor unions, religious groups, and movement conservatives; the ideological fervor of party activists; and a more mobilized and organized nomination politics were the apparent relevant conditions.

Although these effects were complex, one major, long-term development obviously had broad impact. The first detectable movement toward polarization occurred in the hard-fought party battles in Congress in the early 1980s over President Reagan's ambitious conservative agenda.[41] In the standard accounts, this was an elite conflict that began the process of polarization. However, Reagan's nomination for president had been the product of a populist conservative insurgency—one that had defeated Republican establishment candidates to nominate both Barry Goldwater in 1964 and Reagan in 1980.[42] In addition, Reagan's most divisive proposal—a huge, "supply-side" tax cut—had originated as a Republican campaign strategy.[43] The sharp partisan ideological conflict of the Reagan presidency was a manifestation of polarized populism.

## A Deeper Look: Independent Sources of Mass and Elite Polarization

To think about the development of polarization merely as a matter of reciprocal influences—masses leading elites, or elites leading masses—leads to an impasse in the manner of a century-old comic strip: "After you, my dear Alphonse!" "You first, my dear Gaston!"[44] Some other influence is needed to get polarization started and keep it going. A third issue in clarifying the sources of polarized conflict, therefore, is what independent or so-called *exogenous* factor drove the changes.[45] What would make politicians more ideologically extreme, other than their electoral constituencies? What would make ordinary citizens more ideologically extreme, other than polarized political elites?

To bolster his account of an elite-mass disconnect, Fiorina attempts an answer.[46] He points to certain institutional reforms of the 1970s— especially the rise of primary elections as the principal mechanism for party nominations, along with other measures that promoted citizen participation in elections and policymaking—as the main source of elite polarization. He argues that these reforms swept aside traditional party activists, motivated largely by material benefits such as patronage jobs, and replaced them with a new, more ideologically and policy-oriented style of politician and activist. In elected office, these ideologically committed politicians have ignored the moderate preferences of their constituencies to indulge their own, more extreme personal convictions.

The logic of this explanation, however, is murky. It is not clear why having to compete in a primary election should make a politician more concerned about policy and ideology and less concerned about winning elections and enjoying the perquisites of office. It is, after all, essentially just another hurdle to clear in winning office. In any case, there has been no apparent general trend toward Congress members ignoring their electoral interests to act on their personal beliefs. In the massive abuse of budget earmarks, the polarized Congress has indulged some of the most gluttonous, election-seeking, pork-barrel politics in the history of Congress.[47]

There is a stronger independent explanation for polarization among ordinary citizens—one that concerns the fragmentation of the news media and the resulting ideological specialization of news.[48] The origins of this development were purely technological and economic. Cable or satellite transmission can support many more television signals than over-the-air broadcasting. For economic reasons, the more broadcasters compete for viewers, the more they will appeal to specialized tastes, including ideological tastes. Conservative talk radio grew rapidly after the late 1980s; the Rush Limbaugh show was nationally syndicated in 1988. In the late 1990s, Fox News began attracting a large conservative TV audience. And the TV news audience has gradually abandoned the established news networks (CBS, NBC, and ABC news)—which seek a broad audience by presenting politically balanced coverage. In the 2000s, avid consumers of political news have increasingly selected outlets—including highly opinionated political blogs—whose political perspective they agree with.[49] As Iyengar and Bennett point out, contemporary patterns of media consumption strongly promote polarization.[50]

The timing of ideological polarization among citizens appears to be broadly consistent with this primarily citizen- and media-based account. As Wood and Jordon's analysis of voluminous data from five survey organizations demonstrates, the steady divergence of Democratic and Republican mass opinion did not begin until the late 1980s—well after the most divisive period of the Reagan administration—and has been stronger among Republicans, moving to the right, than among Democrats, moving to the left (Figure 9.5).

The search for influences capable of starting and sustaining a trend toward polarization points toward the development of the media and politically engaged citizens' exposure to increasingly biased political information. It points, therefore, to populist, mass-constituency sources of polarized politics.

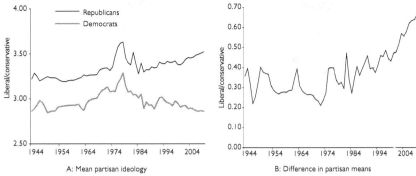

*Figure 9.5* Divergence in citizens' ideology by party identification, 1944–2010[51]

## Polarized Policymaking: Who Shapes Policy Decisions?

Regardless of what caused the polarization of American politics, we also want to know how policymakers make decisions in a polarized setting. Do political elites act on their own ideological beliefs and policy preferences? Or do they defer to party activists, the party base, or other mass constituencies? The distinction matters, even if the policymakers stake out ideologically extreme positions either way. It sometimes makes a major difference whether, for example, liberal Democratic legislators make serious judgments about the merits of a policy decision (perhaps asking, "What does Paul Krugman think?") or rather they merely estimate the reactions from liberal constituency groups ("What does MoveOn.org want?").

Scholars have debated how members of Congress weigh policy goals, on one hand, and electoral goals, on the other.[52] Few have doubted, however, that members respond to opinion in their constituencies as a central element of electoral strategy.[53] As mentioned earlier, Jacobs and Shapiro seek to overturn this consensus with respect to the recent period of polarized politics.[54] In their view, a marked feature of polarized politics is that politicians ignore the public and act on their own, often extreme, ideological and policy views. In contrast, I argue for a historically normal or even increased influence of mass constituencies in polarized politics.

Two theoretical considerations point toward increasing mass influence. First, changes in the technology of communication (e-mail, Internet news, political blogs, Facebook, Twitter, and others) and in strategies of political advocacy (the expansion of issue advertising on television, radio and, more recently, *YouTube*, among other outlets) have lowered the bar for ordinary citizens to achieve influence on policymaking. In particular, these developments have made it easier to follow policy issues and react to politicians' decisions about them.[55] They have also made it easier for policy entrepreneurs to find and communicate with large groups of people who have similar views. These effects are greatest for citizens with strong policy opinions. However, even for unengaged swing voters, the increased exposure to opinionated news coverage and issue-oriented campaign advertising has made it easier to vote on the basis of issues.[56]

Second, since the late 1990s, an additional basis for mass influence has emerged: highly competitive national elections, with frequent changes in party control of Congress and the presidency.[57] For most of the period from the New Deal to the 1990s, Congress had an apparently stable, long-term Democratic majority. Since the Republican victory in the 1994 midterm elections, however, control of Congress has been almost constantly in play from one election to another. Added to the increased policy differences between the parties, the intense competition has induced an extraordinarily strong pursuit of party election victories. In general, therefore, the policy-relevant attitudes and beliefs of ordinary citizens are likely to be more important in policymaking than in earlier periods.

It would be a mistake to suppose that scholars must have pinned down the level of mass influence on policymaking through empirical research. In the largest, most closely related body of work, they have used statistical approaches, with measures of public opinion and policy outcomes, to assess how majority opinion affects policy decisions.[58] A few studies have even asked the more difficult question of whether policymaking institutions have become more responsive to public opinion, or less responsive, over time.[59] Although findings vary, the broader studies find substantial effects of public opinion on policy outcomes.

Ultimately, however, such research cannot distinguish between populist and elite-driven policymaking. The reason, as Jacobs and Page point out, is simple: The studies do not have measures of the policy preferences of other political actors to match the measures of public opinion.[60] Because public opinion and other preferences may often move in the same directions for the same reasons, a policy that looks like a response to public opinion may actually be inspired by organized interest groups or self-initiated by political elites.

In one pertinent research strategy, Joseph Hinchliffe and I, writing about the politics of the 1970s, undertook case studies on a series of issues that shared a distinctive feature: Each issue reflected a long-term conflict between a strong majority of public opinion, on the one hand, and some competing source of influence, on the other—nonpartisan experts, organized interest groups or, in one case, elected officials themselves.[61] That is, they were in large part cases of mass-versus-elite rather than liberal-versus-conservative conflict. In exploring them, we found a series of clear victories for the popular side.

For example, citizens had preferred larger Social Security benefits since the creation of the program in 1935.[62] By contrast, financial experts attached higher priority to ensuring the program's financial stability. The Social Security Act Amendments of 1972 abandoned the cautious management of earlier periods and provided by far the largest benefit increases in the history of the program.

Speculating somewhat boldly, we inferred from the several, similar cases that public opinion had had greater influence in the 1970s than in earlier periods.

Because the Quirk-Hinchliffe analysis—a modest study in any case—dealt with the decade prior to the onset of polarization, we do not know whether the findings remain pertinent. In my view, however, research that focuses on conflicts between mass and elite preferences is crucial to understanding the forces that drive policymaking in this era.[63]

In the study I have mentioned, Jacobs and Shapiro report a massively researched investigation of a single policy issue—the Clinton administration's unsuccessful 1993–1994 health care reform—and make the case for the elite-driven account of polarized policymaking.[64] The most important evidence is simple. They note that although the national public in 1993 approved the general idea of universal health care, it was also highly concerned about the costs of achieving it and ambivalent about major reform.[65] If either Clinton or the congressional Republicans had wanted merely to appeal to the center, therefore, they would have put forth a cautious, incremental reform measure. In fact, neither side opted for that approach. Clinton pushed an ambitious program that would have guaranteed high-end health coverage for all Americans while creating a national network of purchasing cooperatives to control costs. The Republicans set out simply to kill the Clinton proposal, without offering an alternative plan to expand coverage. Centrist, incremental reform was not on the agenda for either party.

Furthermore, Jacobs and Shapiro argue, public opinion played a very limited role in the entire debate. Both the White House and the Republicans polled constantly. However, in numerous interviews, participants on both sides reported they had used polls only in developing rhetorical strategies, not in making policy decisions. In short, it was an episode of politicians acting freely on their own beliefs and preferences, without regard for constituency opinion—what Fiorina called "mass-elite disconnect."

Jacobs and Shapiro certainly refute the common stereotype of politicians, fingers to the wind, immediately adjusting their policies to the most recent trends in national polls. However, they overlook some apparent influences of mass opinion.[66] First, by their account, President Clinton personally insisted that his reform plan provide the same, costly and often wasteful health coverage that was generally received by employees of Fortune 500 corporations. The "gold-plated coverage" magnified the already severe obstacles to making the plan financially plausible. In all likelihood, Clinton's decision was intended to avoid a public perception, however unwarranted, of stingy coverage.[67] Second, although neither party proposed the kind of incremental reform that might have appealed to the center of national opinion, both Clinton and the Republicans responded to narrower, more ideologically mobilized constituencies. In simply opposing any major reform, for example, Republican leaders catered to the party base in Republican states and districts and thus to Republican members.

Finally, in the end, mass opinion determined the outcome of the debate. There were, of course, responsible objections to the Clinton plan, but Republican and insurance-industry attacks on the plan—often grossly misleading—played to the fears, scarce attention, and limited information of most citizens.[68] They succeeded in swinging majority public sentiment from initial support of the Clinton plan to opposition. As a result, many ambivalent or undecided Congress members withdrew support, and the Democratic congressional leadership abandoned the plan without bringing it to the House or Senate floors.

Taking the several sorts of studies together, the evidence is consistent with major effects of mass constituencies on policymaking. Given the limited efforts to study effects of narrower, more ideological constituencies or to focus on issues of mass versus elite conflict, it does not permit a definitive judgment.

### Emerging Evidence of Polarized Populism

While scholars debate, political life goes on—and sometimes provides greater clarity. In the last few years, a series of political events have made the populist sources of polarized conflict increasingly evident. President Obama and the Democrats in Congress have shown some of the manifestations. In the 2009–2010 debate on the Obama administration's health care reform, Democratic mass constituencies—especially liberal groups and labor unions—blocked the adoption of any potentially effective cost-control measures. They also pressed the White House and liberal Democrats in Congress to demand a "public option" for health care insurance and coverage of abortion services, even though both were strongly opposed by Republicans and moderate Democrats. With a populist-style disregard for political constraints, the liberal Democrats pushed these demands to a point that almost resulted in killing the most important liberal domestic measure in more than forty years.[69]

However, the more notable recent episodes have been on the conservative side and associated with the rise of the Tea Party movement—a mass-based, conservative protest movement that had a strong influence in the Republican Party beginning in 2010.[70] I will discuss selected episodes from the congressional elections of 2010 and 2012, the late-2011 negotiations on deficit reduction and the federal debt limit, and the 2012 Republican presidential nomination campaign. In a word, conservative activists and the Republican base have pushed Republican candidates and elected officials far to the right, with dramatic consequences for elections and policymaking.

During the 2010 congressional election campaign, the Tea Party movement was a major force in Republican primary elections for the House and Senate. A network of citizens' groups in all regions of the country, mostly organized within a two-year period, the Tea Party held well-attended protest rallies, campaigned for favored candidates and, according to polls, had broad support among Republican voters. In the congressional primaries, Tea Party activists pushed hard-right candidates for nomination and challenged Republican incumbents who were perceived as moderate.

In Arizona, the Tea Party opposed the re-nomination of senior Republican senator and former presidential candidate John McCain in favor of an ideologically purer candidate. Although McCain had maintained a strong conservative voting record, he had earned a reputation as a maverick for his occasional bipartisan leadership on issues such as campaign finance and immigration. After falling behind the Tea Party candidate in the polls, McCain discovered conservative orthodoxy, even renouncing his own proposals on immigration, and narrowly won the Republican nomination. McCain was then reelected to the Senate, but Tea Party–supported Republicans nominated for the Senate in two other states proved too extreme for the general electorate and lost otherwise winnable seats to Democratic opponents, costing Republicans control of the Senate. At the same time, Tea Party activism helped the Republicans take over the House, installing about thirty new members with strong ties to the movement.

In the 2012 election cycle, Utah Republican Senator Orrin Hatch—another leading conservative with an occasional impulse toward bipartisan problem solving—had to fight for re-nomination against a strict conservative Tea Party candidate. In the year before the primary, Hatch raised his rating by a leading conservative group from a slightly wobbly 89 percent to a perfect 100 percent. Tea Party populism had pushed two of the most influential senators—elites among the elite—toward more extreme conservative positions.

In fall 2011, an extraordinary episode of polarized populism brought the country to its knees.[71] Congress needed to pass an increase in the federal debt limit to permit additional borrowing needed for the government to meet its budgetary commitments and make payments that were coming due on existing debt. Because of the universally acknowledged disastrous consequences of a default on federal debt, there had never been significant uncertainty about the passage of any of the sixty-eight previous debt-limit increases since 1960.[72] Led by members with ties to the Tea Party, however, many Republicans, especially in the House, tried to use the threat of blocking the debt-limit increase to force a hard-line conservative approach to deficit reduction. Republicans demanded deep cuts in Medicare, Medicaid, and other domestic spending and yet offered no tax increases to boost revenues or balance the proposal. In effect, the Republicans, who controlled only one policymaking institution (the House), proposed to dictate terms to the Democrats, who controlled the other two institutions (the Senate and the presidency). The Republic demand was something like the smaller of two children proposing to take all of the marbles.

After that offer failed, Republican leaders, desperate to reach an agreement and avoid the party's being held responsible for default, found much of the party rank-and-file unwilling to cooperate. When the top House Republican, Speaker John Boehner, worked out a compromise with the president and

Senate Democrats that included some tax increases, the House Republicans voted down the Speaker's bill, an embarrassment for the party. Some of the Tea Party Republicans—displaying a populist indifference to the anxieties of bankers, bureaucrats, and party leaders—pronounced themselves perfectly willing to bring about default rather than accept even the smallest tax increase. Judging from reporters' accounts, many of them held that view in complete sincerity, but the intransigence also reflected the uncompromising demands of the kinds of constituents who showed up at their town-hall meetings. As Republican consultant Frank Luntz told the House freshman Republicans in a gathering, "[Your] base is going to kill you if you vote to raise the debt ceiling."[73] In the end, the Republicans were forced to back down, approving the debt limit extension without the unilateral concessions they had demanded from the Democrats while suffering a blow to the party's reputation.[74] As another consequence of the political brinkmanship in dealing with serious fiscal problems, U.S. government bonds lost their AAA rating for the first time.

The 2012 Republican presidential nomination campaign was the most obtrusive demonstration of polarized populism to date. Republican leaders and commentators grew deeply anxious about the party's chances in November as a large field of candidates competed in catering to the most demanding conservative primary electorate ever observed. Amid constant rhetoric about the need to correct long-term deficits, every major Republican candidate promised major tax cuts, with even the wealthiest Americans benefiting generously. They also took hard-line conservative positions on abortion, gay rights, and immigration; denied the reality of climate change; and rejected belief in evolution. (Only the long-shot, moderate candidate Jon Huntsman strayed—tweeting, "I believe in evolution and trust scientists on climate change. Call me crazy.") In a widely discussed moment in a televised debate, a moderator from *Fox News* asked the eight Republican candidates which of them would refuse a deficit-cutting deal with the Democrats consisting of $10 in spending cuts for each $1 in tax increases—a fantasy offer from any realistic Republican standpoint. Every candidate raised a hand.[75]

By the time Mitt Romney, a former moderate governor of a liberal state, had locked up the nomination, he had accumulated a list of hard-right positions that, in the view of most observers, would considerably harm his chances in the November election. Nomination campaigns often have that effect to some degree, but the Republican primary electorate had pushed the candidates to such extremes that former First Lady Barbara Bush deplored "the worst Republican nomination campaign ever."[76]

Polarized populism thus has shaped some of the major political developments of recent years. To be sure, the Tea Party movement had led to an unusual level of popular activism on the conservative side, but this elevated ideological activism, in my view, only revealed with greater clarity ideologically charged constituency pressures on political elites that normally have been less visible.

These recent manifestations of polarized populism should induce far greater efforts by scholars to clarify the influence of ideologically mobilized mass constituencies, and the complex interactions between masses elites, in the development and workings of polarized politics.

## Polarized Populism and the Future of American Politics

I will first sum up briefly and then discuss the implications of my account for the future of American politics. There are two central points. First, even though political elites, especially members of Congress, showed a broad movement toward greater polarization well before the mass public, that does not indicate that elites drove polarization, for their own reasons. By the 1990s, strong constituency foundations for polarized politics had developed. More fundamental, the polarization among elites had responded to a variety of narrowly based, ideologically mobilized mass constituencies that began to alter politicians' incentives by the 1960s. In particular, the elite-polarizing effect of the Reagan presidency was the product of a two-decades-old populist insurgency in the Republican Party. Broadly based polarization among citizens appears to be associated with changes in the structure of the media that began in the late 1980s and 1990s.

Second, even though the president and congressional party leaders do not shape their respective agendas by designing policies to reflect the current midpoint of national public opinion, that finding does not show that policymakers in a polarized setting act on their own ideological and policy views. Rather, they respond to those same narrowly based, ideologically mobilized mass constituencies—of which Tea Party activists and Republican state, district, and primary electorates are currently the most powerful examples. As a result, policymakers are inclined to neglect serious, responsible deliberation and expert advice. They are also prone to partisan deadlock. And the resolution of deadlock, if any, often depends on which side wins a battle of largely disreputable popular rhetoric. The further consequence, as I noted at the outset, is that American government appears unable to address its serious fiscal and policy challenges and may be headed toward long-term decline.

In a sense, one could summarize my analysis with a well-known line from the comic strip *Pogo*: "We have met the enemy, and he is us."[77] The problems of polarized politics reflect, at bottom, changes in the American citizenry. More people have become interested in politics—something that nearly all commentators, including political scientists, have long advocated. It turns out, however, that most people who take the time to follow politics closely become intense supporters of one of the parties and have strong policy views that are generally compatible with their party preference. As important, these politically engaged partisans mostly avoid or dismiss information that would complicate or moderate their ideological or policy views—an unfortunate practice for democracy that the media and technology increasingly accommodate. And they hold politicians accountable, above all, for unyielding devotion to the partisan mission.

What, if anything, can be done? There is, of course, no option of somehow discouraging citizens' engagement with politics. A democracy is not secure without engaged citizens, nor, in a country with freedom of speech, the press, and association, are effective means evidently available for making political rhetoric more deliberative or for exposing people to more balanced sources of information. These are worthy objectives—which various constructively inclined foundations, institutes, and other entities already pursue—but we cannot expect dramatic gains with respect to them.

Rather, the most promising avenues for moderating the effects of polarized politics concern political institutions. One such avenue is to reform the central policymaking institutions—Congress, the presidency, or both—with a view toward making them work more effectively under conditions of intense partisan conflict. One measure that the Senate itself can put into effect—abolishing or sharply limiting the Senate filibuster—would prevent partisan deadlock in certain circumstances. However, the constitutional structures of American government—in particular, the separately elected House, Senate, and presidency—limit the potential for such a strategy. As long as elections often result in divided party control of the central policymaking institutions, American government will not work effectively with highly polarized party conflict.

The other institutional approach is to reform certain features of electoral arrangements. Unlike the situation with the constitutional Separation of Powers, individual states can make relevant changes to these arrangements. In fact, a handful of states have recently adopted new primary-election rules that potentially give an advantage to more moderate candidates. California's "top-two" system—used for the first time in 2012—puts all candidates for a given seat or office, regardless of party, together on the same primary ballot and allows any voter to cast a vote for any one of them; the top two candidates go on to compete in the general election. A moderate Democrat, for example, can draw support from Republican and Democratic voters.

With similar objectives in mind, Mann and Ornstein recommend that the United States adopt mandatory voting—creating an actual obligation (enforced by a small penalty) for citizens to appear at the polls.[78] Several major democracies, among them Australia, have established this requirement. It would massively increase voter turnout, from the current level of about 50 percent for general elections to a figure near 95 percent, and would especially increase the participation of weaker partisans and independents. In addition to the direct benefits of broader, more equal participation, it thus would give a strong boost to moderate candidates.

Appropriate reforms of electoral arrangements, then, might enable the political system both to sustain a sizable contingent of highly engaged, ideologically motivated, and fiercely partisan voters—in many ways, despite their deliberative shortcomings, indicators of a healthy democracy and yet, also to elect much larger numbers of moderate, pragmatic members of Congress—disposed toward the bipartisan cooperation that the constitutional system requires. Given the increasingly widespread alarm about the workings of the political system, the country may soon be ready to contemplate such reforms.

## Notes

1  Top items represented an array of sources, including Fox Business News, the Brookings Institution, and Real Clear Politics.
2  David Stockman, "Four Deformations of the Apocalypse, New York Times, July 31, 2010; Robert J. Samuelson, "Why There's a Debt Stalemate," *Washington Post*, November 20, 2011 http://www.washingtonpost.com/opinions/why-theres-a-debt-stalemate/2011/11/18/gIQAUqH5fN_story.html
3  Ezra Klein, "In Supercommittee, Dems Moved Right and Republicans Moved Righter," *Washington Post*, November 22, 2011. http://www.washingtonpost.com/blogs/ezra-klein/post/wonkbook-which-party-gave-more-ground-in-the-supercommittee/2011/11/22/gIQAVugkkN_blog.html.
4  The chapter develops and extends arguments that I presented in a series of articles in *The Forum*: Paul J. Quirk, "Politicians Do Pander: Mass Opinion, Polarization, and Law Making," *The Forum*: Vol. 7: Issue. 4, 2009, Article 10; "A House Dividing: Understanding Polarization," The Forum. Vol. 9: Issue. 2, 2011, Article 12; "Polarized Populism: Masses, Elites, and Partisan Conflict," The Forum. Vol. 9: Issue. 1, 2011, Article 5. Several passages draw significantly on those articles.
5  Among countless works expressing this judgment, see Thomas E. Mann and Norman Ornstein, *It's Even Worse Than It Looks*, New York: Basic Books, 2012. For a popular source, see Fareed Zakaria, "Why Political Polarization Has Gone Wild (and What to Do About It), CNN Blog, July 24, 2011, http://globalpublicsquare.blogs.cnn.com/2011/07/24/why-political-polarization-has-gone-wild/
6  This note explains generally how polarization is measured. For members of Congress, the measures of ideology use roll-call votes to quantify each member's consistency of support for liberal or conservative policies. The most important are Poole and Rosenthal's remarkably valuable, though strangely named, NOMINATE measures, which permit comparisons of individual or aggregate ideological scores over time. For an explanation of the measures, see Keith T. Poole and Howard Rosenthal, *Congress: A Political History of Roll Call Voting* (New York: Oxford University Press, 1997), Chapters 3 and 11. For the data and various updated figures and analysis, see http://voteview.uh.edu/dwnomin.htm. For ordinary citizens, the measurement is simpler: There are two types of survey measures: One uses opinions on several issues to assess the same consistency. Another simply asks respondents to identify their position on a scale that runs from "very conservative" to "very liberal." *Polarization of the parties* refers to conditions in which Democratic politicians or voters are uniformly and strongly liberal and Republican politicians or voters are uniformly and strongly conservative.
7  Pietro S. Nivola and David W. Brady, eds., *Red and Blue Nation? Consequences and Correction of America's Polarized Politics* (Washington, D.C.: Brookings Institution, 2006); Mann and Ornstein, *It's Even Worse Than It Looks*; Nolan McCarty, "The Policy Consequences of Political Polarization." In *The Transformation of the American Polity*, ed. P. Pierson and T. Skocpol. (Princeton, NJ: Princeton University Press, 2007). For a provocative contrarian view, see David R. Mayhew, *Partisan*

*Balance: Why Political Parties Don't Kill the U.S. Constitutional System* (Princeton, NJ: Princeton University Press, 2012.)

8  Morris P. Fiorina and Samuel J. Abrams, *Disconnect: the Breakdown of Representation in American Politics*. Norman, Oklahoma: University of Oklahoma Press, 2009. See also Morris P. Fiorina, Samuel J. Abrams, and Jeremy C. Pope, *Culture War? The Myth of a Polarized America*, 3d. ed. (New York: Longman, 2010).

9  Lawrence R. Jacobs and Robert Y. Shapiro, *Politicians Don't Pander: Political Manipulation and the Loss of Democratic Responsiveness* (Chicago: University of Chicago Press, 2000).

10  Alan I. Abramowitz, *The Disappearing Center: Engaged Citizens, Polarization, and American Democracy*. New Haven: Yale University Press, 2011. See also Alan I. Abramowitz and Kyle L. Saunders, "Ideological Realignment in the U.S. Electorate." *Journal of Politics* 60, 1998, pp. 634–652; "Why Can't We All Just Get Along? The Reality of Polarized American." *The Forum* 3 (June) 2005.

11  Source: Gary C. Jacobson, "No Compromise: The Electoral Basis of Legislative Gridlock," Prepared for the conference on "Legislative Gridlock: 2012 and Beyond," New York University, March 21–22, 2012, p. 13. See also, Matthew Levendusky, *The Partisan Sort* (Chicago: University of Chicago Press, 2009); Sean M. Theriault, *Party Polarization in Congress*. New York: Cambridge University Press, 2008.

12  David Brooks, Government and the age of innocence, *New York Times*, May 19, 2012. http://www.nytimes.com

13  Samuel J. Eldersveld, "Elites." *Oxford Companion to the Politics of the World*. ed. Joel Krieger. (New York: Oxford University Press, 1993), 263–264.

14  Daniel Carpenter, *Reputation and Power: Organizational Image and Pharmaceutical Regulation at the FDA* (Princeton, NJ: Princeton University Press, 2010); Martha Derthick and Paul J. Quirk, *The Politics of Deregulation* (Washington, DC: Brookings Institution, 1985).

15  Kay Lehman Schlozman, Sidney Verba, Henry E. Brady, *The Unheavenly Chorus: Unequal Political Voice and the Broken Promise of American Democracy* (Princeton, NJ: Princeton University Press, 2012). In contrast with my approach, Fiorina, *Disconnect*, Ch. 1, and Theriault, *Party Polarization in Congress*, categorize party activists—specifically, those who attend the national party conventions (on whom survey data are available)—as elites, although they do not discussing the rationale for doing so. These individuals fit neither of my criteria for an elite. They do not have significant influence; their main job is to demonstrate enthusiasm and vote for the candidates they are pledged to vote for. And they are mostly volunteers, not full-time political professionals. I view convention delegates as merely a sample of the most active ordinary citizens.

16  Jacobs and Shapiro, *Politicians Don't Pander*; Fiorina, *Disconnect*.

17  Jacobs and Shapiro, *Politicians Don't Pander*, Ch. 3.

18  I assume here that the party base is roughly measured by the number of people who call themselves *strong Democrats* or *strong Republicans*. In the 2006 General Social Survey, roughly one-third of respondents identified themselves as strong Democrats or strong Republicans (author's calculation). In addition, turnout in congressional primary elections on average is about one-third of turnout in general elections; see David W. Brady, Hahrie Han, and Jeremy C. Pope, "Primary Elections and Candidate Ideology: Out of Step with the Primary Electorate? *Legislative Studies Quarterly*, 32: 2007, 79–105. It is not easy to determine the numbers of citizens who engage in various political activities. For the best survey estimates, see Schlozman, Verba, and Brady, *The Unheavenly Chorus*. Roughly 6 percent of American adults make contributions to election campaigns. In the 2008 presidential election, more

than 2.25 million individuals made small contributions (up to $200) to one of the candidates seeking the Democratic or Republican nomination for president. (Estimated by author from Campaign Finance Institute, Table 1, Sources of Funds for Presidential Candidates, 2007–2008, http://www.cfinst.org/pdf/federal/president/2010_0106_Table1.pdf

19  A vast literature deals with the ways in which citizens respond to the lack of individual incentive to invest effort in information gathering or deliberation. A common perspective emphasizes the general effectiveness of "low-information rationality." See Arthur Lupia and Mathew McCubbins, *The Democratic Dilemma: Can Citizens Learn What They Need to Know?* (New York: Cambridge University Press, 1998). For a critique of that approach, see James H. Kuklinski and Paul J. Quirk, "Reconsidering the Rational Public: Cognition, Heuristics, and Mass Opinion". Editors: Arthur Lupia, Mathew McCubbins, Samuel Popkin, *Elements of Reason.* (New York: Cambridge University Press, 2000), 153 – 182.

20  Some analyses some additional causes, especially redistricting (in the House) and patterns of migration and geographic sorting. See Theriault, *Party Polarization in Congress*; Levendusky, *The Partisan Sort.* In this chapter, I focus on the more general distinction between mass and elite sources. Note that both redistricting and geographic sorting are mechanisms of polarized populism; that is, they result in more polarized demands from mass constituencies.

21  Jacobson, *Divider.*

22  Fiorina, *Disconnect*, Ch. 1.

23  Source: Morris P. Fiorina, *Disconnect: The Breakdown of Representation in American Politics*, page 6. Data from Poole and Rosenthal, Voteview.com

24  Jacobson, "No Middle Ground"; see also Abramowitz, *Disappearing Center*; Levendusky, *The Partisan Sort*; and Theriault, *Party Polarization in Congress.*

25  Source: Adapted from Morris P. Fiorina, *Disconnect: The Breakdown of Representation in American Politics*, page 13.  Data from Gallup Poll's Liberal-Conservative Self-Identification scale

26  Jacobson, "No Middle Ground."

27  Abramowitz, *Disappearing Center*, Ch. 7.

28  Source: Alan I. Abramowitz, *The Disappearing Center: Engaged Citizens, Polarization, and American Democracy*, pp. 39, 42. American National Election Survey data. The third panel uses a different scale than the other two.

29  Jacobson, "No compromise."

30  Source: Gary C. Jacobson, "No Compromise: The Electoral Basis of Legislative Gridlock," Prepared for the conference on "Legislative Gridlock: 2012 and Beyond," New York University, March 21–22, 2012, p. 13.

31  For analyses that take into account these complications, see Edward G. Carmines and James A. Stimson, *Issue Evolution: Race and the Transformation of American Politics* (Princeton: Princeton University Press, 1989); Gary C. Jacobson, *A Divider, Not a Uniter* 2d. ed. (New York; Longman, 2011); David Karol, *Party Position Change in American Politics: Coalition Management* (New York: Cambridge University Press, 2009).

32  Richard F. Fenno, *Home Style: House Members in Their Districts* (Boston: Little, Brown, 1978; Susan Herbst, 1998. *Reading Public Opinion: How Political Actors View the Democratic Process*, Chicago: University of Chicago Press, 1998.

33  Gary C. Jacobson, "Presidents, Partisans, and Polarized Politics," in *Can We Talk? The Rise of Rude, Nasty, Stubborn Politics*, ed. Daniel M. Shea and Morris P. Fiorina (New York: Pearson, forthcoming); David Karol, *Party Position Change in American Politics: Coalition Management*, (New York: Cambridge University Press, 2009), Ch. 4.

34  James Q. Wilson, *The Amateur Democrat*. Chicago: University of Chicago Press, 1962; Aaron Wildavsky,"The Goldwater Phenomenon: Purists, Politicians, and the Two-party System," *Review of Politics* 27: 393–99,1965; Gary Miller and Norman Schofield; Geoffrey C. Layman, Thomas M. Carsey, John C. Green, Richard Herrera, Rosalyn Cooperman, "Activists and Conflict Extension in American Party Politics," *American Political Science Review* Vol. 104, No. 2 May 2010, 324–346.

35  These views fail to register for several reasons: that standard polls are not designed to measure extreme views or intense commitment; that their sample sizes do not permit describing any views of a small segment of the electorate with precision; that the surveys do not use interview time to identify unusual types of participation; and finally, that respondents tend to exaggerate their participation in politics.

36  Seth Masket, *No Middle Ground: How Informal Party Organizations ControlNominations and Polarize Legislatures*. Ann Arbor: University of Michigan Press, 2011.

37  Quirk, Forum review essay. Paul J Quirk, "A House Dividing: Understanding Polarization," *The Forum*: Vol. 9: Issue 2, (2011), Article 12.

38  John H. Aldrich, *Why Parties? A Second Look* (Chicago: University of Chicago Press, 2011).

39  See Fenno, *Home Style*, on the importance of the social interactions of members with their constituents.

40  According to a careful statistical study by Cains-Wrone, Brady, and Cogan, Congress members whose voting records are more moderate do better than more extreme members in both their share of the two-party vote and their probability of reelection; see Brandice Canes-Wrone, David W. Brady, and John F. Cogan. 2002. "Out of Step, Out of Office: Electoral Accountability and House Members' Voting." *American Political Science Review* 96(01): 127–140. Moreover, and very interesting, the electoral advantage of a more moderate record has held relatively constant over the period from 1956–1996, even as Congress members have become dramatically more polarized. A reasonable interpretation is that constituency demands, overall, have become more polarized; but that members, on the whole, have kept up with the trend; and that, at all times, they have gone slightly further toward the extremes, on average, than the constituencies demanded. As I note in the text, this may reflect the leverage of mobilized constituents from direct contact with the members.

41  Barbara Sinclair, *Party Wars: Polarization and the Politics of National Policy Making* (Norman, OK: University of Oklahoma Press, 2006).

42  Donald T. Critchlow, *The Conservative Ascendancy: How the GOP Right Made Political History* (Cambridge, MA: Harvard University Press, 2007); Andrew E. Busch, *Reagan's Victory: The Presidential Election of 1980 and the Rise of the Right* (Lawrence, KS: University of Kansas Press, 2005).

43  Herbert Stein, *Presidential Economics: The Making of Economic Policy From Roosevelt to Clinton* (Washington, DC: AEI Press, 1994).

44  See "Alphonse and Gaston," *Wikipedia*. http://en.wikipedia.org/wiki/Alphonse_and_Gaston.

45  I use the term "exogenous" here for the benefit of professional readers, for whom it is actually useful shorthand. It refers in this context to a causal factor outside the reciprocal relationship between masses and elites.

46  Fiorina, *Disconnect*, Ch. 4.

47  Gail Russell Chaddock, 'Pork barrel' spending: A big liability for lawmakers in 2010 election? *Christian Science Monitor*, August 19, 2010. http://www.csmonitor.com/USA/Elections/2010/0819/Pork-barrel-spending-A-big-liability-for-lawmakers-in-2010-election.

48 Hamilton; Prior. Diana Owen. "Media Fragmentation." Sage Handbook of Political Communication. Ed. Holli A. Semetko and Margaret Scammell. Newbury Park, CA: Sage Publications, 2011. Diana Owen. "Talk Radio." *The Encyclopedia of Political Science*. Ed. James E. Alt, Simone Chambers, Geoffrey Garrett, Margaret Levi, Paula D. McClain. Washington, D.C.: CQ Press with the assistance of the American Political Science Association, 2011: 1643–1644.

49 Eric Lawrence, John Sides, and Henry Farrell, "Self-Segregation or Deliberation? Blog Readership, Participation, and Polarization in American Politics," *Perspectives on Politics* Vol. 8/No. 1 March 2010, 143–157.

50 Shanto Iyengar and Kyu S. Hahn, "Red Media, Blue Media: Evidence of Ideological Selectivity in Media Use, *Journal of Communication*, 59 (2009), 19–39. W. Lance Bennett and Shanto Iyengar, "A New Era of Minimal Effects? The Changing Foundations of Political Communication," *Journal of Communication*, 58 (2008), 707–731.

51 Source: B. Dan Wood and Soren Jordan, "Electoral Polarization: Definition, Measurement, and Evaluation," Paper delivered at the 2011 meeting of the American Political Science Association, Seattle, WA, September 1–4, 2011. Data mainly from Gallup Poll, supplemented by data from four other polling organizations.

52 The classic statements of the leading alternatives are Richard F. Fenno, *Congressmen in Committee* (Boston, Little, Brown, 1973), which attributes three main goals—reelection, good policy, and influence in government; and David R. Mayhew, *Congress: The Electoral Connection* (Yale University Press, 1974), which argues that only reelection generally motivates members' behavior. I take Fenno's, multi-goal view. Since both views expect strong effects of constituency opinion, however, either is compatible with polarized populism.

53 Some works point to significant biases and distortions in that response, however. Mayhew, *Electoral Connection* argued that members' "position taking" often represents only the appearance of action on behalf of constituents goals. Bartels argues that Congress members represent primarily the upper-income citizens in their districts: Larry M. Bartels, *Unequal Democracy: The Political Economy of the New Gilded Age* (Princeton, NJ: Princeton University Press, 2008).

54 Jacobs and Shapiro, *Politicians Don't Pander*, Ch. 3.

55 Richard Davis and Diana Owen, *New Media and American Politics*, New York: Oxford University Press, 1999.

56 John Geer emphasizes the advantage, in particular, of negative advertising in facilitating issue voting. *In Defense of Negativity: Attack Ads in Presidential Campaigns*. (Chicago: University of Chicago Press, 2006).

57 Sinclair, *Party Wars*.

58 James A. Stimson, Michael B. MacKuen, and Robert S. Erikson, "Dynamic Representation," *American Political Science Review* 89:1995, 543–65; Stuart N. Soroka and Christopher Wlezien, *Degrees of Democracy: Politics, Public Opinion, and Policy* (New York: Cambridge University Press, 2009); for a recent review, see Paul Burstein, "Public Opinion, Public Policy, and Democracy," in K.T. Leicht and J.E. Jenkins (eds.), *Handbook of Politics: State and Society in Global Perspective* (Springer Science+Business Media LLC, 2010), 63–78.

59 Alan D. Monroe, "Consistency Between Policy Preferences and National Policy Decisions." *American Politics Quarterly* 7: 1979, 3–18; "Public Opinion and Public Policy. 1980–1993." *Public Opinion Quarterly* 62: 1998, 6–28.

60 Lawrence R. Jacobs and Benjamin I. Page, "Who Influences U.S. Foreign Policy," *American Political Science Review* 99: 2005, 107–123.

61  Paul J. Quirk and Joseph Hinchliffe, "The Rising Hegemony of Mass Opinion," *Journal of Policy History*, Vol. 10, No. 1 (1998), pp. 19–50. The lineup of opposing forces was apparent from polls, from the content of the proposals, or from the rhetoric of policy advocates, among other things; and the issues had existed in similar form for many years.

62  Our analysis was based on the account in Martha Derthick, *Policymaking for Social Security*, although Derthick did not directly address the role of mass opinion.

63  On how to think about this research, see Quirk, *Politicians Do Pander*.

64  Jacobs and Shapiro, *Politicians Don't Pander*.

65  For the issues discussed here, see Jacobs and Shapiro, *Politicians Don't Pander*, Chapters 3 and 4.

66  Quirk, *Politicians Do Pander*.

67  Although Jacobs and Shapiro acknowledge that Clinton's decision was consistent with public attitudes, they deny that those attitudes affected it. They do not, however, present evidence on the point.

68  Jacobs and Shapiro, *Politicians Don't Pander*, Ch. 4.

69  David M. Herszenhorn, Liberals Urge Reid to Keep Public Option, *New York Times*, November 16, 2009, http://prescriptions.blogs.nytimes.com/2009/11/16/senate-liberals-demand-reid-hold-firm-on-public-option.

70  For a study of the Tea Party movement and its impact, see Theda Skocpol and Vanessa Williamson, *The Tea Party and the Remaking of Republican Conservatism* (New York: Oxford University Press, 2012). See also Nicol C. Rae, "The Return of Conservative Populism: The Rise of the Tea Party and Its Impact on American Politics," Paper presented at the Annual Meeting of the American Political Science Association, Seattle, Washington, September 1–4, 2011.

71  The debt limit episode is described in Mann and Ornstein, *It's Even Worse Than It Looks*, Ch. 2. A journalist's account, focusing on Republican Congress members, is Robert Draper, *Do Not Ask What Good We Do: Inside the U.S House of Representatives* (New York: Free Press, 2012).

72  Mann and Ornstein, *It's Even Worse Than It Looks*, 5.

73  Draper, *Don't Ask Us What Good We Do*, 225.

74  Draper, *Don't Ask Us What Good We Do*, 257

75  Hendrik Hertzberg, "Huntsman Shows His Hand," *New Yorker*, August 20, 2011, http://www.newyorker.com/online/blogs/hendrikhertzberg/2011/08/huntsman-shows-his-hand.html#ixzz1zdgUnucn

76  Ashley Parker, "2012 Presidential Race Is 'the Worst I've Ever Seen,' Barbara Bush Says," *New York Times*, March 5, 2012.

77  *Pogo* was drawn by Walter Kelly, who modified a famous statement made by the American Commandant Oliver Perry after a marine battle in the War of 1812: "We have met the enemy, and they are ours."

78  Mann and Ornstein, *Even Worse Than It Looks*, Ch. 6.

# Chapter 10

# The Motivational Underpinnings of Political Participation

*Joanne M. Miller*

At the heart of democratic theory and practice is the notion that citizens participate in the political process, but scholars have long observed that not everyone participates equally. The question of who engages in politics and why remains a puzzle. Abundant research points to the "cost" of participating or individual resources, such as education, to help citizens overcome such costs, but Joanne Miller believes these studies miss a critical factor by ignoring the psychology of political participation. She designs an ambitious set of studies to demonstrate that personal motives matter and that the decision to become politically active depends on whether individuals believe that participation will help them meet their goals. Some motives, such as the desire to express personal values or group identity, might lead people to join a protest as a way of being "public" about their politics. Miller's work draws on "prospect theory" to show that people who feel threatened are more likely to engage in the political process than those who think they have something to gain. Her research is a particularly good example of using laboratory and field experiments to understand causal relationships. This chapter raises many philosophical and practical questions about the social-psychological foundations of democracy, the sources of bias in political representation, and how civic education may foster political engagement.

> It would clear the air of a good deal of cant if instead of assuming that politics is a normal and natural concern of human beings, one were to make the contrary assumption that whatever lip service citizens may pay to conventional attitudes, politics is a remote, alien, and unrewarding activity. Instead of seeking to explain why citizens are not interested, concerned and active, the task is to explain why a few citizens are.
>
> —Robert A. Dahl (1961, p. 279)

Studies of political participation are ubiquitous in political science. Normative questions about the role of citizens in a democracy, the representativeness of democracies, and the role of civic education in fostering good democratic citizens can be addressed by examining who, when, why, how, and with what effect citizens participate in democratic governance. Essentially, political activity is a *behavior*. And like any other behavior, people must make a conscious decision to participate. Current theory and empirical research boil this decision-making process down to one (or sometimes two) components: "*Can* I participate?" and "Have I been given the *opportunity* to participate?" In contrast, my research argues that motivation is the driving force of participation. Rather than "Can I participate?" I contend that people first ask themselves "Do I *want* to participate?" Incorporating theories of motivation fundamentally changes our thinking about political participation and the role citizens play in democratic governance. Re-conceptualizing the decision-making process in this way can help to explain many things that current models cannot, such as (1) why people higher in socioeconomic status are more likely to participate, (2) the choices people make among the myriad participation options available, (3) why people choose to participate at all when the tangible benefits seem to outweigh the costs, (4) why people choose to participate in some years and not others, and (5) why some mobilization efforts succeed whereas others fail.

This chapter is organized as follows. First, I review past research on the causes of political participation, focusing on the dominant political science perspectives to date. I conclude this section by suggesting that these theories overemphasize "ability" explanations of participation (*can* people participate?) at the expense of "motivation" explanations (do they *want* to participate?). Next, I draw on the psychology literature to define motivation and describe a series of specific motives that may be related to political participation. Finally, I review my research on the motivational underpinnings of political participation and conclude that a theory of participation that has motivation at its core can provide a more nuanced understanding of the process by which citizens choose, or choose not to, have a voice in democratic governance.

## Theoretical Issues and Existing Evidence about Political Participation

More than a century ago, the psychologist William James speculated about the number of things that could be attended to at one time and described the world as "one great blooming, buzzing, confusion."[1] People react to their complicated, ever-changing environment by paying careful attention to only a few stimuli at any time. One of the enduring questions about human nature concerns how people make decisions among the myriad competitors for their cognitive and behavioral energy. Within the realm of democratic politics the question is, "Why do people choose to focus their cognitive and behavioral energy on participating in the political process?" This question is of fundamental importance in a democracy, and there is a long tradition of trying to answer it in political science. What the four dominant theories and models in political science (*socioeconomic status, rational choice, mobilization,* and *civic voluntarism*) have in common is either an implicit or explicit view of participation as a trade-off between costs and benefits.

Participation in the political process can be costly: To contribute money to an organization or a candidate, one must have the necessary financial resources; to volunteer to work on a political campaign, one must have free time. It can also require considerable skills or at least confidence that one possesses those skills. To write an effective letter to a political leader, people must have (or believe they have) good communication skills; to register to vote, one must know when, where, and how to do so.

Given the resources necessary to engage in even the lowest levels of political activity, it should not be surprising that among the individual-level determinants of activism are indicators of individuals' actual or perceived *ability* to become active, as specified by the *socioeconomic status approach* (SES).[2] At the most basic level, people with more available resources such as free time and disposable income are less taxed by participation and are, therefore, more likely to become active.[3] In addition, age is positively correlated with political participation because people acquire the necessary resources to become active, such as political knowledge, skills, and money, as they grow older.[4] And Caucasians and men are more likely to be politically active in part because they enjoy financial advantages over their non-Caucasian and female counterparts.[5] Highly educated people who are better equipped with civic skills are more likely to become active than less educated people. Presumably, this is not only because such skills are objectively necessary for participation but because they confer a subjective sense of confidence that one's efforts can be successful.[6]

Whereas the SES approach focuses on the skills and resources that make it easier for people to bear the costs of participation, *rational choice theory* argues even more explicitly that citizens are self-interested actors who weigh the costs and benefits before deciding whether to become active. According to Downs, each citizen "approaches every situation with one eye on the gains to be had, the other eye on the costs, a delicate ability to balance them, and a strong desire to follow wherever rationality leads him."[7] The theory has been applied primarily to one form of political participation—voter turnout. Because voting is costly and the returns from voting are usually extremely low, the theory predicts that most people will not vote. They will instead "free-ride" by reaping the benefits of others' participation.[8] However, even though voter turnout in this country is not very high (hovering around 55 percent), many more people vote than would be predicted by the purest version of the theory, in which the utility of voting is solely determined by whether one's single vote will or will not affect the outcome of the election.[9]

Another approach to the study of why people participate in politics focuses on mobilization efforts by candidates and political organizations.

The *mobilization model* argues that any theory of political participation is incomplete without a consideration of strategic mobilization—how, when, and why political elites choose to mobilize American citizens into political life.[10] Consistent with the theory, people who are contacted by a party or candidate are more likely to write a letter to a Congress member, sign a petition, and make a political contribution. Contact from an interest group or a social movement is also predictive of political participation. And people are more likely to vote if they have been contacted by a party or candidate, an interest group, or a social movement.[11]

Verba, Schlozman, and Brady's *civic voluntarism model* combines features of the SES approach, rational choice theory, and the mobilization model to posit that time and money, civic skills, and recruitment to politics are at the root of political participation.[12] The authors provide survey evidence of the role resources play in promoting a variety of political activities. In addition, they show how certain resources are closely linked with specific activities (e.g., income increases the likelihood that people will contribute money to a political organization but does not determine whether people will vote). According to Verba et al., "a resource centered explanation of political activity... enhances the SES model by providing an interpretation of the way that model works. Resources explain why people of higher education or income or occupation are, in general, more active."[13] And the civic voluntarism model improves on rational choice theories by highlighting "the resources necessary to bear the costs of various kinds of activities and the way in which a given configuration of resources enhances, or places constraints on, the ability to participate in politics."[14]

## What's Missing from Our Knowledge about Political Participation?

These four models certainly tell us a lot about who chooses to engage in politics. We have learned that people who have greater financial resources and greater skills and knowledge and who are asked to participate by candidates or groups are more likely to get politically involved, whether it be through voting, contributing money, volunteering, demonstrating, or the like. As a result of this important research we know much about the representational biases inherent in who chooses to become involved in democratic governance: Those who participate are more likely than not to be Caucasian, male, highly educated, and of higher SES. The heavenly chorus does, indeed, sing with a strong upper-class accent,[15] but models such as the ones reviewed in the previous section tell us less about *why* people chose to become politically active in the first place. Even the wealthiest person in the world will not contribute money to a political candidate unless he or she *wants* to do so. In my research, I argue that the consequence of leaving out motivation is a distorted picture of political participation.

A self-referential example will help to illustrate the difference between my approach to the study of political participation and that of past research. Within the first few months of my graduate student career, I realized that to maintain any semblance of sanity, I needed to leave the ivory tower bubble and make new, non-academic friends (no offense to my graduate student colleagues, some of whom are still my closest friends). So, I started attending the weekly volunteer night for a local grassroots political organization. For months, every Wednesday night I sat at a long table with about a dozen volunteers, folding literature and stuffing, sealing, and addressing envelopes. If I had been asked to complete a public opinion survey at the time, I would have reported that I volunteer for a political organization, that I care about the issue, and that I am a Caucasian woman with a yearly income of less than $10,000 and work more than sixty hours per week (oh, the life of a graduate student!). Viewed through the lens of the models reviewed in the previous section, my participation is an anomaly. I was not approached by anyone and asked to participate; I sought out the activity. I barely had any free time at all and, given how poor I was, the free time I did have would probably have been better spent working at the local coffee shop.

After a few months I abruptly stopped attending volunteer night. My belief in the cause had not changed. I did not suddenly have less free time or less income (how could I have *less*?). Resource models of participation cannot explain why I stopped participating any more than they can explain why I began. I stopped because, honestly, I did not enjoy the company of the other volunteers. And since the primary reason for participating was to make new friends, once I figured out that was not going to happen, I stopped going. I did not start volunteering because I had the resources to do so, and I did not stop volunteering because of a lack of resources. The lifecycle of my participation can be explained only through the lens of motivation, which is underemphasized by the four dominant participation models in political science.

There are some exceptions to the general conclusion that political participation theories have ignored motivation, most notably work on selective incentives,[16] altruism,[17] and identity[18] (some of which is reviewed in the next section). However, past research on these motives has been inadequate for the development of a general motivational model of participation for two reasons. First, no systematic, empirical comparison of different motives, alongside traditional resource-based explanations, currently exists. Second, the existing conceptualizations of motivation in political science have been derived from an examination of usually a single participatory act (e.g., voting, the civil rights movement, or membership in organizations). In other words, we do not know whether one motive is more effective than any other at instigating participation and/or whether some motives lead to certain types of participation whereas others lead to different behaviors. Moreover, studies have yet to be conducted that enable us to directly compare how well resources versus motives do at explaining participation and whether resources and motives combine in interesting ways to predict things that neither is able to do on its own. My research tries to be more comprehensive. The basic assumption underlying my studies is that citizens are *purposive* political actors whose participation decisions are based first and foremost on beliefs about whether participation will get them the things that they want the most. In this approach, resources are secondary but not insignificant. Specifically, resources may amplify or constrain the type and amount of activity in which a person engages, conditioned first and foremost on motivation (e.g., to the extent that people do not have much disposable income, they may not be able to contribute money to a candidate, no matter how much they want to do so).

## What Is Motivation?

There are many conceptual definitions of motivation in the psychology literature.[19] What they have in common is the notion that *motivation drives behavior*. Specifically, "motivation, the activation of internal desires, needs, and concerns, energizes behavior and sends the organism in a particular direction aimed at satisfaction of the motivational issues that gave rise to the increased energy."[20] As such,

> a basic characteristic of motivation analyses is the assumption that one salient feature of behavior in situations is that the person is an active participant, an originating striving source with needs, desires, hopes, fears, and not simply a wet computer through which information enters, is processed, and is emitted as behavior.[21]

One approach to predicting behavior within a motivational framework is the expectancy × value model.[22] According to this approach, behavior is a multiplicative function of the value of the outcome (or, the strength of the motive) and the likelihood that the behavior will satisfy the motive.[23] This general framework leads to a number of specific predictions: (1) People will not always engage in the behaviors that are available to them; (2) when they do engage in a behavior, they may not expend maximum effort; (3) different motives are likely to lead to different behaviors, depending both on how much a person values the motive and how effective she or he thinks the behavior will be at satisfying the motive. For example, someone who moves across the country may very well be motivated to engage in behaviors that help him or her make new friends. In this instance, voting is not going to be high on the list of potential behaviors (if on the list at all), because the behavior is not one that is likely to help the person make new friends; and 4) persistence of the behavior over time will be related to beliefs about the action's effectiveness.[24]

Although the concept of motivation has historically received less attention in political science than in other disciplines such as psychology,[25] it has emerged over the past two decades as an important concept for understanding political cognition.[26] This research recognizes that people's cognitive capacities are limited: They cannot effectively process every piece of political stimuli to which they are exposed. Moreover, choosing to focus cognitive energies in one direction means forgoing other, maybe equally desirable, directions. As such, people are "cognitive misers": They are stingy about where and when to focus their cognitive energies. Political scientists have explored how motivation affects the types and amount of information people seek about political candidates and the impact of that information on political attitudes.[27] I argue that people are not only stingy about their cognitive energies but stingy about their *behavioral* energies. In other words, people will be less likely to engage in behaviors that they do not believe will be effective at getting them what they really want, even if they have all the resources in the world to "waste" on frivolous behaviors that have little chance of success.

What types of motives are likely to underlie political participation? Interestingly, research from different disciplines, using different methodologies, and focusing on different contexts, tend to converge on three types of motives. For example, studies on why people join organizations (such as professional associations) identify three motives: material, solidary, and purposive.[28] Material incentives are tangible rewards for participation (ones with monetary value). Solidary incentives are intangible rewards derived primarily from the social act of coming together as a group. Purposive incentives are also intangible, derived from the goals of the organization itself, such as getting a particular law passed or an organizational rule adopted.[29] In addition to the social and material (both tangible and intangible) motives, some scholars point to the desire to express one's attitudes or values (independent of whether anything tangible or intangible is received as a result of the expression) as being an important determinant of action.[30]

Social psychologists studying collective political action and volunteerism have settled on a typology of motives similar to that of political scientists. For example, researchers have focused on three motives that determine protest behavior: instrumental (the desire to obtain social or political change), identity (the desire to be a member of, or express one's membership in, a valued group), and ideology (the desire to express one's views).[31] In their research on what motivates AIDS volunteers, Snyder and his colleagues identified six motives, three of which echo the ones already discussed: utilitarian, to obtain tangible benefits; social, to make or maintain friends; and value-expressive, to express one's values to others.[32]

This tripartite classification of motives is also reflected in interviews of activists. The motives for activism most commonly offered in these interviews include making money (material), the community of friends and obtaining the respect of others (social), and doing the right thing and living up to their principles (expressive).[33] Another interview study found that material benefits (e.g., advancing in one's career) were related to contacting a governmental official; social gratifications (e.g., the chance to meet people and the excitement of politics) were most often cited for working in a campaign, participating in a protest, and being a member of community board or political organization; and instrumental motives (e.g., the chance to influence policy) instigated a wide range of political activities.[34]

In summary, theory and findings from disparate lines of research converge on a typology of three classes of motives: instrumental, social/identity, and expressive. However, individual-level empirical research on why people participate in politics has not systematically examined the impact of these motives alongside the conventional resource perspective.

### How Motives Predict Political Participation

I focus on the role of instrumental, social/identity, and expressive motives in individuals' decisions to become politically active. Through surveys and experiments, I test a series of hypotheses about the motivational underpinnings of political participation.

#### Project 1: The Impact of Threat and Opportunity as Motives for Participation

The instrumental motive is typically characterized as the desire to obtain a tangible reward. From this perspective, citizens become active to *obtain* something they lack, such as money, a job promotion, a change in public policy, and so on. However, research in political science, psychology, and neuroscience suggests that the desire to *protect* something one already has might be an even stronger motive to act. According to prospect theory, people are generally more motivated to avoid losses than to acquire gains.[35] In essence, many people appear to hate losing something more than they enjoy gaining it. Another self-referential example may help to clarify this distinction. For a variety of reasons, my husband and I do not go to casinos very often. But, on the rare occasions that we do, under no circumstances will we play at the same blackjack table. This is because I am much more motivated to avoid losses than he is. This frustrates him to no end, as I am content to sit at the table all night and never deviate from the minimum bet. "Bet more money and you'll have a chance to win more," he will say. My response is always the same: "Yeah, but if I bet more money, I'll have a chance to lose more." Relatively speaking, it upsets me much more to lose $20 than it would make me happy to win $20. My husband approaches gambling from the domain of gains (focusing on his motivation to win), and I approach gambling from the domain of losses (focusing on my motivation not to lose).

Moving from gambling to public policy (some might argue that they are not dissimilar endeavors), we can think of people being motivated to engage in political behaviors that can help them avoid losses in policy areas that they care about (e.g., policy changes that they oppose) or being motivated to engage in behaviors that can help them acquire policy gains (e.g., policy changes that they favor). Consistent with prospect theory, research supports the assertion that political action can be motivated by perceptions of political threats.[36] For example, Protestant middle-class citizens appeared to engage in the Temperance movement because they feared that the drinking habits of lower-class immigrants compromised the moral character of society and threatened its very foundations.[37] In the same way, the threat of nuclear war inspired activism among people who perceived that threat most powerfully.[38]

Other suggestive evidence of the role of threat in inspiring activism involves trends over time in activist support for environmental groups. Controlling for many factors and correcting for inflation, financial contributions to such organizations were higher during the Reagan and Bush Sr. administrations than during the Carter administration or the first two years of the Clinton administration.[39] And membership in the Sierra Club and the Audubon Society grew much less rapidly during the Kennedy and Johnson administrations than during the Nixon and Ford administrations.[40] Given this wealth of suggestive evidence, I conduct three studies, using different methods and focusing on different issues, to examine both sides of the instrumental coin—the threat of a loss and the opportunity for a gain. All three studies converge on the conclusion that *perceptions of threat are more powerful than perceptions of opportunity* in motivating political participation.

For one study, I conduct a *survey* of the attitudes and political behaviors of a representative sample of adults living in Ohio.[41] I assess respondents' attitudes toward environmental protection and their perceptions of political actors' views—whether they thought the President, members of Congress, and U.S. businesses were working hard to strengthen or weaken environmental protection laws, or keep them as they are.[42] People who thought political actors were working hard to advocate an undesired policy position (i.e., a weakening of environmental protection laws) were coded as perceiving policy change threat. People who thought political actors were working hard to advocate a desired policy position (i.e., a strengthening of environmental protection laws) were coded as perceiving policy change opportunity. Participation was assessed by asking respondents how much money they had recently contributed to a group that was working to advocate their desired environmental protection policy position. I found that policy change threat was a significant predictor of financial contributions to interest groups, whereas policy change opportunity was not (Figure 10.1). These results were even stronger among people in higher income categories. Importantly, contrary to what resource-based theories would predict, income in and of itself was not related to financial contributions. Only when income was combined with the perception of policy change threat did it have any impact at all.

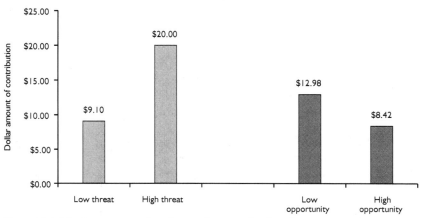

*Figure 10.1* The impact on policy change threat and policy change opportunity on contributions to environmental groups

Although suggestive that the desire to protect something one has (i.e., preventing a loss) is more motivating of political behavior (specifically, financial contributions to an interest group) than the desire to get something one wants (i.e., obtaining a gain), the first study does not provide strong evidence of the *causal* impact of the threat motive. The issue here is that both motives and participation were measured in a survey at the same point in time. Thus, I can conclude from this study that perceptions of threat are positively correlated with contributions (i.e., as one "goes up" so does the other). The observed correlation between perceptions of threat and financial contributions is plausibly the result of policy change threats causing contributions (i.e., people perceive a threat and, as a result, become active on the issue). However, it could also be true that contributions cause perceptions of threat. In other words, the action could come first. Specifically, people may be more likely to notice threats in the political world as a way to justify why they contributed in the first place (i.e., "I must have contributed for a good reason. In fact, look at all the bad things that will happen if we don't win this fight!").[43]

The best way to test causal hypotheses about the impact of motives on participation (or any causal hypothesis, for that matter) is to conduct an experiment in which motives are manipulated (i.e., respondents are randomly assigned to one or another treatment or control condition) and political participation is measured. Experiments are particularly useful for a research question such as mine because they allow me to vary only the particular motive to which each respondent is exposed (more on how I do this later) and to hold everything else constant (the type of appeal, the type of activity being solicited, etc.). As long as respondents are randomly assigned to receive one of the conditions (i.e., every person has an equal chance of being assigned to each condition, and therefore any variations between people are "evened out" among the conditions), any differences between the groups after being exposed to the motive manipulation can be unambiguously attributed to the manipulation itself (e.g., hearing about X motive *caused* people to be more willing to donate money to a candidate than hearing about Y motive). My second and third studies, therefore, use experimental designs to test the causal impact of the threat and opportunity motives on participation.

The second study is a *field experiment* that manipulates motives and measures the political behavior of people going about their daily lives who did not know that they were participating in a study.[44] Respondents were randomly assigned to receive (in the postal mail) one of three solicitation letters from the National Abortion and Reproductive Rights Action League (NARAL) of Ohio. Some were randomly assigned to receive a letter from NARAL describing the actions Congress members were currently taking to *increase* restrictions on abortion (policy change threat for those likely to become NARAL members). Others were randomly assigned to receive a letter from NARAL describing the actions Congress members were currently taking to *decrease* restrictions on abortion (policy change opportunity for those likely to become NARAL members). Others received a letter that did not discuss Congressional activity. Each letter asked respondents to make a financial contribution to NARAL. Consistent with the findings of the first study, threat predicted financial contributions, whereas opportunity did not.[45]

Both studies—the survey and the field experiment—show that the threat motive is more powerfully related to political participation (as measured by financial contributions to interest groups) than the opportunity motive. The case is closed, right? Not so fast. The astute reader will note that although I chose different issue attitudes (pro-environment and pro-choice) and behaviors (financial contributions to environmental organizations and financial contributions to the NARAL), the experiments both tap the left side of the ideological spectrum. For this reason, my third study assesses the generalizability of the effect of the threat motive (i.e., how widely these findings apply) by examining an issue on the conservative side of the ideological spectrum.

This study is a traditional *"laboratory"* experiment (in the sense that respondents know that they are participating in a research study) in which the experimental manipulations were embedded in the context of a public opinion survey.[46] The manipulations were designed to alter perceptions of policy change threat and opportunity with regard to gun control. The experiment has three parts. In Part I, a nationally representative sample of adults was asked a series of questions to determine whether they supported or opposed gun control. In Part II, the respondents were randomly assigned to receive information about one of various different legislative initiatives that were being pursued in Congress at the time the data were collected. Some respondents were told about Congressional efforts to *increase* restrictions on gun access, other respondents

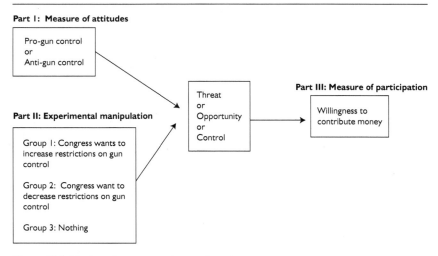

**Part I: Measure of attitudes**

Pro-gun control
or
Anti-gun control

**Part II: Experimental manipulation**

Group 1: Congress wants to increase restrictions on gun control

Group 2: Congress want to decrease restrictions on gun control

Group 3: Nothing

Threat
or
Opportunity
or
Control

**Part III: Measure of participation**

Willingness to contribute money

*Figure 10.2* Design of gun control experiment

were told about Congressional efforts to *decrease* restrictions, and a third group (the control group) was not told anything about gun control legislative efforts. In Part III, respondents were asked how much money they would be willing to contribute to pro- or anti-gun control organizations. Combining the respondents' expressed attitudes toward gun control from Part I and the condition to which they were assigned in Part II yields three groups: (1) policy change threat (anti–gun control respondents who were told of Congressional efforts to increase restrictions and pro–gun control respondents who were told of Congressional efforts to decrease restrictions); (2) policy change opportunity (anti–gun control respondents who were told of Congressional efforts to decrease restrictions and pro–gun control respondents who were told of Congressional efforts to increase restrictions); and (3) a control group of respondents who were not told any information about Congressional efforts (Figure 10.2).

This third study complements the second by assessing the robustness of the effect of policy change threat for a different issue (gun control) and by examining activism on both sides of the gun control controversy—pro–gun control and anti–gun control—rather than on only one side of an issue (pro–environmental protection or pro–abortion rights). The results confirm the findings of the previous studies. Both pro- and anti–gun control respondents for whom the threat motive was made salient expressed a willingness to contribute more money than those in the opportunity or control groups. And consistent with the survey study regarding contributions to environmental groups, income mattered only in conjunction with threat (to amplify participation among the affluent respondents in the threat conditions compared to their less affluent counterparts).

## The Impact of the Value-Expressive, Social/Identity, and Self-Interest Motives

The results of the first three studies suggest that the threat motive inspires financial contributions to interest groups. We can have particular confidence in this conclusion because of the methodological *triangulation* employed in the array of studies. Positive effects of policy change threat appear using a survey, a field experiment, and a laboratory experiment. In addition, the effect of the threat motive is observed for three issues—environmental protection, gun control, and abortion—and with various different sorts of measures. The appearance of the same effect across differently constructed studies provides robust support for the findings.

To understand whether motivation plays a broader and more fundamental role in decisions about whether to become politically active, I test a wider range of motives and behaviors. Moving beyond the threat motive, Study 1 uses a survey to measure the value-expressive, social, and self-interest motives and respondents' political behavior. In Study 2, I use an experimental design to focus on the value-expressive, American identity, and self-interest motives. Both studies test the impact of the motives on four political activities: (1) likelihood of voting, (2) willingness to volunteer for a candidate running for office, (3) willingness to contribute money to a candidate, and (4) willingness to participate in a protest, march, or demonstration.

For Study 1, I collected and analyzed survey data that asked a nationally representative sample about the importance of the value-expression ("express your personal values, convictions or beliefs"), social ("spend time with your friends or meet new people"), and self-interest ("obtain things that you want, such as an advance in your career, more money, prestige, or a better way of life for you and your family") motives in guiding their decisions about what to do with their free time and disposable income. The study was designed to test the following general hypothesis: The impact of various motives on participation will vary depending on the specific form of participation examined. That is, different motives will be positively correlated with different types of participation aimed at satisfying the motive *even after taking into account the explanatory power of traditionally examined resource variables.*[47]

Study 2 tested the same general hypothesis within the context of a survey experiment that respondents completed via computer. A nationally representative sample of adults was randomly assigned to one of three motive conditions—value-expression, American identity, or self-interest—or a control condition to examine the causal impact of each motive on the likelihood or willingness to engage in the same four activities as in Study 1: voting, volunteering, contributing money, and protesting. After answering some basic survey questions about some political attitudes, respondents were told:

We're interested in your thoughts and attitudes about some materials created by a new organization that is trying to convince people to get involved in politics. Please read the materials on the next few screens and follow the instructions. The survey will continue after you have read the organization's materials.

They were then randomly assigned to one of four conditions: value-expression, American identity, self-interest, or a control condition in which no motive was mentioned.[48]

Respondents read through a series of screen shots of a pamphlet produced by an organization called "Democracy Rocks" aimed at convincing people to get involved in politics (see Appendix A for the pamphlets for each condition). The first, fifth, and sixth screens were the same for each respondent (and the control condition was composed of only those three screens). The second, third, and fourth screens comprised the manipulation. The second screen answered the question posed in the first, "Why should *you* get involved in politics?" The answer depended on the specific motive condition to which the respondent was assigned. The third screen asked respondents to think for a minute about how politics is related to the motive and asked respondents to type their thoughts in the box provided. This screen serves both as a manipulation check and as a way to ensure respondents paid at least a minimal amount of attention to the materials. The fourth screen reiterated how politics could enable people to satisfy the motive to which they were randomly assigned.

After reading the screen shots, respondents were asked how likely or willing they would be to vote, volunteer for a candidate, contribute money to a candidate, and participate in a protest, march, or rally. As with the first study, the survey also measured traditionally examined antecedents of participation (education, income, civic skills, mobilization, and political interest).

To test whether motives affected participation in the two studies, I estimated statistical models that predicted willingness to participate in each activity with the measured motives (Study 1) or dummy variables to compare respondents assigned to each motive condition with those assigned to the control condition (Study 2) and the traditionally examined resource variables (income, education, civic skills, mobilization, and political interest). The statistical models tell us whether motives predict each political activity above and beyond what may be predicted by the resource variables.

Figure 10.3 displays the results for the survey. The figure shows the difference in the predicted value of willingness to participate in the activity (measured on a 1 to 5 scale), comparing respondents for whom the motive is high in importance to those for whom the motive is low in importance. In other words, a positive number (represented by the bars that extend above the zero line on the chart) indicates that people for whom the motive is very important express greater willingness to engage in the activity than people for whom the motive is

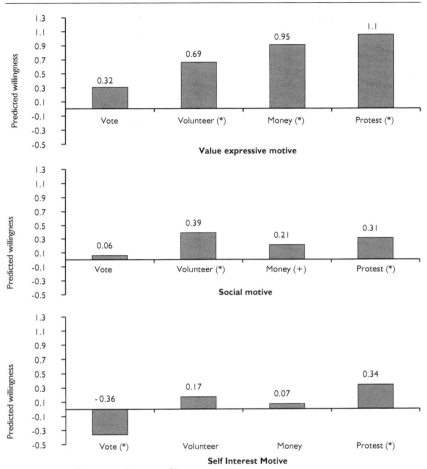

* indicates the coefficient is significant at $p < .05$
+ indicates the coefficient is significant at $p < .10$

*Figure 10.3* Study One (survey): relationship between motives and willingness to participate

less important. A negative number indicates that people for whom the motive is very important express less willingness to engage in the activity than people for whom the motive is less important.

The top panel in Figure 10.3 shows the results for the value-expressive motive. Those who indicated that the motive was very important to them expressed greater willingness to volunteer for a candidate, contribute money to a candidate, and participate in a protest, march, or rally in the near future than those for whom the value-expressive motive was less important. This motive was not, however, related to the expressed likelihood of voting in the next election.

The middle panel shows the results for the social motive. Here, we see that the social motive is positively related to volunteering, protesting and, to a lesser extent, contributing money (the relationship between the social motive and willingness to contribute money does not quite reach conventional levels of significance, meaning that we can be less confident that the relationship is real). As with value-expression, the social motive is not related to likelihood of voting.

The third panel shows the results for the self-interest motive. Here, the pattern is quite different. Self-interest is positively related to willingness to participate in a protest, march, or rally and not at all related to volunteering or contributing money. Interestingly, self-interest is *negatively* related to voting. In other words, people who say that it is important to them that any activity on which they spend their free time or disposable income helps them get the material things that they want say that they are *less* likely to vote than those for whom self-interest is not as important in guiding their behavioral choices (this is consistent with rational choice theory, which posits that voting is not rational from a self-interested perspective).

Taking these results as a whole, we can conclude that there is an important explanatory role for motivation in our understanding of political participation. The evidence thus far is supportive of the "expectancy × value" motivational framework. Recall that the "expectancy × value" model predicts that people for whom a motive is important (i.e., who value the motive) will also consider the extent to which engaging in a particular behavior will be effective at satisfying the motive (i.e., who have a high degree of expectancy). Viewed within this framework, the results of Study 1 show that motives are correlated with behaviors in sensible ways and help us distinguish who is more likely to participate in which activities.

People who place a high degree of importance on value-expression (compared to those who place less importance on the motive) are more willing to engage in activities that enable them to express their values, either publicly (volunteering, protesting) or privately (contributing money). People for whom the social motive is important are more likely to participate in social activities (volunteering and protesting) and, to a lesser extent, the non-social activity of contributing money. And people who place a high degree of importance on the self-interest motive either view politics as ineffective at satisfying their instrumental goals (save for protesting, which is a bit of an anomaly) or possibly even counterproductive (in the case of voting).

However, the correlational nature of these data make it impossible to determine whether the motives are actually *causing* people to want to participate. The reverse interpretation is equally plausible—that participation causes a change in the importance people place on various motives as a post hoc justification for why they got involved in the first place (or, a third alternative

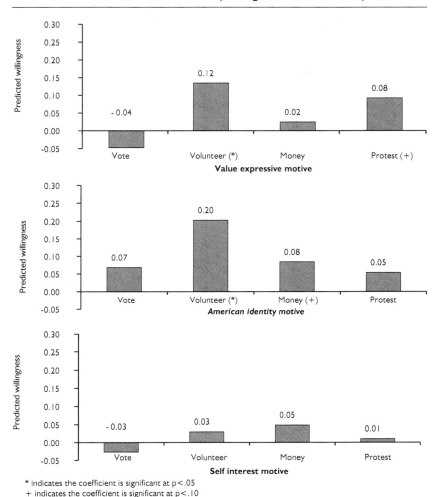

* indicates the coefficient is significant at p<.05
+ indicates the coefficient is significant at p<.10

*Figure 10.4* Study Two (experiment): difference between control condition and motive condition in predicting willingness to participate

is that some unmeasured variable is causing both motive importance and willingness to participate and that the observed correlations between motives and activities are spurious). The experimental design of Study 2 can give us more leverage on the causality question, because people are randomly assigned to read about one motive or another, and their willingness to participate in various political activities is subsequently measured.

The results of the experiment are displayed in Figure 10.4. The figure shows the difference between the predicted value of willingness to participate in the activity (again measured on a 1 to 5 scale) between the experimental group and the control group. Positive numbers indicate that those in the experimental group expressed greater willingness to engage in the activity than those in the control group. Negative numbers indicate that those in the control group expressed greater willingness to engage in the activity than those in the experimental group. The top panel compares respondents in the value-expression condition to the control condition, the middle panel compares those in the American identity condition to the control condition, and the bottom panel compares self-interest to control.

Compared to respondents in the control condition, respondents in the value-expression condition expressed a greater willingness to volunteer for a candidate and participate in a protest, march or rally (the two of the four activities that enable people to express their values publicly). This is consistent with the correlational results displayed in Figure 10.3. Respondents in the American identity condition (compared to the control condition), expressed greater willingness to engage in two activities related to electoral politics—volunteering for a candidate and contributing money to a candidate—but not the unconventional (and, by some characterizations, "anti-establishment" act of protesting). Interestingly, there was no effect of the American identity condition on expressed likelihood of voting—the quintessential "civic duty" act in a democracy (more on this below). And, largely consistent with the correlational study, the self-interest condition had no effect on expressed willingness to engage in any of the activities (compared to the control condition).

Before concluding, two aspects of these results warrant some discussion. First, not only do these findings indicate that motives can, in fact, explain between-person variance in political participation above and beyond what resources can explain, but motives are likely to be better predictors than resources of who is going to engage in which types of activities. Simply put, resource variables are not nuanced enough to allow researchers to predict, with any level of certainty, whether, for example, Person X is more likely to participate in a protest or is more likely to vote (beyond showing that people with higher incomes are more likely to contribute money than people with lower incomes, and people with more free time are more likely to participate in activities that require a greater time commitment).[49] Differences in the "motive profiles" of individuals can be leveraged to provide a better understanding of who is going to choose which activity at any given time.

Second, the reader has no doubt noticed a glaring non-finding across the two studies. None of the motives measured in Study 1 or manipulated in Study 2 is related to voting at all (save for the negative effect of self-interest in Study 1). This is somewhat surprising and could be interpreted as a nail in the coffin for any argument that motivation matters for understanding political participation. If motives are important, why are they not related to the most quintessential political act in America? A preliminary but intriguing answer to this question relates to recent scholarship in political science that finds that a significant proportion of the variation in people's propensity to vote can be explained by biology. That is, people exhibit genetic variation in their likelihood of voting.[50] If voting is, in a sense, "hardwired," this could be a possible explanation for why motivation plays less of a role in determining who is more or less likely to vote.[51]

## Conclusion

The costs to political participation in the United States can be considerable and are higher than in other developed democracies. This, in combination with evidence of steep declines in social capital and citizen participation, makes the motivational question ever more imperative. There are many reasons why somebody with a wealth of resources may choose not to participate. Most relevant to my research, he or she may not think that participating in politics will be an effective way to further his or her goals, regardless of her or his ability to do so.[52] Therefore any theory of political participation is inadequate without a careful consideration of motivation.[53]

In addition to providing a more complete (and more accurate) understanding of political participation, models that incorporate motivational parameters alongside resources have broader implications for our understanding of other aspects of democratic political life. Incorporating motivation, for example, can help to explain fluctuations in public policy.

If threat turns out to be the most powerful motivator, then we might expect only a small group of citizens to speak out on an issue at any one time. This would help to explain why policy change occurs so slowly (to the frustration of many!). It is because the vocal minority is operating to *prevent* change. And the composition of this vocal minority might shift dramatically with changes in the political context. Sometimes, the context reassures one segment of the population (which causes them to taper their participation) while it simultaneously threatens another (which causes them to engage).

Alternatively, if identity is the most powerful motivator, changes in public policy might be tied to changes in civic education programs aimed at linking civic duty with citizens' identities or to fluctuations in the identities that are activated by different policy proposals (e.g., policies that make it easier for employers to refuse to cover contraception in their employee's insurance plans may activate women's identities, or policies to increase gun control restrictions might activate the identity of gun owners, thus motivating activism accordingly).

Motivational models can also contribute to normative theories about the effectiveness of democracy. For a democracy to function properly, citizens must actively participate in the political process—to make their voices heard. If only a small proportion of the citizenry chooses to participate, democratic governance leads to "rule by some of the people," as public officials hear a distorted message about what citizens want. And, indeed, for years academics and commentators alike have decried not only the steep declines in political participation over the last half century but the representational biases inherent in participation: Those who participate are more likely than not to be white, male, highly educated, and of higher socioeconomic status. Although models that focus either solely or primarily on resources have shown us that these biases exist, they can do less in the way of contributing possible prescriptions to alleviate these biases at the individual level (because resources tend to be more static). Motivations, conversely, can be learned, changed, and strengthened. Because motivational models can explain and predict *why* citizens become active in the first place, they can provide guidance for civic education programs and other efforts aimed at increasing minority representation. Successful strategies should emphasize changing motives and strengthening existing ones.

## Acknowledgments

The research described in this chapter was funded by grants from the Ohio State University, the University of Minnesota, and the National Science Foundation. The author would like to thank Chris Galdieri, Sarah Treul, and Vincent Vecera for their research assistance.

## Notes

1 James, William. 1890. *The Principles of Psychology*. New York: Dover.
2 See, for example, Verba, Sidney and Norman H. Nie. 1972. *Participation in America: Political Democracy and Social Equality*. New York: Harper & Row.
3 Rosenstone, Steven J. and John Mark Hansen. 1993. *Mobilization, Participation, and Democracy in America*. New York: MacMillan Publishing Co.; Verba, Sidney, Kay Lehman Schlozman, and Henry E. Brady. 1995. *Voice and Equality: Civic Voluntarism in American Politics*. Cambridge: Harvard University Press.
4 Campbell, Angus, Philip E. Converse, Warren E. Miller, and Donald E. Stokes. 1960. *The American Voter*. New York: Wiley; Miller, Warren E. and J. Merrill Shanks. 1996. *The New American Voter*. Cambridge: Harvard University Press; Rosenstone and Hansen 1993.
5 Rosenstone and Hansen 1993; Verba and Nie 1972; Verba et al. 1995.
6 Dahl, Robert. 1961. *Who Governs? Democracy and Power in an American City*. New Haven: Yale University Press; Rosenstone and Hansen 1993; Verba and Nie 1972; Verba et al. 1995.
7 Downs, Anthony. 1957. *An Economic Theory of Democracy*. New York: Harper & Row, pp. 7–8.
8 Olson, Mancur. 1965. *The Logic of Collective Action*. Cambridge: Harvard University Press.
9 Green, Donald P. and Ian Shapiro. 1994. *Pathologies of Rational Choice Theory: A Critique of Applications in Political Science*. New Haven: Yale University Press;

Uhlaner, Carole J. 1989. "Rational Turnout: The Neglected Role of Groups." *American Journal of Political Science* 33(2): 390–422.

10  Rosenstone and Hansen 1993, p. 5.

11  Berelson, Bernard R., Paul F. Lazarsfeld, and William N. McPhee. 1954. *Voting: A Study of Opinion Formation in a Presidential Campaign*. Chicago: The University of Chicago Press; Chong, Dennis. 1991. *Collective Action and the Civil Rights Movement*. Chicago: University of Chicago Press; Guth, James L., Lyman A. Kellstedt, Corwin E. Smidt, and John C. Green. 1998. "Thunder on the Right? Religious Interest Group Mobilization in the 1996 Election." In *Interest Group Politics*, ed. Allan J. Cigler and Burdett A. Loomis. Washington, D.C.: CQ Press; Key, V. O. 1964. *Politics, Parties, and Pressure Groups*. New York: Thomas Y. Crowell Co.; Lee, Taeku. 2002. *Mobilizing Public Opinion: Black Insurgency and Racial Attitudes in the Civil Rights Era*. Chicago: University of Chicago Press; McAdam, Doug. 1985. *Political Process and the Development of Black Insurgency, 1930–1970*. Chicago: University of Chicago Press; Rosenstone and Hansen 1993; Schlozman, Kay Lehman and John T. Tierney. 1986. *Organized Interests and American Democracy*. New York: Harper & Row.

12  Verba et al. 1995; see also Burns, Nancy, Kay Lehman Schlozman, and Sidney Verba. 2001. *The Private Roots of Public Action: Gender, Equality, and Political Participation*. Cambridge: Harvard University Press.

13  Verba et al. 1995, p. 282.

14  Verba et al. 1995, p. 285.

15  Schattschneider, Elmer E. 1960. *The Semi-Sovereign People: A Realist's View of Democracy in America*. NY: Holt, Rinehold ,and Winston, p. 35.

16  Chong, 1991; Clark, Peter B. and James Q. Wilson. 1961. "Incentive Systems: A Theory of Organizations." *Administrative Science Quarterly* 6 (September): 129–166; Oberschall, Anthony. 1973. *Social Conflict and Social Movements*. New Jersey: Prentice-Hall; Olson 1965; Riker, William H. and Peter C. Ordeshook. 1968. "A Theory of the Calculus of Voting." *American Political Science Review* 62(1): 25–42; Salisbury, Robert H. 1969. "An Exchange Theory of Interest Groups." *Midwest Journal of Political Science* 13(1): 1–32; Wilson, James Q. 1973. *Political Organizations*. New York: Basic Books.

17  Dawes, Robyn M., Alphons J. C. van de Kragt, and John M. Orbell. 1990. "Cooperation at the Benefit of Us—Not Me, or My Conscience." In *Beyond Self-Interest*, ed. Jane Mansbridge. Chicago: University of Chicago Press; Keohane, Robert O. 1990. "Empathy and International Regimes." In *Beyond Self-Interest*, ed. Jane Mansbridge. Chicago: University of Chicago Press; Mansbridge, Jane. 1990. "On the Relation of Altruism and Self-Interest." In *Beyond Self-Interest*, ed. Jane Mansbridge. Chicago: University of Chicago Press; Sears, David O. and Carolyn L. Funk. 1990. "Self-Interest in Americans' Political Opinions." In *Beyond Self-Interest*, ed. Jane Mansbridge. Chicago: University of Chicago Press; Tyler, Tom R. 1990. "Justice, Self-Interest, and the Legitimacy of Legal and Political Authority." In *Beyond Self-Interest*, ed. Jane Mansbridge. Chicago: University of Chicago Press.

18  Teske 1997

19  For a review, see Pittman, Thane S. 1998. "Motivation." In *The Handbook of Social Psychology (v.1, fourth edition)*, ed. Daniel T. Gilbert, Susan T. Fiske, and Gardner Lindzey. Boston: McGraw-Hill.

20  Pittman 1998, p. 549.

21  Pittman 1998, p. 550.

22  For reviews, see Feather, Norman T. 1990. "Bridging the Gap Between Values and Actions." In *Handbook of Motivation and Cognition* (v. 2), ed. E. Tory Higgins and

Richard M. Sorrentino. New York: Guilford; Kuhl, Julius. 1986. "Motivation and Information Processing: A New Look at Decision Making, Dynamic Change, and Action Control." In *Handbook of Motivation and Cognition (v. 1)*, ed. and Richard M. Sorrentino and E. Tory Higgins. New York: Guilford.

23  I view motives as being different from benefits in an important way. Specifically, motives are features of *people*, whereas benefits are features of *activities*. As such, simply recognizing that an activity has a potential benefit is unlikely to instigate behavior unless the person has a pre-existing motivation to obtain that benefit.

24  Pittman 1998.

25  Atkinson, John William and Norman T. Feather. 1966. *A Theory of Achievement Motivation*. New York: Wiley; Festinger, Leon. 1957. *A Theory of Cognitive Dissonance*. Evanston: Row, Peterson; Heider, Fritz. 1958. *The Psychology of Interpersonal Relations*. New York: Wiley; Neuberg, Steven L. and Susan T. Fiske. 1987. "Motivational Influences on Impression Formation: Outcome Dependency, Accuracy-Driven Attention and Individuating Processes." *Journal of Personality and Social Psychology* 53(3): 431–444; Seligman, Martin E. P. 1975. *Helplessness: On Depression, Development, and Death*. San Francisco: Freeman; Weiner, Bernard. 1986. *An Attributional Theory of Motivation and Emotion*. New York: Springer-Verlag; White, Robert W. 1959. "Motivation Reconsidered: The Concept of Competence. *Psychological Review* 66(5): 297–333.

26  Lau, Richard R. 1990. "Political Motivation and Political Cognition." In *Handbook of Motivation and Cognition* (v. 2), ed. E. Tory Higgins and Richard M. Sorrentino. New York: Guilford; McGraw, Kathleen M. 2000. "Contributions of the Cognitive Approach to Political Psychology." *Political Psychology* 21(4):805–832 (see also Lane, Robert E. 1969. *Political Thinking and Consciousness: The Private Life of the Political Mind*. Chicago: Markham Publishing Co.).

27  Lau, Richard R. 1995. "Information Search During an Election Campaign: Introducing a Process-Tracing Methodology for Political Scientists." In *Political Judgment: Structure and Process*, ed. Milton Lodge and Kathleen M. McGraw. Ann Arbor: University of Michigan Press; Lau, Richard R. and David P. Redlawsk. 1997. "Voting Correctly." *American Political Science Review* 91(3): 585–598; Lodge, Milton, and Charles S. Taber. 2000. "Three Steps Toward a Theory of Motivated Political Reasoning." In *Elements of Reason: Cognition, Choice, and the Bounds of Rationality*, ed. Arthur Lupia, Mathew D. McCubbins, and Samuel L. Popkin. Cambridge, UK: Cambridge University Press; McGraw, Kathleen, Mark Fischle, Karen Stenner, and Milton Lodge. 1996. "What's in a Word? Bias in Trait Attributions of Political Leaders." *Political Behavior* 18(3): 263–281; Stroh, Patrick K. 1995. "Voters as Pragmatic Cognitive Misers." In *Political Judgment: Structure and Process*, ed. Milton Lodge and Kathleen M. McGraw. Ann Arbor: University of Michigan Press; Taber, Charles S., Milton Lodge, & Jill Glathar. 2001. "The Motivated Construction of Political Judgments. In *Citizens and Politics*, ed. James H. Kuklinski. Cambridge, UK: Cambridge University Press (see also Kunda, Ziva. 1990. "The Case for Motivated Reasoning." *Psychological Bulletin* 108(3): 480–498).

28  Clark, Peter B. and James Q. Wilson. 1961. "Incentive Systems: A Theory of Organizations." *Administrative Science Quarterly* 6(September): 129–166.

29  Clark and Wilson 1961, p. 135.

30  Chong 1991; Salisbury 1969.

31  Klandermans, Bert. 2003. "Collective Political Action." In *Oxford Handbook of Political Psychology*, ed. David O. Sears, Leonie Huddy, and Robert Jervis. Oxford: Oxford University Press.

32  See, for example, Clary, E. Gil, Mark Snyder, Robert D. Ridge, John Copeland, Arthur A. Stukas, Julie Haugen, and Peter Miene. 1998. "Understanding and Assessing the Motivations of Volunteers: A Functional Approach." *Journal of Personality and Social Psychology* 74(6): 1516–1530.

33  Teske 1997.

34  Verba et al. 1995.

35  Kahneman, Daniel, and Amos Tversky. 1979. "Prospect Theory: An Analysis of Decision Under Risk." *Econometrica* 47 (March): 263–291.

36  Marcus, George E., W. Russell Neuman, and Michael B. MacKuen. 2000. *Affective Intelligence and Political Judgment*. Chicago, IL: University of Chicago Press.

37  Gusfield, Joseph E. 1963. *Symbolic Crusade: Status Politics and the American Temperance Movement*. Urbana, IL: University of Illinois Press.

38  Tyler, Tom R., and Kathleen M. McGraw. 1983. "The Threat of Nuclear War: Risk Interpretation and Behavioral Response." *Journal of Social Issues* 39 (Spring): 25–40.

39  Lowry, Robert C. 1997. "The Private Production of Public Goods: Organizational Maintenance, Managers' Objectives, and Collective Goals." *American Political Science Review* 91 (June): 308–323; Richer, Jerrell. 1995. "Green Giving: An Analysis of Contributions to Major U.S. Environmental Groups." *Discussion Paper 95–39*. Washington, DC: Resources for the Future.

40  Mitchell, Robert Cameron. 1979. "National Environmental Lobbies and the Apparent Illogic of Collective Action." In *Collective Decision Making: Applications from Public Choice Theory*, ed. Clifford S. Russell. Baltimore, MD: Johns Hopkins University Press.

41  Miller, Joanne M. 2000. "Threats and Opportunities as Motivators of Political Activism." Unpublished doctoral dissertation. Ohio State University.

42  As it turned out, very few respondents said that they wanted to see environmental protection laws weakened, so my analyses are limited to the large majority of respondents who were pro-environmental protection.

43  Bem, Daryl J. 1967. "Self-Perception: An Alternative Interpretation of Cognitive Dissonance Phenomena." *Psychological Review* 74: 183–200; Festinger, Leon. 1957. *A Theory of Cognitive Dissonance*. Stanford, CA: Stanford University Press.

44  Miller, Joanne M. and Jon A. Krosnick. 2004. "Threat as a Motivator of Political Activism: A Field Experiment." *Political Psychology* 25(4):507–523.

45  Interestingly, opportunity had a significant, positive effect on the decision to express one's views on the issue to the President, whereas threat did not. This finding is consistent with the notion that different motives will lead to different types of participation.

46  Miller, Joanne M., Jon A. Krosnick, Alexander Tahk, Allyson Holbrook, and Laura Lowe. 2010. "The Impact of Policy Change Threat on Financial Contributions to Interest Groups." Unpublished manuscript.

47  Specifically, respondents were asked how important each of the three motives were in helping them to decide: 1) how they spend their free time *in general*, 2) how they spend their disposable income *in general*, 3) how they spend their free time on *volunteer or political activities*, and 4) how they spend their disposable income on *volunteer or political activities*. Responses to the four questions were summed to create an index for each motive. The survey also measured traditionally-examined antecedents of participation (education, income, civic skills, recruitment, and political interest) in order to isolate the independent effects of motivation. Finally, respondents were asked how likely or willing they would be to vote, volunteer for a candidate, contribute money to a candidate, or participate in a protest, march, or rally in the near future.

48  There are a variety of ways one could manipulate motives in the context of this type of experiment. One option would be to randomly assign respondents to conditions aimed at increasing the salience of each motive. For example, respondents in a value expression salience condition could be asked to answer a variety of questions about their personal values, convictions, and beliefs before going on to answer questions about political participation. Respondents in an American identity salience condition could be asked to answer questions about what it is like to be an American before answering questions about political participation, and so on. Presumably, respondents in each motive salience condition would say that they would be more willing to participate in activities presumed to be effective at satisfying the motive than respondents in a control condition in which no motive is made salient. Alternatively, respondents could be randomly assigned to conditions aimed at persuading them that each motive should be important to them personally (in essence, "creating" the motive in some people and not in others). This could be done by assigning people to read an excerpt of a speech that provides strong arguments for why each motive is important. Finally, respondents could be randomly assigned to conditions aimed at persuading them that participating in politics is an effective way to satisfy each motive. I chose the third option, because my goal was to mimic the real-world process of hearing about different reasons for why a person should become politically active. People can be exposed to reasons for becoming politically active through conversations with friends or relatives, or through the news media or their schooling. And politicians and interest groups can try to mobilize citizens through persuasive messages that focus on one or more reasons to become active. The current study manipulates motives using this sort of persuasive communication.

49  Verba et al. 1995.

50  Fowler, James H., Laura A. Baker, and Christopher T. Dawes. 2008. "Genetic Variation in Political Participation." *American Political Science Review*, 102(2): 233–248.

51  There is also recent work that suggests that voting is a habitual behavior (and therefore presumably less affected by variations in motives). See, for example, Aldrich, John, Jacob M. Montgomery, and Wendy Wood. 2011. "Turnout as Habit." *Political Behavior* 33: 535–563.

52  Gamson, William A. 1968. *Power and Discontent*. Illinois: The Dorsey Press, p. 96.

53  McGraw 2000, p. 820.

# Part III

# Politics and Policy

# Chapter 11

# The Politics of Immigration in a Nation of Immigrants

## Jack Citrin and Matthew Wright

The fraught issue of immigration raises fundamental questions about what it means to be American. Being a nation of immigrants is part of the national mythology, yet, Americans remain ambivalent about immigrants and immigration policy. Drawing on public opinion and historical analysis, Jack Citrin and Matthew Wright delineate the political conundrum: Americans are generally well disposed toward immigration and its economic benefits but fear loss of national culture and identity. Their work reveals the historical continuities on the immigration issue since the Founding and recurrent anxieties among Americans about whether immigrants will assimilate. Their analysis illustrates clearly how public opinion, which tends to favor more restrictive immigration policies, differs with the views of many elites, who prefer an open policy, which they refer to as "liberal cosmopolitan." The chapter helps put in perspective recent efforts by some states to pass laws to keep illegal immigrants out and the seemingly confused response of the federal government to deal with the issue of illegal immigration. It also addresses issues of political power and party politics as the share of the electorate with origins from Latin America and Asia grows.

In 1783, George Washington pledged that "America is open to receive not only the Opulent and respectable Stranger, but the oppressed and persecuted of all Nations and Religions."[1] The message has endured, and America's self-definition has, throughout history, been that of a nation of immigrants, treating the Statue of Liberty and Ellis Island as iconic symbols of the country's identity. Indeed, immigration is part of the narrative that distinguishes America from most other liberal democracies and has continuously affected the country's demography, economy, foreign policy, and religious and cultural practices. As of 2010, America's immigrant population had surpassed the 40 million mark, a record high in absolute terms, with more than 14 million arriving since 2000.

Yet, ambivalence about immigration is another continuing strand in America's story. Global economic forces resulting in the push of privation and the pull of opportunity have been the primary drivers of mass migration to the United States. Yet, whatever the economic consequences of immigration, immigration brings "strangers" into "our" land, raising anew question of who "we" are and how to meet the challenge of *e pluribus unum*. Each major wave of immigration in American history has provoked such questions. Today, it is the "Fourth Wave" of immigrants—since 1965, predominantly newcomers from Latin American and Asian countries—who spark a fierce debate about the cultural and economic consequences of the changing composition of society. Will the new immigrants learn English? Consume more government services than they pay for through taxes? Take jobs away from native workers? Will they adapt to the American way of life, and what will happen if they retain their original cultures instead of assimilating? And what should be done about the huge number of immigrants who are in the country illegally?

Against this background, the fundamental policy dilemmas concerning who should be allowed to come to America, how many should come, and on what terms have animated immigration policy since the Founding. In this chapter, we emphasize the way public opinion constrains policy choices and how immigration has created divisions in party politics with important implications for electoral outcomes in the future. Americans have mixed views about immigration despite the judgment of most experts that immigration is "good" for the county. Our account of contemporary immigration politics stresses both historical continuities and the way in which this issue dovetails with debates about national identity, social solidarity, and economic needs.

## Dimensions of Disagreement

The positions taken by politicians and interest groups can be arrayed along two axes: One pendulum swings from cosmopolitanism, which welcomes migrants from all backgrounds, to nativism, a perspective that seeks either to restrict immigration or to limit it to those who would reinforce the cultural homogeneity of the population. The second dimension of conflict centers on immigrant rights and responsibilities, with disagreement about their access to public services on the same basis as citizens and their obligation to Americanize as in the idea of the melting pot. The cosmopolitan liberal version of American identity expressed great faith in the ability of American society to assimilate newcomers or diverse origins and optimism about the immigrant's desire to join what David Hollinger has called the "Circle of We."[2] By contrast, nativism favored limiting immigration to people of Anglo-Saxon stock and insisted that other newcomers would have to shed their native skins and learn to "speak American" and "think American," as Theodore Roosevelt put it.

Daniel Tichenor has combined these two dimensions—openness to entry versus restricting access and expansive rights for aliens versus limited civil and social rights for noncitizens—to identify four distinct perspectives on immigration, each with a historically identifiable coalition.[3] The cosmopolitans favor expansive immigration with broader civil and social rights for aliens; among their supporters are various ethnic organizations such as the American

Jewish Committee and the Mexican American Legal Defense Fund. The free market restrictionists are peopled by major business interests and such political and economic luminaries as Ronald Reagan and Bill Gates, who support immigration in principle but favor a narrower set of rights for aliens, partly out of cost considerations. Tichenor calls Thomas Jefferson and civil rights leaders such as Frederick Douglass and Barbara Jordan "egalitarian nationalists." They, along with the American Federation of Labor in the late nineteenth century and the Sierra Club more recently, have opposed expansive immigration policies on the ground that it hurt the employment of native workers, especially blacks, and threatened the environment with a rapidly increasing population. Finally, the classic restrictionists or nativists opposed immigration and easy access to citizenship for those newcomers who were admitted. Cultural homogeneity is their siren song, expressed in the nineteenth century by the "Know-Nothing" Party and more recently by pundits such as Patrick Buchanan, academics including Samuel Huntington, and interest groups such as the Federation of Americans for Immigration Reform.[4]

In recent years, the political economy of immigration has become much more one-sided and expansionist than public attitudes. Virtually all the major interest groups—manufacturers, high-tech companies, agriculture, ethnic activists, including black civil rights leaders, the principal lawyers' organizations, the Catholic church, and even more of the major labor unions— have, for various self-interested and tactical reasons, come to favor a liberal admissions policy and tolerate the de facto residence in the country of what now is estimated at more than 12 million illegal immigrants.[5] Yet, more than forty years of polling shows that the public has consistently favored decreasing the number of legal immigrants and expressed deep concern about the entry of people illegally.

Though opinions do fluctuate with the unemployment rate, Peter Schuck summarizes public attitudes toward immigration as follows:

> Americans like immigrants more than like immigration, favor past immigration more than recent immigration, prefer legal immigrants to illegal ones, support immigrants' access to education and health benefits but not to welfare or Social Security. Americans feel diversity strengthens American society, but overwhelmingly resist any concept of multiculturalism that discourages immigrants from learning and using the English language.[6]

There is, then, a political disconnect between expansionist immigration politics and restrictionist public opinion, which, frustrated by the veto politics of the legislative arena at the national level, resorts to initiatives and populist laws in selected states. Before commenting on the policy dilemmas produced by this disconnect, we turn to a brief historical overview of immigration in American history.

## Cosmopolitanism versus Nativism from 1789 to 1965

Diversity was a feature of America's ethnic makeup from the beginning. Even so, those of English stock dominated, both numerically and culturally, making up 49.2 percent of the total population and 60 percent of the whites in the first, 1790 Census. Blacks constituted 19.3 peercent of the total nationally, and Germans, Scotch-Irish, Irish, Dutch, French, and Swedes made up the rest.[7] Some looked at this variety through rose-colored glasses. For example, Tom Paine wrote that America was made up of many nations, not just England, and Ralph Waldo Emerson stated that "American democracy has no genealogy. Its family tree is not easily traced." [8] In Federalist 2, John Jay viewed the census figures through the dual lenses of English dominance and social unity:

> Providence has pleased to give this one connected country to one united people: a people descended from the same ancestors, speaking the same language, professing the same religion, attached to the same principles of government, very similar in manners and customs....To all accounts we have uniformly been one people.[9]

Jay knew full well that the country around him was more diverse than he was letting on. He and other leaders of the new American nation knew there would be immigration but assumed that newcomers would have to absorb the dominant British values. For example, Jefferson warned against acts that would allow migrants to maintain among "us" foreign dialects and customs. He worried further that non-English "continentals" would be unable to absorb America's democratic creed.[10] Similarly, Benjamin Franklin (Pennsylvania) spoke darkly about the pernicious effect of Pennsylvania's large German minority:

> Why should Pennsylvania, founded by the English, become a Colony of *Aliens*, who will shortly be so numerous as to Germanize us instead of our Anglifying them, and will never adopt our Language or Customs, any more than they can acquire our Complexion.[11]

Despite these nativist worries, the need to forge a sense of distinctive we-feeling that separated the new nation from the mother country with which so much was shared pushed the founding elite to define American identity broadly in terms of a commitment to liberal political principles rather than ancestry. This inclusive narrative meant that anyone could have full-fledged membership in the national community provided he or she adopted the country's civic creed; immigrants would become Americans once they learned English and absorbed the country's democratic values.

Neither immigration nor naturalization (the process by which immigrants become legal citizens) figures prominently in the new nation's founding documents and, in the first fifty years of the Republic, immigration was entirely unregulated at the federal level. There was a recognition from the outset that population growth was needed for economic expansion: Alexander Hamilton's *Report on Manufactures* (1791) saw immigration as a solution to America's "dearness of labor" problem. Furthermore, all "free whites" could naturalize after living in the country for only five years. Born out of Jefferson's desire to secure the vote for immigrants (mostly French and Irish) who had allied with him against the Federalists, this relatively lax provision—coupled with the advent of mass suffrage and Jacksonian democracy in the 1820s and 1830s—would ultimately provide European immigrants with enormous political power.

With no federal restriction on immigration whatsoever and an easy path to citizenship, there was a steady yet modest migration from 1790 until the late 1830s. After 1830, however, the "push" of famine and economic distress in Europe and the "pull" of improving conditions in the United States turned the stream into a torrent: Immigration between 1830 and 1850 reached unprecedented levels both in absolute terms and relative to the United States' native population. More alarmingly to some, this new wave was largely composed of Irish Catholics and Germans, groups viewed as different from (and threatening to) the country's hegemonic Anglo-Protestant values, the foundation of national unity and social order.

Between 1830 and 1850, immigration was so prominent that the 1850 U.S. Census introduced the distinction between native- and foreign-born, and the count revealed that the foreign-born among the white population was 11.5 percent in the nation as a whole; by 1860, this proportion had reached 15 percent, the highest in the country's history.[12] Anxieties about the religious and linguistic differences between immigrants and natives engendered dark warnings about the loyalty of the newcomers to the Pope rather than their new country. These anxieties sparked the electoral successes of the anti-immigrant, anti-Catholic "Know-Nothing" party and a renewed effort to restrict immigration through legislation to limit passengers to the United States and the spread of local measures to promote assimilation such as requiring the reading of the Protestant bible in public schools prohibiting the teaching of foreign languages, and extending the period before naturalized citizens could vote. Opposition from the business community, who favored access to cheap immigrant labor, and politicians with ties to German and Irish voters limited the scope of nativist successes, a political dynamic that recurs to this day.

After the Civil War, the confrontation over immigration turned to the Chinese, who had begun to come to the Pacific West after the Gold Rush first as miners and then as laborers on the railroads. The growth of Chinese labor seemed to jeopardize the achievements of white workers and this, along with racial prejudice, spawned efforts both to limit immigration and deny citizenship rights to Chinese in the United States. In 1875, Congress passed the first substantive act limiting immigration and, in 1882, the Chinese Exclusion Act effectively ended Chinese immigration and encouraged the deportation of Chinese laborers.[13] Resentment at job competition was clothed in racialist rhetoric about the incapacity of the "yellow" man to live according to democratic principles; Chief Justice Hugh Murray of California's Supreme Court called the Chinese "a race of people whom nature has marked as inferior […] differing in language, opinions, color, and physical conformation."[14] The Chinese themselves, who, unlike "white" immigrant groups had never been permitted the right to naturalize and exert political pressure through voting, were virtually powerless against this onslaught.

Westward expansion and industrialization continued to attract labor to the United States. "Send us your huddled masses," proclaimed Emma Goldman, and millions from Eastern and Southern Europe heeded the call. In terms of sheer numbers, the flow of immigrants now referred to as the "Third Wave" peaked between 1900 and 1910, when nearly 9 million arrived, a number that was approached again only in the 1990s and one that relative to overall population size remains unmatched.[15] Once again, beyond the vast numbers coming ashore, it was the *character* of immigration that preoccupied restrictionists. Now inflows were dominated not by the "old" immigrant groups that had arrived in numbers in the past but by "new" immigrants from Southern and Eastern Europe, whose arrival revived the idea that true Americanism required conformity to the majority in religion, language, and manners. At this juncture, too, Social Darwinism furnished an additional "scientific" justification for giving a narrow ethnocentric cast to American identity.[16]

Steeped in the racial nativism of the era, restrictionists sought to limit immigration and re-balance it in favor of traditional source countries. World War I further whipped up anti-German sentiment and finally secured the passage of literacy requirements for naturalization in addition to spawning laws outlawing teaching foreign languages in public schools. An "Americanization" movement championed by Progressive elites insisted on cleansing immigrants of their native customs and requiring them not just to be committed to democratic principles but to speak English, improve their personal hygiene, eschew alcohol, and go to church.[17]

By the end of World War I, the Social Darwinism of the "Gilded Age" was in full flower. For example, in a 1919 article for the *Journal of Heredity*, Prescott Hall (head of the influential Immigration Restriction League) wrote

> Immigration restriction is a species of segregation on a large scale, by which inferior stocks can be prevented from both diluting and supplanting good stock. Just as we isolate bacterial invasions, and starve out the bacteria by limiting the area and amount of their food supply, where its over multiplication in a limited area will, as with all organisms, eventually limit its numbers.[18]

In addition to these racist views, concerns about the political radicalism of the Eastern European immigrants grew stronger after the Russian Revolution brought Communists to power.

In this context, nativist influence reached its peak with the passage of the Immigration Act of 1921 and the Johnson-Reed (National Origins) Act of 1924. These laws provided for an annual limit of 150,000 Europeans who could immigrate, a complete prohibition on Japanese immigration, and quotas based on the contribution of each nationality to the overall population in 1890. These new laws shifted the country's demographic makeup back toward the racial and ethnic status quo of the period before the Third Wave, assuaging native anxieties and effectively removing language and immigration issues from the national agenda for the next forty years. The hiatus in immigration also arguably facilitated the assimilation of those already here, as it stemmed the flow of newcomers with the language and customs of the "old" country.

World War II and its aftermath liberalized immigration policy in several important ways: It spurred the creation of a guest worker program with Mexico for temporary farm workers (known as the "Bracero Program"), led to the end of Chinese and Japanese exclusion, and encouraged the admission of refugees from Communist countries. Still, the watershed in American immigration did not come until 1965 with the passage of the Immigration and Nationality Act (also known as the Hart-Celler Act). Spurred by the change in attitudes toward minorities created by the civil rights movement, this legislation represented the triumph of cosmopolitan liberalism. By ending the national origins quotas, it was the death knell for immigration based on ancestry. The 1965 Act established the policy regime that remains intact today, replacing national origins quotas with overall hemispheric "caps" using family reunification as the main basis for allocating visas, adding skills preferences categories, and a quota reserved for refugees. The Hart-Celler Act was, at the time, seen as a low-profile reform. A product of elite compromise, it was viewed by its proponents, including President Johnson, as a largely symbolic action that would help reunite families separated by war without dramatically altering the number and origins of immigrants.[19] However, making family reunification rather than national origin the basis for visa preferences meant that the new immigrants would increasingly resemble their immediate predecessors. A father from a particular country sent for his wife, children, and parents. Once citizens, spouses used the next level of visa preferences to send for their siblings. A process of "chain migration" then allowed each sibling to spawn a new cluster of immigrants by bringing in their own spouses, children, and in-laws. So once the young Hispanic, Asian, and African immigrants began to arrive, the size of these ethnic groups in the United States grew exponentially.[20]

The effect of this migration pattern has been profound. Between 1960 and 2010, the proportion of the U.S. population that was foreign-born more than doubled, growing from 5.4 percent (9.7 million people) to 13.1 percent (38.5

million people).[21] Due to their relative youth and higher fertility as compared to the native-born, new immigrants and their offspring accounted for half of the U.S. population growth between 1990 and 2010.[22] In California, New York, and Florida, the favorite destinations of new arrivals, immigrants now comprise 27 percent, 21 percent, and 19 percent of the population, respectively.[23]

Not only did the new regime reopen gates welded shut after 1924 but it transformed the ethnic composition of American society by creating a massive influx of newcomers, both legal and illegal from Latin America, Asia, the Caribbean, and Africa. Between 1970 and 2010, about 29 million immigrants came to the United States. Well more than half came from either Mexico or Central America. Asia contributed more than a fourth, whereas less than 15 percent of immigrants arriving after the passage of the 1965 came from the previously most important originating sources, Europe and Canada, combined. [24] Mexico now is the source of about two-thirds of all immigrants to the United States.

In the decade between 1990 and 2000, the Latino population jumped 58 percent, more than four times the nation's overall population growth. Latinos in 2000 made up 13 percent of the U.S. population, compared to 9 percent in 1990, and are increasingly widely distributed throughout the country.[25] The trend is continuing. Between 2000 and 2010, the Latino share of the population grew by another 3 oercent in the country as a whole and by 6 percent in California. More than one-half of America's foreign-born residents today are Latinos from Central and South America. More than 30 percent are from Mexico. Mexicans also are estimated to comprise 58 percent of the nation's illegal immigrants, a group of more than 12 million people. [26]

The nation's Asian population has also surged, doubling between 1970 and 2010. The largest increase between 2000 and 2010 was among those from the Indian subcontinent, due in part to the influx of skilled immigrants to work in high-tech companies, but Chinese comprise the largest group of foreign-born residents of Asian origin.[27] Asians also have moved outside the traditional loci of immigration such as Los Angeles, San Francisco, and New York. In the meantime, whites and, to a lesser extent, blacks have moved away from states with high concentrations of immigrants-whites to the nation's hinterland and blacks to the South.[28]

Figure 11.1, drawn from U.S. Census figures, shows the change in the size of the main ethnic groups in America between 1980 and 2010. The growth in the Latino and Asian population is even greater in destination states such as California and New York, and continuing immigration together with higher fertility rates among the relatively young immigrant groups will accentuate these trends.

Demography shapes political destiny, and just as the enfranchisement of previous waves of immigrants shifted the political fault lines in the nineteenth century, so the growth and spread of the Latino population is making itself felt in politics. For example, legislative reapportionment has generally created

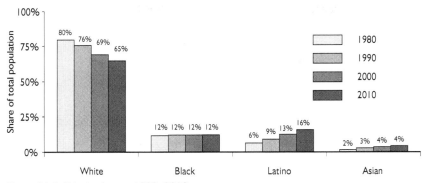

*Figure 11.1* Ethnic change 1980–2010

more safe seats for Democrats and Latino candidates. The increasing number of Latino and Asian citizens also puts into play new voters for whom immigration policy may be an important litmus test. After Governor Pete Wilson made the centerpiece of his reelection campaign support of Proposition 187, a citizen's initiative that denied illegal immigrants access to most public services, Republicans in California experienced an enduring loss of Latino backing. By contrast in 2004, President Bush's more liberal views about immigration helped win the Republicans about 40 percent of the Latinos' vote nationally, a significant increase from the previous election. This proportion declined to 31 percent in 2008, and anti-immigration rhetoric and support for state laws targeting illegal immigrants among many Republican politicians has further reduced Latino support for the party. Given the trends that are gradually making America a "majority-minority" nation, an all-white party ultimately will be unable to win a national majority, and some Republicans are scrambling to appeal to the Latino population by emphasizing traditional family and entrepreneurial values rather than restrictionist policies.[29] As in the case of politics before the Civil War, the electoral power of immigrant groups constrains the nativist impulses of a large segment of mass opinion.

## The Emergence of the Pro-immigration Coalition

Reacting to the anti-immigration tone of public opinion, in 1990 President George H. W. Bush proposed a reform that would have restrained the level of growth in immigration. Instead, as Peter Schuck has shown, the legislative dynamic produced an act "that raised legal admissions to 50 percent above pre-1986 levels, eased controls on temporary workers, made the diversity visas program permanent, and limited the government's power to deport for ideological reasons."[30] The 1990 Act remains the core of immigration policy today; astonishingly, it was passed during a recession, when anti-immigration sentiment generally intensifies.

The passage of the 1990 Act revealed the power of the interest group coalition that continues to press for more legal immigrants and the continued presence of illegal immigrants to this day. Growers demanding agricultural labor are a main impetus for Latin-American migrants, just as they have been since early in the twentieth century, and they exert enormous political influence in the populous and electorally important states such as California, Texas, New York, and Florida. Other business- and university-related groups also depend on immigration for engineers, programmers, researchers, doctors, and nurses, and they too press for more legal immigration. Ethnic groups lobby for easier access for relatives and refuges from their countries of origins. Religious organizations join in for both humanitarian reasons and the desire to recruit new members. Unions, long suspicious of the impact of immigration on their members, also are joining the expansionist coalition, recognizing the potential for replenishing their ranks as membership from more "traditional" industries declines and even in some cases supporting amnesty for illegal immigrants. Finally, black civil rights organizations have shifted positions, partially out of solidarity with liberal allies and partly due to their tactical cooperation with Latino and other pro-immigrant groups on other issues.

Against this formidable lineup stand the relatively unorganized views of general opinion and the pressure of state and local governments responding to the resentment of electorates, the perceived fiscal burden of education, health, and welfare services for immigrants, and annoyance about the laxity of federal enforcement. Local ordinances and state laws targeting illegal immigration encounter immediate resistance. For example, recent state laws in Arizona and Alabama that empower the police to demand that people stopped for traffic violations produce evidence of their legal status and punish employers for hiring illegal immigrants are heading for resolution in the Supreme Court.

## Public Opinion

In 1965, Gallup asked a national sample of Americans whether immigration should be kept at its present level, increased, or decreased.[31] At the moment of the transformative reform ending nativism, 40 percent opted for the same level of immigration, 33 percent wanted a decrease, and only 9 percent said they wanted the higher levels of immigration that almost immediately followed. This seeming disconnect between public opinion and public policy has persisted in the forty-five years since. Anti-immigration sentiment reached its zenith during the recession of 1994, soon after the expansionist 1990 Act had taken effect. In that year's Gallup Poll, as shown in Figure 11.2, fully 62 percent wanted immigration decreased, with 28 percent preferring the same level of immigration and just 7 percent favoring more. The proportion favoring more immigration has grown somewhat in recent years, but a plurality (roughly 42 percent) still favors a decrease. Other surveys, including the respected American National Election

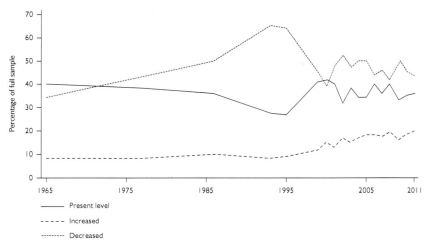

*Figure 11.2* American public opinion on desired level of immigration, 1965–2011

Note: "In your view, should immigration be kept at its present level, increased, or decreased?"
Source: Gallup.

Study, using slightly different wording, have recorded largely similar results. In sum, there is only a small number advocating the more liberal immigration policy favored by most elites, although it should be noted that favoring the same level of immigration when that level permits the entry of more than 1 million a year newcomers is hardly a call for restriction.

The U.S. native-born population has always been wary of large-scale immigration from groups that are linguistically, culturally, and racially outside of the "mainstream," and this remains true today. When asked whether there were too many immigrants coming from Europe, Africa, Asia, Latin America, or Arab countries, Gallup consistently found (from 1984 to 2006) that newcomers from Europe were most welcome followed by those from Asia, and Latin America. For example, in 2002, the proportions of the public saying "too many" were 27 percent for Europe, 32 percent for Africa, 43 percent for Asia, 49 percent for Latin America, and 55 percent for Arab countries. The opposition to Arab immigrants doubtless reflected the impact of 9/11 and, four years later, opposition to Arab migration had slipped to about 45 percent, whereas more than 53 percent said there were too many immigrants from Latin America. Given that people of European stock are the largest ethnic group in the country, this pattern of preferences probably reflects the tendency of people to favor those with a similar background, but it is instructive that opposition to immigration is centered on those groups that are providing most of the newcomers.

As to social and political differences in opposition to immigration, polls repeatedly show greater tolerance among the young and better-educated

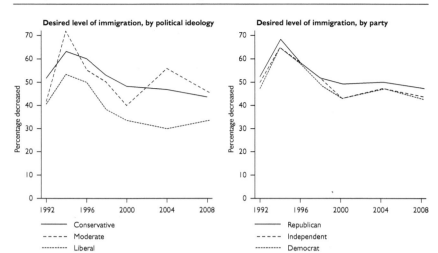

*Figure 11.3* American public opinion on preferred level of immigration, by party identification and ideological self-placement

Notes: "Do you think the number of immigrants from foreign countries who are permitted to come to the United States to live should be increased a little, increased a lot, decreased a little, decreased a lot, or left the same as it is now?" Source: National Election Studies.

segments of the population. Race is not a major factor in beliefs about the proper level of immigration: A 2007 Gallup poll found that 46 percent of whites and 44 percent of blacks said that immigration should be decreased, and this gap had narrowed since 2001. Predictably, Latinos were much more favorable to immigration: In the same 2007 Gallup poll, only 26 percent of these respondents wanted less immigration.

Figure 11.3 compares the attitudes of Democrats and Republicans and self-identified liberals and conservatives. Congressional voting on important immigration legislation, including the 1990 Immigration Act, showed a wide partisan divide, with Democrats much more likely to have favored liberalizing immigration. Indeed, at the elite level, party differences on immigration policies have widened in keeping with the widely observed polarization on other matters. For example, more Republicans in the House (85%) than Democrats (74%) voted for the landmark Hart-Celler Act. However, on the Immigration Act of 1990, which set the parameters in place today, the pattern was reversed, with 67 percent of Democrats and 53 percent of Republicans voting aye. This vote does, however, indicate less intra-party unity than on the related issue of language rights where Republicans almost unanimously voted against facilitating bilingualism.[32] In the general public, however, partisan differences are small. In the 2008 American National Election Study, 50 percent of Republicans compared to 44 percent of both Democrats and Independents favored decreasing immigration, a small difference, and the size of this gap had not grown since 1992 despite some evidence of part polarization on many other issues. Liberals and conservatives were much further apart than party identifiers, with 55 percent of self-identified conservatives advocating a decrease in immigration compared to just 29 percent of liberals in 2004. This was the largest gap recorded since the American National Election Studies (ANES) began asking the question in 1992 but, in 2008, the gap had narrowed to just 15 percent, perhaps because Obama and McCain did not make immigration a salient campaign issued. Nevertheless, partisan differences on immigration do exist, and we shall show that they are more intense on the matter of illegal immigration. These differences help explain the dilemma facing Republican leaders: Their most ardent followers are hostile to immigration whereas important interest group allies in the business world favor a freer global supply of labor. Partisan pressure mobilized by the blogosphere can also hinder the emergence of a legislative compromise.

Most Americans agree that the overall effects of immigration on America have been favorable and that earlier waves of immigrants have successfully assimilated.[33] In recent surveys, a majority believe that immigrants should "blend into the mainstream" rather than "maintain their own cultures," but when given an option to say both, about 20 percent choose that option, suggesting that the public believes cultural assimilation and cultural pluralism are not incompatible.[34] Still, one domain in which there is an unbending consensus deals with language. Americans overwhelmingly (79% in a 2004 Gallup poll) believe that speaking English is very important for making one a "true" American, and this sentiment is reflected in widespread support for laws making English the country's "official" language.[35] Yet, the value of learning English is fully accepted by immigrants themselves, and the facts are that by the third generation, most immigrants are monolingual in English, although this pattern of assimilation is a little slower among those from Mexico.[36]

Economists believe that the net benefit of immigration to economic growth is positive, although modest relative to the size of the economy as a whole.[37] There is an ongoing debate about the effects on employment and wages among native workers, with some arguing that the infusion of so many low-skill workers has reduced opportunities and pay for Americans with low levels of education. Figure 11.4 shows that the general public is less sanguine than the experts: In a 2007 Gallup Poll, 32 percent said that immigration had reduced job opportunities for themselves and their family; 42 percent said that the effect on the economy in general was negative; and 52 percent felt that the immigration had made the situation in the country's taxes worse. In no year does the proportion of respondents claiming that immigration makes any of these things "better" come close that choosing the "worse" option; the ratio runs from 2:1 (in favor of "worse") on the economy in general to 4:1 on taxes.

The perceived "criminality" of immigrants registers strongly in public opinion. The 2007 Gallup Poll found that 56 percent of the public believed immigration

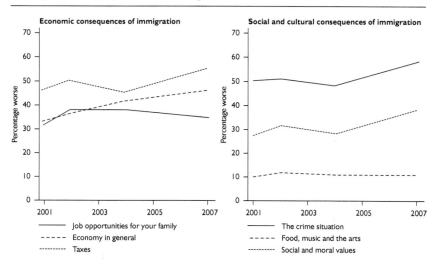

*Figure 11.4* American public opinion on the perceived consequences of immigration

Notes: "For each of the following areas, please say whether immigrants to the United States are making the situation in the country better or worse, or not having much effect. How about ...?" Source: Gallup.

had made the crime problem worse, and in no year does the proportion of respondents claiming that it has made the problem better break into double digits. Though a plurality of Americans feel that immigration has "not much effect" on the country's social and moral values, roughly one-third (depending on the year) agree that immigration has made the country worse along these lines, and fewer than a fourth argue that it has made the country better. Americans appear least worried about immigration's effect on food, music, and the arts, with a mere 8 percent to 10 percent selecting the "worse" option. As one would predict, those who perceive the consequence of immigration as negative are far more likely to favor decreased immigration, a pattern that repeats itself in all countries outside the United States.[38] Nevertheless, the pattern of beliefs about immigration suggests that many are ambivalent and that support or opposition may shift depending on economic and political events.

As stated earlier, immigration poses questions about who should belong to the national community. How one imagines America's identity shapes attitudes toward immigration policy. One reason that the United States has a more liberal immigration policy than virtually all European countries is that Americans are less likely to believe that "it is better for a country if almost everyone shares the same customs and traditions" and more likely to believe that "it is better for a country if there are a variety of religions among its people."[39] This tolerance of diversity is associated with a greater willingness to admit immigrants. Americans are more likely to endorse inclusive civic criteria such as respect for the law, treating people equally, or feeling American than ethnic or ascribed traits such as believing in God, being white, or being born in the United States as important for maing one "a true American."[40] And studies repeatedly show that the cosmopolitan liberal conception of national identity reduces feelings of cultural threat and promotes acceptance of immigration, whereas nativism, the residual belief in a white, Christian America, leads to the desire to restrict the influx of newcomers who today are mostly non-white.

This of course raises the question of whether sheer prejudice is a factor in country opposition to increased immigration of mainly non-white groups. A recent study by Donald Kinder and Cindy Kam argues that ethnocentrism, defined as both pride in one's own ethnic group and hostility toward other ethnic groups, is consistently an important source of anti-immigrant sentiment among both whites and blacks, predicting preferences for less immigration, stricter border control, restricted access to welfare benefits for immigrants, and English as the country's official language. Among Latinos, by contrast, in-group pride predicts a desire for increasing the level of immigration and spending less on border control.[41]

Though the gap between public and elite positions on the immigration issue is wide, it may diminish in the future. Demographic change due to the increase in second- and third-generation immigrants, cohort replacement, and the spread of education should reduce restrictionist sentiment in the mass public over time. More significant, however, may be the continuing inculcation and reinforcement of the cosmopolitan liberal conception of American identity, one that values a common culture that accepts pluralism within the crucible of a democratic civic religion.

## Immigrant Assimilation

Throughout American history, many have worried that newcomers would either fail or outright refuse to assimilate and become fully integrated into American society. Today, those worried about the consequences of immigration frequently ask whether the Hispanic and Asian immigrants of today will blend into the "melting pot" as their European predecessors ultimately did,[42] or will changes in the legal, economic, and political climate of the late twentieth century limit political, cultural, and economic assimilation? Assimilation means to become similar to; in the present context, this means the narrowing of differences between native and immigrant groups. Assimilation necessarily refers to change over time. Ethnic differences erode as immigrants and their offspring are exposed to and absorb the habits and customs of their new country and are able to take advantage of opportunities for mobility. In principle, of course, assimilation can be a two-way process, with the native population learning superior skills or cultural practices from immigrants. How else would pizza, salsa, sushi, and karaoke have become staples of popular culture?

Milton Gordon's seminal *Assimilation in American Life* distinguished between structural assimilation—the large-scale entry of native minorities and immigrants into the economic, social, and political institutions of the "host" society and ultimately leading to intermarriage—and cultural assimilation, involving learning English and adopting the dominant values and customs of American popular culture. In the political domain, cultural assimilation implied identifying oneself as an American both subjectively and through naturalization, patriotism, and endorsing the country's democratic and constitutional principles. Gordon believed that structural assimilation— residential integration, economic progress, political engagement, and intermarriage—would inevitably lead to cultural assimilation but that cultural assimilation is easier and faster because it can be achieved without the approval of the majority group. Circumstances in which structural integration lags behind cultural assimilation in a particular ethnic group often stimulate discontent and protest.[43]

Because assimilation (or integration) takes place over time, it is difficult to measure. There are few large-scale longitudinal studies tracking the same individuals, so scholars rely on cross-sectional comparisons of relevant groups at different points in time. And it is reasonable to expect specific immigrant groups to assimilate at different rates, depending on their cultural similarity with the native population, the skills and resources they bring with them, and the legal and informal obstacles they confront in the United States. In this regard, the traditional idea of "straight-line" assimilation holds that successive generations of immigrant generations, whatever their national origins, will climb the ladder of integration and increasingly resemble one another. In this optimistic scenario, third-generation Latinos should be more similar to native-born whites than to recent Latino immigrants. However, sociologists Alejandro Portes and Min Zhou, among others, suggest that today's immigrants face a less favorable labor market than their predecessors of a century ago. They posit a segmented path to assimilation with two destinations: the traditional mainstream culture of a white middle-class and the oppositional culture of a minority underclass, rejecting educational achievement for gang membership, crime, and violence.[44]

There is a vast literature on immigrant integration that is continuously updated with the appearance of each decennial census. A comprehensive recent study by Jacob Vigdor concludes that just as in the nineteenth century, today's immigrants improve their economic position as they spend time—usually no longer than ten years—in the American workforce. The children of immigrants tend to attain higher occupational status than their parents, but this varies across groups according to the concentration of skills needed in a multifaceted labor market.[45] In addition, the dynamism of the U.S. economy produces a relatively low unemployment rate among immigrants, certainly as compared to European countries.

Market forces also have helped speed the linguistic assimilation of immigrants. Most new immigrants do learn English, although few prefer to speak it at home. And the acquisition of English understandably varies with the language skills people come with. Vigdor's evidence is that late–twentieth-century immigrants knew more English than their late–nineteenth-century predecessors but also that the most recent immigrants have poorer language skills than the cohorts who arrived in the 1970s. Mexican immigrants, the largest group, lag in both the knowledge of English and the speed of learning it than other groups such as Vietnamese and Chinese,[46] but over the next two generations, linguistic assimilation becomes virtually universal in all groups.

Intermarriage is perhaps the last barrier in assimilation, as this brings different groups into one family. And the latest evidence is that intermarriage is growing in all ethnic groups. In 2010, 10 percent of newlywed whites reported marrying someone of a different race or ethnicity. The comparable figures for blacks, Latinos, and Asians were 17 percent, 23 percent, and 28 percent, respectively.[47] Immigrants generally marry people of the same ethnicity but, with each successive generation, this tendency declines.

Turning to political assimilation, it is important to address Samuel Huntington's fears about the consequences of massive Latino immigration. He writes that "the ultimate criterion of allegiance is the extent to which immigrants identify with the United States as a country,"[48] and it is reasonable to ask whether strong ethnic and national identities collide as when Latino fans root for Mexico and boo the American national anthem at an international soccer game.

A Pew Latino Survey conducted in 2006 provides more reassuring evidence about assimilation to an American identity. Respondents were asked whether they preferred to describe themselves primarily as someone from their country of origin, as a Latino-Hispanic, or as an American. Among foreign-born Latinos, only 7 percent identified themselves first as American but, by the third generation, this proportion rose to 56 percent.[49] In addition, in each Latino immigrant generation, speaking English increases the tendency to identify oneself as an American and, significantly, bilingual respondents are more similar to their English-speaking than their Spanish-speaking counterparts. By the third generation, identifying as an American is the plurality choice of bilingual Latinos.[50]

A more direct test of emotional identification is a question that asked people whether in their politics they thought of themselves as mainly a member of their ethnic group, as just an American, or both. Latino respondents preferred the hyphenated identification to calling themselves just an American, but this tendency was diminished among the native-born, additional evidence of assimilation. Finally, an array of surveys conducted between 1988 and 2004 showed that the choice of a hyphenated identity does not collide with feelings of patriotism among Latinos and, more important, that when asked about their pride in being an American and their love of the American flag, after adjusting for differences in age and years of formal education, native-born Latinos gave *more* patriotic answers than whites. Globalization and multiculturalism may be gnawing away at traditional forms of American patriotism, but immigration is not an important factor in any erosion of national attachment.

## The Problem of Illegal Immigration

The most heated question in current immigration policy is what to do with the estimated 12 million residents living here illegally. Perversely, this problem originated on a large scale in the wake of most liberal immigration reform in U.S. history: the Hart-Celler Act of 1965. Though devastatingly restrictive with respect to immigration from Europe, the National Origins Act of 1924 had left migrants from Western Hemisphere countries completely exempt from quota restrictions. Hart-Celler's provision for overall hemispheric caps on immigration now meant that, for the first time in U.S. history, official limits would be placed on the numbers that could come from Canada and Latin American countries. Combined with the termination of the Bracero Program in 1964, the immense logistical challenge of securing the United States's southern border, and the country's relative ineffectiveness in doing so, illegal immigration has soared in the decades since 1965.

The public is convinced that there is a need for government action: A January 2012 Gallup Poll found that for the first time since they asked the question, a majority (53 percent) of the public said it was "extremely important "to halt the flow of illegal immigrants into the U.S." Concern was higher among whites than non-whites and among older than younger Americans, but the largest gap was between partisans, with 68 percent of Republicans compared with 42 percent of Democrats feeling this way. There is greater party polarization on illegal immigration than on the proper level of *legal* migration. Alongside growing concern about the problem is anxiety about the absence of a solution. The same January 12 Gallup Poll found that 43 percent of respondents felt it was extremely important to develop a plan to deal with "the large number of illegal immigrants." Furthermore, 55 percent felt it was more important to halt the flow of illegal immigrants compared to 43 percent who said it was more important to deal with immigrants currently in the United States illegally. The 2008 ANES indicated substantial partisan and ideological differences regarding how to deal with the illegal immigration problem. For example, 72 percent security, compared to 57 percent of Democrats and 48 percent of liberals. There are similar differences in the degree of support for a path to citizenship for illegal immigrants already in America. Indeed, this issue is more polarizing that the question of how many legal immigrants should be admitted.

Since the cheap labor provided by illegal immigration benefits so many, the animus against them may seem puzzling. One explanation is that the very term *illegal* is freighted with heavy negative symbolism. There is a hurdle in simply accepting breaking the law, and this cultural norm is why immigration advocates insist on renaming "illegals" as "undocumented aliens." The presence of so many illegal immigrants also conjures up the image of a weak government, unable to fulfill the essential task of protecting the nation's borders. And concern may also be heightened by the tendency of the public to overestimate the number of illegal immigrants in the country. A 2006 national study by John Sides and Jack Citrin found that the average estimate for the proportion of illegal immigrants in the overall American population was an astonishing 21 percent, more than six times the number provided by the U.S. Census.[51] Finally, as the Kinder and Kam study suggested, one cannot discount prejudice against the largely ill-educated, non-English-speaking, brown Latinos who comprise the majority of the category. Given these concerns, it may not be surprising that a Pew national poll in February 2011 found that 72 percent of whites approved of Arizona's law requiring police to verify the legal status of anyone they detain if they suspect the person is in the country illegally. More generally, Gallup found in a January 2012 poll that roughly two-thirds of the public is dissatisfied with how the government is handling the illegal immigration problem.

Thus, it is easy to see why there may be public resistance to the idea of any proposal that seems to reward lawbreakers. Yet, so long as the economic asymmetry between the United States and neighboring countries remains, there will always be an influx of people seeking economic opportunity and willing to risk crossing the porous border illegally rather than wait for a permanent visa. Other sources of illegal immigration are lax enforcement against employers for hiring illegals, but this issue has less salience for the public than the seemingly unstoppable border crossings from Mexico. Slowing the influx is a separate matter from dealing with illegals already here, many for many years. This Gordian knot has been impossible to cut. The 1986 Immigration and Control Act was an effort to provide legalization for some agricultural workers, but its implementation was fraud-ridden and, as illegal immigration continued to increase due in large part to the opposition of business interests to the enforcement provisions, this Reagan-era legislation came to symbolize a failure not to be repeated.

In 2006, a new outburst of opposition to illegal immigration produced a legislative proposal in Congress known as H.R. 4437. This bill called for raising penalties for illegal immigration and the classification of illegal immigrants and anyone who helped them enter or remain in the United States as felons. The proposal engendered heated opposition, sparked months of mass rallies by supporters of the immigrants, and generated an alternative legislative proposal by President Bush. This law advocated enhanced border control, a

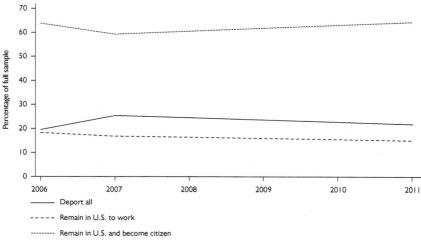

*Figure 11.5* Public opinion on dealing with illegal immigrants presently in the country

Notes: "Which comes closest to your view about what government policy should be toward illegal immigrants currently residing in the United States? Should the government—[deport all illegal immigrants back to their home country, allow illegal immigrants to remain in the United States in order to work, but only for a limited amount of time, or allow illegal immigrants to remain in the United States and become U.S. citizens, but only if they meet certain requirements over a period of time]?" Source: Gallup.

guest worker program, and a path to legalization and American citizenship for the millions of illegal immigrants already in the country. President Bush's effort failed, largely due to opposition to the legalization plan from within his own party. Consensus could not be reached on the trigger date for legalization, the eligibility criteria, the need for documentation and safeguards against fraud, the rules governing a path to citizenship, employer sanctions for those who hired illegals, and so forth. [52]

There is pervasive recognition that mass deportation is not feasible. Figure 11.5 shows that Gallup Polls from 2006 to 2011 consistently found that more than 60 percent of the public favored allowing illegal immigrants to remain in the United States and become U.S. citizens if they met certain requirements over a period of time. Once again, there are partisan differences about this policy, with Democrats more favorable about easing the path to legalization. Still, no one has found a magic thread to guide politicians through the labyrinth of bureaucratic and cultural obstacles. Illegal immigration provides the cheap labor that benefits the economy. At the same time, the political costs of enforcing our rhetorical commitment to the rule of law are formidable. As long as this imbalance exists and market forces in Mexico and the United States are unchanged, the influx of illegal immigration and the political conflicts it elicits will remain on the national agenda.

## Policy Choices

America is indeed a nation of immigrants, and it continues to be a beacon for people seeking freedom and opportunity. Immigration has made and remade America's economy and culture. Ending immigration is neither feasible nor desirable, but neither is the liberal utopia of open borders. The policy choices remain whom to admit, how many, and on what terms. Even though a plurality of the public say that immigration should be decreased, more than 55 percent in the same 2011 Gallup Poll say that immigration has been good for America. Current law favors family reunification over the Canadian "points system," which gives points to applicants based on their age, language skills, education, work history, and the like. This "designer" system is tailored to meet economic demand in Canada, and opposition to immigration has been tempered by controlling the number of visas to reflect employment conditions. There are American advocates for such a system. The public is divided, with half of those with a definite opinion in a 2007 Gallup Poll saying that people highly educated and skilled applicants should be given priority and the other half favoring visa preferences for applicants who have family members already living in the United States. The same poll found support for linguistic homogeneity, with 77 percent agreeing that proficiency in English should be a requirement for immigrants wishing to remain in the United States.

This pattern of opinion should warn the advocates of a free market in immigrant labor that they face widespread concern about cultural unity. To retain democratic legitimacy, immigration policy must respect the ideal of *e pluribus unum*. Hence, policies that go beyond merely responding to labor demand to encouraging and rewarding progress toward assimilation and citizenship are worth considering.[53]

Where so many European democracies confront the specter of aging and declining populations that threatens their hallowed welfare state, immigration has added vitality and innovation to American life. To be sure, immigration is not problem-free, and the impacts on local economies, population growth, and infrastructure cannot be ignored. More significant, however, is the need to openly acknowledge that immigration does stoke fears about national identity. As long as the nation-state remains the principal unit of democratic legitimacy, forging a common identity in a multi-ethnic society poses a significant challenge. America's good fortune is the deeply rooted presence of a cosmopolitan liberal conception of nationhood that accommodates newcomers. Yet, that formula for unity needs to be buttressed by policies such as language training, civic education, and naturalization rules that spread and speed up the process of psychic and political integration, a task made more urgent by the presence of centrifugal economic and cultural forces at home and abroad.

The American political system favors stability, not change. Organized interests, aided by a legislative process that rewards intense minorities generally can protect existing advantages. In the realm of immigration policy, the expansionist regime remains intact despite the disconnect with public opinion, because it delivers concrete benefits to a range of powerful groups while the costs, often psychological rather than tangible, are dispersed among an unorganized, if numerically large, public for whom other issues tend to be more salient on Election Day. At the same time, comprehensive reform to deal with the problem of illegal immigration seems remote. There is significant opposition to anything that smacks of amnesty, particularly among Republicans in the electorate and Congress, and once again the policy-making process favors the status quo. Muddling through with incremental changes in response to economic and political events may be the most likely scenario for immigration reform in the future. Yet, the interplay of demographic change and political power, economic need, and gaps in education argues for a more sustained effort to achieve comprehensive change. Whether a fractured political system is up to the task remains the country's major challenge.

## Notes

1   Quoted from Daniel Tichenor (2002). *Dividing Lines: The Politics of Immigration Control in America*. Princeton: Princeton University Press, p.51.
2   David Hollinger (1993). "How Wide the Circle of 'We'? American Intellectuals and the Problem of the Ethnos Since World War II," *The American Historical Review* (98): 317–337.
3   Tichenor, *Dividing Lines*.
4   Samuel Huntington (2004). *Who are We? Challenges to American National Identity*, New York: Simon and Shuster is the most cogent presentation of this position.
5   This is the standard estimate based on U.S. Census's approximate calculations. See Peter Schuck, "Immigration" in Peter Schuck and James Q. Wilson eds. (2007). *Understanding America*, New York: Public Affairs Press, p. 361.
6   Peter Schuck (2007). "The Disconnect between Public Attitudes and Public Policy on Immigration, in Carol Swain ed. *Debating Immigration*, New York: Cambridge University Press, p.19.
7   Schuck, "Immigration" p.342.
8   Quoted in Tichenor, op. cit.
9   John Jay, *The Federalist #2*, http://avalon.law.yale.edu/18th_century/fed02.asp.
10  Quoted in Aristide Zolberg (2006). *A Nation by Design: Immigration Policy in the Refashioning of America*, New York, Russell Sage Foundation, p. 81.
11  Quoted from Roger Daniels (2002). *Coming to America: A History of Immigration and Ethnicity in American Life (2nd Edition)*. New York: Harper Perennial, pp.109–110.
12  Ibid. p.129.
13  Lawrence Fuchs (1990). *The American Kaleidoscope, Race, Ethnicity and the Civic Culture*, Middletown: Wesleyan University Press
14  Quoted from Tichenor, p.89.
15  Zolberg, Chapter 7.
16  See, for example: Rogers Smith, (1997). *Civic Ideals: Conflicting Visions of Citizenship in U.S. History*. New Haven: Yale University Press, pp.347–410; John Higham (2008) [1955]. *Strangers in the Land: Patterns of American Nativism, 1860–1925*. New Brunswick: Rutgers University Press, pp.131–157.

17  Higham discusses this in detail.
18  Quoted from Tichenor, p.144
19  Tichenor, Daniel (2002). *Dividing Lines: The Politics of Immigration Control in America*. Princeton: Princeton University Press.
20  *Ibid.*
21  Schmidley, A. Dianne (2001). "Profile of the Foreign-Born Population of the United States: 2000." *U.S. Census Bureau, Current Population Reports, Series P23–206*. Washington, D.C.: U.S. Government Printing Office. *Migration Policy Institute* at www.migrationinformation.org/datahub/acscensus.cfm#
22  Camarota, Steven A. (2011). "Immigrants in the United States 2010: A Snapshot of America's Foreign-Born Population." *Center for Immigration Studies*. Available online at http://www.cis.org/articles/2011/
23  Gryn, Thomas A. and Larsen, Luke J. (2009). "Nativity Status and Citizenship in the United States: 2009." *American Community Survey Briefs*. October. Available online at http://www.census.gov/prod/2010pubs/acsbr09-16.pdf.
24  Camarota, Steven (2001), *Supra, fn. 40*.
25  Guzman, Betsy (2001). "The Hispanic Population: Census 2000 Brief." *U.S. Census Bureau*: C2KBR/01-3. Available online at http://www.census.gov/prod/2001pubs/c2kbr01-3.pdf
26  Passel, Jeffrey (2011). "Mexican Immigration to the U.S.: The Latest Estimates." Available online at http://migrationin.ucdavis.edu/cf/files/2011-may/passel-new-patterns-in-usimmigration.pdf.
27  Barnes, Jessica S. and Bennett, Claudette E. (2002). "The Asian Population: Census 2000 Brief." *U.S. Census Bureau*: C2KBR/01-16. Available online at http://www.census.gov/prod/2002pubs/c2kbr01-16.pdf.
28  *Ibid.*
29  Laura Meckler "GOP tries to woo Hispanics: After Tough Rhetoric on Immigration in Primary, a Push to Win Key Constituency," *Wall Street Journal*, April 2, 2012, p.A1.
30  Schuck, "The Disconnect...." op. cit., pp. 22–23.
31  All Gallup polling data referenced below can be accessed through www.gallup.com/poll/1660/Immigration.aspx.
32  www.voteview.com
33  Schuck, "Immigration," p.368.
34  Jack Citrin, Cara Wong, and Brian Duff, "The Meaning of American Identity," in Richard D. Ashmore, Lee Jussim and David Wilder eds. (2001) *Social Identity, Intergroup Conflict and Conflict Resolution*, New york: Oxford University Press.
35  Jack Citrin, David O. Sears, Cara Wong, and Christopher Muste, (2001). "Multiculturalism in American Public Opinion, *British Journal of Political Science*, Volume 31, no. 2.
36  Richard Alba and Victor Nee 2003). *Remaking the American Mainstream: Assimilation and Contemporary Immigration*, Cambridge, Mass: Harvard University Press, ; Alejander Portes & Ruben Rumbaut (2006). *Immigrant American: A Portrait* (3rd edition). Berkeley: University of California Press.
37  George J. Borjas, (1999). *Heaven's Door: Immigration Policy and the American Economy*. Princeton: Princeton University Press.
38  John Sides and Jack Citrin (2007). "European Attitudes Toward Immigration: The Role of Interests, Identities, and Information," in *British Journal of Political Science*, Volume 37, no.3
39  Jack Citrin and John Sides (2008) "Immigration and the Imagined Community in Europe and the United States," in *Political Studies*, Volume 56, no. 1.

40   Elizabeth Theiss-Morse (2009), *Who Counts as an American?: The Boundaries of National Identity?* New York: Cambridge University Press; Jack Citrin, Beth Reingold and Donald Green, (1990), "American Identity and the Politics of Ethnic Change," in *Journal of Politics,* Volume 52, no.4

41   Donald R. Kinder and Cindy D. Kam (2009), *Us Against Them: Ethnocentric Foundations of American Opinion,* Chicago: University of Chicago Press, pp. 137–144.

42   Richard Alba & Victor Nee (2003). *Remaking the American Mainstream,* op. cit.

43   Milton M. Gordon (1964). *Assimilation in American Life: The Role of Race, Religion, and National Origins.* New York: Oxford University Press.

44   Alejandro Portes & Min Zhou (1993). "The New Second Generation: Segmented Assimilation and Its Variants," *Annals of the Academy of Political and Social Science* (530): 74–96.

45   Jacob L. Vigdor (2010). *From Immigrants to Americans: The Rise and Fall of Fitting In.* New York: Rowman and Littlefield, p.75; Alba and Nee, op. cit.

46   Ibid.

47   The *Wall Street Journal,* February 17, 2012, p.A2.

48   Samuel Huntington, *Who Are We?,* op. cit. p. 241

49   Jack Citrin, Amy Lerman, Michael Murakami, Kathryn Pearson (2007). "Testing Huntington: Is Hispanic Immigration a Threat to American Identity?" ,in *Perspectives on Politics,* Volume 5, no. 1.

50   Ibid. p. 41

51   John Sides and Jack Citrin, "Does Telling it Like it Is Matter?: The impact of Information on Public Opinion about Immigration Policy", paper presented at the 2007 Annual Meeting of the American Political Science Association.

52   Schuck, "Immigration," p.367

53   Vigdor, op. cit. outlines the idea of an "assimilation bond" to create incentives for the integration of immigrants.

# Chapter 12

# Race, Ethnicity, and Politics
## Controversies and New Directions

*Jennifer R. Garcia and Katherine Tate*

The election of a black president carries strong symbolism about the advancement of black political power in the United States and leads some to argue that America is now "post-racial." And yet, as Jennifer Garcia and Katherine Tate explain, race and ethnicity remain influential factors shaping politics in America. Though much has changed in a positive direction, research continues to show significant disparities between whites and minority groups in terms of political representation, attitudes, and behavior. Garcia and Tate trace these developments historically, and illustrate how descriptive representation continues to play a compelling part in giving voice to blacks and Latinos, even as formal barriers decline in granting the rights of citizenship to minorities. Despite attitudinal changes among whites, the Tea Party movement reflects in part the ongoing racialized views of many Americans. Importantly, this chapter points to the power of institutions to shape political behavior. For example, as blacks gain positions in Congress, they tend to moderate their views as they adjust to procedural and partisan constraints of seeking and holding power. This research raises fresh questions about how an Obama presidency, and the rise of minority leadership in government, might affect racial attitudes and behavior of Americans from different races and ethnicities.

The election of African American Barack Obama as president in 2008 led to some pronouncements that America has moved decisively away from its tragic, racial past. Some are now calling America "post-racial," where racial group memberships and racial divisions are less relevant. The U.S. Constitution defines America as egalitarian, where individuals are equal under the concept of one person, one vote. However, citizens of color were systematically denied fundamental rights and privileges under the original Constitution. Historians and political scientists have generally sought to minimize the role of race and ethnicity in American society and politics. In this chapter, we ask whether race and ethnicity continue to impact American politics. First, we review the research establishing how America represented a racial state, one where race and ethnicity were used in laws and public policy to advance the interests of whites over others. Not surprisingly, today whites have a wealth advantage that is twenty times greater than for blacks and Latinos.[1] Second, we review the current work on the racial divide in American elections and the debate over whether America is now post-racial. The role of race and ethnicity in the political system has changed over time. No longer are there formal political barriers to minority political incorporation, yet the influence of race and ethnicity persists. Though there has been a decline in overt racism and an increase in the election of minority political officials, negative racial attitudes remain pervasive and minority representation limited. Ultimately we argue that race continues to play a significant role in American politics.

## Race and Ethnicity in the American Government

The 2008 election of Barack Obama as the nation's first black president is symbolic of the dramatic growth that minorities are making in political offices and positions of power all across the country. The number of black elected officials has skyrocketed from an estimated 1,500 in 1970 to more than 10,500 by 2011.[2] In 2011, 5, 850 Latinos were elected to public office, and nine Latinos were serving in statewide offices.[3] In 2011, a record number of 3,000 Asian Americans were serving as elected or appointed officials in government as well, including a state governor and two U.S. senators.[4] One American Indian served in the 112th Congress. The National Caucus of Native American State Legislators reports that eighty elected officials are American Indian, Alaska Native, or Native Hawaiian across nineteen states.[5] Minorities in the United States generally refer to these four groups, covered with African Americans under the 1975 extension of the 1965 Voting Rights Act, which will be further discussed.

The significance of these minority political advancements is complicated as, for a long period in American history until the pivotal post–World War II era, Americans often ignored the problems blacks, American Indians, Asian Americans, and Latinos experienced, consigned by law as unequal citizens. Their lack of descriptive representation in government was also generally ignored and, when it was brought up, triggered a sharp debate among political scientists.

The illiberal roots of American democracy in the original Constitution are not often taught. Few writers point out that the original Constitution was rigged in favor of slave-holding interests. Even during the 112th Congress, elected in 2010, when members decided that they wanted to read the entire Constitution at the start of the first session, the new Republican House majority refused to read the parts that exposed the racial foundation granting slave-holding interests disproportionate power. Critics complained that the Republicans wanted to "sanitize the Constitution."

Even when read aloud, however, the significance of these slavery provisions is easy to ignore. The framers strengthened the institution of slavery in the

Constitution without mentioning the words "slave" or "slavery." Article I counted slaves as three-fifths of a "person" in the allocation of seats in the House and Electoral College. The three-fifths compromise is sometimes misunderstood as purely symbolic. On the contrary, as Garry Wills writes in *Negro President*, because slaves were counted as three-fifths of a person for the purposes of enumeration (the allocation of seats to the states), slave states had one-third more seats in the U.S. Congress than their free population warranted.[6] Slave states also had more votes in the Electoral College because of their slave populations. Ten of the fifteen presidents before the Civil War owned slaves, including the nation's first president, George Washington. Nevertheless, popular biographies and textbook accounts of early American presidents generally fail to mention these facts.

Though the three-fifths compromise is briefly mentioned in textbooks, the denial of citizenship to American Indians, Asian Americans, and Latinos is often not mentioned at all. The original constitution refers to American Indians as "not taxed," and thus not counted in the allocation of seats and votes. Because of these constitutional provisions, courts held that tribal Indians were not citizens; the U.S. government was likened to a guardian until the Indian Citizenship Act of 1924 was passed.[7] Without political rights, Indians were compelled to sign treaties in which they ceded virtually all their land, first in the East for new lands in the West, then eventually in the West to restricted areas. Furthermore, the fact that American Indians were not counted for the purposes of enumeration was used to deny citizenship and voting rights to American Indians until Congress passed the 1924 Citizenship Act.

In the 1857 *Dred Scott* decision, Chief Justice Taney, writing for the majority, said that members of the African race were not considered to be included as citizens of the United States under the original constitution. This view from the high court that the Constitution established a republic for white people only was affirmed in *Ozawa v. United States*. In 1922, the Supreme Court ruled that federal law could continue to deny Asians the right to naturalize and become citizens because "The intention was to confer the privilege of citizenship upon that class of persons whom the fathers knew as white, and to deny it to all who could not be so classified." This ruling meant that many Asian immigrants could not naturalize until 1952, when the Naturalization Act of 1790, which denied citizenship to non-whites, was formally repealed by Congress. Meanwhile, more than 1 million white immigrants gained citizenship from 1907 to 1920 under the racially restrictive laws.[8] However, Asians *born* on American soil were entitled to U.S. citizenship under the Fourteenth Amendment—*U.S. v. Wong Kim Ark* (1898).

The will of the white majority to deny minority groups citizenship was persistently strong throughout the history of this nation. Citizenship confers constitutional protection of one's rights in society, including freedom from government persecution and the right to sue fellow citizens, businesses, and even the government itself. These political rights, in turn, confer access to social and economic benefits and privileges in society. The original constitutional features, laws, and policies were designed, as Linda Faye Williams writes, to advantage whites over other groups and confer "white privilege."[9] As Rogers M. Smith argues, instead of expressing purely pluralism, American citizenship laws have always expressed an illiberal desire to keep America "white."[10]

Citizenship denial combined with racially discriminatory laws limited the ability of Asians in America to benefit from the "blessings of liberty." California especially sought to close the door for economic opportunities to Asian Americans. In 1913, lawmakers did this by prohibiting the sale and leasing of land in the state specifically to "aliens not eligible to naturalize," meaning non-white aliens, rather than simply "noncitizens," which would have included Europeans. The Japanese farmers who put land in their children's names were prosecuted as aliens leasing the land. In 1948, the Supreme Court held that the prosecution of a Japanese American for unlawfully "leasing land" to his Japanese citizen father was unconstitutional under the Fourteenth Amendment (*Oyama v. California*).

Mexicans were also denied citizenship rights by states after the United States formally acquired Arizona, New Mexico, California, Colorado, Texas, Nevada, Utah, Kansas, Oklahoma, and Wyoming from Mexico in 1848. Under the Treaty of Guadalupe Hidalgo of 1848, Mexican citizens were given one month to retain Mexican citizenship or become U.S. citizens. However, though all Asian immigration was banned, the door to undocumented Mexican immigration was left open due to the cheap labor provided by Mexican immigrants. Although granted entry into the country, Mexicans were not granted the protections and benefits of citizenship, resulting in many instances of exploitation.[11] Mexicans and Latinos faced severe discrimination in the Southwest where school children were kept in segregated schools away from white school children until 1946–1947, when this segregation was successfully challenged in a California court in *Mendez v. Westminster*. They were discriminated against by local governments in the provision of local goods, such as access to pools and parks. There was wage and employment discrimination against Latinos as well.

By the end of World War II, concern about illegal immigration led to a 1950 law that made it a felony to import, transport, or harbor illegal aliens. However, the law also specifically said that the employment of undocumented workers did not constitute "harboring."[12] Further hostility toward Mexican workers led to a severe crackdown when, in 1954, the Immigration and Naturalization Service conducted raids in the Southwest and deported all those unable to prove their legal status in this country. In 1954, 1 million Mexican workers were rounded up and deported. Finally, in 1965, Congress passed an immigration reform act that opened the door equally to Asia and other non-European nations. Clearly, the U.S. interest in serving as a clear leader in international affairs meant that it could no longer keep its immigration laws suggesting the inferiority of non-whites of the world. The 1965 Immigration and Nationality Act ended the formal racial discrimination in U.S. immigration policy, but still left those from Latin American and the Caribbean at a disadvantage in obtaining legal immigration visas.[13]

With the end of formal racial restrictions on citizenship, the battle moved more squarely to voting rights. The Constitution left the decision of who could vote to the states. Thus, voting rights varied widely from state to state. Though many states had property requirements, by the time of the Civil War, all white males could vote. In contrast, a number of states denied the right to vote to women and blacks. Their formal political exclusion continued until the establishment of the Fifteenth and Nineteenth Amendments, which mandated the franchise be extended to blacks and women. The Fifteenth Amendment, adopted in 1870, forbids states to deny the right to vote on the basis of "race, color, or previous condition of servitude." Despite the Fifteenth Amendment to the U.S. Constitution, which enfranchised blacks, southern voter registration boards used poll taxes, literacy tests, and other bureaucratic impediments to deny African Americans their new political rights. Southern blacks also risked economic reprisal and physical violence when they tried to register or vote. As a result, African Americans had little if any political power, either locally or nationally. In 1947, the estimated percentage of registered blacks voters in Alabama was 1.2 percent, whereas throughout the South, black registration at that time was estimated at 12 percent. By 1956, black voter registration in the South had risen to 24.9 percent. In 1964, however, in the State of Mississippi, black registration was thought to be only 6.7 percent.[14] In addition to vote denial tactics, states with populous minority populations used racial gerrymandering, run-off requirements, and other electoral laws to dilute the voting power of minorities in their states.[15] The intent was to keep elective government lily-white and responsive only to the interests of the white majorities, who also favored laws discriminating against citizens of color in the provision of public goods, such as justice, schools, housing, parks, and police and fire protective services. This changed after the 1965 Voting Rights Act was adopted, as it forced states and localities to create some opportunities for candidates supported by minorities to win elective office.

## The New Political Empowerment Movements

Race relations in the United States have progressed, but not without upheaval. The political majority was challenged forcefully by movements to bring about minority rights. The formation of civil rights organizations, such as the NAACP in 1911, was important in the development of these movements. For Asian Americans, there was an emergence of political organizations in the early 1900s aimed at fighting stereotypes.[16] Latino civil rights organizations, such as the League of United Latino American Citizens founded in 1929, fought for citizenship rights and racial equality. Mexican American organizations, particularly in the Southwest, continue to pursue a variety of political causes aimed at addressing the interests of Latinos.[17] There were also Latino labor union organizations and interest groups that sought to influence U.S. policy towards their respective homelands. The black church was crucially involved as well.[18] Doug McAdam explains that the decline of the cotton crop in the South and the Great Migration of blacks to the North were important catalysts for a national campaign for equal rights as blacks in the North had access to the ballot and used their new voting power to lobby for civil rights.[19] For Richard M. Valelly, a critical turning point for African Americans was the presidential leadership of Harry Truman. He writes that Truman was the "first openly civil rights–oriented Democratic president."[20] Still, Valelly also states that the Democratic Party was deeply divided over race and, at that time, the Democratic Party's active support of civil rights existed in the "eye of the needle" as blacks still needed to organize extra-politically and independently to push their civil rights agenda through Washington. In 1965, blacks, through their civil rights movement led by Martin Luther King, were able to get Congress and President Johnson to pass the Voting Rights Act. Most recently in 2006, President Bush signed into law a twenty-five-year extension of the 1965 Voting Rights Act. It remains law, in other words, until 2032.

The Voting Rights Act pertained only to blacks until 1975, when four language minority groups were added. Section 203 provides language assistance to voting-age citizens who are not fluent in English. The language minority groups covered by Section 203 are American Indians, Alaska Natives, Asians, and Spanish-heritage citizens. Other language groups were not included because there is no evidence showing that they were massively discriminated against by states when trying to vote and participate in the American political process. Though it remains a powerful check against minority vote dilution by the states, especially in light of the continued demographic transformations favoring Latinos, Asians, and blacks, the Voting Rights Act also remains powerfully important to language minorities in this country.

## Controversies in Political Science: The Role of Race in Representation and Voting

The end of formal racial barriers to citizenship, voting, and immigration by 1965 suggested that America no longer had a political system dominated unfairly by white citizens. Acknowledging, however, the large racial and ethnic disparities in black and Latino rates of incarceration, segregation in public schools, and high rates of poverty, some suggest that these disparities reflect economic conditions and no longer the will of the American public to consign minority groups to a lower place in society because of their race and ethnicity under American laws and policies. Though progress has been made, this "end of racism" view in American politics remains contested. With respect to political institutions, scholars have argued that policies and politics remain shaped by race and ethnic considerations.[21] There is an ample set of publications showing that minority legislators, in fact, bring to government agendas more focus on minority concerns than their white colleagues. The numerical underrepresentation of minorities, therefore, limits their political and social equality. With respect to political behavior, scholarship reveals that political attitudes and voting patterns of Americans remain strongly shaped by racial factors, including prejudice.[22]

Early studies of the elections of blacks and Hispanics to local government found that the political incorporation of these groups leads to policy responsiveness for minorities.[23] Still, there has been a longstanding debate among political theorists about the benefits of descriptive representation. Opponents of descriptive representation generally argue that women and minorities might be better off in the long run pursuing the representation of their interests ideologically rather than racially or through group representation. Ethnic and racial divisions are dangerous in societies and are routes to war and genocide.[24] Furthermore, even strong proponents of descriptive representation argue that once systemic barriers to political participation have been eliminated for minority groups, the need for descriptive representation should "disappear."[25] Some have argued that strong procedures, such as quotas, to yield descriptive representation should be used cautiously and not be made permanent.[26]

Because these arguments against descriptive representation have been used by opponents of the Voting Rights Act, a wealth of scholarship has emerged challenging claims that descriptive representation is unimportant. Research finds that controlling for political party, region, and other factors, white legislators are more opposed to liberal legislation that targets African Americans.[27] Furthermore, white legislators are less racially oriented than black members, meaning that they do not as frequently raise racial issues that disproportionately affect racial and ethnic minorities in policy making.[28] These issues can be explicitly racial, as is the case with affirmative action, or implicitly racial, such as the issue of welfare. Examining the content of bills sponsored by members of the 103rd Congress, Canon finds that 95 percent of the substantive bills sponsored and 88 percent of the symbolic bills sponsored by white members had no racial content, compared to 58 percent and 46 percent, respectively, of bills initiated by black members.[29] Canon concludes that "While white members certainly can represent black interests…the white members in the 103rd Congress who represented districts that were at least 25 percent black did not show much interest in racial issues."[30]

Scholars have argued that descriptive representation improves the representation of minorities in other substantive ways.[31] Research finds that black legislators are more aggressive in voicing concerns that pertain to minority interests than their white colleagues at race and ethnic hearings in the 107th Congress. Indeed, according to one study, whites appear better represented substantively than blacks and Latinos.[32] Using survey data from the 2000 National Annenberg Election Study, which included more than 5,000 blacks and 5,000 Latinos, the study found that white representatives are closer to white voters on issues than they are to blacks and Latinos.[33] However, issue proximity of minority citizens to minority legislators is very close. In fact, when represented by minority legislators, blacks are as well represented as whites. Finally, because dyadic representation, the correspondence between a representative's policy positions and a specific constituency, is problematic, with scholars arguing that representation constitutes more than congruency on a few policy areas, the study also examines collective representation by comparing spending preferences of voters across eight areas to actual federal expenditures from 1972 to 2003. The results show that the U.S. federal government favored whites' spending preferences in the aggregate more than the two minority groups' preferences.

Constituency work matters, too. One study finds that women and blacks elected to city councils are more likely than males and whites to devote additional hours to constituency service.[34] These group differences remained statistically significant even after controlling for the elected official's political party, among other things. In addition, black House members are still more likely to locate their offices in black neighborhoods and hire black staffers, illustrating how a legislator's race affects his or her representational decisions beyond roll-call voting.[35]

Then, of course, there is some empirical work disputing these claims. A study of ten members of Congress found no difference in the racial composition of staff members across the black and white members whose districts were heavily black.[36] The author reported that white members had district offices in minority communities as well and concluded that white members were just as effective as blacks in representing black constituencies. Furthermore, there are growing claims that political behavior is changing as minorities win more descriptive representation in government. Some studies find that minority elected officials are actually quite diverse. A close study of representative activities of five African American House legislators finds significant differences in their representational styles.[37] Another finds that the Congressional Black Caucus is increasingly ideologically diverse, especially since its growth after the creation of new majority-minority districts in 1992 and after 1992.[38]

Despite some work illustrating similarities across racially diverse officeholders, the accumulated empirical evidence demonstrates black elected officials have a distinctive record with respect to policy agendas, votes on bills, staff composition, campaigns, and self-descriptions. Furthermore, African Americans in the electorate remain politically distinctive in survey polls. Descriptive representation continues to matter, therefore, as blacks are more likely to speak to the concerns that blacks have, and as blacks continue to have interests distinctive from those of whites. Thus, while researchers continue to search for evidence of black empowerment—reductions in the economic and social disparities that exist in the United States—plainly the election of blacks have increased government responsiveness to black interests. Though many prefer to side with the normative claim that race is not important in the political representation of citizens in a democratic system, research has established that it is. Blacks lacked equal and full representation in government until members of their racial group won elective office.

## Change and Persistence of Racial Attitudes among White Voters

Discriminatory laws and policies against communities of color represented the will of the white majority. However, by the end of the Civil Rights movement, white attitudes had massively changed. Surveys showed that few (around 10 percent of Americans) supported the unequal treatment of blacks and minorities by backing such policies as segregation laws and anti-miscegenation laws.[39] So few expressed overt racism of the past that, by the 1970s and 1980s, such questions were dropped from standard surveys. Nevertheless, the field remains in a fierce debate over the continuing role of racial prejudice in American political behavior. Some argue that a new form of racial prejudice explains white hostility toward affirmative action programs and welfare policies.[40] In contrast, others argue that much of the opposition to liberal racial policies, such as affirmative action, is based on conservative political values, such as individualism and a commitment to a limited government.[41]

To address the ongoing debate about the persistence of racial prejudice, we examine the voting behavior of white Americans. We demonstrate that racial prejudice continues to play a significant role in American political behavior even as attitudes changed after World War II. For example, the southern strategy of the GOP emerged fully in the 1968 presidential campaign of Richard Nixon to win votes on the basis of white southern opposition to civil rights policies. In the previous midterm election of 1966, about one-third of the South's House districts went to the Republicans. The backlash was attributed, in part, to President Johnson's Great Society agenda, which included a rewrite of immigration law and the creation of Medicare but, most important, the passage of 1964 and 1965 civil rights legislation that transformed the South politically. Urban rioting by blacks after King's assassination in 1968 became a campaign issue. Nixon exploited white voters' fears of the growing political power and demands of African Americans. He pushed for "freedom of choice" plans, where parents choose which school to send their children to, and opposed busing, which contributed to a decline in the Democratic vote from 61 percent in 1964 to 43 percent in 1968. Governor George Wallace, the segregationist from Alabama, ran as an Independent as well in 1968, picking up five Southern states. Racial conservatism arguably gave the GOP a "lock" on the Electoral College. Republicans won five of the next six presidential elections from 1968 to

1988, losing only in the aftermath of Watergate in 1976.[42] The Republican Party has benefited from racial conservatism and has exploited race in some national campaigns,[43] but is trying to diversify its base, having an African American lead its Republican National Committee in 2009. However, suspicions of racially based appeals persist. In the 2012 presidential GOP primaries, some claimed that one candidate, Newt Gingrich, made a racially coded attack when he called Obama a "food stamps president."

In 2008, the nation elected its first black president with 53 percent of the vote, leading some to assert that an era of post-racial politics had finally emerged. To the contrary, much evidence suggests that race played a significant role in the election of the forty-fourth president. Studies show that the presence of a viable African American presidential candidate invoked racial attitudes, thereby influencing voter behavior on Election Day.[44] One study finds that the salience of Obama's race reduced his vote share among whites in the general election by 3 percentage points.[45] Although surveys show that expression of overt racism has declined over the past several decades, evidence suggests that this does not necessarily reflect a decline in racial prejudice. Rather, it reflects a change in the public's lack of acceptance of overt racism.[46] In its place, a new, more subtle form of racism has emerged, known as *symbolic racism.*[47]

Rooted in anti-black affect (negative feelings and attitudes toward blacks) and traditional American values, symbolic racism stems from a belief that African Americans violate cherished aspects of the American creed, such as individualism and hard work.[48] Symbolic racism has been demonstrated to influence white public opinion on issues with racial implications, such as affirmative action and welfare, and voting behavior in elections. Support for black political candidates is negatively influenced by symbolic racism among whites.[49] Conversely, the most racially resentful whites, those who score high on the symbolic racism scale, are more likely to support white candidates who invoke racial attitudes through their use of code words.[50] Following this, recent research has shown that symbolic racism significantly influenced the 2008 presidential election. For instance, one study finds that those most racially resentful were more than 70 percentage points more likely to support Sen. John McCain, the Republican nominee, than Obama.[51]

The position of Barack Obama as the first viable African American presidential candidate evoked "profound racial hopes and fears alike."[52] Despite Obama's effort at portraying himself in racially neutral terms,[53] the "simple perceptual salience of his race" invoked racial attitudes among the electorate.[54] Studies have shown that racial attitudes affected the election in several ways. First, it has been argued that the unusually long primary contest between Barack Obama and Hilary Clinton was due to the influence of negative racial attitudes.[55] Those more racially resentful were more likely to support Clinton than Obama and were slower to switch their support to Obama once he became the presumptive Democratic nominee.[56] Second, public opinion on issues became more racialized, that is, racial attitudes influenced political preferences over the course of the campaign as Obama's position on those issues, such as health care and tax policy, became better known.[57] Finally, the general election outcome itself was influenced by racial attitudes.

One study finds that explicit prejudice among whites negatively affected their support for Obama in 2008.[58] Whites who expressed high rates of prejudice had a predicted probability of voting for Obama that was 15 percent to 24 percent less than whites who expressed little to no prejudice.[59] Another study demonstrated that symbolic racism was one of the primary factors that influenced support for and opposition to Obama in both the primary and general elections.[60] The most racially resentful were not only more likely to oppose Obama, they were 70 percent more likely to vote for Senator John McCain compared to racial liberals. Obama, however, was able to win the election in large part due to the support he received from racial liberals, that is, those who wanted to express their "symbolic support" for the first African American president.[61] Although many claim that Obama's election transcended race, one study concluded that the 2008 presidential election was "more racialized from start to finish than any other presidential campaign in modern history."[62]

Variations in turnout during the 2008 election also indicate that race played a significant role. Numerous studies have shown that turnout among racial minorities is significantly lower than for whites. A 2004 Census Bureau survey shows that whites vote at about a 10-percent higher rate than African Americans, and nearly a 50-percent higher rate than Asian Americans and Latinos. However, in 2008, voter turnout among minorities, particularly blacks and Latinos, increased to all-time highs (Figure 12.1). Furthermore, statistics from the U.S. Census Bureau indicate that black voter turnout increased by

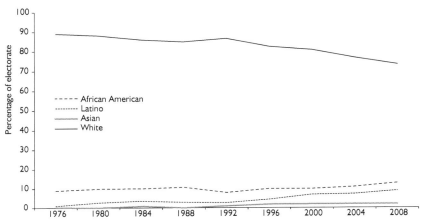

*Figure 12.1* Turnout in presidential elections: percent of electorate by race/ethnicity, 1976–2008[63]

roughly 8 percent and Latino voter turnout by around 7 percent from the previous presidential election in 2004. In comparison, white turnout increased by slightly more than 1 percent, and Asian American turnout increased by about 4 percent.

The increase in minority voter turnout may be attributed to the presence of a viable black presidential candidate. Though some have argued that the discrepancy between white and minority turnout can be explained by socioeconomic factors such as income and education,[64] others have shown that these resource-based factors do not fully account for the disparity between white and non-white voters.[65] Rather, psychological factors such as feelings of political efficacy and trust might provide a better explanation. For example, descriptive representation has been shown to increase political engagement among African Americans and Latinos.[66] The presence of a viable co-ethnic candidate has been shown to increase voter turnout among blacks[67] and Latinos.[68] Others have demonstrated that descriptive representation increases voter turnout, in part, because co-ethnic candidates spend more time and resources trying to mobilize minority voters.[69]

The presence of a viable African American presidential candidate in 2008 mobilized blacks across the country. Though blacks have consistently supported the Democratic Party since the 1940s, their nearly unanimous support for Barack Obama, with 95 percent of blacks voting for him in the general election, was an all-time high. A majority of Latinos (67 percent) and Asians (62 percent) also supported Obama, whereas only 43 percent of white voters supported him.

A closer examination of minority voting behavior over time reveals distinctive patterns across racial and ethnic groups. First, as seen in Figure 12.2, African Americans have consistently supported the Democratic Party, with at least 83 percent or more of black voters supporting the Democratic

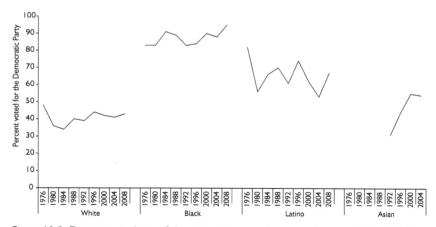

*Figure 12.2* Democratic share of the two-party vote by race/ethnicity, 1976–2008[70]

presidential candidate since 1976. This appears to provide support that African Americans tend to vote as a collective bloc. Stemming from a long history of discrimination, racial oppression, and segregation, this sense of "linked fate"[71] has established a strong group identity among African Americans and impacts when and how they vote. However, Latinos and Asian Americans do not have as strong of group consciousness as African Americans.[72] Both are pan-ethnicities, meaning that they are composed of a variety of different national origin groups. They come from several different countries, cultures, religions and, to a certain extent, speak different languages. Not only is there a tremendous amount of diversity within these groups, but as a large proportion are first- or second-generation immigrants, they tend to lack a sense of shared history that has played such a fundamental role in the development of African American group consciousness.

When examining patterns of support for presidential candidates, it is clear that there is much more variation in the voting behavior of Latinos and Asians. Figure 12.2 shows that though a majority of Latinos have supported the Democratic presidential candidate since 1976, this support has fluctuated over the past several elections and, for the most part, does not come close to matching levels of cohesion depicted by African Americans. Although some evidence suggests that Latinos, like African Americans, support the Democratic Party, convincing new research has begun to call these findings into question.[73] As for Asian Americans, they show even more diversity in voting behavior. Prior to 2000, a majority of Asians supported the Republican presidential candidate. This trend, however, appears to be reversing, with Obama receiving the highest percent of Asian voter support among any presidential candidate. Though neither Latinos nor Asians vote as a collective bloc similar to blacks, studies have found that Latinos demonstrate somewhat higher rates of group cohesion than Asian Americans.[74] There is no direct relationship between partisan support and being Asian American. In fact, partisanship among Latinos and Asians varies by age, length of residence in the United States, and national origin.[75]

More recently, scholars have begun to question how individuals who identify as multiracial differ from monoracial individuals in their political behavior and attitudes. One scholar argues that there is something fundamentally distinct about multiracial political attitudes; however, these differences vary greatly depending upon one's race.[76] For instance, Masuoka finds that multiracial whites tend to be much more liberal on racial issues than monoracial whites. Stemming from historical conceptions of race in the United States, whereby individuals were categorized as either white or non-white by the one-drop rule, and continued racial marginalization, multiracial whites are influenced by their minority identities. However, monoracial Asians tend to be more racially liberal than multiracial Asians. Ultimately, she finds that multiracial whites, blacks, and Latinos are significantly more supportive of the Democratic Party than monoracial whites.[77] Due to the growing number of Americans who choose to identify as multiracial, more scholarly attention should be given to understanding their political behavior.

Considering the role that race played in the election of Barack Obama, does race continue to impact his presidency? A good deal of evidence suggests that race continues to influence the Obama presidency. Much like during the campaign, racial attitudes influenced the public's view of Obama's job performance during the first year of his administration.[78] Those most racially conservative were less optimistic about Obama's performance than the most racially liberal Americans. The racialization of Obama has also encroached into the policy realm of his presidency. For instance, health care reform became more racialized once Obama entered the debate.[79] A study shows that, in part, opposition toward health care reform stemmed from negative racial attitudes toward a "black president's agenda."[80] Furthermore, through accusations that Obama is a Muslim or that he was born outside the country, Obama's political opponents have continuously tried to establish his "otherness." This, scholars have argued, has droned up fears and anxiety among white Americans who worry that their position in society may be vulnerable.

In February 2009, the Tea Party, which supports conservative values such as limited spending and small government, emerged on the political scene. Although this wing of the Republican Party had been present for years, the election of the first black president mobilized them into full force, indicating a central role for race within the Tea Party movement.[81] Other scholars contend that the election of the first black president, "and the change it symbolizes, represents a clear threat to the social, economic, political and social hegemony to which supporters of the Tea Party had become accustomed."[82] Essentially, whites are fearful that their position atop the racial hierarchy is in jeopardy. Surveys show that racial resentment among members of the Tea Party is high.[83] Tea Partiers are, in fact, more likely to be resentful of blacks and immigrants, which is linked to ethnicity, particularly Latinos.[84] This resentment may be a factor in the Tea Party's strong opposition to President Obama.[85]

Some argue that policy positions of the Tea Party are harmful to racial and ethnic minorities.[86] Those Tea Partiers in office, or running for office, tend to support English-only policies and restrictive immigration policies, such as Arizona's SB 1070, which allows police to racially profile individuals they suspect of being undocumented immigrants. Furthermore, the Tea Party opposes social programs such as welfare, which tend to benefit minorities, while at the same time supporting programs such as Social Security and Medicare. Opposition to these policies stems from resentment toward those "undeserving groups" who are receiving government "handouts."[87] At the core, this "Tea Party dichotomy of the 'freeloader' versus the 'hardworking taxpayer' has racial undertones that distinguish it from a simple reiteration of the American creed."[88] Though the national Tea Party publicly condemns any expression of racism, racial prejudice has been present at some Tea Party events. For instance, after the passage of the

Affordable Care Act on March 30, 2010, which is part of the health care reform initiated by the Obama administration, members of the Tea Party protested outside of the Capitol building. As Rep. John Lewis and Rep. Emanuel Cleaver, both African American members of the House, were walking up the steps of the Capitol, participants at the protest spit and yelled racial epithets at them. By no means do these accounts suggest that all members of the Tea Party are racially prejudiced; however, it does suggest that "a closer look at the immediacy of racism in America today" is warranted.[89]

## New Directions in the Study of Race, Ethnicity, and Politics

Despite impressive data showing policy gains for minorities through minority office holding and incorporation, minority empowerment theories have attracted a small set of critics. Some question the ability of minority officeholders to use politics to greatly transform the lives of minority citizens—to lift them up in society and eliminate racial and ethnic disparities. This skepticism exists because the political process by design is inherently too conservative for minority groups to advance genuine change through their politics. The "dominant groups," explains Rodney Hero, "use the political system to maintain and enhance their power and status," whereas "minorities pursue policies to try to achieve a modicum of equality."[90] Furthermore, he contends, a legacy of the formal and informal exclusion of blacks and Latinos from politics continues to constrain their influence. Added to this, the politics espoused by minority groups is often the least popular, as the white majority generally opposes minority redistributive policy demands by framing such policies as inconsistent with American values.[91] Minority politics are also greatly constrained by the fiscal limits of local governments, which cannot support redistributive policies.[92] Others argue that the political process is dominated by conservative, business interests, which minority mayors have learned to accommodate.[93] Thus, though minority incorporation has produced other policy changes, research has found that urban fiscal policies were not altered after minority incorporation.[94]

Blacks and Latinos may not be able to get much from incorporation in government because of institutional constraints, two-party politics, and lingering racism. However, minority incorporation or empowerment theories have not advanced much beyond the assertion that minority influence increases as their numbers in office increase. However, political incorporation is a two-sided process. Not only do minorities struggle for representation in the political system, fighting established groups and racism as newly incorporated groups, they also struggle over how to lead. Incorporation favors political moderation and, thus, whether through actual purges and replacement or accommodation, black moderates are expected to advance over black radicals. Institutions shape the behavior of political elites as much as elites pursue their individual goals. Thus, there is a dialectic between new elites and established institutions. Tate finds that African American representatives in the U.S. House have become more moderate over time because of institutional constraints and rising ambitions.[95] Incorporation theories fail to acknowledge the arsenal of rules and procedures that are used by those in power to overcome conflict. Parties are institutions having mechanisms of political control. Furthermore, the U.S. Congress has complex rules, procedures, and norms. Through reform, the influence of parties increased in the House. Parties provide committee assignments for members and select leaders, such as committee chairs, who support their goals. They also compel cooperation from the rank-and-file through the provision of opportunities, goods, and exchanges such as logrolls that otherwise are not available. Presidents, as heads of the national party, have also used their authority to influence members of Congress. They enter into legislative politics prior to the introduction of policies that they care about as bills on the floor.[96] Institutions matter; they affect elite behavior.

Thus, in time, incorporation in the political system is expected to produce political moderation as minorities politically advance. Operating under a winner-take-all election system, the policy agendas of dominant American parties are not often radical. Newly incorporated groups find that they need to accommodate the policy interests of parties to advance and become more effective legislators. They enter into centralized leadership where the collective fate of the party is as important as their groups' efforts to increase their share of seats. Writing in the aftermath of the Socialist Party's decisive support of German imperialism, Robert Michels insists that political parties have oligarchical and conservative tendencies.[97] Thus, incorporation is a dynamic, contested process between radicals and moderates.

At the level of the electorate, there are signs that political incorporation reduces the radicalism of minority voters. Tate finds that since the 1970s, African Americans are less staunchly liberal on government spending to provide a guaranteed standard of living for every American and on spending programs to help minority groups advance.[98] Additionally, Latinos who have been in the United States longer tend to be less supportive of policies that benefit immigrant communities.[99]

Questions remain, however, as to whether the political incorporation of new immigrant groups will lead to moderate politics or whether the color line will sustain more liberal, ethnic politics. Due in large part to high rates of immigrants among Asians and Latinos, both groups demonstrate high levels of nonpartisanship.[100] Some research shows that the voting behavior of nonpartisans is indistinguishable from the voting behavior of moderate partisans.[101] Following this, the high rate of nonpartisans among Asians and Latinos may result in more moderate politics. In contrast, other research has shown that Asians and Latinos respond well to group-specific mobilization efforts, which have tended to be liberal.[102] New research will continue to assess these questions.

# Conclusion

The field of political science traditionally has ignored the role of race and ethnicity in American politics,[103] even as it was a stark and critical feature of American government, embedded in the original constitution and federal, state, and local laws. As these racially discriminatory laws were finally struck down by the courts and banned by federal laws during the post–WWII era, the field remains engaged in a debate over how much race and ethnicity continue to matter politically in the United States. Throughout this chapter, we have argued that race and ethnicity continue to play a significant role in American politics. Though some Americans express the view that the United States has become colorblind, the historical and empirical work highlighted in this chapter suggest otherwise. Obama's election, therefore, raises many questions regarding how his presidency has affected racial attitudes and the political behavior of minorities. Despite the great gains minorities have achieved in political office holding, one cannot easily dismiss race and ethnicity as no longer relevant in American politics, considering the persistent economic and social disparities experienced by minorities today.

At the same time, there is work suggesting that the political system still functions to bind minorities to the majority. How much influence do minorities have in a system with conservative, majoritarian tendencies is a new direction of research in minority politics. It remains essential that scholars in political science continue to study the impact of race and ethnicity in the American political system.

# Notes

1  "Wealth Gaps Rise to Record Highs Between Whites, blacks, Hispanics," by Rakesh Kochhar, Richard Fry, and Paul Taylor, *Pew Research Center*, July 26, 2011, see http://pewresearch.org/.
2  See The Joint Center for Political and Economic Studies' website, www.jointcenter.org.
3  See the website of the National Association of Latino Elected and Appointed Officials (NALEO) for these data, http://www.naleo.org/directory.html.
4  See Don Nakanishi and James Lai, Eds.,*The National Asian Pacific American Political Almanac, 14th Ed.* Los Angeles, CA: UCLA Asian American Studies Center, forthcoming.
5  See the website of the National Caucus of Native American State Legislators, http://www.nativeamericanlegislators.org.
6  Wills, Garry, *Negro President: Jefferson and the Slave Power* (Boston: Houghton Mifflin, 2003). See also, Katherine Tate, Kevin L. Lyles, and Lucius J. Barker, "A Critical Review of American Political Institutions: Reading Race into the Constitutional 'Silence' on Race. in *African American Perspectives on Political Science*, Wilbur C. Rich, Ed.(Philadelphia: Temple University Press, 2007); Lucius J. Barker, Mack H. Jones, and Katherine Tate, *African Americans and the American Political System, 4th Edition* (Englewood Cliffs, NJ: Prentice Hall, 1999).

7   Wilkins, David E. and Heidi Kiiwetinepinesiik Stark, *American Indian Politics and the American Political System, 3rd Edition* (Lanham, MD: Rowman & Littlefield Publishers, Inc., 2011); Paula D. McClain and Joseph Stewart Jr., *Can We All Get Along?: Racial and Ethnic Minorities in American Politics, 5th Ed.* (Boulder, CO: Westview Press, 2010).

8   Ngai, Mae M, "The Architecture of Race in American Immigration Law: A Reexamination of the Immigration Act of 1924," *Journal of American History* 86:1 (June 1999): 67–92.

9   Williams, Linda Faye, *The Constraint of Race: Legacies of White Skin Privilege* (University Park, PA: The Pennsylvania State University Press, 2003) and see also, Ira Katznelson, *When Affirmative Action Was White: An Untold History of Racial Inequality in Twentieth-Century America.* (New York: W. W. Norton, 2005).

10   Smith 1999.

11   In 1917, Puerto Ricans were granted citizenship, but are not permitted to vote in American elections from the island.

12   Reimers, David M., *Still the Golden Door: The Third World Comes to America, 2nd Edition.* (New York: Columbia University Press, 1992), 52.

13   Ngai, Mae M., *Impossible Subjects: Illegal Aliens and the Making of Modern America.* (Princeton, NJ: Princeton University Press, 2005).

14   James E. Alt, "The Impact of the Voting Rights Act on Black and White Voter Registration in the South," in *Quiet Revolution in the South: The Impact of the Voting Rights Act, 1965–1990*, Chandler Davidson and Bernard Grofman, Eds. (Princeton, NJ: Princeton University Press, 1994).

15   Richard L. Engstrom, "Racial Discrimination in the Electoral Process: The Voting Rights Act and the Vote Dilution Issue," in *Party Policies in the South*, Robert Steed, Laurence Moreland, and Ted Baker, Eds. (New York: Praeger, 1980); Chandler Davidson and Bernard Grofman, Eds., *Quiet Revolution in the South: The Impact of the Voting Rights Act, 1965–1990.* (Princeton, NJ: Princeton University Press, 1994).

16   Pei-te Lien, *The Making of Asian America Through Political Participation* (Philadelphia: Temple University Press, 2001); Lien, Pei-te, Conway, Margaret and Janelle Wong, *The Politics of Asian Americans: Diversity and Community* (New York: Routledge, 2004).

17   Benjamin Márquez, *Constructing Identities in Mexican American Political Organizations: Choosing Issues, Taking Sides* (Texas: University of Texas Press, 2003).

18   Aldon Morris, *The Origins of the Civil Rights Movement: Black Communities Organizing for Change* (New York: Free Press, 1984).

19   Doug McAdam, *Political Process and the Development of Black Insurgency, 1930–1970, 2nd Ed.* (Chicago: University of Chicago Press, 1999).

20   Richard M. Valelly, *The Two Reconstructions: The Struggle for Black Enfranchisement* (Chicago: University of Chicago Press, 2007), 149.

21   David Canon, *Race, Redistricting, and Representation* (Chicago: University of Chicago Press, 1999); Katherine Tate, *Black Faces in the Mirror, African Americans and Their Representatives in the US Congress* (Princeton, NJ: Princeton University Press, 2003); David Lublin *The Paradox of Representation: Racial Gerrymandering and Minority Interests in Congress* (Princeton, NJ: Princeton University Press, 1999); Mary Hawkesworth, "Congressional enactments of race-gender: Toward a Theory of Race-Gendered Institutions." *American Political Science Review* 97: 529–550 (2003); Katrina L. Gamble, "Black Voice: Deliberation in the United States Congress." *Polity* 43: 291–312 (2011); King, Desmond S. and Rogers M. Smith, *Still a House Divided: Race and Politics in Obama's America* (Princeton: Princeton University Press, 2011).

22  Michael Tesler and David O. Sears, *Obama's Race: The 2008 Election and the Dream of a Post-Racial America* (Chicago: University of Chicago Press, 2010); David O. Sears and Donald R. Kinder, "Racial Tension and Voting in Los Angeles" in *Los Angeles: Viability and Prospects for Metropolitan Leadership*, W.Z. Hirsch, Ed. (New York: Praeger, 1971); Donald R. Kinder and David O. Sears, "Prejudice and Politics: Symbolic Racism Versus Racial Threats to the Good Life." *Journal of Personality and Social Psychology* 40,3: 414–431, 1981; David O. Sears, Carl P. Hensler, and Leslie K. Speer, "Whites' Opposition to "Busing": Self-Interest or Symbolic Politics?" *American Political Science Review* 73,2: 360–384, 1979; Martin Gilens, *Why Americans Hate Welfare: Race, Media, and the Politics of Antipoverty Policy* (Chicago: University of Chicago Press, 2000).

23  Browning, Rufus P., Dale Rogers Marshall, and David H. Tabb, *Protest is Not Enough: The Struggle of Blacks and Hispanics for Equality in Urban Politics* (Berkeley and Los Angles, CA: University of California Press, 1984); Kenneth J. Meier and Joseph Stewart Jr, *The Politics of Hispanic Education* (Albany: State University of New York Press, 1991); Kenneth J. Meier, Eric Gonzalez Juenke, Robert Wrinkle, and J. L. Polinard, "Structural Choices and Representational Biases: The Post-Election Color of Representation," *American Journal of Political Science* 49:4 (2005): 758–768; Kerry L. Haynie, *African American Legislators in the American States* (New York: Columbia University Press, 2001); Albert K. Karnig and Susan Welch, *Black Representation and Urban Policy* (Chicago: University of Chicago Press, 1980); Robert R. Preuhs, "The Conditional Effects of Minority Descriptive Representation: Black Legislators and Policy Influence in the American States," *Journal of Politics* 68:3 (2006): 585–599; Robert R. Preuhs, "Descriptive Representation as a Mechanism to Mitigate Policy Backlash: Latino Incorporation and Welfare Policy in the American States," *Political Research Quarterly* 60:2 (2007): 277–292; see also Peter K. Eisinger, "Black Empowerment in Municipal Jobs: The Impact of Black Political Power," *American Political Science Review*, Vol. 76 (1982): 380–392.

24  Anne Phillips, *The Politics of Presence: The Political Representation of Gender, Ethnicity, and Race* (New York: Oxford University Press, 1995).

25  Jane Mansbridge, "Should Blacks Represent Blacks and Women Represent Women? A Contingent 'Yes,'" *Journal of Politics* 61:3 (1999): 628–657.

26  See, for example, Iris Marion Young, *Inclusion and Democracy* (New York: Oxford University Press, 2000).

27  Kenny J. Whitby and George A. Krause, "Race, Issue Heterogeneity and Public Policy: The Republican Revolution in the 104th US Congress and the Representation of African-American Policy Interests," *British Journal of Political Science*, 31:3 (2001): 555–572.

28  David T. Canon, *Race, Redistricting, and Representation* (Chicago: University of Chicago Press, 1999): 200.

29  Canon.

30  Canon.

31  Richard L. Hall, *Participation in Congress* (New Haven, CT: Yale University Press, 1996); Gamble, Katrina L., "Black Political Representation: An Examination of Legislative Activity within U.S. House Committees." *Legislative Studies Quarterly* 32 (2007): 421–47; Michael Minta, "Legislative Oversight and the Substantive Representation of Black and Latino Interests in Congress," *Legislative Studies Quarterly* 34:2 (2009): 193–218.

32  John D. Griffin and Brian Newman, *Minority Report: Evaluating Political Equality in America* (Chicago: University of Chicago Press, 2008).

33  John D. Griffin and Brian Newman, *Minority Report: Evaluating Political Equality in America* (Chicago: University of Chicago Press, 2008).

34  Thomas, Sue, "The Effects of Race and Gender on Constituency Service," *Western Political Quarterly* 45:1 (1992): 169–180.

35  Christian Grose, *Congress in Black and White* (New York: Cambridge University Press, 2010): 108; Janie Lorber, "Black Caucus Studies Racial Makeup of House Committee Staffs," *New York Times*, July 9, 2009.

36  Carol M. Swain, *Black Faces, Black Interests: The Representation of African Americans in Congress* (Cambridge, MA: Harvard University Press, 1993).

37  Richard F. Fenno, *Going Home: Black Representatives and Their Constituents* (Chicago: University of Chicago Press, 2003).

38  Canon.

39  Howard Schuman, Charlotte Steeh, and Lawrence Bobo, *Racial Attitudes in America: Trends and Interpretations* (Cambridge, MA: Harvard University Press, 1985).

40  Donald R. Kinder and Lynn M. Sanders, *Divided by Color: Racial Politics and Democratic Ideals* (Chicago: University of Chicago Press, 1996); Donald R. Kinder and David O. Sears, "Prejudice and Politics: Symbolic Racism versus Racial Threats to the Good Life," *Journal of Personality and Social Psychology* 40 (1981): 414–431; Martin Gilens, *Why Americans Hate Welfare: Race, Media, and the Politics of Antipoverty Policy* (Chicago: University of Chicago Press, 1999).

41  Paul M. Sniderman, Richard A. Brody, and Philip Tetlock, *Reasoning and Choice: Explorations in Political Psychology* (New York: Cambridge University Press, 1991); Paul M. Sniderman and Thomas Piazza, *The Scar of Race* (Cambridge, MA: Harvard University Press, 1993); Paul M. Sniderman and Edward G. Carmines, *Reaching Beyond Race* (Cambridge, MA: Harvard University Press, 1997).

42  Lublin, David, *The Republican South: Democratization and Partisan Change* (Princeton, NJ: Princeton University Press, 2004).

43  Tali Mendelberg, *The Race Card: Campaign Strategy, Implicit Messages, and the Norm of Equality* (Princeton, NJ: Princeton University Press, 2001).

44  Michael Tesler and David O. Sears, *Obama's Race: The 2008 Election and the Dream of a Post-Racial America* (Chicago: University of Chicago Press, 2010); Simon Jackman and Lynn Vavreck, "Primary Politics: Race, Gender, and Age in the 2008 Democratic Primary," *Journal of Elections, Public Opinion, and Policy* 20:2 (2010); Spencer Piston, "How Explicit Racial Prejudice Hurt Obama in the 2008 Election," *Political Behavior* 32 (2010): 431–451; Brian Schaffner. "Racial Salience and the Obama Vote," *Political Psychology* 32, 6: 963–988 (2011).

45  Brian Schaffner, "Racial Salience and the Obama Vote," *Political Psychology* 32, 6: 963–988 (2011)

46  Kinder and Sanders; David O. Sears, "Symbolic Racism," *Eliminating Racism: Profiles in Controversy*, P.A. Katz and D.A. Taylor, Eds. (New York: Plenum Press 1988); Lawrence D. Bobo, "Whites' Opposition to Busing: Symbolic Racism or Realistic Group Conflict?" *Journal of Personality and Social Psychology* 45 (1983): 1196–1210.

47  David O. Sears and Donald R. Kinder, "Racial Tension and Voting in Los Angeles" in *Los Angeles: Viability and Prospects for Metropolitan Leadership*, W.Z. Hirsch, Ed. (New York: Praeger, 1971).

48  Sears and Kinder; David O. Sears and John B. McConahay, *The Politics of Violence: The New Urban Blacks and the Watts Riots* (Boston, MA: Houghton-Mifflin, 1973); John B. McConahay and J. Hough Jr., "Symbolic Racism," *Journal of Social Issues* 32 (1976): 23–45; Kinder and Sanders; David O. Sears and P.J. Henry, "The Origins of Symbolic Racism," *Journal of Personality and Social Psychology* 85:2 (2003): 259–275.

49  Donald R. Kinder and David O. Sears, "Prejudice and Politics: Symbolic Racism versus Racial Threats to the Good Life," *Journal of Personality and Social Psychology* 40 (1981): 414–431.

50 Susan E. Howell, "Racism, Cynicism, Economics, and David Duke," *American Politics Quarterly* 22 (1994): 190–207; Kinder and Sanders; Tali Mendelberg, *The Race Card: Campaign Strategy, Implicit Messages, and the Norm of Equality* (Princeton, NJ: Princeton University Press 2001).

51 Michael Tesler and David O. Sears, *Obama's Race: The 2008 Election and the Dream of a Post-Racial America* (Chicago: University of Chicago Press, 2010): 61.

52 Michael Tesler and David O. Sears, *Obama's Race: The 2008 Election and the Dream of a Post-Racial America* (Chicago: University of Chicago Press, 2010): 35.

53 Eduardo Bonilla-Silva, *Racism Without Racists: Color-blind Racism and Racial Inequality in the Contemporary Era*." 3rd Ed. (Maryland: Rowman and Littlefield Publishers, Inc., 2010); Valeria Sinclair-Chapman and Melanye Price, "Black Politics, the 2008 Election, and the (Im)Possibility of Race Transcendence," *PS: Political Science and Politics* 41 (2008): 739–745.

54 Tesler and Sears.

55 Simon Jackman and Lynn Vavreck, "Primary Politics: Race, Gender, and Age in the 2008 Democratic Primary," *Journal of Elections, Public Opinion, and Policy* 20:2 (2010): 153–186.

56 Simon Jackman and Lynn Vavreck, "Primary Politics: Race, Gender, and Age in the 2008 Democratic Primary," *Journal of Elections, Public Opinion, and Policy* 20:2 (2010): 153–186.

57 Tesler and Sears.

58 Spencer Piston, "How Explicit Racial Prejudice Hurt Obama in the 2008 Election," *Political Behavior* 32 (2010): 431–451.

59 Piston.

60 Tesler and Sears.

61 Tesler and Sears.

62 Tesler and Sears: 52.

63 Source: Roper Center http://www.ropercenter.uconn.edu/elections/presidential/presidential_election.html

64 Louis DeSipio, *Counting on the Latino Vote: Latinos as a New Electorate* (Charlottesville, VA: University Press of Virginia, 1996).

65 Steven J. Rosenstone and John Mark Hansen, *Mobilization, Participation, and Democracy in America* (New York: Macmillian, 1993).

66 Bobo and Gilliam; Gilliam; Tate.

67 Kenny J. Whitby, *The Color of Representation: Congressional Behavior and Black Interests* (Ann Arbor: University of Michigan Press, 1997).

68 Matt A. Barreto, "¡Sí Se Puede! Latino Candidates and the Mobilization of Latino Voters," *American Political Science Review* 101:3 (2007): 425–441. Matt A. Barreto, *Ethnic Cues: The Role of Shared Ethnicity in Latino Political Participation.* Ann Arbor, MI: University of Michigan Press, 2010; Kevin Hill, Dario Moreno, and Lourdes Cue, "Racial and Partisan Voting in a Tri-Ethnic City: The 1996 Dade County Mayoral Election," *Journal of Urban Affairs* 23 (2001): 291–307; Rodney Hero and Susan Clarke, "Latinos, Blacks and Multi-ethnic Politics in Denver: Realigning Power and Influences in the Struggle for Equality," in *Racial Politics in American Cities*. Eds. Rufus P. Browning, Dale Rogers Marshall, and David H. Tabb.(White Plains, NY: Longman, 2003).

69 Matt A. Barreto, "¡Sí Se Puede! Latino Candidates and the Mobilization of Latino Voters," *American Political Science Review* 101:3 (2007); Lien, Pei-te, Conway, Margaret and Janelle Wong, *The Politics of Asian Americans: Diversity and Community* (New York: Routledge, 2004).

70 Source: Roper Center http://www.ropercenter.uconn.edu/elections/presidential/presidential_election.html

71  Michael C. Dawson, *Behind the Mule: Race, Class and African American Politics*. (Princeton: Princeton University Press, 1994); Katherine Tate, *From Protest to Politics*. (Cambridge: Harvard University Press and the Russell Sage Foundation, 1994).

72  Natalie Masuoka, "Together They Become One: Examining the Predictors of Panethnic Group Consciousness Among Asian Americans and Latinos," *Social Science Quarterly* 87 (2006), 5: 993–1101.

73  Barreto 2007.

74  Masuoka 2008.

75  Zoltan Hajnel and Taeku Lee. *Why Americans Don't Join The Party* (Princeton, NJ: Princeton University Press, 2011); Janelle S. Wong, "The Effects of Age and Political Exposure on the Development of Party Identification Among Asian American and Latino Immigrants in the United States." *Political Behavior* 22: 4 (2000): 341–371; Bruce E. Cain, D. Roderick Kiewiet, and Carole J. Uhlaner, "The Acquisition of Partisanship by Latinos and Asian Americans," *American Journal of Political Science* 35 (May 1991): 390–422.

76  Natalie Masuoka, "Political Attitudes and Ideologies of Multiracial Americans: The Implications of Mixed Race in the United States." *Political Research Quarterly* 61 (2008): 253–267.

77  Masuoka 2008: 261.

78  Tesler and Sears.

79  Tesler and Sears: 156.

80  Michael Tesler and David O. Sears, *Obama's Race: The 2008 Election and the Dream of a Post-Racial America* (Chicago: University of Chicago Press, 2010)

81  Vanessa Williamson, Theda Skocpol, and John Coggin, "The Tea Party and the Remaking of Republican Conservatism," *Perspectives on Politics* 9:1 (2011): 25–43.

82  Barreto, Matt A., Betsy L. Cooper, Benjamin Gonzalez, Christopher S. Parker, Christopher Towler. 2011. "The Tea Party in the Age of Obama: Mainstream Conservatism or Out-Group Anxiety?" *Political Power and Social Theory* 22, p. 9.

83  Christopher Parker, "2010 Multi-state Survey on Race and Politics." University of Washington Institute for the Study of Ethnicity, Race and Sexuality, unpublished paper (2010). http://depts.washington.edu/uwiser/racepolitics.html

84  Baretto et al.

85  Williamson, Skocpol, and Coggin: 28.

86  Baretto et al.

87  Ibid.

88  Williamson, Skocpol, and Coggin: 34

89  Barreto et al.: 10.

90  Rodney Hero, *Latinos and the U.S. Political System: Two-Tiered Pluralism* (Philadelphia: Temple University Press, 1992): 204.

91  Kinder and Sanders.

92  Paul Peterson, *City Limits* (Chicago: University of Chicago Press, 1981).

93  Clarence Stone, *Regime Politics: Governing Atlanta, 1946–1988* (Lawrence, KS: University Press of Kansas, 1989).

94  John P. Pelissero, David B. Holian, and Laura A. Tomaka, "Does Political Incorporation Matter? The Impact of Minority Mayors Over Time," *Urban Affairs Review* 36:1 (2000): 84–92.

95  Katherine Tate, *Concordance: Black Lawmaking in the U.S. Congress from Carter to Obama* (Ann Arbor: University of Michigan Press, forthcoming).

96  Matthew N. Beckmann, *Pushing the Agenda: Presidential Leadership in U.S. Lawmaking, 1953–2004* (New York: Cambridge University Press, 2010).

97  Robert Michels, *Political Parties: A Sociological Study of the Oligarchical Tendencies of Modern Democracy* (New Brunswick, NJ: Transaction Publishers, 1999).

98  Katherine Tate, *What's Going On? Political Incorporation and the Transformation of Black Public Opinion* (Washington, DC: Georgetown University Press, 2010).

99  Regina Branton, "Latino Attitudes toward Various Areas of Public Policy: The Importance of Acculturation," *Political Research Quarterly* 60: 2 (2007): 293–303; see also, M. V. Hood, III, Irwin L. Morris, and Kurt A. Shirkey, "'!Quedate o Vente!': Uncovering the Determinants of Hispanic Public Opinion toward Immigration," *Political Research Quarterly* 50: 3 (1997): 627–647; Gabriel R. Sanchez, "The Role of Group Consciousness in Latino Public Opinion," *Political Research Quarterly* 59:3 (2006): 435–336.

100  Hajnal and Lee.

101  Miller, Arthur H. and Martin P. Wattenberg. 1983. "Measuring Party Identification: Independent or No Partisan Preference?" *American Journal of Political Science* 27,1: 106–121.

102  Matt Barreto (2007) finds that the presence of co-ethnic candidates help mobilize Latinos around ethnic politics.

103  Ernest J. Wilson III, "Why Political Scientists Don't Study Black Politics, but Historians and Sociologists Do," *PS: Political Science and Politics* 18: 3 (1985): 600–607.

# Chapter 13

# Parties, Leaders, and the National Debt

*Daniel J. Palazzolo*

There is widespread agreement that the United States is headed for a train wreck of massive proportions if its leaders do not address the problem of the national debt. However, the nation's leaders appear unable to agree to terms about a potential solution, a dynamic that poses fundamental concerns about the capacity of the constitutional system and ability of citizens to self-govern. The conventional wisdom holds that politicians are chiefly concerned about reelection, so they refuse to make tough choices that might offend constituencies and powerful interest groups. Of particular consequence is the growing polarization of the parties and inability to find common ground. Dan Palazzolo's analysis provides some cause for hope while offering a concise description for how the nation got into the debt crisis. Most theories of Congress predict stalemate on budget policy. Palazzolo's historical approach, using "process tracing," highlights situations in which crises, shifts in public opinion, changes in institutional procedures, and shrewd actions of leaders might lead to bipartisan outcomes. In other words, structural constraints, such as polarization and electoral incentives, do not necessarily prevent leaders from acting to solve the nation's problems. Palazzolo's case study analysis challenges theories that rely too heavily on single-factor explanations of policy outcomes. It calls for scholars to study politics with a deeper and nuanced understanding of the character of problems and ability of political leaders to move beyond the constraints of politics as usual.

Just days before his inauguration as the forty-fourth President of the United States in January 2009, Barack Obama described the urgency of dealing with the national debt and future spending on entitlement programs for senior citizens, Medicare and Social Security:

> What we have done is kicked this can down the road. We are now at the end of the road and are not in a position to kick it any further. We have to signal seriousness in this by making sure some of the hard decisions are made under my watch, not someone else's.[1]

After two consecutive years of unprecedented budget deficits, Republican congressional candidates campaigned against the president's economic policies and the rising debt in the 2010 midterm election campaigns, won a majority of seats in the House of Representatives, and elected Representative Paul Ryan (R-WI) to be Chair of the House Budget Committee. As he was about to introduce the House Republican budget in April 2011, Ryan recycled the president's metaphor to frame the choice facing policy makers: "It all comes down to this: Either you fix this problem now…or you pick the president's path, which is do nothing, punt, duck, kick the can down the road, and then we have a debt crisis and then its pain for everybody." [2]

The views expressed by Obama and Ryan illuminate a puzzle of contemporary budget politics: Though leaders of both parties know that the federal debt is unsustainable and entitlement programs need to be reformed, major policy solutions are bypassed, and the debt continues to fester. Why, according to Obama, had policymakers before him "kicked the can down the road?" Why had the president, according to Ryan, joined the game? If they agree on the urgency of the problem, why cannot Obama and Ryan—and the two parties they represent—agree to a solution? What does the persistent debt say about the capacity of our constitutional system and the ability of leaders to address the nation's most pressing challenges?

According to the prevailing wisdom of Washington politics, the puzzle is easily solved, and we know how the story will end. The political parties are so polarized and so unwilling to risk losing elections that they avoid the necessary compromises on taxes and spending that would reduce the debt. [3] Even if leaders of opposite parties, such as Obama and Ryan, agree that reducing the national debt is a priority, they disagree fundamentally about how to accomplish that goal. [4] Politics take over, and reducing the debt is subordinated to other budget priorities defended by the two parties: Republicans argue for lowering taxes and maintaining a strong national defense, Democrats for investing in social progress and protecting entitlement programs. [5] Rather than compromise, the parties blame the other side for failing to address the problem, and the debt grows. Ultimately, if partisan polarization prevails, the country loses. At the least, a debt crisis will cause chronic inflation and sluggish economic growth for decades; in the worst case, the United States may experience a major stock market collapse, hyperinflation, double-digit interest rates, and even political instability. [6]

Yet, though political scientists have done extensive quantitative analysis to show that congressional parties have become *more* polarized over the past three decades, several scholars have shown that the role of parties in the policy-making process is more complicated than polarization theories suggest and that we do not fully understand the effects of partisan polarization on specific policy issues. Moreover, though the worst consequences of the debt are certainly possible, the budget process does not always end in gridlock. Thus, we should complement structural explanations of partisan politics derived from quantitative analysis of a large number of undifferentiated issues with case studies of particular issues.

The new direction to budget politics proposed here applies an existing mode of analysis—process tracing—to explain bipartisan deal making in an era of polarized parties.[7] I design hypotheses to determine the extent to which the expectations of party polarization theory apply to the budget deficit. Then by drawing from case studies of budget reforms in the 1980s and 1990s and tracing the sequence of events that led to the passage of the 2011 Budget Control Act, I show how crises, procedural deadlines, changes in public opinion, and the choices and actions of leaders affect deficit politics. Process tracing produces evidence of partisan polarization and exceptions to partisanship in deficit politics. Before deploying this approach, we need to draw a clearer picture of the scope, causes, and potential effects of the debt problem and review scholarly approaches to the topic.

## Debt Dilemma

Not all deficits are created equal. Although annual budget deficits are nothing new in American politics, the deficits we face today are much more difficult to address than ever before. According to James Savage, deficits were held in check from the Founding era at least until the Great Depression because Congress and the president held to the longstanding norm of balancing the budget.[8] Aside from funding wars, the federal government of the United States did not raise or spend much money.[9] Wars were financed by taxes or bonds paid off over time, and recessions were ultimately followed by economic recoveries. In the 1930s, the size and scope of the federal budget changed as the role of government changed.[10] New Deal programs created in the 1930s financed jobs that reflected Keynesian fiscal policy whereby government sought to stimulate economic growth by creating consumer demand in a depressed economy. The New Deal also featured social welfare programs for the poor, the unemployed, and the elderly, including the creation of Social Security in 1935.[11] Yet, those programs and subsequent wars in the twentieth century caused only temporary budget deficits. The publicly held debt grew to nearly 109 percent of GDP during World War II but dropped rapidly after the war ended (Figure 13.1).[12] Until the 1960s, the vast bulk of federal spending was "discretionary," meaning that spending levels could be changed annually through the congressional appropriations process. Spending allocations for most programs changed incrementally.[13]

Yet, after a landslide victory in the 1964 election, President Lyndon Johnson and Democratic majorities in Congress enacted Great Society legislation, including entitlement programs that expanded mandatory spending.[14] Johnson and Congress adopted two government health care programs—Medicare for the

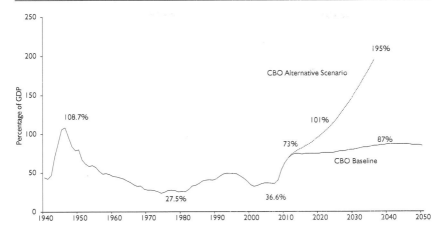

*Figure 13.1* Publicly held debt as a percentage of GDP: CBO baseline and alternative, 1940–2050[15]

elderly and Medicaid for the poor—and numerous other mandatory programs from food stamps to student loans. Under Johnson and his successor, Republican President Richard Nixon, Congress regularly increased Social Security benefits and, under Nixon, it indexed numerous programs for inflation. In little more than ten years, policy makers of *both parties* dramatically increased the welfare state (see Table 13.1).

Eventually, a budget based primarily on discretionary programs that could be controlled by altering annual spending levels became dominated by mandatory spending that varies with uncontrollable conditions. Thus, if unemployment increases, so does spending for unemployment compensation, food stamps, and income support; if inflation grows, so does spending for programs indexed for inflation; if health care costs grow, so do the costs of Medicare and Medicaid; and so on. The only way to control mandatory spending is to change the laws that determine eligibility for program benefits.

The transformation from discretionary to mandatory programs is illustrated in Figure 13.2. In 1965, before the passage of Medicare and Medicaid and the rapid expansion other entitlements, the portion of discretionary spending in the federal budget was more than twice the size of mandatory spending; twenty years later, the portion of discretionary spending marginally exceeded mandatory spending; and by 2011, mandatory spending had greatly surpassed discretionary spending in the federal budget. Mandatory spending also grew dramatically in relation to the U.S. economy. From 1965 to 2011, mandatory spending tripled from 4.6 percent to 13.5 percent of gross domestic product (GDP), whereas discretionary spending actually declined from 11.3 percent to 9 percent of GDP.

*Table 13.1* Creation and expansion of entitlement benefits: 1960s and 1970s

| Program created | Year | Program indexed for inflation | Year |
| --- | --- | --- | --- |
| Food Stamps | 1964 | Civil Service Retirement | 1962 |
| Medicaid | 1965 | Military Retirement | 1963 |
| Medicare | 1965 | Coal Miners Disability | 1969 |
| Student Loans | 1965 | Food Stamps | 1971 |
| Supplemental Security Income (SSI) | 1972 | Social Security (OASDI) | 1972 |
| | | Medicaid | 1973 |
| | | Supplemental Security Income (SSI) | 1974 |
| | | Railroad Retirement | 1974 |
| *Social Security benefit increases* | | | |
| 7% Increase | 1965 | | |
| 13% Increase | 1967 | | |
| 15% Increase | 1969 | | |
| 10% Increase | 1970 | | |
| 20% Increase | 1972 | | |
| 11% Increase | 1973 | | |

Sources: Dennis S. Ippolito, *Why Budgets Matter: Budget Policy and American Politics* (University Park: Penn State Press, 2003), Chapter 6; Dennis S. Ippolito, *Uncertain Legacies: Federal Budget Policy from Roosevelt to Reagan* (Charlottesville: University of Virginia, 1990), 175; Kent Weaver, *Automatic Government: The Politics of Indexation* (Washington DC: Brookings, 1988), 43.

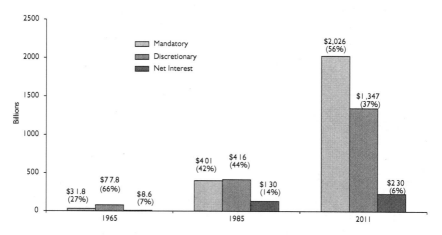

*Figure 13.2* Federal spending by major category: 1965, 1985, and 2011[16]

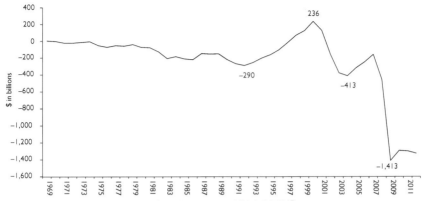

*Figure 13.3* Nominal budget deficits/surpluses: 1964–2012[17]

On the revenue side of the budget, the government raises money mainly through income, corporate, and payroll taxes,[18] but it also loses revenue through tax expenditures (i.e., "provisions of the Federal tax laws which allow a special exclusion, exemption, or deduction from gross income or which provide a special credit, a preferential rate of tax, or a deferral of tax liability").[19] Unlike entitlement programs that emerged mainly in two large waves during the 1930s and 1960s, tax expenditures developed gradually over time, beginning with mortgage interest deduction in 1913.[20] The current tax code contains about 200 tax expenditures for individuals and corporations that cost more than $1.1 trillion per year.[21] The five most costly tax expenditures for 2008 granted exclusions for health care insurance ($288 billion), retirement income ($120 billion), state and local taxes ($74 billion), mortgage interest deductions ($67 billion), and charitable contributions ($47 billion).[22]

The shift toward mandatory spending and the growth of tax expenditures, combined with the economic effects of high unemployment and inflation, produced chronic budget deficits after 1969 (Figure 13.3). The deficits were exacerbated by tax cuts and defense spending increases in the early 1980s. Yet, after a series of modest deficit reduction agreements in the 1980s and three larger deals—1990, 1993, and 1997—the budget was balanced for four straight years (1998–2001).[23] However, fiscal restraint did not last long. Beginning in 2001, several unfunded initiatives— tax cuts, spending for wars in Iraq and Afghanistan, prescription drug coverage for Medicare beneficiaries, and economic stimulus measures consisting of domestic spending increases and "temporary" tax cuts—combined with two recessions drove annual deficits to unprecedented levels.[24] Thus, the national debt rose sharply (Figure 13.1). Moreover, because recurring deficits are "structural" (i.e., they result from spending that exceeds revenue even when the economy is healthy), economic growth alone will not solve the problem.[25]

In December 2010, the Commission on Fiscal Responsibility and Reform, created by President Barack Obama to identify solutions to chronic deficits and the rising national debt, reported: "Our nation is on an unsustainable fiscal path. Spending is rising and revenues are falling short, requiring the government to borrow huge sums each year to make up the difference. We face staggering deficits."[26] Annual budget deficits have exceeded $1 trillion every year from 2009 to 2011, and the national debt, which surpassed $15 trillion at the outset of 2012, currently grows at a rate of more than $3.2 million per minute and $4.6 billion per day.[27] The national debt held by the public nearly doubled from 33 percent of GDP in 2001—the last year the federal budget was balanced—to 62 percent in 2010. Without major spending reductions and/or tax increases, publicly held debt will approach 90 percent of GDP by 2020, at which time just the cost of interest on the debt will reach $1 trillion.[28] Unlike after World War II, when the government had a plan to restore fiscal balance, future demographic trends will put immense pressure on federal spending. By 2011, the baby boomers began retiring at a rate of 10,000 individuals per day. The number of people older than age sixty-five is projected to grow from about 40.2 million (13 percent of the population) in 2010 to 64 million (18 percent of the population) in 2025 and to 88.5 million (more than 20 percent of the population) in 2050. As Figure 13.1 illustrates, under the alternative Congressional Budget Office scenario, the national debt will soar after 2020.[29]

The fiscal consequences of the disparity between workers who pay taxes and retirees who earn benefits are almost unfathomable. In 2008, when the fiscal situation was much better than it was four years later, the Government Accountability Office (GAO) estimated that future unfunded liabilities of the federal government exceeded $53 trillion dollars.[30] In other words, due mainly to an increasingly dependent aging population and rising health care costs, the government has made $53 trillion worth of promises (primarily to future recipients of Medicare, Medicaid, and Social Security) that it has no plan to pay for.[31] To put this number into perspective, former Comptroller General David Walker reported if we "…put aside and invest today enough to cover these promises tomorrow. It would take approximately $455,000 per American household—or $175,000 for every man, woman, and child in the United States."[32]

In sum, the debt dilemma consists of three components: large annual deficits that require additional borrowing, a complex tax code that drains revenues, and massive unfunded commitments to a growing dependent population. Moreover, elected officials face a daunting political reality: The programs and tax policies that drive the debt are very popular, strongly supported by the organized interests, and intensely debated by leaders of the two political parties.

## Scholarly Approaches

With the emergence of deficits in the 1970s and 1980s, scholars sought to identify the political causes of large, chronic budget deficits and explain why policymakers struggled to develop policies to reduce the deficit. Those studies focused on the effects of interest groups, public opinion, political parties, and budget rules on deficit reduction policy. As the parties became more polarized around tax and spending issues, a phenomena that began in the 1980s but became more consequential as time when on, scholars focused on the extent to which partisan polarization affected Washington politics in general, including deficit politics. From the onset of deficit politics, scholars have also debated the functionality of the U.S. Constitution by considering the degree to which congressional leaders and the president are capable of addressing major problems. Toward this end, the literature on budget politics includes analysis of cases in which the budget process produced deficit reduction policies that ultimately led to a balanced budget in 1998.[33] Yet, since deficits returned to unprecedented levels, the debt has skyrocketed, and the parties have become increasingly polarized, questions about whether and how we can govern are back.

Rooted in pluralist theories of American politics, one theory claims that "Special interest politics is the main cause of excessive spending and deficit expansion."[34] Jonathan Rauch used longitudinal data from a range of sources to illustrate relationships between the growth of groups, lobbyists, campaign contributions, and entitlement benefits. The advent of benefit programs and tax expenditures described earlier contributed to the growth of organized interest groups, a condition Rauch refers to as "hyperpluralism."[35] Organized groups have an economic incentive to defend government programs because the groups can survive only if the programs survive. Thus, interest groups fought very hard to block attempts to cut spending or raise taxes. [36]

Though interest groups demonstrated the ability to stymie budget reforms, other scholars argue that their influence should not be overstated. In his account of Social Security reform, Aaron Wildavsky pointed out:

> In 1982…despite strong opposition of civil service unions, members were required to contribute to social security, which was subtracted from their pensions. The unions did everything right politically; they launched a major campaign against inclusion. The trouble was their little juggernaut was overwhelmed by a much bigger one, the gripping concern that social security retirement might become insolvent.[37]

In 1986, well-heeled corporate lobbyists wound up on the losing end of the Tax Reform Act, and many individual tax preferences were traded in for a consolidation of tax rates.[38]

For Wildavsky, and his co-author Joseph White, who wrote an extensive account of budget battles through the 1980s, the primary reason for persistent deficits could be traced to contrasting views held by members of Congress about how best to represent public opinion.[39] Americans want Congress to reduce deficits, but they also opposed raising taxes or cutting entitlement programs. Therefore, either the same people held contradictory policy preferences or, more likely, elected officials represented different "publics"—one that felt more strongly about taxes, the other about spending. Bound to represent their constituents, most members of Congress worried about deficits, but some favored cutting spending, others raising taxes. Both positions seemed perfectly legitimate and consistent with public opinion, but, taken together, they posed a collective action problem. The problem remains today. But since surveys show that the public holds conflicting preferences, leaders can choose either to exploit differences over taxes and spending or seek consensus around a common goal of deficit reduction. Leaders may also interpret election results to mean that the public wants the parties to compromise or, conversely, that it wants one party to carry out a deficit reduction plan.[40]

In terms of evaluating the role of party in policy making during the 1980s and 1990s, scholars primarily considered the effects of party control of the White House and Congress. Those who adhered to the responsible party school of thought argued that a single party needed to control both branches of government for government to pass major legislation.[41] Yet, David Mayhew found that party control of government had no effect on passage of major legislation from World War II through 1990. As two of the three major deficit reduction deals of the 1990s passed under divided party government, Mayhew's finding seemed to apply to the budget. As Charles Jones observed, because significant deficit reduction plans require elected officials to vote for unpopular choices, government may work better when responsibility for policy is diffused across the parties, rather than assumed by one of the parties.[42]

Studies that highlight the adverse effects of groups, public opinion, and parties on deficit reduction policy assume that electoral goals are preeminent in the minds of decision makers. To the extent that members of Congress are single-minded seekers of reelection,[43] they would naturally avoid tax and spending choices that are opposed by organized groups and are unpopular with voters. Political scientists who assume that members of Congress and party leaders are motivated by multiple goals—including reelection, making good public policy, and gaining influence within Congress—illustrate how leaders might pursue strategies that were designed to solve public problems and that may or may not have a direct electoral benefit.[44] Richard Fenno used a qualitative case approach—a combination of interviews, observations, and analysis of events—to describe how Senator Pete Domenici, Republican Chair of the Senate Budget Committee, sought to build consensus around a range of policy choices through deliberation, negotiation, and compromise.[45]

Leadership efforts to build consensus will vary with short-term conditions. Using case study analysis, Paul Light showed how a crisis in funding Social Security ultimately forced a few policy makers from both parties to develop a plan outside of the public view in 1983.[46] Daniel Franklin describes how a Republican president and Democratic congressional leaders forged a major deficit reduction deal in 1990 under the pressure of automatic budget cuts.[47] By tracing the budget process through a single, successful case, I showed how changes in public opinion and election results encouraged a Democratic president and Republican congressional leaders to negotiate a budget deal in 1997. In all three cases, policymakers had failed to reach agreement in previous trials, and leaders ultimately took advantage of congressional rules and procedures that facilitate passage of major legislation.[48] Thus, under the right conditions, leaders can build majorities within and across party lines in favor of deficit reduction and in spite of interest group demands, partisan differences, public opinion, and concerns about reelection.

Of course, when deficits returned after 2001, for the next decade—with the exception of the Budget Control Act of 2011—the only budget outcomes to explain were policies that increased deficits or failed to control deficit spending.[49] To the extent that leaders matter in terms of deficit politics, the choices and actions of presidents George W. Bush and Barack Obama, and the acquiescence of party leaders in Congress, contributed to the size of the national debt for most of this period. Yet, according to the conventional wisdom, the primary culprit is the rise in partisan polarization, a process that began as far back as 1970 but has gained strength over time. As Ronald Brownstein puts it: "The central obstacle to more effective action against our most pressing problems is an unrelenting polarization of American politics that has divided Washington and the country into hostile, even irreconcilable camps."[50]

Partisan polarization is typically defined as an alignment between ideological views and partisan affiliation. As summarized by Nolan McCarty, Keith Poole, and Howard Rosenthal, "There are two complementary facets to the polarization story. First, at the level of individual members of Congress, moderates are vanishing. Second, the two parties have pulled apart. Conservatives and Liberals have become almost perfect synonyms for Republicans and Democrats."[51] To support those conclusions, McCarty, Poole, and Rosenthal use of a comprehensive indicator of roll call voting by members of Congress—the DW Nominate score—that measures the voting records of members of Congress along a liberal/conservative dimension.[52] Other scholars use these data and measures of party unity and interest group ratings to show that members of Congress have become more polarized along party lines.[53]

Though roll-call vote studies provide substantial evidence of increased party polarization,[54] scholars debate the causes and consequences of polarization. According to one view, polarization stems from the voters. Either because of gerrymandering of congressional redistricting,[55] choices by Americans of like minds to live near one another,[56] or changes in political attitudes,[57] most congressional districts are either predominantly Democratic or predominantly Republican. When elected representatives act upon their constituents' opinions on public policy, they coalesce with members of their own party, who represent constituents with similar beliefs, and against members of the opposite party, who represent constituents with different beliefs.[58] Alan Abramowitz explains, because "members of Congress generally reflect the views of their parties' electoral bases . . . Polarization in Congress reflects polarization in the American electorate."[59] According to another school of thought, partisan polarization is primarily a result of growing ideological differences among the "political class" or political elites—party and group activists, elected officials, and the news media. Morris Fiorina, a leading proponent of this view, has argued that the public has not become polarized or at least not nearly as much as members of Congress.[60]

A third view, advanced by Sean Theriault, finds that increased party polarization in Congress is not so much caused by voters, elites, or redistricting but results primarily from the way party leaders use powers of agenda setting and rule making in the House and by rules and filibusters in the Senate.[61] Theriault's conclusion coincides with other studies that argue that the degree of partisan polarization in Washington, the linkage between partisanship and electoral factors, and the effects of polarization on policy making are often overstated. Joseph Cooper and Garry Young and Charles Jones point out that, even in the era of polarized parties, many bills are passed by bipartisan and cross-partisan majorities.[62] David Rohde argues that the influence of party in the legislative process is conditional; the degree of partisanship depends on the extent to which the parties divide on particular issues.[63] Steven Smith argues that, although members of Congress are motivated by reelection and party leaders seek to win a majority of seats in the legislature, leaders also seek to advance their party's policy interests and respond to national problems.[64] Other scholars argue that the goals, choices, and actions of party leaders independently affect the degree to which partisanship shapes policymaking and institutional change.[65] Taken together, these studies suggest that the congruence between voters and their representatives is not neatly or tightly held together by party allegiance on all issues, at all times, and by all leaders.

Political scientists also have mixed views of the extent to which party polarization affects the ability of the president and Congress to address major issues. Though Fiorina concludes that the consequences of party polarization for successful policymaking are uncertain and deserve further study,[66] Abramowitz deduces that polarization affects policymaking; a polarized electorate gives members of Congress little incentive to work across party lines.[67] Several political scientists, including Sarah Binder and Thomas Mann and Norman Ornstein look mainly at the effect of polarization on the institutional well-being and reputation of Congress, but they also conclude that rising levels of polarization, combined with divided party control of government, increases chance of policy stalemate.[68] By contrast, in a study of major legislation introduced by presidents since World War II, David Mayhew argues that parties have not undermined representation or the separation of powers, and most legislation reflects the general preferences of the American public. Moreover, it remains an open question whether increased partisan polarization subverts the ability of Congress and the president to achieve policy goals under divided party control.[69]

## Deficit Politics and Party Polarization From a Process Tracing Approach

Arguments about the causes and consequences of party polarization are typically based on quantitative analysis of a large number of cases from selected survey data and comprehensive measures of roll-call voting in Congress, but how do we determine the extent to which deficits politics, in particular, are polarized along party lines? My research involves process tracing, a method that begins with prior knowledge or regularities of political phenomena, closely traces and describes the sequence of events in the development of policy outcomes, identifies relevant causal variables to explain those outcomes, and designs hypothesis tests using qualitative or quantitative data. Though space limitations prevent a complete description of process tracing methodology or a detailed account of failed and successful budget agreements, we can test specific hypothesis about deficit politics suggested by the literature on polarization and highlight the key features of the 2011 budget battle.[70]

### Hypothesis 1: Parties in Congress

The first hypothesis deals with the degree to which the parties are polarized on budget votes in Congress. Since polarization began in the 1980s and grew over time, we should expect more cross-partisan and bipartisan deficit reduction agreements in the 1980s than the 1990s and thereafter. As the center of the ideological spectrum shrunk over time, so should partisan cooperation and agreement. In particular, more Republicans should have been amenable to tax increases in the 1980s compared with the 1990s and beyond.[71] Those patterns generally hold up, though some of the results do not reflect the expectations of polarized parties.

From 1982 to 1989, when the forces of partisan polarization had not completely set in, a Republican president and a Congress with at least one chamber controlled by Democrats enacted eight acts that reduced deficits by either increasing taxes and/or cutting spending (a total of four packages included some form of revenue increase, either by closing loopholes or increasing excise taxes). Four of eight acts amounted to very small budget savings, though the combined effect of the other four exceeded $500 billion in deficit reduction over fifteen years. In spite of the savings, since the deficit persisted throughout the Reagan presidency, one could certainly argue that the progress toward deficit reduction was not sufficient. Moreover, in 1986, Congress and the president also enacted the Gramm-Rudman-Hollings law, which sought to impose automatic spending cuts to meet specified deficit targets leading to a balanced budget over five years. The Gramm-Rudman-Hollings law was a sign that advocates of deficit reduction had capitulated to the forces of gridlock by putting in place procedures to do the job that elected officials could not.[72]

Deficit reduction agreements in the 1990s and the Budget Act of 2011 are more difficult to explain with a single theory. From 1990 to 1997, three major deficit reduction deals, each containing a mixture of taxes and spending cuts, were passed and produced $1.2 trillion in deficit reduction. Congress also passed a welfare reform bill in 1996 that projected savings of $54 billion over five years. The 1993 budget deal fits squarely into the party polarization narrative: The Democrats had control of government and passed a major budget deal with no Republican votes. Yet, the 1990 and 1997 budget agreements are harder for polarization theories to deal with because both were passed by bipartisan majorities under divided government during the polarized era.

As noted, previous case studies of the budget process showed that situational factors—concerns about the economic effects of deficits or the national debt, deadlines that forced action, and/or public opinion—motivated leaders to push for an agreement in spite of obvious differences between the parties. Leaders made deficit reduction a priority (often working through setbacks), sought to frame choices in the most favorable terms, and either found ways to accommodate the policy goals of their partisan bases or risked dissent from their partisan constituents, interest groups, or the general public. For instance, faced with dramatic automatic spending cuts under the Gramm-Rudman-Hollings law in 1990, President Bush made a move that was clearly unanticipated by theories of partisan polarization: He reneged on a 1988 campaign promise not to raise taxes. Bush said that "getting this deficit down, continuing economic expansion and employment in this country" trumped his "no new taxes" pledge, admitting: "I knew I'd catch some flak on this decision, but I've got to do what I think is right."[73] Right or wrong, Bush split the Republican Party in Congress.

Roll-call votes on congressional budget resolutions since 1997, the last year majorities of both parties voted together, illustrate partisan polarization.[74] Every year from 1998 to 2011, huge majorities of Republicans voted in unison and in opposition to huge majorities of Democrats on House budget resolutions. Over those fourteen years, an average of 98 percent of House Republicans voted together and against 97 percemt of Democrats. A similar pattern held in the Senate, where an average of 97 percent of Republicans voted together and opposite an average of 94 percent of Democrats.[75]

In sum, judging by the acts of Congress, partisan polarization might be considered a normal aspect of deficit politics, especially after 1997. However, the exceptions are too numerous to ignore and, through process tracing methods, scholars have noted the effects of crises, procedural requirements, shifts in public opinion, and the actions of leaders on budget outcomes.

### Hypothesis 2: Parties and Public Opinion

A second hypothesis relates to public opinion on budget issues. According to Abramowitz, public opinion data should reveal clear differences among party identifiers across a range of tax, spending, and deficit reduction issues: Democrats should hold liberal opinions and Republicans conservative opinions. Abramowitz finds that two positions—privatizing Social Security and cutting the capital gains tax—correlate highly with conservative ideology, particularly among engaged citizens.[76] Yet a broader array of survey items indicates that Democrats and Republicans divide along party lines on some spending and tax questions and converge along others.[77] Viewed through this wider lens, public opinion might be considered either a source of partisan polarization or an opportunity for bipartisan cooperation.

To begin with, Americans, including both Democrats and Republicans, are concerned about deficits and debt. As deficits increase, so does the portion of the public who believes deficit and debt are major priorities (Figure 13.4). According to a January 2012 report by the Pew Center for the People and the Press, "reducing the budget deficit" ranked as the third highest priority from a list of twenty-two issues.[78] And, although Republicans (84%) were more likely than Democrats (66%) to say that "reducing the budget deficit" was a

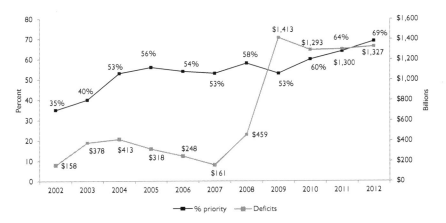

*Figure 13.4* Annual deficits and percent of public who say the deficit/debt is a priority[79]

"top priority," overwhelming majorities of both parties were concerned about deficits and debt.[80]

However, partisan identifiers differ strongly on strategies for dealing with deficits. During the budget debate in the July of 2011, a poll on deficit reduction strategies conducted by Gallup found that Republicans (67%) were twice as likely as Democrats (33%) to support "only or mostly with spending cuts" and six times less likely to support "only or mostly with tax increases." [81] Results from questions on tax policy also reveal clear partisan divisions. Republicans (35%) are three times more likely than Democrats (12%) to say that "cutting taxes" is "the best approach for Congress and the president to take in dealing with the US economy."[82] When asked whether "government should or should not redistribute wealth by heavy taxes on the rich," Republicans opposed such taxes by a margin of 41 percent, whereas Democrats favored them by a margin of 45% percent.[83]

Yet, when it comes to entitlement programs, polls show more convergence than differences between partisans. A January 2011 *USA/Today* Gallup survey found at least 60 percent of Democrats and Republicans oppose spending cuts in Medicare or Social Security. The same percentage of Democrats and Republicans (34%) favored cutting Social Security, and Republicans (40%) were only slightly more in favor of cutting Medicare than Democrats (36%).[84] In spite of opposition to cuts, Americans believe those programs are either at or nearing a crisis point. A 2011 Gallup Poll found that 34 percent of Americans believed that the costs of Medicare and Social Security were "already creating a crisis," and another 33 percent said they would create a crisis "within 10 years."[85] Moreover, though Republicans (76%) and Independents (70%) were more likely than Democrats (54%) to say the programs were in a crisis within ten years or less, majorities of both parties see a crisis pending.

Majorities of both parties also support certain specific ideas to "address concerns with the Social Security system," though the extent of support varies by party affiliation.[86] When given a list of policy options, majorities of both parties agreed that two approaches were "good ideas": (1) "requiring higher income workers to pay Social Security on all wages" and (2) "limiting benefits for wealthy retirees." More than 70 percent of Democrats favored those two ideas, whereas 60 percent of Republicans favored the first, and 55 percent favored the second. Most ideas for reforming Social Security are unpopular with both Democrats and Republicans, and there is virtually no difference of opinion between them.[87]

Thus, we should not be surprised when a Democratic president proposes higher taxes on the wealthy and cuts in defense spending. Likewise, Republican leaders oppose tax increases and advocate cutting government spending. In taking those positions, leaders are reflecting the opinions of their primary constituents. Conversely, we can also see why either party may hesitate to cut spending for Medicare and Social Security. Yet, given the public's sense that those programs are reaching a crisis point, bipartisan support for certain ideas to reform Social Security, and a general agreement that reducing the deficit/debt is a top priority, elected officials of both parties also have incentives to deal with those issues.[88]

## Hypothesis 3: Parties and Groups

A third hypothesis relates to the congruence between the interests of groups with a stake in the budget and the preferences of political parties in Congress. Fiorina argues that the rise in elite polarization has tied the interests of particular groups more closely to each of the political parties.[89] If so, data on campaign contributions should reveal that groups give regularly to the same party. Yet, as in the case of public opinion, the results are mixed. Campaign finance data show that certain industries consistently contribute either to Republican or Democratic candidates. For each election cycle from 1990 to 2010, political action committees from the communications and electronics industries typically contributed more to Democrats than Republicans. Lawyers and lobbyists gave twice as much, and labor unions gave between seven and thirteen times as much, to Democrats as to Republicans. Meanwhile, construction, energy and natural resources, agribusiness, and transportation interests routinely contribute between two and three times as much to Republicans as to Democrats.[90] Yet, group campaign contributions do not always cut along party lines. For instance, many corporate political action committees (including those from finance/real estate/insurance, health, and defense interests) contribute more to whichever party holds a majority in Congress.[91]

Moreover, looking beyond campaign contributions, both parties are cognizant of groups that represent the large numbers of people who receive entitlement benefits and tax expenditures (see Table 13.2).[92] The number of Americans who depend on government entitlement programs grew from 21.7 million (11.7% of the population) in 1962 to 67.3 million (21.8% of the population) in 2010.[93] Many of those entitlements, and especially the tax expenditures, go to middle- and upper-middle-income Americans.[94] Politicians in both parties like to flatter the public by berating the "special interests" that rule Washington. However, given the link between organized group interests and the large numbers of Americans who benefit from government programs, there is very little distance between the great body of the American people and the so-called "special interests." As Rauch points out, "They are, in fact us—you and me."[95]

In sum, the congruence between Republicans and several business organizations and Democrats and unions, attorneys, and media-related groups suggest a link between some groups and parties. However, other groups swing their support in favor of the party that controls Congress, and neither party seems to own or wants to offend groups that represent millions of Americans who benefit from the tax expenditures that cost revenues and entitlements that drive up spending.

*Table 13.2* Numbers receiving selected tax expenditures and entitlement benefits

| Tax Expenditures | |
| --- | --: |
| Americans with private health insurance (2010) | 195,874,000 |
| Households with tax subsidized retirement account (2010) | 80,250,000 |
| Tax filers claiming a home mortgage interest deduction (2009) | 36,541,819 |
| Tax filers claiming a charitable contribution (2009) | 37,243,302 |
| Tax filers claiming a child tax credit (2009) | 23,563,012 |
| Tax filers claiming student loan interest deduction (2009) | 9,718,995 |
| Tax filers claiming a tuition/fees deduction (2009) | 2,422,642 |
| | |
| *Entitlement Benefits* | |
| Social Security recipients (2011) | 55,000,000 |
| Medicare recipients (2011) | 49,000,000 |
| Medicaid recipients (2011) | 60,000,000 |

Sources: See endnote 92

## Observations from the Budget Control Act of 2011

If there are cases of bipartisan and cross-partisan deal making in a polarized era and slack in the relationships between parties, groups, and voters, we might find more clues to the puzzle of deficit politics by tracing a process that produces a major deficit reduction agreement. By describing the sequence of events and actions in the budget process in 2011, we can identify the factors that affected the choices and outcomes. A complete application of process tracing would include a comprehensive timeline of events and more detailed analysis of proposals, actions by various actors, and decisions (i.e., empirical information drawn from news accounts, government documents and interviews). Obvious limits prevent such detail here, but we can trace the process enough to determine the extent to which polarization affected the outcome. The process that culminated in the Budget Control Act of 2011reveals evidence of party polarization and the limits of polarization as an explanation for deficit politics. In an atmosphere of crisis, leaders continue to seek bipartisan and cross-partisan approaches to the debt problem.

As the Democratic nominee for president in 2008, Barack Obama campaigned against Bush's fiscal policy and the excessive partisanship in Washington. Shortly after an overwhelming victory in the 2008 elections that gave Democrats control of the White House and Congress, President Obama and congressional Democrats pursued a Keynesian policy of deficit spending designed to stimulate the economy. In February of 2009, Congress passed the American Recovery and Reinvestment Act, popularly referred to as the "stimulus bill," a $787 billion package of tax cuts and spending increases. Not a single Republican voted for the bill in the House.[96] The political situation changed dramatically after the 2010 midterm elections, when the Republicans won sixty-one House seats and majority control of the body.[97] The leaders of the two parties began 2011 on separate planets but, after budget deadlines and concerns about the debt forced them, together they agreed to a deficit reduction plan that was historic in scale, yet modest in relation to the size of the debt.

When President Obama presented the Fiscal Year 2012 budget in January 2011, he ignored the recommendations of the Commission he had appointed a year earlier to reduce the debt and asked Congress for a bill to raise the statutory ceiling on the national debt, which was due to expire that summer. However, newly elected "Tea Party" Republicans in the House and Senate informed party leaders that they would oppose raising the debt ceiling, at least without a major plan to reduce the debt.[98] In April, House Republicans, led by Budget Committee Chair Ryan (R-IL), drafted a budget resolution that cut spending by nearly $6 trillion over ten years. The plan proposed to reduce Medicare costs by replacing the government's fee-for-service program with a "premium support" plan whereby eligible senior citizens would receive a credit for purchasing private health insurance.[99] On April 15, the House passed the budget resolution by a vote of 235 to 193; Republicans voted 235 to 4 in favor, and all 189 Democrats voted against the budget.

On April 13, just days before the House voted on the budget resolution, President Obama rebuked Ryan's Medicare plan and stated: "It's not going to happen as long as I am President."[100] He made a counter offer that cut the budget by $4 trillion over ten years through a combination of tax increases and spending cuts and called on congressional leaders to form a bipartisan group with Vice President Joe Biden to work out a budget agreement.[101] In just two years, President Obama's fiscal policy took a 180-degree turn, from a strategy to stimulate the economy with massive deficit spending, to a proposal to reduce the debt. With annual deficits exceeding $1 trillion, polls registering public concern about deficits and debt, and a consensus among policy experts that the debt was unsustainable, deficit reduction vaulted to the top of the policy agenda.

The threat of default on the national debt and a downgrade in the credit rating of U.S. Treasury securities compelled the White House and congressional leaders of both parties to negotiate a budget deal. Just one day before the Treasury would run out of authority to borrow, Congress passed the Budget Control Act of 2011, which cut spending by $900 billion and established a joint bipartisan congressional committee to find another $1.5 trillion of savings by the end of the year. In the House, Republicans voted 174 to 66 in favor of the bill, and Democrats split evenly 95 to 95; in the Senate, majorities of both parties supported the agreement: Democrats voted 46 to 7, and Republicans voted 28 to 19 in favor of the bill.[102]

In addition to the roll-call votes, several aspects of the process did not reflect the expectations of partisan polarization. First, during the summer of 2011, President Obama and Republican Speaker of the House John Boehner came close to forging a deal that would have increased taxes and reformed Medicare and Social Security.[103] In his speech to the House, Boehner noted, "I stuck my neck out a mile. And I put revenues on the table, in order to try to come to an agreement..."[104] Second, a group of Senators called the "Gang of 6"—three Republicans and three Democrats—negotiated a package of entitlement and tax reforms that would have saved $3.7 trillion over ten years.[105] Third, once the joint congressional committee's work was underway, a bipartisan group of 100 members of the House lobbied the committee to "go big," indicating that they would vote for legislation that contained spending cuts and new revenues that saved $4 trillion, more than twice the $1.5 billion prescribed by the agreement.[106] Fourth, during the super-committee negotiations, a group of business organizations, including the National Association of Manufacturers, the Business Roundtable, and the U.S. Chamber of Commerce, urged the committee to find additional savings: "We believe it is crucial to act expeditiously to rein in spending, reform the tax code, reduce the deficit, and stabilize and ultimately lower America's level of debt...Congress must reform entitlement programs and comprehensively restructure the U.S. tax code."[107] Fifth, conservative Republican Pat Toomey (R-PA) agreed to $300 billion in new revenues in exchange for lower tax rates, and Democrats broached the issue of entitlement reform.[108] Fifth, as the parties were negotiating the deal, a Gallup Poll found that more than 60 percent of Americans, including majorities of Republicans and Democrats, wanted their leaders to "agree to a compromise plan, even if it is a plan you disagree with."[109] Finally, as 2011 drew to a close, Ryan and Senate Democrat Ron Wyden (D-OR) announced a bipartisan plan to reform Medicare.[110]

Yet, in spite of those developments and the fact that Congress and the President agreed to the largest deficit reduction package in history, partisan polarization constrained the scale and scope of budget savings.[111] By 2011, the debt had grown so large that the law's $2.4 trillion in projected savings over ten years was not enough to slow the rising debt to a sustainable level.[112] In addition, the budget savings were limited to discretionary spending; nothing was done to reform the tax code or entitlements. Democratic Minority Leader Nancy Pelosi (D-CA) singled out entitlement policy in her speech in favor of the bill on the House floor: "...the most important assignment given to the Democratic leadership going to the table: Make sure there are no cuts in benefits in Medicare, Medicaid and Social Security. That was achieved."[113] Moreover, although policymakers eluded gridlock in the summer, party polarization prevailed later that year. Negotiators on the joint congressional committee considered a range of tax and entitlement options, but they reached a stalemate over taxes and adjourned without an agreement.[114] Under the terms of the Budget Control Act, those savings would come from automatic spending cuts scheduled for 2013. Most Americans, including a majority of Republicans and a sizeable portion of Democrats, blamed both parties for the committee's failure.[115]

## Conclusion

The nation's struggle over the federal debt can be understood only by grappling with the complex role of party politics in the budget process. As institutions that seek primarily to gain political power by winning elections, parties must be responsive to the priorities and opinions of their primary constituents. To the extent that Democratic and Republican voters have grown apart on spending and tax issues and interest groups line up on either side of the divide, party leaders are bound to reflect opposing perspectives on the budget and will struggle to reconcile their differences. At the same time, however, party leaders cannot ignore the general public's concern about the debt and the popularity of the programs that drive up that debt. They must also be aware of the increasing number of Americans who identify as Independents,[116] polls that reflect a public interest in compromise, and the consensus among policy experts about the need for entitlement and tax reform. At the very least, leaders must pay attention to factions within their parties that make the debt a priority, promote policy reforms that reduce debt, and support bipartisan negotiations.

From the vantage point of process tracing, the relationship between partisanship and the debt dilemma reveals a mixed picture. Though partisan polarization is clearly evident in budget politics, the relationships between public opinion, interest groups, and elected officials are not as tightly linked as one might expect from theories that explain partisan polarization. Moreover, although partisan polarization limits the capacity of leaders to negotiate deficit reduction agreements across party lines, it does not incapacitate them. Under certain situations—perceived crises, legislatively imposed deadlines, and public concern about the debt—party leaders may raise the deficit above other budget priorities, take political risks, and negotiate agreements that advance spending cuts or tax increases.

Looking forward, the stakes could not be higher. Former Chairman of the Joint Chiefs of Staff, Admiral Michael Mullen announced in August of 2010: "The most significant threat to our national security is our debt."[117] Public concerns about debt and the future of entitlements are only going to increase as the political and economic effects of the European debt crisis unfold and the reality of an aging and dependent baby boom population sinks in. Of course, the United States is not in the same condition as countries such as Portugal, Italy, Greece, or Spain. However, in 2010, the United States had the eleventh highest debt-to-GDP ratio of the thirty-four countries in the Organization for Economic Co-Operation and Development.[118]

Evidence from the process-tracing approach suggests that the future of deficit politics is likely to continue to reflect a mixture of polarized politics and attempts to address the debt problem. Party leaders have some discretion in terms of how the process unfolds. Given the polarizing forces in American politics, party leaders can always retreat to the priorities of their base donors, groups, and voters. Yet, if they focus on solving the debt problem, leaders may loosen their ties to primary constituents, expand their conception of representation, and frame policy choices in ways that protect their parties' electoral goals and advance constructive approaches to debt reduction. They may justify deviations from partisan priorities by expressing concerns about the debt's effects on the nation's children or grandchildren, suggesting that their obligations as representatives extend beyond the voters that participate in the next election. Instead of talking about entitlement reform in terms of cutting spending for the elderly, leaders could agree to "preserve and strengthen Social Security and Medicare." [119] In spite of the increased partisan polarization since the 1970s, there is still enough flexibility in the relationships among voters, groups, and elected representatives for party leaders to advance reforms that control entitlement spending and reduce the debt. The questions are: Will they choose to do so, and will their efforts be sufficient to avoid the worst effects of a debt crisis?

## Acknowledgments

I would like to thank Kate Lawrenz, Tom Morris, Sarah Palazzolo, Randall Strahan, John Whelan, Ray La Raja, and anonymous reviewers for their helpful comments; I am, of course, responsible for any errors or mistakes.

## Notes

1 Michael D. Shear, "Obama Pledges Entitlement Reform President-Elect Says He'll Reshape Social Security, Medicare Programs," *Washington Post*, January 16, 2009, http://www.washingtonpost.com/wp-dyn/content/article/2009/01/15/AR2009011504114_pf.html.
2 Nicholas Ballasy, "Ryan: Debt on Track to Hit 800 Percent of GDP; 'CBO Can't Conceive of Any Way' Economy Can Continue Past 2037," *CNS News*, April 6, 2011, http://cnsnews.com/news/article/ryan-debt-track-hit-800-percent-gdp-cbo-cant-conceive-any-way-economy-can-continue-past.
3 I substantiate this point with reference to literature on partisan polarization further along, but for arguments about how partisan politics block solutions to the debt problem, see George Hager and Eric Pianin, *Mirage* (New York: Random House, 1997); and Peter G. Peterson, *Running on Empty* (New York: Farrar, Straus, and Giroux 2004).
4 See Joseph White and Aaron Wildavsky, *Deficit and the Public Interest: The Search for Responsible Budgeting in the 1980s* (Berkeley: University of California Press, 1989).

5   If advancing policy and political goals are not enough to divide the parties, in tough
    economic times, those choices can be justified as a way to stimulate economic
    growth. Republicans often say, "You should never raise taxes in a recession," or
    Democrats: "We need public investments to grow the economy."

6   Laurence J. Kotlikoff and Scott Burns, *The Coming Generational Storm* (Boston: MIT
    Press, 2004). See also, Congressional Budget Office, "Federal Debt and the Risk of a
    Fiscal Crisis," July, 17 2010, http://www.cbo.gov/doc.cfm?index=11659&zzz=41052;
    and Congressional Budget Office, "CBO's 2011 Long Term Budget Outlook," June
    22, 2011, http://cbo.gov/publication/41486.

7   See David Collier, "Understanding Process Tracing," *PS: Political Science and
    Politics*, Vol. 44, No. 4 (October 2011): 823–830.

8   James D. Savage, *Balanced Budgets and American Politics* (Ithaca, New York:
    Cornell University Press, 1988). Donald Kettl argues that Keynesian economics did
    not undermine the balanced budget norm, but it did alter the concept of balancing
    the budget. Under Keynesian economics, the government's primary goal would be
    to "balance the economy" rather than "balance the budget." Thus, deficits were an
    acceptable means of stimulating the economy. See Donald F. Kettl, *Deficit Politics:
    Public Budgeting in Its Institutional and Historical Context* (New York: Macmillan
    Publishing Company, 1992), Chapter 2.

9   For a history of key developments in budget policy, see Dennis S. Ippolito, *Why
    Budgets Matter: Budget Policy and American Politics* (University Park, PA: The
    Pennsylvania State University Press, 2003).

10  For an overview of social policy developments from the 1930s through the 1970s,
    see Dennis S. Ippolito, *Uncertain Legacies: Federal Budget Policy from Roosevelt to
    Reagan* (Charlottesville, VA: University of Virginia Press, 1990), Chapter 5.

11  See Martha Derthick, *Policymaking for Social Security* (Washington, D.C.:
    Brookings Institution, 1979).

12  The annual budget deficit is calculated by subtracting total federal outlays (i.e.
    spending) from total revenues. For example, for Fiscal Year 2011, which ended
    September 30, 2011, the Office of Management and Budget estimated that
    government outlays were about $3.8 trillion, revenues were about $2.5 trillion, and
    the deficit was about $1.3 trillion. Office of Management and Budget, *Historical
    Tables, Table 1.1—Summary of Receipts, Outlays, and Surpluses or Deficits: 1789–
    2016*, http://www.whitehouse.gov/omb/budget/Historicals. The national debt is
    the total amount of money the federal government owes to its borrowers, which
    amounts to the accumulation of annual deficits plus interest from 1789 to the
    present. The debt is typically reported in two ways: the "publicly held debt," which
    includes debt obligations to creditors outside of the federal government, and the
    "total debt," which includes all publicly held debt plus the debt that comes from
    borrowing within federal government accounts. For instance, when the Social
    Security Trust Fund runs a surplus, the government purchases special issue
    Treasury securities to the Fund; in essence, the government is borrowing from
    itself. Since future debt depends partly on assumptions about the revenue and
    spending effects of current law and prospective changes in those laws, Figure 13.1
    estimates two possible debt scenarios. The Congressional Budget Office (CBO)
    "extended" baseline assumes current law will continue, whereas an "alternative"
    baseline assumes certain expected changes in law. See note 29 for more details.

13  Congressional appropriations committees controlled spending. Richard F. Fenno,
    Jr., *The Power of the Purse: Appropriations Politics in Congress* (Boston: Little, Brown
    and Company, 1966), Chapters 1 and 8; Aaron Wildavsky, *The New Politics of the
    Budgetary Process* (Glenview IL: Scott, Foresman and Company, 1988), Chapter 3.

14   Entitlements refer to programs under which "the U.S. government is legally required to make the payments to persons or governments that meet the requirements established by law (2 U.S.C. § 622(9))." Entitlements are considered mandatory spending, which "refers to budget authority that is provided in laws other than appropriation acts..." Government Accountability Office, *A Glossary of Terms Used in the Federal Budget Process*, September 2005, (GAO-05-734SP), 47 and 66, http://www.gao.gov/new.items/d05734sp.pdf.

15   Source: Congressional Budget Office, "CBO's Long-Term Budget Outlook," June 22, 2011, http://cbo.gov.publication/41486.

16   Source: Office of Management and Budget, *Historical Tables*, Table 8-5-Outlays for Mandatory and Related Programs, 1962–2016 and Table 8.7-Outlays for Discretionary Programs, 1962–2016, http://www.whitehouse.gov/omb/budget/Historicals.

17   Source: Office of Management and Budget, *Historical Tables*, Table 1.1-Summary of Receipts, Outlays, and Surpluses or Deficits: 1979–2017 (Washington, DC: OMB, 2012) http://www.whitehouse.gov/omb/budget/Historicals.

18   In 2011, 47% of receipts to the Federal government came from individual income taxes, 35.5% for payroll (social insurance), and about 8% from corporate taxes; the remainder comes from excise taxes and miscellaneous fees. Office of Management and Budget, *Historical Tables, Table 2.2-Percentage of Receipts by Source: 1934–2017*, http://www.whitehouse.gov/omb/budget/Historicals.

19   Joint Committee on Taxation, *Estimates of Federal Tax Expenditures for Fiscal Years 2011–2015*, January 17, 2012, 3, http://www.jct.gov/publications.html?func=startdown&id=4386.

20   Christopher Howard, *The Hidden Welfare State* (Princeton: Princeton University Press, 1997), 177.

21   The number of tax expenditures have doubled since 1986, "Leonard E. Burman and Marvin Phaup, "Tax Expenditures, the Size and Efficiency of Government, and Implications for Budget Reform," September 2011, http://www.nber.org/chapters/c12563.pdf.

22   David M. Walker, *Comeback America: Turning the Country Around and Restoring Fiscal Responsibility* (New York: Random House, 2009), 107.

23   Daniel J. Palazzolo, *Done Deal?: The Politics of the 1997 Budget Agreement* (New York: Chatham House, 1999), Chapter 2.

24   Kathy Ruffing and James R. Horney, "Economic Downturn and Bush Policies Continue to Drive Large Projected Deficits," *Center on Budget and Policy Priorities*, May 10, 2011, http://www.cbpp.org/cms/index.cfm?fa=view&id=3490.

25   Concord Coalition ,"The Structural Deficit: What is It, Why do We Have One, and Why Should We Worry About It?," February 27, 2012, http://concordcoalition.org/issue-briefs/2012/0227/structural-deficit-what-it-why-do-we-have-one-and-why-should-we-worry-about-i.

26   The National Commission on Fiscal Responsibility and Reform, *The Moment of Truth*, December 2010, http://www.fiscalcommission.gov/sites/fiscalcommission.gov/files/documents/TheMomentofTruth12_1_2010.pdf.

27   Andrew Malcolm, "New National Debt Data: It's Growing About $3 Million a Minute, Even During His Vacation," *LA Times*, August 23, 2011, http://latimesblogs.latimes.com/washington/2011/08/obama-national-debt.html.   (For today's running debt total, see http://www.usdebtclock.org/.)

28   The National Commission on Fiscal Responsibility and Reform, *The Moment of Truth*.

29   Figure 13.1 charts two scenarios. (1) The CBO extended baseline assumes tax cuts will expire, the alternative minimum tax and tax provisions in the Patient and

Affordable Care Act (PACA) of 2010 would result in increased revenues in relation to the GDP, and discretionary spending will remain flat. (2) The CBO alternative scenario anticipates changes in current law that are likely to occur, including extension of tax cuts and other changes that will bring revenues to the historical average of 18% of GDP since 1960. It also assumes that Medicare reimbursement rates will continue at current levels, policies in PACA that restrain spending will not take effect until after 2021, and discretionary spending will not fall below its average. Congressional Budget Office, "CBO's Long-Term Budget Outlook," June 22, 2001, http://cbo.gov/publication/41486. For more detailed analysis of different scenarios for the debt, see Government Accountability Office, "Long-Term Federal Budget Simulation: Fall 2011 Update," http://www.gao.gov/special.pubs/longterm/pdfs/2011fed_fiscal_simulation_charts_slides.pdf.

30  The GAO is Congress' independent, nonpartisan "watchdog" agency that monitors federal spending. David W. Walker, "Long-Term Fiscal Outlook: Action is Needed to Avoid the Possibility of a Serious Economic Disruption in the Future," Statement of Comptroller General of the United States, Testimony Before the Committee on the Budget, U.S. Senate, January 29, 2008, 6, http://www.gao.gov/assets/120/118810.pdf.

31  It is important to note that the combination of demographic changes and health care costs, not just demographic changes, will drive the cost of Medicare and Medicaid in the future. Congressional Budget Office, "Key Factors Affecting Long-Term Growth in Federal Spending," June 29, 2009, http://www.cbo.gov/publication/24931.

32  Walker, "Long-Term Fiscal Outlook: Action is Needed to Avoid the Possibility of a Serious Economic Disruption in the Future."

33  Daniel P. Franklin, *Making Ends Meet: Congressional Budgeting in the Age of Deficits* (Washington DC: CQ Press, 1993); John L. Hilley, *The Challenge of Legislation: Bipartisanship in a Partisan World* (Washington: Brookings, 2008). Paul Light, *Artful Work: The Politics of Social Security Reform* (New York: Random House, 1985); Palazzolo, *Done Deal? The Politics of the 1997 Budget Agreement.*

34  Steven R. Eastbaugh, *Facing Tough Choices: Balancing Fiscal and Social Deficits* (Westport, CT: Praeger, 1994), 37.

35  Jonathan Rauch, *Demosclerosis: The Silent Killer of American Government* (New York: Random House, 1994), Chapter 3.

36  Rauch refers to this problem as "demosclerosis," a disease in the body politic born of expansion of interest groups and fed by their capacity to halt the system from making policy changes that reduce government benefits. Rauch, *Demosclerosis: The Silent Killer of American Government*, Chapters 1 and 6.

37  Aaron Wildavsky, *The New Politics of the Budgetary Process*, 273.

38  Jeffrey H. Birnbaum and Alan S. Murray, *Showdown at Gucci Gulch* (New York: Random House, 1987); and Randall Strahan, *New Ways and Means: Reform and Change in a Congressional Committee* (Chapel Hill, NC: University of North Carolina Press, 1990), Chapter 7.

39  See Joseph White and Aaron Wildavsky, *Deficit and the Public Interest: The Search for Responsible Budgeting in the 1980s* (Berkeley: University of California Press, 1989), especially Chapter 22.

40  In 1997, for instance, leaders of both parties agreed that the results of the 1996 election—a continuation of a Democratic presidency and Republican Congress—indicated the public wanted compromise. Palazzolo, *Done Deal? The Politics of the 1997 Budget Agreement.*

41  James L. Sundquist, ed. *Beyond Gridlock: Prospects for Governance in the Clinton Years* (Washington: Brookings, 1993).

42  Charles O. Jones, *The Presidency in a Separated System*, 2nd ed. (Washington DC: Brookings Institution, 2005), Chapter 2. For Mayhew's findings, see David R. Mayhew, *Divided We Govern* (New Haven: Yale University Press, 1991).

43  David R. Mayhew, *Congress: The Electoral Connection* (New Haven: Yale University Press, 1974)

44  Richard Fenno discovered the relevance of multiple goals in his study of congressional committees. Richard F. Fenno, Jr., *Congressmen in Committees* (Boston: Little, Brown, 1973). For a discussion of how this framework applies to party leaders, see Steven S. Smith, *Party Influence in Congress* (New York: Cambridge University Press, 2007).

45  Richard F. Fenno, *The Emergence of a Senate Leader: Pete Domenici and the Reagan Budget* (Washington: CQ Press, 1991).

46  Light, *Artful Work: The Politics of Social Security Reform.*

47  Franklin, *Making Ends Meet: Congressional Budgeting in the Age of Deficits.*

48  Budget reconciliation rules are typically used to package together a broad array of spending and tax law changes and avoid Senate filibusters. John B. Gilmour, *Reconcilable Differences?* (Berkeley: University of California Press, 1990).

49  Though as Sarah Binder notes, in 1999 the two parties reached stalemate over how to spend a surplus. Sarah A. Binder, *Stalemate: Causes and Consequences of Legislative Gridlock* (Washington, DC: Brookings Institution Press, 2003).

50  Ronald Brownstein, The *Second Civil War: How Extreme Partisanship Has Polarized Washington and Polarized America* (New York: Penguin, 2007), p. 11.

51  Nolan McCarty, Keith T. Poole, and Howard Rosenthal, *Polarized America: The Dance of Ideology and Unequal Riches* (Cambridge, MA: MIT Press, 2006), p. 3.

52  Until the advent of DW Nominate scores, scholars used group ratings of ideology, most notably Americans for Democratic Action (ADA) scores. For a discussion of various measures of ideology, see McCarty, Poole, and Rosenthal, *Polarized America: The Dance of Ideology and Unequal Riches.*

53  Morris P. Fiorina, with Samuel J. Abrams and Jeremy C. Pope, *Culture War? The Myth of a Polarized America*, 2nd ed. (New York: Pearson, 2006, Chapter 2); Sean M. Theriault, *Party Polarization in Congress*, (New York: Cambridge University Press, 2008), Chapter 2.

54  Though note that Keith Krehbiel suggests that DW Nominate scores may overstate the degree to which Members of Congress have become more polarized. Keith Krehbiel, "Comment" in Petro S. Nivola and David W. Brady, eds., *Red and Blue Nation?* Volume Two (Washington: Brookings Institution, 2008), 93–99; see also Sean Trende, "What Has Made Congress More Polarized?" *Real Clear Politics*, May 11, 2012, http://www.realclearpolitics.com/articles/2012/05/11/what_has_made_congress_more_polarized.html.

55  Juliet Eilperin, *Fight Club Politics: How Partisanship is Poisoning the House of Representatives* (Lanham, MD: Rowman & Littlefield, 2006).

56  This view contrasts with the redistricting perspective, by highlighting the ways Americans have sorted themselves into homogenous voting blocks. Bruce I. Oppenheimer, "Deep Red and Blue Congressional Districts," in *Congress Reconsidered*, 8th ed. Lawrence C. Dodd and Bruce I. Oppenheimer (Washington DC: CQ Press): 135–57; Bill Bishop, *The Big Sort: Why the Clustering of Like-minded America is Tearing Us Apart* (New York Houghton Mifflin, 2008).

57  Alan I. Abramowitz, *The Disappearing Center: Engaged Citizens, Polarization, and American Democracy* (New Haven, CT: Yale University Press, 2010), 52–53.

58  David W. Rohde, *Parties and Leaders in the Postreform House* (Chicago: University of Chicago Press, 1991); Gary C. Jacobson, "Party Polarization in National Politics: The

Electoral Connection," in *Polarized Politics: Congress and the President in a Polarized Era*, eds. Jon R. Bond and Richard Fleisher (Washington: CQ Press, 2000), 9–30.

59  Abramowitz, *The Disappearing Center: Engaged Citizens, Polarization, and American Democracy*, 7 and 157.

60  Fiornia's analysis consists of public opinion among individuals and across states and over time based mainly on National Election Studies and the General Social Surveys. Fiorina, with Abrams and Pope, *Culture War? The Myth of a Polarized America*. McCarty, Poole and Rosenthal, agree with Fiorina's view that polarization is mainly an elite phenomenon, though they also find a closer alignment between the voting preferences of congressional constituents and members of Congress.

61  Congress, see Theriault, *Party Polarization in Congress*.

62  In a bipartisan coalition, majorities of both parties vote together,whereas in a cross-partisan coalitions, a minority of one party votes together with a majority of the other party. Joseph Cooper and Garry Young, "Party and Preference in Congressional Decision Making: Roll Call Voting the House of Representatives, 1889–1999," in *Party, Process and Political Change in Congress*, eds. David W. Brady and Mathew D. McCubbin (Stanford, CA: Stanford University Press, 2002), 64–106; Jones, *The Presidency in a Separated System*, 2nd ed., 25–31.

63  Rohde, *Parties and Leaders in the Postreform House*. See also, John H. Aldrich and David W. Rohde, "The Consequences of Party Organization in the House: The Role of Majority and Minority Parties in Conditional Party Government," in *Polarized Parties: Congress and the President in a Partisan Era*, eds., Jon R. Bond and Richard Fleisher (Washington DC: CQ Press, 2000), 31–72.

64  Changing political circumstances, especially the size and ideological composition of the party, and the policy agenda also affect the ability of leaders to maintain party unity. Smith, *Party Influence in Congress*.

65  For a good review of this literature and a compelling case for the influence of leaders in congressional politics, see Randall Strahan, *Leading Representatives: The Agency of Leaders in the Politics of the U.S. House* (Baltimore: The Johns Hopkins University Press, 2007). See also, Eric Schickler, *Disjointed Pluralism: Institutional Innovation and the Development of the U.S. Congress* (Princeton: Princeton University Press, 2001).

66  Morris P. Fiorina with Samuel J. Abrams, *Disconnect: The Breakdown of Representation in American Politics* (Norman: University of Oklahoma Press, 2009), 160.

67  Abramowitz, *The Disappearing Center: Engaged Citizens, Polarization, and American Democracy*, 161.

68  Binder, *Stalemate: Causes and Consequences of Legislative Gridlock*; Thomas E. Mann and Norman J. Ornstein, *The Broken Branch: How Congress is Failing America and How to Get It Back on Track* (New York: Oxford University Press, 2006).

69  David R. Mayhew, *Partisan Balance: Why Political Parties Don't Kill the U.S. Constitutional System* (Princeton: Princeton University Press, 2011).

70  For more details of process tracing, see Collier, "Understanding Process Tracing."

71  Darrell West, *Congress and Economic Policymaking* (Pittsburgh: University of Pittsburgh Press, 1987), Chapter 3.

72  It is worth nothing that Senator Gramm was a conservative Republican from Texas, Senator Rudman was a moderate Republican from New Hampshire, and Fritz Hollings was a conservative Democrat (on most issues) from South Carolina.

73  Pamela Fessler," Bush's Sudden Shift on Taxes Gets Budget Talks Moving," *CQ Weekly*, June 30, 1990, 2029, http://newman.richmond.edu:2271/cqweekly/document.php?id=wr101409762&type=toc&num=246&.

74 The 1997 budget resolution was approved by a bipartisan coalition: 89% of House Republicans and 65% of House Democrats voted for it, and 75% of Senate Republicans and 82% of Senate Democrats voted in favor.

75 For three of the fourteen years the Senate did not vote on a budget resolution.

76 Using data from a 2006 Cooperative Congressional Survey, Abramowitz finds that among voters, the liberal/conservative ideological position is highly correlated with opinions on capital gains taxes (.537) and privatizing Social Security (.545); the correlation is much weaker among nonvoters: .255 and .205, respectively. Abramowitz, *The Disappearing Center: Engaged Citizens, Polarization, and American Democracy*, 52–53.

77 I emphasize "broader" sample of survey items; space constraints prevent a comprehensive review of polling questions. I have selected topics that are most relevant to the debt dilemma and cite findings from recent surveys.

78 Only "strengthening the nation's economy" and "improving the job situation" (82%) ranked higher. "Defending Against Terrorism" was tied for third with "reducing the deficit." Pew Center for the People and the Press, "Public Priorities: Deficit Rising, Terrorism Slipping," January 23, 2012, http://www.people-press. org/2012/01/23/section-1-the-publics-policy-priorities/.

79 Sources: Pew Center for the People and the Press, "Public Priorities: Deficit Rising, Terrorism Slipping," January 23 2012. http://www.people-press.org/2012/01/23/ section-1-the-publics-policy-priorities/; and Office of Management and Budget, *Historical Tables*, Table 1.1-Summary of Receipts, Outlays, and Surpluses or Deficits: 1979–2017 http://www.whitehouse.gov/omb/budget/Historicals.

80 The report points out that the opinions of partisans are affected by the party of the president: Democrats were more likely than Republicans to rate the deficit as a top priority when President Bush was in the White House. Republicans have been more concerned about the deficit while President Obama has been in office. Pew Center for the People and the Press, "Public Priorities: Deficit Rising, Terrorism Slipping."

81 Only 3% of Republicans compared with 20% of Democrats preferred "only or mostly with tax increases." Jeffrey M. Jones, "On Deficit, Americans Prefer Spending Cuts; Open to Tax Hikes," *Gallup*, July 13, 2011, http://www.gallup.com/poll/148472/Deficit-Americans-Prefer-Spending-Cuts-Open-Tax-Hikes.aspx.

82 "Reducing the deficit/debt" was one of four responses to the question. The others were: increasing taxes on the wealthy," "cutting taxes," or "increasing stimulus spending." Jeffrey M. Jones, "Americans Prioritize Deficit Reduction as an Economic Strategy," *Gallup*, November 30, 2010, http://www.gallup.com/poll/144956/Americans-Prioritize-Deficit-Reduction-Economic-Strategy.aspx.

83 Among Republicans, 28% said government should and 69% said government should not "redistribute wealth…" whereas among Democrats, 71% said should and 26% said should not. Frank Newport, "Democrats, Republicans Differ Widely on Taxing the Rich," *Gallup*, April 14, 2011, http://www.gallup.com/poll/147104/Democrats-Republicans-Differ-Widely-Taxing-Rich.aspx.

84 Frank Newport and Lydia Saad, "Americans Oppose Cuts in Education, Social Security, Defense," *Gallup*, January 26, 2011, http://www.gallup.com/poll/145790/Americans-Oppose-Cuts-Education-Social-Security-Defense.aspx. Not surprisingly, previous studies have shown high levels of public support for Medicare and Social Security. Paul Light, *Artful Work: The Politics of Social Security Reform*, 2nd ed. (New York: Random House, 1985), Chapter 6; Benjamin I. Page and Robert Y. Shapiro, *The Rational Public* (Chicago: University of Chicago Press, 1992): 118–21 and 129; Christopher Howard, *The Welfare State Nobody Knows* (Princeton: Princeton University Press, 2007): 113–14; Jennifer Baggette, Robert Y.

Shapiro and Lawrence R. Jacobs, "Poll Trends: Social Security-An Update," *Public Opinion Quarterly*, 59, no. 3 (Autumn, 1995): 420–42.

85  Jeffrey M. Jones, "Americans See Medicare, Social Security 'Crisis' Within 10 Years," *Gallup*, May 2, 2011, http://www.gallup.com/poll/147380/Americans-Medicare-Social-Security-Crisis-Within-Years.aspx.

86  Jeffrey M. Jones, "Americans Look to Wealthy to Help Save Social Security," *Gallup*, July 29, 2010, http://www.gallup.com/poll/141611/Americans-Look-Wealthy-Help-Save-Social-Security.aspx.

87  Less than half of all Democrats and Republicans responded "good idea" to each of following three policy recommendations: reducing amount of early retirement benefits, increasing the age at which people are eligible for full benefits, and reducing retirement benefits for people who are under age 55. The main partisan difference was found on the item, "increasing Social Security taxes on all workers." Again, less than half of all Democrats and Republicans thought it was a "good idea," though Democrats (43%) favored this option more than Republicans (26%). Jones, "Americans Look to Wealthy to Help Save Social Security."

88  As noted below, Paul Ryan's public campaign to reduce Medicare spending is evidence that at least some leaders are not shying away from entitlement reform.

89  Fiorina with Abrams, *Disconnect: The Breakdown of Representation in American Politics*, 137–38.

90  Campaign finance data can be found "Industries," Center for Responsive Politics, http://www.opensecrets.org/industries/index.php.

91  For evidence of how majority control affects the contribution strategies of corporate and trade PACs, see Gary W. Cox and Eric Mager, "How Much is Majority Status in the U.S. Congress Worth?" *American Journal of Political Science*, 93, no. 2 (June 1999): 299–309; and Thomas J. Rudolph, "Corporate and Labor PAC Contributions in House Elections: Measuring the Effects of Majority Party Status," *The Journal of Politics*, 61, no. 1 (February 1999): 195–206. For recent data comparing contributions for certain industry groups when the majority parties change in Congress, see "Interest Groups," Center for Responsive Politics," http://www.opensecrets.org/industries/index.php.

92  The sources for Table 13.2 are: for insurance, United States Census Bureau, *Annual Social and Economic (ASEC) Supplement: Health Insurance Coverage Status and Type of Coverage by Selected Characteristics: 2010 All Races*, 2011, http://www.census.gov/hhes/www/cpstables/032011/health/h01_001.htm; for retirement savings, Holden, Sarah and Daniel Schrass, "The Role of IRAs in U.S. Households' Saving for Retirement, 2010," *Investment Company Institute* 19 (December 2010): 3, http://www.ici.org/pdf/fm-v19n8.pdf; for home mortgage deduction, United States Internal Revenue Service, *Statistics of Income 2009: Individual Income Tax Returns*, July 2011, http://www.irs.gov/pub/irs-soi/09inalcr.pdf; for charitable contributions, child tax credit, and education tax credit and deduction, United States Internal Revenue Service, *Statistics of Income 2009: Individual Income Tax Returns* (July 2011), http://www.irs.gov/pub/irs-soi/09inalcr.pdf; Social Security, United States Social Security Administration, Social Security Basic Facts (October 2011), http://www.ssa.gov/pressoffice/basicfact.htm; Medicare, Kaiser Family Foundation, *Medicare at a Glance* (November 2011), http://www.kff.org/medicare/upload/1066-14.pdf; for Medicaid, Kaiser Family Foundation, *Medicaid's Long-Term Care Users: Spending Patterns Across Institutional and Community-based Settings*, (October 2011), http://www.kff.org/medicaid/upload/7576-02.pdf .

93  This study only counts people who are dependent on mandatory spending (not tax expenditures). Rob Bluey, "Chart of the Week: 1 in 5 Americans are Dependent

on Government," February 12, 2012, http://blog.heritage.org/2012/02/12/chart-of-the-week-1-in-5-americans-are-dependent-on-government/. The report coincides with a similar study published in the *New York Times*, see Binyamin Appelbaum and Robert Gebeloff, "Even Critics of Safety Net Increasingly Depend On It," *New York Times*, February 12, 2012, http://www.nytimes.com/2012/02/12/us/even-critics-of-safety-net-increasingly-depend-on-it.html?_r=1&pagewanted=all.

94  Christopher Howard, *The Welfare State Nobody Knows* (Princeton: Princeton University Press, 2007), Chapters 2 and 10. In fact, the share of government benefit payments going to the lowest fifth of the population has declined from 54% to 36% from 1980 to 2010. Appelbaum and Gebeloff, "Even Critics of Safety Net Increasingly Depend On It." Several high profile tax expenditures also predominantly benefit Americans with high incomes: e.g. education tax credits, and tax deductions for medical expenses, real estate, charitable contributions, student loans, and mortgage interest. Joint Committee on Taxation, *Estimates of Federal Tax Expenditures for Fiscal Years 2011–2015*, January 17, 2012, 48–52, http://www.jct.gov/publications.html?func=startdown&id=4386

95  Rauch, *Demosclerosis: The Silent Killer of American Government*, 48.

96  Just three Republicans voted for the bill in the Senate, and one of them, Arlen Specter (R-PA), later switched to the Democratic Party.

97  The Republicans also gained six Senate seats, though Democrats retained a 53–47 majority in the Senate.

98  John Cranford," Taking the Federal Debt Ceiling to Its Limit," *CQ Weekly*, January 24, 2011, 200, http://newman.richmond.edu:2271/cqweekly/document.php?id=weeklyreport112-1000003798545&type=toc&num=159&.

99  The plan also proposed replacing the federal entitlement under Medicaid with a block grant of funds to the states. For more details of Ryan's budget, see Paul M. Kawzak, "GOP Touts House Budget Chairman's Proposal; Democrats Vow to Fight Back," *CQ Weekly*, April 11, 2011, 808, http://newman.richmond.edu:2271/cqweekly/document.php?id=weeklyreport112-000003849545&type=toc&num=59&.

100  Jackie Calmes, "Obama's Deficit Dilemma," *New York Times*, February 27, 2012, http://www.nytimes.com/2012/02/27/us/politics/obamas-unacknowledged-debt-to-bowles-simpson-plan.html?_r=2.

101  Paul M. Krawzak and Joseph J. Schatz, "Skirmishing Begins on Deficit Reduction," *CQ Weekly*, April 18, 2011, 870, http://newman.richmond.edu:2271/cqweekly/document.php?id=weeklyreport112-000003855219&type=toc&num=103&.

102  For an account of how the agreement came together at the last hour, see Joseph J. Schatz, "Debt Deal Brings Relief, Frustration," *CQ Weekly*, August 8, 2011, 1756, http://newman.richmond.edu:2271/cqweekly/document.php?id=weeklyreport112-000003924863&type=toc&num=73&.

103  Jackie Calmes, "Obama's Deficit Dilemma."

104  Joseph J. Schatz, "A Deal in Which Nobody Wins," *CQ Weekly*, Aug. 8 2011, 1740.

105  "Gang of Six Focuses on Spending Cuts," *CQ Weekly*, July 25, 2011, 163, http://newman.richmond.edu:2271/cqweekly/document.php?id=weeklyreport112-000003916180&type=toc&num=143&.

106  Paul M. Krawzak and Richard E. Cohen, "No Deficit Deal; Revenue at Issue," *CQ Weekly*, November 7, 2011, 2334, http://newman.richmond.edu:2271/cqweekly/document.php?id=weeklyreport112-000003976655&type=toc&num=28&.

107  John Stanton, "Industry Groups Push Super Committee to Go Big," *Roll Call*, Sept 29, 2011, http://www.rollcall.com/news/industry_groups_push_super_committee_to_go_big-209056-1.html.

108  Joseph J. Schatz, "After the Fall of the 'Supercommittee,'" *CQ Weekly*, Nov 28, 2011, 2490.

109 Frank Newport, "Americans, Including Republicans, Want Debt Compromise," *Gallup*, July 18, 2011, http://www.gallup.com/poll/148562/Americans-Including-Republicans-Debt-Compromise.aspx. As the joint congressional committee began deliberations, *Gallup* also found that most Americans wanted the parties to compromise, though people who identified with the Tea Party were more likely to say that it is more important for political leaders to "stick to beliefs" than to compromise. Frank Newport, "Americans Again Call for Compromise in Washington," *Gallup*, September 26, 2011, http://www.gallup.com/poll/149699/Americans-Again-Call-for-Compromise-Washington.aspx.

110 Ron Wyden and Paul Ryan, "A Bipartisan Way Forward," *Wall Street Journal*, December 15, 2011, http://online.wsj.com/article/SB10001424052970203893404577098681919780636.html.

111 For a good review of the politics and policy developments of the budget in 2011, see Lori Montgomery, "Washington's Year of Drama Leaves Little Done Regarding Debt," *Washington Post*, December 27, 2011, http://www.washingtonpost.com/business/economy/washingtons-year-of-drama-leaves-little-done-regarding-debt/2011/12/23/gIQAB6kRLP_story.html.

112 Robert Bixby, "Debt-Limit Deal Avoids Default But Does Not Solve Fundamental Fiscal Problems," August 1, 2011, http://www.concordcoalition.org/tabulation/debt-limit-deal-avoids-default-does-not-solve-fundamental-fiscal-problems.

113 Joseph J. Schatz, "A Deal in Which Nobody Wins," *CQ Weekly*, Aug. 8 2011, 1740.

114 Schatz, "After the Fall of the 'Supercommittee'," 2490, http://newman.richmond.edu:2271/cqweekly/document.php?id=weeklyreport112000003988680&type=toc&num=137&.

115 55% of Americans, including 60% of Republicans and 61% of Independents blamed both parties "equally," whereas 41% of Democrats blamed both parties and 50% of Democrats blamed Republicans. Jeffrey M. Jones, "Americans Blame Both Sides of 'Supercommittee' for Failure," *Gallup*, November 22, 2011, http://www.gallup.com/poll/150935/Americans-Blame-Sides-Supercommittee-Failure.aspx.

116 Jeffrey M. Jones, "Record-High 40% of Americans Identify as Independents in '11," *Gallup*, January 9, 2012, http://www.gallup.com/poll/151943/Record-High-Americans-Identify-Independents.aspx.

117 "Mullen: Debt is top National Security Threat," *CNN*, August 27, 2010, http://articles.cnn.com/2010-08-27/us/debt.security.mullen_1_pentagon-budget-national-debt-michael-mullen?_s=PM:US.

118 This ranking is based on 2010, the year with the latest available data. Central Government Debt, http://stats.oecd.org/Index.aspx?DatasetCode=GOV_DEBT.

119 For the effects of issue framing on public opinions about government spending, see William G. Jacoby, "Issue Framing and Public Opinion on Government Spending," *American Journal of Political Science* 44, no. 4 (October 2000): 750-67.

# Chapter 14

# What War's Good For

## Minority Rights Expansions in American Political Development

*Robert P. Saldin*

Paradoxically, wars appear to have a positive effect on domestic politics. Yet, we often fail to see the connection because scholars tend to separate foreign and domestic policy in their analyses. Robert Saldin, however, explains how wars have helped facilitate the extension of rights to previously marginalized groups in America. Employing an historical approach, Saldin traces changes in the nation's culture, institutions, and policies regarding citizenship, all of which are linked to foreign wars. He identifies key periods of change, or "critical junctures," that alter expectations about citizenship and shape future directions. Just as the World Wars helped extend citizenship for women and blacks, recent wars in Afghanistan and Iraq have done much to change policies toward gays in the military. Saldin argues that both practical and moral considerations lead to change. His chapter makes a broader argument about how change occurs in the American political system and how major events have the capacity to stimulate political change. This research raises important questions about how international conflict may influence domestic issues regarding the role of government, taxation, privacy, and higher education.

How do foreign wars affect domestic political life? This is not a new question. Indeed, the role war plays in society has been a central and enduring theme in Western political reflection. Everyone from ancient political philosophers to the American Founders have contributed to the discussion. In the United States, the events of September 11, 2001 and the wars that followed in Afghanistan and Iraq returned the question to prominence. However, understanding the relationship between foreign affairs and domestic political life is often frustrated by a common impulse to treat the two realms separately, as though they exist in isolation. The *New York Times*, for instance, splits its front page into "National" and "International" sections—a demarcation no less stark than that separating the "Sports" and "Styles" sections. This tendency to disconnect the foreign from the domestic is also standard practice in the political arena. Even presidential debates adhere to this formulation, with certain debates centering on foreign policy and others dedicated to domestic policy. The separation is also the norm for faculty and students on college campuses. Political science departments and the courses they offer are divided into rigid subfields including "American Government" and "International Relations," and students are usually required or encouraged to concentrate in a particular subfield.

In one sense, of course, the distinction between domestic politics and foreign affairs makes perfect sense. After all, the United States has its own unique history, culture, and political institutions that are worth studying in their own right. And debates over, say, American foreign policy toward the Middle East would seem to have little to do with domestic social policies such as health care and education. However, in another sense, the strict separation between domestic politics and foreign affairs is overstated and amounts to little more than an artificial construction. And all too frequently, this rigid paradigm can blind us to the critical ways in which domestic politics and foreign affairs intersect with and influence one another.

The political science subfield known as American political development (APD)[1] offers a natural home for considering the influence of war on domestic politics. The study of APD is grounded in the observation that American government and its various features have been constructed piece by piece over time. To understand American politics, then, requires attention to the historical and developmental processes that have shaped the nation's institutions, policies, culture, and political thought. The subfield is particularly attentive to key periods of change. One reason why historical processes are important is because they establish trajectories, thereby altering the set of available options and shaping the context of future debates. Taken cumulatively, knowledge of these processes allows us to identify the patterns that typically play out within a given area of political life.

In a practical sense, APD-style research is often similar to that of the professional historian. APD scholarship typically features historical accounts grounded in a wide range of primary and secondary source material. Compared to other political scientists, the APD scholar is much more likely to conduct archival research and forego the quantitative research methods that are central to other subfields. Indeed, the relatively new field of APD was founded in the 1980s partially in a reaction against the methods-driven research associated with behavioral social science that had come to dominate the study of American politics by the late 1970s. However, unlike pure political history, political scientists in the APD mold are ultimately oriented toward social science objectives—such as generalizing, categorizing, identifying patterns, and building theories—that help to illuminate the present and suggest frameworks for thinking about the future. In short, APD scholarship is grounded in the conviction that history is an invaluable resource for understanding American political life.

This chapter employs an APD-style approach to consider the relationship between wars and minority rights. Though wars have wide-ranging effects, this relationship is worth considering because it is important in itself and because the pattern in these historical cases offers leverage for understanding how foreign affairs can shape American domestic politics more broadly. Wars have a counterintuitive track record of recalibrating the terms of American citizenship for minorities. Each of America's major wars over the last 100 years offered critical boosts to marginalized groups.

## Wartime Rights Expansions from World War I through the "War on Terror"

The standard view of democratization in America suggests that the extension of new rights came about through an inevitable, progressive process in which social movements—most notably the Civil Rights Movement—nudged history through a natural, egalitarian process to an enlightened endpoint.[2] To the extent war is considered in this context, it is generally seen as a force for slowing down or temporarily reversing the march toward that endpoint. As one leading scholar has put it,

> The United States has a long and unfortunate history of overreacting to the perceived dangers of wartime. Time and time again, Americans have allowed fear and fury to get the better of them. Time and time again, Americans have suppressed dissent, imprisoned and deported dissenters, and then—later—regretted their actions.[3]

There can be no doubt that governments tend to abuse rights during wartime. And this universal norm is certainly evident throughout American history, notably including forcibly relocating Native Americans, suspending habeas corpus during the Civil War, the World War I–era imprisoning of political dissidents, the internment of Japanese descendants during World War II, and, more recently, abusing prisoners at Abu Ghraib prison in Iraq.

However, there is another tradition concerning wars and democratic rights that—despite being more important in the long run—tends to be underappreciated and less well known. Wars have had a peculiar and counterintuitive way of facilitating the extension of rights to marginalized minority groups, thereby enhancing and improving American democracy. Wars' democratizing power has long been recognized in other contexts. The ancient Greek philosophers Thucydides and Aristotle, for instance, noted that oligarchies often offered commoners increased equality and democracy in return for their wartime service.[4] The pattern is evident in the American case as well.[5] Wars have helped enhance and improve American democracy through the extension of new rights to women, African-Americans, youths, and the gay community after these groups contributed to a war effort. There is a consistent process that plays out. Prior to each war, marginalized minorities have unsuccessfully sought expanded rights. Then a war alters the political environment in a way that provides these fledgling movements with the final, critical push for enactment.

### *"The War to End All Wars" and Women's Suffrage*

The initial phase of American feminism emerged in the mid-1800s out of the anti-slavery and Prohibition movements and was, above all else, focused on gaining voting rights for women. For decades, these efforts yielded little. It was not until the 1890s that several Western states permitted women access to the ballot. But even though states such as Wyoming and Colorado still wear their seemingly progressive moves as badges of honor, the policy changes actually had more to do with cynical power politics than principled egalitarianism. Granting women access to the ballot was an effective means of boosting the political heft of long-entrenched families amid an influx of a largely male population of transients and fortune seekers.[6] At the peak of the Progressive movement a couple decades later, early feminists had gathered enough support to get their cause heard before Congress, but votes on a constitutional amendment in 1914, 1915, and 1916 failed to muster simple majorities, to say nothing of the required two-thirds threshold.[7]

When the United States entered World War I, though, an opportunity presented itself. Up to this point, one of the key arguments against expanding the franchise held that women were not worthy of voting rights because, unlike men, they were not subject to putting their lives on the line in defense of the homeland.[8] The Great War did not see many women literally join the battle, but it did see them make essential contributions to the war effort. Though historical attention has focused on World War II's iconic Rosie the Riveter and the female masses she represented, women were every bit as critical to the U.S. war effort in this earlier crisis: 25,000 of them went to Europe to serve in various official and unofficial capacities, including substantial work on the frontlines. Nurse Edith Ayres of Base Hospital #12 on the *USS Mongolia* was the first of more than 350 servicewomen to die in the line of duty when a deck gun exploded on May 20, 1917. Back on the home front, the National American Woman Suffrage Association (NAWSA) played a crucial organizing role, helped facilitate volunteer efforts, assembled and distributed food, sold bonds, produced clothing, and aided the Red Cross. As individuals, women contributed economically to the war effort, and a massive advertising campaign urged them to join the depleted American workforce. Captions on posters proclaimed women to be "Our Second Line of Defense" and displayed images of women at work under slogans such as "The Girl Behind the Man Behind the Gun," "For Every Fighter a Woman Worker," or "Our Boys Need Sox, Knit Your Bit."[9] More than 1 million women answered this call from a nation in need by working jobs outside the home, many of which were directly connected to wartime industrial mobilization. The transition from homemaking or employment in "traditional" female professions, such as servants or laundresses, was not a comfortable one. Women worked long hours in difficult conditions, were paid substantially less than men, and were viewed as temporary employees.

However, their wartime service did not go unnoticed. President Woodrow Wilson experienced an illustrative and politically important shift in thinking. A longtime opponent of women's suffrage and gender equality in general, Wilson had said just a few years prior to the war that he was "definitely and irreconcilably opposed to woman suffrage" and that he thought a "woman's place was in the home, and the type of woman who took an active part in the suffrage agitation was totally abhorrent."[10] Yet women's wartime service forced Wilson to reconsider. (He also may have been influenced by the NAWSA's shrewd support of the war and of his presidency in difficult times.)[11] Reversing his earlier position and emphasizing women's role in the war effort, Wilson proclaimed his support for women's suffrage at the NAWSA national convention.[12] In 1917, he went farther by discarding his previously preferred states-rights approach and formally endorsing a constitutional amendment. Wilson had come to see women's suffrage as not only "an act of right and justice" but as "a vitally necessary war measure."[13] In an impassioned speech before the Senate, Wilson stated that

> We have made partners of the women in this war; shall we admit them only to a partnership of suffering and sacrifice and toil and not to a partnership of privilege and right? This war could not have been fought…if it had not been for the services of women.[14]

Months later, the amendment eclipsed the necessary two-thirds threshold in both chambers of Congress, and the states ratified it shortly thereafter. Just two years before, it had fallen well short of even a simple majority on Capitol Hill.

### "The Good War" and African American Voting Rights

During World War II, African American soldiers were initially held back from combat situations because they were thought to be unreliable in battle and prone to fleeing or providing aid to the enemy, but manpower shortages quickly forced a reconsideration. For the U.S. Army Air Force, the campaign in North Africa compelled the hasty organization of black units, including the famous Tuskegee Airmen. The Army held out longer but, after the Battle of the Bulge in 1944, it too was forced to revamp its policy concerning African American soldiers. Limitations on black enrollment were discarded. African American platoons were formed and, though these units remained segregated, black soldiers came to fight side by side with white units in the same companies.

More than 1 million blacks served, and—for the first time—a substantial number were placed in combat positions. It is worth stressing that none of these changes within the military structure were undertaken for enlightened, progressive reasons. General George Patton came closer to the mark when he said: "I don't care what color you are, so long as you go up there and kill those Kraut sonsabitches."[15] In short, the country was in need, and African Americans were available and willing to serve. Winning the war had become more important than maintaining a rigid and segregated racial hierarchy.

However, regardless of practical motivations, African American wartime service—like that of women during World War I—had the very real effect of altering white attitudes, at least among those who served alongside blacks. Prior to inserting black units into previously all-white companies, a survey of white officers and noncommissioned officers found that 64 percent reported holding unfavorable feelings about serving next to African American units, but after the integration of these black units into previously all-white companies, 77 percent of the white personnel reported having more favorable feelings. In stark contrast to the prewar assumptions that blacks were weak-willed and cowardly, the white respondents also offered high marks when asked about African American combat performance, with 80 percent giving black soldiers the highest possible rating.[16] Echoing the survey results, one South Carolina soldier said, "When I heard about it I said I'd be damned if I'd wear the same patch they did. After that first day when we saw how they fought I changed my mind. They're just like any of the other boys."[17] Back home, the war was also a unifying force that undermined traditional ethnic divisions. Broad, inclusive conceptions of citizenship were promoted through public and private educational initiatives sponsored by groups ranging from the Office of War Information to Hollywood.[18] These and other campaigns were motivated primarily by a desire to prevent old divisions from subverting the war effort, but their effects were to instill a wider sense of identification with the national community and mission while decreasing nativism and other divisive influences.[19]

A new intellectual climate also reflected World War II's effect on racial attitudes. Most important, the war undercut theories of racial supremacy in America. In the intellectual battle between Western freedom and fascist hierarchy, the United States had a profound weakness: Denunciations of Hitler's ideology appeared hypocritical in the face of Jim Crow subjugation. As *The New Republic* put it, domestic racial discrimination made a "mockery of the theory that we are fighting for democracy."[20] This awkward situation focused new attention on race relations in America. Gunnar Myrdal's *An American Dilemma* garnered wide attention, *Life* magazine proclaimed race to be the country's most vexing social problem, intellectuals embraced the cause of oppressed groups, and scholarly journals reflected a new preoccupation with race. The shift in America's intellectual climate was even evident in popular culture, which produced novels and films depicting heroic black soldiers.[21]

African American organization for expanded civil rights also got a boost from the war and provided key institutional and procedural groundwork for the Civil Rights Movement that followed. Recognizing the opportunity the war provided, the Congress of Racial Equality formed in 1942 and began staging protests to draw attention to segregated public facilities. The organization's commitment to nonviolence developed during these years and became a central and powerful strategy in the decades to come. At the same time, the National Association for the Advancement of Colored People saw its membership increase tenfold and realized the symbolic and practical influence of bringing large numbers of people together as a means of pressuring the government.[22] Numerous black leaders argued that, if the nation required African Americans to sacrifice on its behalf, it ought to pay a reasonable price. As the *Pittsburgh Courier*, a prominent black newspaper, editorialized: "What an opportunity this crisis has been and still is for one to persuade, embarrass, compel and shame our government and our nation…into a more enlightened attitude toward a tenth of its people!"[23]

The key point here is that World War II highlighted racial inequality in the United States, altered the way in which Americans thought about and discussed race, and helped lay the foundation for the Civil Rights Movement. Race was an embarrassment to American assertions of moral supremacy over Nazism and Fascism, and once blacks began serving in large numbers and in harm's way, pressure mounted for ensuring fuller political freedom.

These factors yielded two major policy changes that would have been unthinkable prior to the war. First, the Soldier Voting Act of 1942 nationalized soldiers' right to register and vote absentee and, more important, eliminated the poll tax, which had prevented southern blacks from casting ballots for decades. Previous efforts to eliminate the poll tax in Congress had long been blocked by southern Democrats. The wartime climate, however, changed their calculations. Opposing or filibustering such a bill in peacetime is one thing, but barring men on the frontlines from voting is quite another. Proponents of the measure emphasized this new argument for abolishing the poll tax. Its passage was a turning point in African American voting rights and the first expansion of those rights since Reconstruction.[24]

The second major change came from the Supreme Court. The 1944 *Smith v. Allwright* case prohibited the white primary, reversing a 1935 case that had deemed political parties to be private organizations not subject to the Fifteenth Amendment's protections against racial discrimination. The eight to one *Smith* decision found that the Texas Democratic Party acted unconstitutionally when it prohibited blacks from voting in its primary. The Court acknowledged that no facts pertinent to the case had changed in the nine years since the 1935 ruling but, as Arthur Krock, the *New York Times* Washington bureau chief, wrote: "The real reason for the overturn is that the common sacrifices of wartime have turned public opinion and the court against previously sustained devices to exclude minorities from any privilege of citizenship the majority enjoys."[25] As a result of *Smith*, more than 1 million southern African Americans had registered to vote by 1952, four times more than in 1940. Additionally, *Smith* paved the way for *Brown v. Board of Education* a decade later. The lead attorney for both cases, Thurgood Marshall, called *Smith* his greatest achievement.[26]

### *"The Forgotten War" and Army Desegregation*

In the years after World War II, President Harry Truman built upon the limited integration of the U.S. military that occurred during that conflict. His 1948 issuance of Executive Order 9981 mandated an end to formal segregation in the military and was implemented with relative ease in both the Navy and Air Force.[27] But the Army was a different story. No integration occurred, based on the argument that segregated units were better for morale and efficiency. Some in the Army thought Truman was trying to use the military as a means of forcing racial reforms on an unwilling country through the back door. As General Omar Bradley, the president's Army Chief of Staff, put it: "The Army is not out to make any social reforms. The Army will put men of different races in different companies. It will change that policy when the Nation as a whole changes it."[28]

The Korean War altered Bradley's timeline. In mobilizing for the conflict, separating the races came to be seen as needlessly inefficient. With a long checklist of preparations, basic training camps found it frustratingly impractical to sort hundreds of incoming recruits by race. As a result, officers at Fort Jackson in South Carolina decided to quit segregating their soldiers. The policy shift was viewed as a success, and soon staffers from the Department of the Army were visiting to witness firsthand how Fort Jackson's integration policy was streamlining war preparation and to assess whether the model could be exported to other camps. Integration became the policy of all basic training camps early in 1951.[29]

On the Korean peninsula, a similar process was unfolding. Heavy casualties had created a manpower shortage. Because of lingering questions about African Americans' combat worthiness, they were held back from the frontlines in segregated units. Consequently, white soldiers were left to do the fighting— and dying—early in the war, while blacks idly served in non-combat support positions. The obvious solution was to tap into this large cohort of soldiers to replenish the depleted fighting force. In the words of one officer, "Forces of circumstance" compelled Army integration. "We had no replacements," he explained. "We would have been doing ourselves a disservice to permit [black] soldiers to lie around in rear areas at the expense of still further weakening of our [white] rifle companies."[30] Officers in the field began taking it upon themselves to unofficially integrate their units. When the integrated units performed well, and in the face of continued manpower shortages, the Army's top leadership turned a blind eye, tacitly endorsing the de facto integration.[31]

Once African Americans began fighting and dying with whites, a powerful new argument for formally ending segregation emerged: If blacks were risking their lives for their country while serving in an Army uniform, they should be treated like equals within that institution. At the same time, embarrassing Soviet propaganda called attention to the irony of the United States rhetorically touting freedom and equality while violently suppressing blacks at home and shamelessly segregating those serving their nation oversees. These factors, combined with the efficiency-based considerations, helped push the Army to formally integrate early in 1952. The following year, 95 percent of blacks were in integrated units; the final all-black unit was abolished by 1954.

### "The Lost War" and the Youth Vote

As far back as 1867, shortly after the Civil War ended, New Yorkers unsuccessfully attempted to extend the voting franchise to males age eighteen and older based on the rationale that fighting for one's country sufficiently qualified one to vote. The issue cropped up again as a proposed constitutional amendment during World War II. Though the proposal did not go anywhere at the national level, Georgia independently reduced its voting age to eighteen in 1943. Not coincidentally, the Korean War revived efforts to place eighteen- to twenty-year-olds on the voter rolls in all the other states. Dwight Eisenhower became the first president to call for a constitutional amendment. During his 1954 State of the Union, he said,

> For years our citizens between the ages of 18 and 21 have, in time of peril, been summoned to fight for America. They should participate in the political process that produces this fateful summons. I urge Congress to propose to the States a constitutional amendment permitting citizens to vote when they reach the age of 18.[32]

Despite the general-turned-president's impassioned call for lowering the voting age, Congress was unable to muster the necessary two-thirds majorities. However, Kentucky joined Georgia in 1955 when it unilaterally lowered its voting age to eighteen. In the years after the Korean War, Alaska and Hawaii lowered their age thresholds to nineteen and twenty, respectively, while South Dakota and Idaho considered but rejected making changes.

The next wave of pressure to lower the voting age came during the Vietnam War. Between 1966 and 1971, sixteen states considered but ultimately decided against reducing their age requirements, whereas eight states implemented reductions in 1970 and 1971. The issue was also continuing to gain national traction. "Old enough to fight, old enough to vote" had become a mantra. President Lyndon Johnson offered his support for a constitutional amendment in 1968 but, unlike Eisenhower fourteen years earlier, he was far from alone. In that election year, both the Democratic and Republican platforms endorsed an amendment, as did both parties' presidential nominees, Hubert Humphrey and Richard Nixon.[33]

Senator Birch Bayh held hearings in the Subcommittee on Constitutional Amendments in February 1970. Echoing the arguments made during previous episodes of war-influenced rights expansions, President John Kennedy's former aide Ted Sorensen called the voting age a "moral issue." Though his argument for expanding the franchise was not new, it was among its more strident articulations: "Those between the ages of 18 and 21 have no voice whatsoever in the process which determines whether they live or die. If taxation without representation was tyranny, then conscription without representation is slavery." Other witnesses spoke to the proposed amendment's practical benefits. One expert's study suggested that suffrage would mitigate youthful frustration and violent tendencies. Voting would allow the option of "a direct, constructive, and democratic channel for making their views felt and for giving them a responsible stake in the future of the nation."[34] In 1971, the amendment cruised through Congress with margins of 401 to 19 and 94 to 0 in the House and Senate, respectively. Within months, thirty-eight state legislatures endorsed it as well, making it the Twenty-Sixth Amendment to the U.S. Constitution. Thus, an issue historically attached to wartime domestic politics built up momentum over several decades, becoming policy at the height of one of America's most internally divisive wartime experiences.

### "The War on Terror" and the Demise of "Don't Ask, Don't Tell"

When President Barack Obama signed the Don't Ask, Don't Tell Repeal Act of 2010, the official policy that banned openly gay service members in the armed forces became the most recent casualty of war. Like the cases outlined earlier, the issue of gays in the military had been a longstanding point of contention. Debate over the policy dated back to a political compromise hashed out by the Clinton Administration. After his 1993 inauguration, President Clinton attempted to reverse the ban on gays serving in the military. The initiative crumbled when Congress preemptively passed the Military Personnel Eligibility Act of 1993, which preserved the ban. "Don't Ask" became law when Clinton—not willing to use any additional political capital on the divisive issue—signed the bill, adding a directive that no military personnel or future applicants were to be asked about their sexual orientation. Nonetheless, more than 14,000 military personnel were discharged under Don't Ask. But, over the years, sentiments shifted. Back in 1993, the military brass was adamantly opposed to allowing gays to serve openly. By 2010, however, some important figures became advocates for change. For instance, in an appearance before the Senate Armed Services Committee, the chairman of the Joint Chiefs of Staff,

Admiral Michael Mullen, said, "It is my personal belief that allowing gays and lesbians to serve openly would be the right thing to do."[35]

For supporters of abolishing Don't Ask, the gradual attitude shift created an opening, and the spotlight provided by the Iraq and Afghanistan wars provided a sense of urgency. Leaders of the repeal effort—like those seeking expanded rights during earlier wars—understood that the "War on Terror" had created a window of opportunity for realizing meaningful reform. As Daniel Choi—an Army officer, Iraq veteran, and Arabic linguist who had been dismissed for being gay—argued at a 2010 rally for ending the ban: "If we don't seize this moment, [the repeal of 'Don't Ask'] may not happen for a very long time."[36]

As in the earlier conflicts, a new moral consideration emerged in the wartime context. Eric Alva's story became well known and offered a rallying cry for those seeking to overturn Don't Ask. A Marine, Alva became the first U.S. service member wounded in Iraq when he stepped on a landmine and lost his right leg while on patrol in Basra. Shortly thereafter, he left the Marine Corps, came out as gay, and became a spokesman for overturning the Clinton-era ban. Alva maintained that the wars in Afghanistan and Iraq "allowed an opening." He discovered that his wartime sacrifice compelled others to think twice about Don't Ask. "They say, 'he's made that sacrifice and we should reward him,' and reward not just me, but others."[37] The larger implication was that serving one's country carries significant moral weight. It must be acknowledged and respected. And for marginalized groups who sacrifice for their country, it demands new rights. Like women, African Americans, and eighteen- to twenty-year-olds in earlier generations, the wartime sacrifices of gay soldiers yielded a compelling new moral argument. As Alva said, "For us to turn away a veteran who has served the country—to not say your service is honorable—is a disgrace."[38] And Alva was not the only soldier in the closet. According to research at UCLA's Williams Institute, the American armed forces had more than 65,000 gay service members—about 2 percent of all personnel—prior to the repeal of Don't Ask.[39] And as Alva knew too well, snipers and improvised explosive devices do not distinguish between gay and straight targets.

In addition to the moral consideration, there were also practical concerns with the ban on gays. Adequate staffing in Iraq and Afghanistan was a pressing issue, and there was little margin for error. Because the military was consistently stretched thin, troops were sent on multiple tours, and deployments were extended. In this context, the dismissal of approximately 14,000 military members on the basis of sexual orientation appeared, at best, counterintuitive. Particularly dubious was the discharge of dozens of desperately needed Arabic translators and hundreds of other service members possessing critical abilities requiring years of expensive training. Additionally, there was a big upside to ending Don't Ask: Estimates suggested that allowing gays to openly serve would bring in almost 40,000 new troops.[40] These factors indicated that Don't Ask weakened the American armed forces by needlessly dismissing qualified personnel and had the effect of creating riskier situations for those remaining in the field without their trained and experienced fellow soldiers.

This concern left some commanders who had enforced Don't Ask before the September 11 attacks feeling conflicted. As one retired Marine infantry officer put it:

> For a guy who's been in that seat and had to enforce that policy, it's a black and white issue. If the rule exists that makes it a violation of the uniform code of military justice to come out, then for me as an officer, the policy has to be enforced. But personally, from the perspective that we're at war, this is ridiculous because you're now denying yourself the critical personnel and skills that we need. Forget about how many millions of dollars have been spent on a guy's training, he's fulfilling a critical need. For a military person, it's a crying shame that talented linguists, for instance, are getting kicked out.[41]

He was not alone. In Afghanistan and Iraq, some field commanders—like those in Korea decades earlier who unofficially and quietly started integrating their units during personnel shortages—began turning a blind eye when Don't Ask came up. Shortly before the policy was repealed, one former Air Force staff sergeant who was discharged under Don't Ask and went on to work for the Servicemembers Legal Defense Network, said: "We've seen it happen where a trooper is over there and they come out [as gay]. But they don't get kicked out right then. They let you finish the tour and kick you out when you get back home." In these critical war zones, "Commanders are less willing to enforce the policy. You're seeing that more and more often. They say, 'that's my go-to person, I need you.' They have the experience you need, they're well trained, and they're the only expert in their particular field." Under these conditions, enforcing standards of sexual norms was not a priority. In some cases, the ex–staff sergeant said, service members had "even gone to their commanders and said 'I'm gay,' and the commander [said], 'Go back to work. We don't have time to deal with this.'"[42]

And though the gay rights movement has been gaining momentum, it is far from clear that the Don't Ask policy would have been changed outside the context of the wars in Iraq and Afghanistan. As Alva said,

> You have to wonder, what if we'd never engaged in these wars [in Afghanistan and Iraq]. Would the issue be so up-front? That gave it the umpf it needed. What people started noticing is that these men and women are getting injured and losing arms and legs. And then the idea of discharging people because of sexual orientation seems ridiculous.[43]

Just as the military service of African Americans during World War II and Korea helped shape the ensuing Civil Rights Movement, repealing Don't Ask was important for the gay rights movement. Integrating the Army in the 1950s was only one area of interest for the black community. Likewise, military policy is only one of many rights-based issues for today's gay community. Indeed, employment protections, gay marriage, and gay adoption are seen by many gay advocates as more important than military policy. Yet, history suggests that progress in one area can spark advances in others.

## Conclusion

Over the course of American history, many groups have struggled to realize the fundamental guarantees of freedom enshrined in the Declaration of Independence and the Constitution. Part of the reason for the agonizingly slow pace of change is that the American political system is structured in a way that makes substantive reform exceedingly difficult. It simply is not set up to address problems quickly and efficiently. And that is not all bad. One comparative benefit of the U.S. system is that, once fundamental rights are actually established, they are more secure than in other countries with more malleable systems. But getting over the hill to see the promise of full citizenship realized is a challenge. Typically, it has required something more than a just cause. An attention-focusing crisis or prolonged challenge has often been required to build additional support among political elites and the American public and to make that final, critical push to enactment. Wars have often filled this role and facilitated rights expansions. Because these new war-wrought rights endure, they constitute a more remarkable pattern than that of the largely temporary, albeit appalling and disgraceful, abuses that also seem to be part and parcel of American wars.

There is a clear pattern explaining how wartime contributions from marginalized minority groups—in the trenches oversees or in American factories—led to important and enduring extensions of new democratic rights. Three factors are at work. First, wars strain government and create personnel shortages. They usually require the mobilization of military and civilian labor forces in excess of those needed in peacetime. As a result, the government is compelled to bring previously under-utilized segments of the population into the fold. Frequently, the required tasks involve citizens putting their lives on the line.

Second, this call to service from a government in need injects a new moral consideration into the social equation. Though racial equality and other causes had moral purchase prior to the outbreak of hostilities, these cases were ratcheted up to a higher level once lives were at stake. Putting one's life at risk in defense of the homeland shines a light on the second-class status of marginalized groups and is a moral trump card in the quest for the full rights of citizenship. And this is not just an American phenomenon. Many Western democracies, for instance, granted suffrage rights to women during or in the immediate aftermath of the two World Wars for reasons similar to those that prevailed in the United States.[44]

Finally, wars foster national unity in a way that engenders the extension of new rights. Though wars are often politically controversial, they almost always create cohesion reflected in support for the troops. The team mentality associated with wartime national service has a way of undercutting stereotypes used to justify discrimination. This relationship between war and national unity is an old tale. John Jay, for instance, recounted a version of it in *The Federalist Papers*. The American Revolution, he explained, forced citizens to band together in a shared enterprise and, as a result, strengthened the link between the former colonies.[45] This process can be seen in subsequent American wars as well. The team effort of wartime national service frequently undercuts stereotypes justifying a group's marginalized status. Additionally, political leaders have an incentive to promote cohesion. The relative unity that tends to accompany wars furthers the demand for new rights for marginalized groups that contribute to a shared national project.

In each of the cases explored here, efforts were already under way to secure the rights extensions in question before shots were fired. And with the exception of permitting eighteen- to twenty-year olds to vote and the dismantling of Don't Ask, Don't Tell, it is nearly certain these rights expansions would have eventually been realized even without the influence of war. However, these major foreign conflicts gave the final, decisive push toward implementation by introducing compelling new reasons to extend democratic rights. Additionally, without the war influence, it is far from certain how or when these rights expansions would have been implemented. It is possible that the policy shifts could have been more fully or efficiently implemented, but they just as easily could have been watered down. And it is not clear how delays in enacting these policies would have influenced subsequent rights extensions. With the exception of the youth vote, the advances detailed here were building blocks for future gains. As such, it is quite plausible that inaction at these key junctures would have limited future achievements.

Of course, the relationship between wars and democratic rights is only one of many areas in which domestic politics is influenced by foreign affairs. Further consideration of wars—just one prominent aspect of foreign affairs—reveals other patterns. For instance, wars have recast what government actually does and what the American public expects it to do. Though the United States was founded on the ideal of limited government, wars from the American Revolution to the War on Terror have cut against this ideal and seen the federal government expand its reach. Areas as diverse—and seemingly unrelated to foreign affairs—as tax policy, alcohol regulation, and federal aid for higher education have roots in international conflicts.[46] Wars have also been important influences on the political party system. Though foreign affairs are certainly not always significant factors in elections, they play a major role much more frequently than is often realized. And for Democrats and Republicans alike, wars have played a major role in shaping party ideology.[47]

These kinds of connections are often difficult to see because various institutions—including the political science profession—organize themselves around an arbitrary separation of the domestic and the foreign. Transcending these divisions is important because it permits a rethinking of standard interpretations that may be incomplete or even misleading. As the most disruptive and dramatic aspect of foreign affairs, wars offer an obvious starting point for studying the interaction between foreign and domestic politics. In the case of democratic rights, considering the influence of war should compel a reassessment of traditional explanations of rights expansions and how they come about. However, much work remains to be done in understanding the influence of war on other areas of American public policy and politics. And even that would only be skimming the surface of comprehending how foreign affairs more broadly influences domestic political life.

## Notes

1  Karen Orren and Stephen Skowronek, *The Search for American Political Development* (New York: Cambridge University Press, 2004); Rogan Kersh, "The Growth of American Political Development: The View from the Classroom," *Perspectives on Politics* 3:2 (2005), 335–345.

2  See, for instance E.E. Schattschneider, *A Semisovereign People* (New York: Holt, Rinehart, and Winston, 1960); V.O. Key, *Politics, Parties, and Pressure Groups* (New York: Crowell, 1964); Sidney Verba, Norman H. Nie, and Jaeon Kim, *Participation and Political Equality* (Cambridge: Cambridge University Press, 1978). On the Civil Rights Movement, see Stephen F. Lawson, "Freedom Then, Freedom Now: The Historiography of the Civil Rights Movement," *The American Historical Review* 96:2 (1991), 456–71.

3  Geoffrey R. Stone, *Perilous Times: Free Speech in Wartime, From the Sedition Act to the War on Terror* (New York: W.W. Norton, 2004), 5.

4  Aristotle, *The Politics*, Book 6, Chapters 6–7; Thucydides, *History of the Peloponnesian War*, 3.27.

5  For more on this theme in the American case, see: Mary L. Dudziak, *Cold War and Civil Rights: Race and the Image of American Democracy* (Princeton: Princeton University Press, 2000); Philip A. Klinkner and Rogers M. Smith, *The Unsteady March* (Chicago: University of Chicago Press, 1999); Azza Salama Layton, *International Politics and Civil Rights Policies in the United States, 1941–1960* (New York: Cambridge University Press, 2000); Robert P. Saldin, *War, the American State, and Politics since 1898* (New York: Cambridge University Press, 2011).

6  David E. Kyvig, *Explicit and Authentic Acts: Amending the U.S. Constitution, 1776–1995* (Lawrence: University Press of Kansas, 1996), 227.

7  The two-thirds threshold is required in both the Senate and the House for constitutional amendments. If those hurdles are passed, proposed amendments move on to a second stage requiring 75% of the states legislatures to ratify the amendment.

8  Alexander Keyssar, *The Right to Vote: The Contested History of Democracy in the United States* (New York: Basic Books, 2000), 172–221.

9   George Theofiles, *American Posters of World War I* (New York: Dafran House, 1973), 151, 152, 165.

10  Frank Parker Stockbridge, "How Woodrow Wilson Won His Nomination," *Current History* 20 (1924): 567.

11  Beth A. Behn, "Woodrow Wilson's Conversion Experience: The President, Woman Suffrage, and the Extent of Executive Influence," MA thesis, Department of History, University of Massachusetts, Amherst, 2004.

12  Woodrow Wilson, "An Address in Atlantic City to the National American Woman Suffrage Association," 8 Sept. 1916 in *The Papers of Woodrow Wilson: Volume 38*, ed., Arthur S. Link (Princeton: Princeton University Press, 1984), 161–4.

13  Wilson, "A Statement," 9 Jan. 1918 in *The Papers of Woodrow Wilson: Volume 45*, 545; Wilson, "An Address to the Senate," 30 Sept. 1918, *The Papers of Woodrow Wilson: Volume 51*, 160.

14  Wilson, "An Address to the Senate."

15  Ulysses Lee, *United States Army in World War II Special Studies: The Employment of Negro Troops* (Washington: Department of the Army, 1963), 661.

16  Klinkner and Smith, *The Unsteady March*, 190.

17  Jean Byers, "A Study of the Negro in Military Services," Department of Defense Monograph, June 1947, 172–3.

18  Robert L. Fleegler, "Theodore G. Bilbo and the Decline of Public Racism, 1938–1947," *Journal of Mississippi History* 68:1 (2006), 2–3; Richard W. Steele, "The War on Intolerance: The Reformulation of American Nationalism," *Journal of American Ethnic History* 9 (Fall 1989), 9–35.

19  David H. Bennett, *Party of Fear: The American Far Right From Nativism to the Militia Movement* (Chapel Hill: University of North Carolina Press, 1995).

20  "Back to Jim Crow," *The New Republic* (16 Feb. 1942), 221.

21  Gunnar Myrdal, *An American Dilemma: The Negro Problem and Modern Democracy* (New York: Harper & Brothers, 1944); Klinkner and Smith, *The Unsteady March*; Alan Brinkley, *The End of Reform: New Deal Liberalism in Recession and War* (New York: Knopf, 1995).

22  For more on CORE, the NAACP, and civil rights organizing during World War II, see August Meier and Elliot Rudwick, *CORE: A Study in the Civil Rights Movement, 1942–1968* (Urbana: University of Illinois Press, 1975); Gilbert Jonas, *Freedom's Sword: The NAACP and the Struggle Against Racism, 1909–1969* (New York: Routledge, 2007); Klinkner and Smith, *The Unsteady March*.

23  "Voiceless in Congress," *Pittsburgh Courier* (10 Jan. 1942), 6.

24  For more on the Soldier Voting Act, see Steven F. Lawson, *Black Ballots: Voting Rights in the South, 1944–1969* (New York: Columbia University Press, 1976).

25  *Smith v. Allwright*, 321 U.S. 649 (1944); *Grovey v. Townsend*, 295 U.S. 45 No. 563 (1935); Arthur Krock, "In the Nation: Self Reexamination Continues in the Supreme Court," *New York Times*, 4 April 1944, 20.

26  Keyssar, *The Right to Vote*, 248.

27  Harry S. Truman, "Executive Order 9981," *Public Papers of the President*, Truman Presidential Museum and Library Online archive.

28  Richard M. Dalfiume, *Desegregation of the U.S. Armed Forces: Fighting on Two Fronts, 1939–1953* (Columbia, MO: University of Missouri Press, 1969), 172.

29  Ibid, 203–209.

30  Lee Nicholas, *Breakthrough on the Color Front* (New York: Random House, 1954), 112.

31  Dalfiume, *Desegregation of the U.S. Armed Forces*, 209.

32  Dwight D. Eisenhower, "Annual Message to the Congress on the State of the Union, January 7, 1954," *Public Papers of the Presidents of the United States: Dwight D.*

*Eisenhower, 1954* (Washington: Office of the Federal Register National Archives and Records Service, 1960), 22.

33   Wendell W. Cultice, *Youth's Battle for the Ballot: A History of Voting Age in America* (New York: Greenwood Press, 1992).

34   U.S. Senate, Committee on the Judiciary, Subcommittee on Constitutional Amendments, *Lowering the Voting Age to 18: A Fifty-State Survey of the Costs and Other Problems of Dual-Age Voting*, 92nd Congress, 1st Session, 1971, 8.

35   Elisabeth Bumiller, "Top Defense Officials Seek to End 'Don't Ask, Don't Tell,'" *New York Times* 2 Feb. 2010, available at http://www.nytimes.com/2010/02/03/us/politics/03military.html.

36   Brian Montopoli, "Lt. Dan Choi Arrested at White House During Gay Rights Rally," *CBS News* 18 Mar. 2010, available at http://www.cbsnews.com/8301-503544_162-20000740-503544.html.

37   Interview with Eric Alva, 4 Aug. 2010.

38   Ibid.

39   Gary J. Gates, "Effect of 'Don't Ask, Don't Tell' on Retention among Lesbian, Gay, and Bisexual Military Personnel," The Williams Institute, March 2007, available at http://williamsinstitute.law.ucla.edu/wp-content/uploads/Gates-EffectsOfDontAskDontTellOnRetention-Mar-2007.pdf.

40   Ibid.

41   Interview with retired infantry Marine officer, 16 Aug. 2010. This individual requested anonymity.

42   Interview with David Hall, 17 Aug. 2010.

43   Interview with Alva.

44   These include Britain, Canada, Germany, Austria, Poland, Czechoslovakia, Sweden, Belgium, and the Netherlands during or quickly following the Great War. France, Italy, Hungary, and Japan followed suit in the aftermath of World War II. David R. Mayhew, "War and American Politics," *Perspectives on Politics* 3:3 (Sept. 2005), 478 and 487.

45   John Jay, "No. 2: Concerning Dangers from Foreign Force and Influence," *The Federalist Papers*, ed., Rossiter (New York: Mentor, 1999), 6.

46   For more on war and the American state, see W. Elliot Brownlee, "Tax Regimes, National Crisis, and State-Building in America," *Funding the Modern American State, 1941–1995*, ed., Brownlee (New York: Cambridge University Press, 1996); Robert Higgs, *Crisis and Leviathan: Critical Episodes in the Growth of American Government*, (New York: Oxford University Press, 1987); Mayhew, "Wars and American Politics"; Saldin, *War the American State, and Politics since 1898*; Bartholomew H. Sparrow, *From the Outside In: World War II and the American State* (Princeton: Princeton University Press, 1996); James T. Sparrow, *Warfare State: World War II Americans and the Age of Big Government* (New York: Oxford University Press, 2011).

47   For more on war and the American party system, see Saldin, "Foreign Affairs and Party Ideology in America: The Case of Democrats and World War II," *The Journal of Policy History* 22:4 (2010), 387–422; Saldin, *War the American State and Politics since 1898*; Saldin, "World War I and the 'System of 1896,'" *The Journal of Politics* 72:3 (2010), 825–36.

# Appendix A
## Wordings for Experimental Manipulation for Chapter 10

First Screen (seen by everyone)

Democracy Rocks

Question:

Why Should <u>You</u> Get Involved in Politics?

[Click for the Answer]

Second, Third, and Fourth Screens (VALUE EXPRESSION CONDITION):

Answer:

To Express Your

Personal Values and Beliefs!

   Show your concern for issues that are related to your values

   Work for what you personally believe in

[Click to Learn More]

Democracy Rocks

Think for a moment about how politics is related to the values and beliefs that are important to you personally.  Please type your thoughts about those values and beliefs here:

[Click to Learn More]

Democracy Rocks

Participating in politics will enable you to:

 Show others what you truly believe

 Act on your values

Participate – Express your Personal

Values and Beliefs!

[Click to Learn More]

Second, Third, and Fourth Screens ( AMERICAN IDENTITY CONDITION):

Answer:

To Show that You Are a Good American!

 Do your civic duty

 Express your views as an American

[Click to Learn More]

Democracy Rocks

Think for a moment about what it means to you personally to be a good American. Please type your thoughts about what it means to you to be a good American here:

[Click to Learn More]

Democracy Rocks

Participating in politics will enable you to:

   Do things that are important to Americans

   Express your identity as an American

Participate– Be a Good American!

[Click to Learn More]

Second, Third, and Fourth Screens (SELF INTEREST CONDITION):

Answer:

To Improve Your Standard of Living!

 Help get policies that will make your life better

 You can work on issues that will improve your family's financial situation

[Click to Learn More]

Democracy Rocks

Think for a moment about the ways in which proposals from political candidates or organizations can help improve your and your family's standard of living.  Please type your thoughts about those ways to improve your standard of living here:

[Click to Learn More]

Democracy Rocks

Participating in politics will enable you to:

 Increase your standard of living

 Capitalize on opportunities to improve your finances

Participate– Improve Your Standard of Living!

[Click to Learn More]

Fifth Screen (seen by everyone):

Democracy Rocks

There are thousands of ways
to get involved in politics!

*Democracy Rocks* is a newly formed
nonpartisan national organization.

Our objective is to encourage people to
participate in politics by raising awareness
about the many reasons to get involved and
providing people with all the tools and
tips they need to meet their goals

For more information, go to:
www.democracyrocks.us

[Click to Learn More]

Sixth Screen (seen by everyone):

Democracy Rocks

**6 Ways to Get Involved**

1. **VOTE!** – It's so easy, there's no excuse not to!

2. **Attend a Rally** – Work with people who share your ideas!

3. **Volunteer for a Campaign** – Find a candidate you like and contact the campaign.

4. **Write Letters to Congress** – Tell your representatives exactly what you are thinking.

5. **Involve Your Friends and Family** – Get your friends and family involved with your activities and stay active.

6. **Give Money** – Find a cause that you agree with and send whatever you can afford.

# Index

abortion 19, 23, 24 34, 97, 198, 200; in a study of political behavior 219, 221
Abramowitz, Alan I. 185, 188, 189, 292, 295
Abu Ghraib 314
activism: federal 22, 28, 31; grant 33; intergovernmental 31; judicial 98; national 30, 31
activists 32, 33, 110–13, 119, 186, 191, 193, 194, 198, 201, 292; motivations of 215, 217
Affordable Health Care Act 19, 34, 35, 273
African-Americans *see* Blacks
agenda setting: in Congress 52, 54, 57, 292; and the media 147
American Indian *see* Native American
American political development *see* research methods
American politics 29, 58, 80, 101, 111, 289; as an academic field 57, 313; as corrupt 138; and budget deficits 284; and federalism 20–1, 26, 28, 35; and race 259–60, 275
American Recovery and Reinvestment Act (ARRA) 22, 298
Americans for Tax Reform (ATR) 137–8
antiwar groups 119
Articles of Confederation 62
Asian-Americans 260, 263, 264; in government 260; and group consciousness 271; and immigration 241, 242–3, 249, 261, 262; and intermarriage 251, voting behavior of 269, 270, 271, 274
authority: of Congress 95; of courts 94; division of in federalism 20; of

federal government 27, 31, 95, 98; of presidents 62, 65, 68, 80, 274; president's use of unilaterally 63, 67; separated 63; of states 23, 25, 28–9, 31, 33–4

behavioralism 90, 313; critique of 93
bipartisan 192, 199, 203, 292, 295; and budget politics 284, 293, 294, 296, 298, 299, 300, 301
Blacks 22, 28, 237, 238, 242, 244, 261, 263, 264–8, 272, 273, 274; and constitutional amendments 27, 263; in the government 260, 265–7, 273, 274; and group consciousness 271; and immigration 241, 246, 249; and intermarriage 251; in the military 316–17, 319–20; rights for 263, 314, 318, 320; voting behavior of 269–71, 319
Boehner John 199, 300
budget 33, 55, 67, 76, 192, 194, 199, 299: as balanced 284, 287, 288, 289, 294; deficits 283, 284, 287–90, 294, 296, 299; discretionary spending 285; mandatory spending 285; and polarization *see* polarization; politics of 284; and public opinion 295–7; savings 300; of state governments 25; reforms *see* reform
Budget Control Act (2011) 284, 291, 298–9, 301
bureaucracy 50, 66, 76, 78, 79, 263; discretion of 53
Bush, George H.W. 217, 294
Bush, George W. 34, 67, 70, 76, 78, 113, 243, 253–4, 264; the Bush administration 36, 148